River of God

River of God

An Introduction to World Missions

EDITED BY
DOUG PRIEST AND STEPHEN E. BURRIS

WIPF & STOCK · Eugene, Oregon

RIVER OF GOD
An Introduction to World Missions

Wipf & Stock
An Imprint of Wipf and Stock Publishers
199 W. 8th Ave., Suite 3
Eugene, OR 97401
www.wipfandstock.com

ISBN 13: 978-1-61097-619-0
Manufactured in the U.S.A.

Contents

List of Contributors vii

Foreword by Tetsunao Yamamori ix

Introduction: Navigating the Waters in the River of God   1
         by Stephen E. Burris and Kendi Howells Douglas

1   Preach the Gospel or Feed the Hungry   15
        by Doug Priest

2   Enfleshing Hope: Incarnational Approaches to Emulate   25
        by Ashley Barker

3   The People of God and His Purpose   41
        by Paul K. McAlister

4   Missiological Reading of the New Testament   49
        by Robert Kurka

5   Teaching Them to Obey All That I Have Commanded   63
        by Mark Moore

6   Surging Waters: Global Expansion of the World Christian Movement   78
        by Stephen E. Burris

7   Opening the Floodgates: From Everywhere to Everywhere   93
        by Stephen E. Burris

8   Upon Closer Examination: Status of World Christianity   108
        by Todd M. Johnson and Gina A. Bellofatto

9   Anthropology and Missions: Learning to Understand the Sea of Humanity 125
        by Doug Priest

10   Using Anthropology to Understand Ritual and Symbol   135
        by Doug Priest

11   Rethinking Mission Strategy to Lead Others to the Streams of Life   147
        by Doug Priest

12 Only the Street Knows Your Name   160
    by Kendi Howells Douglas

13 Urban Ministry: The River of God Makes the City Glad   174
    by Linda Whitmer

14 Islam: How Christians Are Learning
        to Create A Bridge Over Troubled Waters   188
    by Robert Douglas

15 Short-Term Missions: A Cup of Cold Water In My Name?   201
    by Donovan Weber and Bill Weber

16 Crossing Language Barriers   213
    by Greg Pruett

17 Stress and Perseverance in Crossing Cultures   228
    by Janice Lemke

18 New Streams: Looking to the Future   241
    by Mike Sweeney

Bibliography   253
Subject Index   263

Contributors

Ashley Barker, Ph.D
 Is the Founder and Director of Urban Neighbors of Hope, a mission that works in five cities of the world, and has been a missionary in the Klong Toey urban slum of Bangkok, Thailand.

Gina A. Bellofatto, M.A.
 Is a Research Associate at the Center for the Study of Global Christianity at Gordon-Conwell Theological Seminary and the senior editorial assistant of the *Atlas of Global Christianity*.

Stephen E. Burris, M.A.
 Is a research missiologist with CMF International, and the pastor of the Golden Valley Christian Church San Bernardino, California, and has done mission service in Zimbabwe, Africa.

Kendi Howells Douglas, D.Miss
 Is the Professor of Cross-Cultural Ministries at Great Lakes Christian College. She has done mission service in Kenya, Japan, Mexico, Dominican Republic, Puerto Rico, Atlanta, Minneapolis, St. Louis, and Detroit.

Robert Douglas, Ph.D
 Is the Director of the Abraham Center at Graduate Institute of Applied Linguistics and has done mission work in Libya, Egypt and Lebanon.

Todd Johnson, Ph.D
 Is the Director of the Center for the Study of Global Christianity at Gordon-Conwell Theological Seminary and editor of the *Atlas of Global Christianity*.

Robert Kurka, D.Min
 Is professor of Theology and Church in Culture at Lincoln Christian Seminary of Lincoln Christian University and Director of the M.A. in Bioethics.

Janice Lemke, B.S.
 Served fifteen years with CMF International in Ukraine, where her husband, Cory, helped establish a training program for church planters. She previously served five years in Kenya with Youth With A Mission.

PAUL MCALISTER, D.MIN

Works with Pioneer Bible Translators in the area of member care and is an adjunct professor at Lincoln Christian University. He is a former instructor in bio-medical ethics at Mayo Clinic and professor of theology at Minnesota Bible College (Crossroads College).

MARK MOORE, PH.D

Is the professor of New Testament and Hermeneutics at Ozark Christian College.

DOUG PRIEST, PH.D

Is the Executive Director of CMF International and has done missionary work in East Africa and SE Asia.

GREG PRUETT, M.A.

Serves as President of Pioneer Bible Translators and was a Bible translator with Pioneer Bible Translators in Guinea, West Africa.

MIKE SWEENEY, PH.D

Is the President and missions professor at Emmanuel Christian Seminary. He served as a Bible translator, translation consultant, and administrator with Pioneer Bible Translators in Papua New Guinea as well as an Honorary Translation Advisor with the United Bible Societies.

BILL WEBER, PH.D

Is a Consultant for Leadership Development with Christian Missionary Fellowship. He served as an urban missionary in Johannesburg, South Africa, working in congregational formation and leadership development.

DONOVAN WEBER, PH.D

Has worked in Christian higher education for the past decade. He holds degrees in ministry, biblical studies and the PhD in educational leadership from Miami University. His research areas are service-learning and short-term missions.

LINDA WHITMER, PH.D

Is the Director of Online Intercultural Studies Programs, B.S., B.A., and M.A., at Johnson University. She has done mission service in Zimbabwe, Africa.

TETSUNAO YAMAMORI, PH.D

Is President Emeritus of Food for the Hungry International, former International Director of the Lausanne Committee for World Evangelization, and Senior Fellow of the Center for Religion and Civic Culture at the University of Southern California.

Foreword

by Tetsunao Yamamori

Early in the summer of 1974, I was doing field research among the Oromo people in Wollega Province of Ethiopia. I had the chance to visit CMF missionaries stationed in three locations in the area. Among them were Mr. and Mrs. Doug Priest Sr. They introduced me to their son, Doug Jr., who was visiting after finishing college. Therefore, it is a special privilege for me to write this Foreword, after almost four decades.

Stephen Burris and Doug Priest are both accomplished authors. Each has several books to his name. Burris is Research Missiologist of CMF International and Pastor of the Golden Valley Christian Church in San Bernardino, California. Priest has been Executive Director of CMF International since 1995. He and his wife Robyn served as missionaries in Kenya, Tanzania, and Singapore.

River of God is an introduction to world missions, as the sub-title indicates, and, according to the editors, this college textbook is aimed at undergraduate students. However, the readers will soon discover that the book is rich in its content far beyond the editors' original plan. It serves as a reader for people with various levels of missiological interest and competence. It deals with cutting-edge issues in missions.

In the Introduction, Stephen Burris and Kendi Howells Douglas introduce the direction of the book. They lay out a new paradigm, Kingdom Missiology, that builds on *shalom* in the Old Testament and as Jesus applied it to the Kingdom of God in the New Testament. The authors' intent is to wed social action (deed) and evangelism (word).

Doug Priest in chapter 1 expounds on issues related to social action vs. evangelism. He asks: "Should we preach the Gospel or feed the hungry?" The implications embodied in this simple question reflect decades of debate and ongoing battles between those who opted for evangelism over social action and those who chose to underscore social action over evangelism. Priest traces the history of how the church has grappled with the relationship between word and deed: Word And Deed, Word Or Deed, Word Over Deed, and Word With Deed. He then refers to what Chris Wright considers to be the correct relationship between the two. Wright speaks of the *ultimacy* of evangelism rather than the *primacy* of evangelism. Rather than prioritizing evangelism over social action, he contends that the correct response to the human predicament must ultimately include evangelism and the declaration of God's Word. The church may respond to the need of the hour, first, like natural disasters and minimal education. But the church's mission is incomplete without touching the spiritual predicament of all humans.

One may proceed to read the book according to the way the chapters are laid out. Each chapter has been written by a specialist on the topic, and each stands alone and is instructive. As I went through the book, however, I began thinking how the remaining chapters might well be organized under five headings. These groupings of chapters all contribute to the understanding of Kingdom Missiology. Under each heading, I wish to make a few comments. Obviously, there is no attempt on my part to be comprehensive; that is the task of the readers.

BIBLICAL/THEOLOGICAL EXPOSITION OF MISSION
(CHAPTERS 3, 4, & 5)

My comment here is simply one of gratitude to Professor Mark Moore (Chapter 5) for his discourse on Jesus' commands. After reading his chapter, I kept on saying to myself: "The one hundred and ten commands! 110 . . . 110 . . . 110!" It will certainly help us to know the commands of Jesus as we are instructed to teach others about them. Thank you, Professor Moore!

EXPANSION OF CHRISTIANITY: A HISTORICAL OVERVIEW
(CHAPTERS 6 & 8)

The two essays (chapters 6 by Stephen Burris and 8 by Todd Johnson and Gina Bellofatto) present a comprehensive picture of the expansion of Christianity from a historical perspective. Burris has conducted a thorough study of classic and current literature on the expansion of Christianity to make his case. Johnson is the director of the Center for the Study of Global Christianity at Gordon-Conwell Theological Seminary and Bellofatto is his research associate at the Center. Both have been involved in a number of projects, the latest being the *Atlas of Global Christianity*. Among missiologists, we say: "If you want to know the statistics of anything, ask Todd." Todd is a serious scholar, brilliant researcher, and astute analyst. Chapter 8 is replete with lessons: insights, trends, and projections. I found it especially helpful to learn the manifold implications of the shift of Christianity to the Global South.

CROSS-CULTURAL UNDERSTANDING
(CHAPTERS 9, 10, & 17)

Chapters 9 and 10 by Doug Priest constitute a mini-course on anthropology, anthropology being the study of humankind. It is sub-divided into four disciplines: archaeology, physical anthropology, linguistics, and cultural anthropology. This academic discipline takes a holistic view of humankind, and for missionaries, the study of anthropology is imperative. Communicating the gospel message clearly is the task of missionaries. They want the message to be understood without ethnocentric hurdles. I included chapter 17 by Janice Lemke in the category of "Cross-Cultural Understanding." Lemke deals with culture stress, an important topic for cross-cultural workers. It can make or break cross-cultural workers. Often people hesitate to talk about it, feeling guilt and embarrassment.

Lemke is a veteran missionary of fifteen years in the Ukraine working side-by-side with her husband. Prior to going to the Ukraine, she spent five years in Kenya as a single missionary. Her practical insights into coping with culture stress will be of help to many would-be cross-cultural workers.

MISSION STRATEGIES
(CHAPTERS 7, 11, 14, 15, 16, 17, & 18)

There are a variety of strategies. This book contains eighteen chapters. Half of the book may be said to deal with strategies (including chapters that belong to "Urban Mission" below). Burris in chapter 7 traces the paradigm shifts of the past 200 years of the "modern missions" period and describes the current shift to be "From Everywhere to Everywhere." Shifts have occurred: (a) Focus on the Coastlands, 1800 (William Carey), (b) Focus on the Interiors, 1865 (Hudson Taylor), and (c) Focus on the Unreached Peoples, 1935 (Cameron Townsend of Wycliffe Bible Translators and Donald A. McGavran who called nearly 3,000 subgroups of people "homogeneous units").

Doug Priest in chapter 11 makes a systematic presentation of strategy: (a) What is missionary strategy?, (b) Components of a strategy, (c) Types of strategies, and (d) Levels of strategy. Then, Priest turns to examining some well-known strategies: (a) The incarnational strategy, (b) The indigenous theory strategy, and (c) The CHE strategy. It will be interesting to track his thinking and develop your own assessments.

I consider Robert Douglas (chapter 14) to be one of the top experts on Islam. He has done mission work in Libya, Egypt, and Lebanon. He has held the directorship of the Zwemer Institute, and is now directing the Abraham Center at the Graduate Institute of Applied Linguistics. I enjoyed reading his chapter. I would, especially, heed his advice related to "Approaches in Ministry to Muslims."

"Short-Term Missions" (chapter 15) is a topic often discussed in churches. I am glad that this chapter is included in the book. In Christian colleges and seminaries, there will be many debates on this topic.

Since the days of Cameron Townsend, remarkable progress has been made in the field of Bible translation, though much is yet to be done. Greg Pruett leads Pioneer Bible Translators. I have observed the growth of that ministry for some time. I am pleased to read Greg's affirmative comment on the Orality Movement. Bible translation and the Orality Movement complement each other.

Mike Sweeney (chapter 18) presents two major missiological shifts, already mentioned in other chapters, and discusses the impact of these global changes on seven areas: (a) missions from everywhere to everywhere, (b) the increasing role of technology in missions, (c) mission entrepreneurialism, (d) foreign-supported indigenous workers, (e) short-term missions, (f) the growth of Pentecostalism, and (g) increased mission networking and partnerships. These seven areas Sweeney identifies will remain as topics of great importance because of their strategic significance. I wish to list two of my books which may contribute to the discussion on (c) and (f).[1]

URBAN MISSION (CHAPTERS 2, 12, & 13)

Urban mission is a continued discussion on mission strategies. In the Church circle, the urban challenges have been unpopular. Like it or not, we cannot ignore the magnitude of the impact of urbanization on the Church and its mission. Three authors have selected to deal with urban mission and strategies: Ashley Barker (chapter 2), Kendi Howells Douglas (chapter 12), and Linda Whitmer (chapter 13).

Barker's incarnational mission has much to contribute to mission strategy in the urban context. The readers will benefit as they review the following incarnational methodologies and models: (a) Incarnation as relocation, (b) Incarnation as crossing cultures, (c) Incarnation as influencing others, and (d) Incarnation as simple lifestyle. Furthermore, Barker delineates strengths and weaknesses of incarnational mission to the benefit of the reader.

Kendi Howells Douglas has done us service in presenting a helpful discourse on inner cities. Due to lack of knowledge, we tend not to differentiate the inner city from the urban area. I have appreciated the chapter by Howells Douglas on two specific points. One is the help I received in understanding incarnational evangelism in the inner city and the other is her fair treatment of the Social Gospel movement.

Linda Whitmer's "Urban Ministry: Change and Need" is an excellent chapter that explores the changing frontier of urban ministry and the way this changing urban world is being addressed by the church. In short, Whitmer deals with holistic ministry in the urban setting.

I shall list for reference the fourth of my four-book series on holistic ministry (1995–1998) that is relevant here.[2]

Now, I must come to a close. The book you are about to read is informative, challenging, inspirational, current, scholarly, and practical. I highly recommend it.

---

1. Tetsunao Yamamori and Kenneth A. Eldred, eds., *On Kingdom Business.* Donald E. Miller and Tetsunao Yamamori, *Global Pentecostalism.*

2. Tetsunao Yamamori, Bryant L. Myers, and Kenneth L. Luscombe, eds. *Serving with the Urban Poor.*

Introduction

NAVIGATING THE WATERS IN THE RIVER OF GOD: A PARADIGM FOR MISSIOLOGY

by Stephen E. Burris and Kendi Howells Douglas

IN RECENT YEARS A great deal of emphasis has been given to a missional reading of the Bible.[1] We applaud this needed re-direction. From beginning to end, the Bible is a record of God's action to redeem fallen creation. This introduction seeks to explore how the church of today can model the ministry of Jesus in action as we confront a world of need. Engel and Dyrness said it this way, "If this defines his agenda, it also must define ours. No fractured worldview here, confining faith to one's individual and personal life. Rather, there is a bold mandate to combine faith with action to overcome injustice and oppression."[2] We are calling this *Kingdom Missiology* for we seek to be the church that faithfully performs the whole work of the kingdom of God to the whole world.

For the last century, at least, there has been a growing, and often rancorous, division between those who place primary emphasis on social action and those who give priority to evangelism.[3] This absurd dichotomy is unbiblical, as the Greek words *sozo* and *sotaria* were used interchangeably in the New Testament for healing but are almost always translated "salvation," in which spiritual salvation was strongly assumed. This was a choice made by translators[4] that was influenced by this false dichotomy and worked to cement it for some. These words are not limited to spiritual salvation, but also mean salvation from economic oppression, psychological oppression, as well as physical and social healing. In this introduction we will explore the mission of God to discern the scope of Jesus' concern for all of human need. We will then look at the mission of the church today using seven categories: 1) compassion, 2) witness, 3) God's action, 4) *missio*

---

1. Books by Wright, *Mission of God*, and *Mission of God's People*; Glasser, *Announcing the Kingdom*; and Bosch, *Transforming Mission* are particularly helpful.

2. Engel and Dyrness, *Changing the Mind of Missions*, 23.

3. An overly simplistic definition of ecumenical and evangelical is that the ecumenical branch of the church gives primary emphasis to social action and the evangelical branch gives primary emphasis to evangelism.

4. Using the word salvation with the intended meaning of spiritual salvation was a choice each translator made again and again.

Dei, 5) holism, 6) incarnation, and 7) transformation.[5] Bosch said it well: "The God who has *compassion* on the stranger, the widows, the orphans, and the poor in Israel is also the God who turns human categories upside down: he uses the weak, the suffering, and those of no consequence as his *witnesses* (martyrs) in the world. Ultimately, however, mission remains God's *mission*, *missio Dei*, since he retains the initiative, creates *history*, and guides it toward fulfillment."[6] A missional[7] reading of the Bible and consequent practice by the church in mission must take into consideration all that Jesus taught and did if it is to be truly biblical. A biblical approach will incorporate all aspects of this paradigm. The starting point will be determined by the context in which ministry is done. Of course our goal remains the same, by following Christ's example and addressing the whole person we are making disciples of all nations.

The consistent thread in Jesus' life was "to seek and save the lost."[8] Additionally, at the very beginning of his ministry he gave us his purpose statement, the Nazareth manifesto.[9] Quoting from Isa 61, Jesus said, "The Spirit of the Lord is upon me, because he has anointed me to bring good news to the poor. He has sent me to proclaim release to the captives and recovery of sight to the blind, to let the oppressed go free, to proclaim the year of the Lord's favor."[10] Jesus also taught using parables that often began the kingdom of God is like . . . most often using everyday events to teach kingdom values.

So how do we bring these two foundational sayings, saving the lost and good news to the poor, of Jesus together? What is the scope of the church's mission in making disciples? Glasser offers help in merging these ideas, seeing them as tributaries that lead to one river, the river of God, when he writes, "There is but one acid test that should be applied to all activities that claim to represent obedience in mission. Do they or do they not produce disciples of Jesus Christ?"[11] So Kingdom Missiology must incorporate all that Jesus did and taught[12] as the scope of the mission for today, with the goal of making disciples. Swanson and Williams give further definition, "Kingdom work involves two aspects. It

---

5. We are indebted to David Bosch, "Reflections on Biblical Models of Mission," 175–90, for several of these categories. Van Engen gives a helpful graphic on how this is interrelated in Fig. 8, *God's Missionary People*, 128.

6. Bosch, "Reflections on Biblical Models of Mission," 187.

7. "Missional thinking embraces the belief that God intends for every one of his children to be living on mission, partnering with him in his redemptive mission in the world." Swanson and Williams, *To Transform a City*, 21.

8. Matt 18:11.

9. Marshall, *New Testament Theology*, 144.

10. Luke 4:18–19. "the coming of the Kingdom is to provide a tangible manifestation of God's attitude toward poverty and injustice. His people will grapple with the injustice that brings exploitation and poverty and will be particularly concerned to help the poor and the suffering. It is on this basis that the poor can rejoice." Glasser, *Announcing*, 216.

11. Glasser, *Announcing*, 13.

12. See Matt 28:18–20, "teaching them to observe all things." See Chapter 5 by Mark Moore in this volume.

involves introducing people to the King (Jesus), and it involves bringing his perspective, his values, and his generative structures into the world in which we live."[13]

So how do we balance what has been previously presented as the ridiculous dichotomy of social action vs. evangelism? Where do we start? Wright gives specific and defensible help when he says,

> almost any *starting* point can be appropriate, depending possibly on what is the most pressing or obvious need. We can *enter* the circle[14] of missional response at any point on the circle of human need. *But ultimately* we must not rest content until we have included within our own missional response the wholeness of *God's* missional response to the human predicament—and that of course includes the good news of Christ, the cross and resurrection, the forgiveness of sin, the gift of eternal life that is offered to men and women through our witness to the gospel and the hope of God's new creation . . . Mission may not always begin with evangelism. But mission that does not ultimately *include* declaring the Word and the name of Christ, the call to repentance, and faith and obedience has not completed its task. It is defective mission, not holistic mission.[15]

Each Christian may not be the one to do the whole task. Paul himself said in 1 Cor 3:6, "I planted, Apollos watered, but God gave the growth." It's okay to just feed someone in the name of mission or evangelism. We don't have to feed them and baptize them all ourselves, as this isn't about us or our egos, it's about God's plan for them; all actions are still evangelism.

Wright also clearly raises a fundamental question for today: "What does the Bible as a whole in both testaments have to tell us about why the people of God exist and what it is they are supposed to be and do in this world? What is the mission of God's people?"[16] That is the missional question, and it's holistic in scope.[17] This backdrop helps us focus on a new missiological paradigm: Kingdom Missiology.

PART 1—BIBLICAL FOUNDATION OF MISSION

Mission in the Old Testament

There are three dominant themes from the Old Testament that are given emphasis: Creation, Exodus, and Exile. Each of these events had special significance in the history of the people of God. Space does not allow us to develop the theme of the people of God here, but it is enough to say that these were to be God's people, his representatives, caring for the things God cares about.

---

13. Swanson and Williams, *To Transform*, 77.

14. See a diagram of this circle in Chapter 1 by Doug Priest in this volume.

15. Wright, *Mission of God*, 318–19.

16. Wright, *Mission of God's People*, 17.

17. Holistic mission is "mission that takes into account the whole of human needs: spiritual, social and personal. Holistic mission includes both evangelism and church planting as well as development and social transformation." Pocock, *Changing Face of World Missions*, 15.

CREATION—ACT I

The Bible begins with the amazing words, "In the beginning God." The rest of the book is the story of that God acting in marvelous ways. A God who creates, rules, forgives, and redeems; a God who loves and cares for his creation; and the God who is above all other gods, Yahweh God, who originates, creates, and sustains. So, what is the Bible about? What is the storyline? What unifies sixty-six books into one story of how God has acted, is acting, and will continue to act? We are advancing the notion that the God who created is the God who saves and redeems, sets captives free. The correct reading of the Bible, therefore, is to see the Creator God as a missionary God.

As we look at the first eleven chapters of Genesis we are reminded that this narrative involves as long a period of time as the remainder of the Old Testament.[18] The beginning of the human race, the fall, the multiplication of that race, the continual struggle between God and humankind over who will be in charge, are all highlighted. As Glasser has pointed out, "The theme of Genesis 1–11 is that the human race in its fallenness tends to destroy God's good creation. And yet God demonstrates that he is the God of grace as well as the God of judgment."[19] As Wright has so clearly asked, "What does the Bible as a whole in both testaments have to tell us about why the people of God exist and what it is they are supposed to be and do in the world? What is the mission of God's people?"[20]

Here we find the absolute origin of the universe and every dimension is present in Gen 1–11. Humans are placed here as stewards of that property. As Wright has pointed out, we need to be careful how we treat the property of the divine owner.[21] "The main point of our ruling the earth is for its benefit, not our own."[22] It should also be noted that this mandate to care for God's creation has never been rescinded. Creation care is still in full force today.

Bavinck points out that Genesis 1:1 is the basis of the so-called great commission in Matt 28:19–20.[23] God's creation is good. The word *good* here is the Hebrew word *tov*—which means more than nice or good—fulfilling the purpose for which it was created. The creation is fulfilling its purpose as the stage on which all the acts of God's redemptive plan for humanity is taking place. Archer rightly said, "The guiding principle throughout the

---

18. Bauer, *The History of the Ancient World*, 3–126, gives a good overview of the development of humankind in these centuries leading up to Abraham, including Sumer, the Nile River Valley, the Indus River Valley, the Yellow River Valley, etc.

19. Glasser, *Announcing*, 53.

20. Wright, *Mission of God's People*, 17. With Costas we ask, "The question is no longer what is the church's 'primary' task, but what is her *total* task. The issue today is not whether or not people are being converted to Christ but whether this is happening as part of a total process: is the church a community totally committed to and involved in the fulfillment of the gospel in the context of the concrete historical situations in which men and women find themselves?" in Costas, *The Church and Its Mission*, 11.

21. Wright, *Salvation Belongs to Our God*, 141.

22. Wright, *Mission of God's People*, 51.

23. Bavinck, *An Introduction to the Science of Missions*, 12. Bavinck also states, "from the first page to the last the Bible has the whole world in view, and its divine plan of salvation is unfolded as pertaining to the whole world." Ibid., 11.

narrative is the covenant of grace, and God's gracious dwellings with true believers from the time of Adam onward."[24]

THE EXODUS—ACT II[25]

"The exodus stands in the Hebrew Scriptures as the great defining demonstration of YHWH's power, love, faithfulness and liberating intervention on behalf of his people."[26] The exodus is more prominent in Israel's history than the creation. The purpose of the law was not to keep the status quo, but laws existed for making justice, delivering the helpless, and restoring order.[27] In this way, the exodus stands for deliverance from whatever enslaves. God's redemptive work in Egypt was to free an immigrant enslaved people so that they may worship God.[28] "The problem was not just that the Hebrews were slaves, but that they were slaves to the wrong master and needed to be transferred into the service of the living God . . . The exodus was not a movement from slavery to freedom, but from slavery to covenant."[29]

God desires the praise of his creation. The exodus account teaches that whatever enslaves,[30] whatever prevents that worship, must be done away with so that praise may be offered to the one true God, the creator of the universe.

THE EXILE—ACT III[31]

The Exile is preparation for a new creation, the *missio Dei*. It begins again with this fresh start. During the captivity in Babylon the people needed to accomplish two things. First, they needed to survive as a people, and second, they were to be a witness to their captors. Ezek 36:22–36 tells of a new cleansing and a new birth. This new land is compared to the Garden of Eden. A cleansed people would then live in a clean land as God's covenant people as a testimony to others who first saw how they profaned God's name and then witnessed how God cleaned them up and made them holy. [32]

SHALOM

Throughout all of Israel's history there is one word that encapsulates—and is used repeatedly when describing Israel's *modus operandi*—*shalom*. The heart of the concept of *shalom* is reconciliation, to God, to each other, and to his creation.[33] Because of sin, all

---

24. Archer, *A Survey of Old Testament Introduction*, 186.

25. Note Exod 19:3–6 and compare to 1 Pet 2:9–10. See also Deut 7:6–8.

26. Wright, *Mission of God*, 75.

27. Exod 15:18. "This is the first significant time the kingdom of God is mentioned in the Bible, and it comes in the specific context of YHWH's victory over those who have oppressed his people and refused to know him (Exod 5:2)." Wright, *Mission of God*, 78.

28. Exod 7:16.

29. Wright, *Mission of God's People*, 101.

30. Regardless of what enslaves, be it political, economic, social, or spiritual.

31. See Ezek 36:19–23.

32. Ezek 36:35.

33. "With reconciliation, being reconciled, peace, it is primarily a matter of removing that which stands in the way of the right relationship between God and (on the most comprehensive sense of the word) the

areas were destroyed or damaged. Only through the reconciliation of God, especially in the death, burial, and resurrection of Christ, can this be restored. Any hope of healing relationships with others, or the healing of creation, is futile until this basic relationship is made whole.

But *shalom* has still deeper meaning. As Slimbach says, "Ancient Israel spoke of this vision or 'great dream' as shalom, Jesus taught it as the kingdom of God. Both terms capture a vision of and for a world 'made right.'"[34] This great dream becomes the kingdom of God demonstrating *shalom* on earth. This is the River of God flowing to the nations. This is incorporated in God's promise to Abraham, "I will bless you, and make your name great, so that you will be a blessing . . . in you all the families of the earth shall be blessed."[35] A blessing and a "world where all individuals and institutions, families and peoples, the natural world in all its richness, and the divine powers that provide ultimate explanation for existence are knit together and fulfilled in mutual respect and delight."[36] There can be no separation of addressing the needs of others when talking about salvation, as pointed out earlier. Jesus' statement in Luke 4:16–19, the Good Samaritan parable, and the judgment passage found in Matt 25:31–46 are merely three examples of how wholeness is intended to function in the kingdom of God.[37] It is in the judgment passage in Matt 25 that Jesus repeatedly states if one fails to care for the "least of these" they have failed to care for Jesus.

> The word *shalom* is used more than 350 times in the Old Testament. It covers a wide range of meanings: wholeness, without injury, undivided, well-being, a satisfactory condition, bodily health, and all that salvation means in its Old Testament usage. If a person or nation has *shalom*, no lack exists in any direction, whether personal or national . . . The equivalent word in the New Testament is peace and is particularly identified with the redemptive work of Christ, bringing the repentant individual into a new relationship with God and neighbors and giving hope for eschatological salvation that will embrace the whole person and the whole *kosmos*.[38]

So the church, as representative of God's *shalom* on earth,[39] his kingdom, here and now, must be involved in these things—feeding the hungry, healing the sick, clothing the naked, and addressing sinful systems and structures that oppress and hold people in bondage—it is our job as his representatives, while we declare the death, burial, and resurrection of Christ. As representatives of the kingdom of God we have an obligation

world; in other words, of the eschatological restoration of all things." in Ridderbos, *Paul: An Outline of His Theology*, 183.

34. Slimbach, "The Mindful Missioner," 155.

35. Gen 12:2–3.

36. Slimbach, "The Mindful Missioner," 155.

37. "God is concerned for social justice. he is strangely moved at the cries of the oppressed, particularly when God's people collectively make neither effort nor sacrifice to relieve their anguish," Glasser, *Announcing*, 25.

38. Glasser, *Announcing*, 130.

39. "The goal is *shalom*—a sense of human welfare and well-being that transcends an artificial distinction between the private and public worlds. *Shalom*, by its very nature, is rooted in justice and compassion." Engel and Dyrness, *Changing*, 93.

to be stewards of what we have been given so that we can minister to those Jesus cares about. "Spreading the kingdom of God is more than simply winning men and women to Christ. It involves working toward shalom and the redemption of structures, individuals, families, and relationships as well as surprising others with unexpected deeds of grace, mercy, and justice (Mic 6:8). The church is called to create an attractive and compelling alternative, showing what life is like when lived under the reign of God."[40]

This holistic view of the kingdom of God helps us to more clearly identify the needs that are particularly obvious in the urban centers of the world, above all in the Majority World. If the church is to be truly the church then we must give full attention to bringing the *shalom* of God's kingdom into the most desperate areas in our world. This is our best chance to bring God's creation back to wholeness and rightness.[41]

Centripetal Model[42]

In the life of Israel there were to be visible qualities that would attract the nations to God. This would involve the demonstration that they were God's people. But it also spoke of the kind of people they were to be. They were to live as the people of God before the watching nations. This emphasis would demonstrate the ethics by which the people of God would live as a testimony to the nations.[43] In short, the people of God are to live in such a way that the proclamation of the good news will have effect, their witness, but also so that those outside watching will be attracted to the worship of God because of the quality of their life and fellowship. It is in this way that Bosch says, "the Church's first missionary responsibility is not to change the world but to change herself."[44] The ethical quality of the church and her fellowship becomes a missional magnetism.

Mission in the New Testament

We are familiar with the missionary passages of the New Testament. Normally we begin with the great commission, Matt 28:18–20. We then expand to include a few additional favorite passages. This approach is lacking in that it often misses the central point that God is a missionary God. Without this basic understanding we cannot adequately understand the mission of the church in the world today. Christ stands in the center of history and connects the old to the new at that center, the concern for the helpless in the Old Testament, the *shalom* model, is concern for the helpless in the New Testament, the kingdom model. Jesus gave us a picture of what the kingdom of God is like in his teachings and mainly in the kingdom parables. Jesus didn't feed everyone, he didn't heal

40. Swanson and Williams, *To Transform*, 81.

41. See in particular Jer 29:7, where they were to seek the peace and welfare of the city—i.e., *shalom*.

42. "Part of the mission of God's people is to have God so much at the centre of who they are and what they do, that there is a centripetal force, God's own gravitational pull, that draws people into the sphere of his blessing." Wright, *Mission of God's People*, 129. Note the centripetal nature included in Solomon's prayer of dedication of the temple, 1 Kings 8:41–43.

43. "The early Christians lived in such a way that the world noticed something different about them, for they had a distinctive lifestyle that could not be ignored." Swanson and Williams, *To Transform*, 84.

44. Bosch, *Witness to the World*, 246.

everyone, but he gave his world, and ours, a new view of life called the kingdom of God. This kingdom melds together the great commission and the Great Commandment. It is the *shalom* of God in action in the church today.

Acts 2:42–47[45]

If the New Testament church is to be our model of faith and practice, then these verses show the kind of activities the church should be involved in today. Four activities—the apostles' teaching[46] and fellowship, to the breaking of bread, and prayer—formed the core in the assembly of the Christians, 2:42. These activities were confirmed with signs and wonders, 2:43. Then comes the surprising part of the story: they sold their possessions and had all things in common, and gave to each as they had need, 2:44–45. This was not common practice, even among the Jews. Luke's description of the disciples as those who "ate their food with glad and generous hearts, praising God and having the good will of all the people," 2:46–47, leads to the growth of the church. "And the Lord added to their number those who were being saved," 2:47.[47] Schnabel is correct when he says, "Luke presents a pragmatic ethic of possessions that places the needs of the poor in the center. He does not idealize a past mode of behavior in the Jerusalem church but describes a way of behavior that is focused on the community and can be practiced in all Christian communities. The view that Luke has a 'bourgeois' concept of the church is wrong. Luke repeatedly reminds his readers that the Jerusalem church (as a model for other churches) expected its wealthy members to sacrifice their private property or encouraged them to sell property voluntarily and with joy."[48]

The fact that Luke records the growth of the church, 2:47, is a significant indicator that the church was doing the right things in both its fellowship and in its outreach, centrifugal and centripetal witness. It should be observed that the quality of the fellowship, and the care for the needs of others, had a direct impact on the church's witness in the community. It still does.

A thorough examination of the verses between Acts 1:8, where Jesus tells the disciples that they will be his witness, up to Acts 2:42–47, and also Acts 4:32–35 and 5:12–16, shows that in no way is the witness of the disciples and the early church limited to verbal proclamation. In fact the example of Acts shows that the witness was both in word and deed. They got their hands dirty. The first century church brought together these twin

---

45. Space does not permit us to examine two additional passages in Acts, 4:32–35 and 5:12–16, that indicates what is described in Acts 2:42–47 was not an isolated exception. The apostles and church described in Acts set about meeting the whole range of human need as a regular part of their witness and testimony.

46. "Luke does not specify the 'apostles' teaching' in Acts 2:42, but he does provide a lengthy account of Peter's preaching. This warrants the conclusion that the sermons and speeches of Peter, who acts as representative and spokesman of the apostles, provide the substance and content of the 'teaching of the apostles.'" Schnabel, *Early Christian Mission*, 409.

47. "It is the Lord whose prerogative it is to add new members to His own community; it is the joyful duty of the community to welcome to their ranks those whom Christ has accepted (cf. Rom 15:7)." Bruce, *The Book of Acts*, 81.

48. Schnabel, *Early Christian Mission*, 413. Marshall suggests "each person held his goods at the disposal of the others whenever the need arose." Marshall, *Acts*, 90.

emphases of ministry assumed as a natural part of making disciples by healing, feeding, caring for, any who had need while at the same time proclaiming the crucified, risen Christ.[49]

Urban Ministry

Urban ministry[50] was a key to the expansion of the church—*shalom* or kingdom mission—throughout the apostolic period, and beyond, as evidenced by Paul's missionary journeys.[51] Typically, Paul would begin his ministry in a new city by going to the synagogue.[52] He then moved to more receptive areas to continue his preaching and ministry, including open air preaching. Paul made great use of household evangelism.[53]

Paul went to prominent cities[54] such as Antioch, Athens, Corinth, and Rome, among others. Many of these cities were among the most influential at the time. Paul maintained flexibility in his methods, but his strategy seems obvious. Schnabel properly observes, "Since Paul wanted to reach all people in a given location, matters of ethnic identity, class, culture or gender did not control his missionary focus."[55] Should this inform mission strategy today? Rather than focus on nations or peoples, isn't it wise to focus our strategies on the influential urban areas of the world? This follows Paul's example and allows *shalom*, as evidenced in the kingdom of God, to be practiced in these most strategic areas as a centripetal force.

PART 2—KINGDOM MISSIOLOGY

How should all of this be lived and practiced in the church today? Building on the work of David Bosch, we seek to define Kingdom Missiology that takes into consideration each of the following seven aspects. They are intrinsically interrelated and interdependent and, as was pointed out earlier, the starting point for mission will likely be different depending on the context in which ministry takes place. We seek to make disciples by bringing *shalom* through the kingdom of God to those who do not yet have the good news of Christ.

---

49. Peter's sermon on Pentecost, Acts 2: 14–36, occurs immediately before this passage. Clearly the church was born on Pentecost. So, the church understood its task to be holistic from the beginning.

50. "If the goal is to 'make disciples of all nations,' missionaries need to go where there are many potential converts, which is precisely what Paul did." Swanson and Williams, *To Transform*, 35.

51. For good treatments of this strategy see, Allen, *Missionary Methods*, Green, *Evangelism in the Early Church*, and Schnabel, *Paul the Missionary*.

52. Allen, *Missionary Methods*, 19.

53. "the household proved the crucial medium for evangelism within natural groupings, whatever member of the family was first won to the faith. It was preferable, of course, if the father was converted first, for then he would bring over the whole family with him." Green, *Evangelism in the Early Church*, 210. See also the Chapter 12 by Kendi Howells Douglas and Chapter 13 by Linda Whitmer in this volume that deal specifically with urban ministry.

54. Allen, *Missionary Methods*, 26.

55. Schnabel, *Paul the Missionary*, 36.

Compassion

Compassion is part of the character of God and Ezek 6:4–7 is an indication of the extent of God's compassion. These verses show God's compassion on the lost and marginalized.[56] God's compassion knows no boundaries.[57] Jesus' words in Luke 4:18–19 serve as both a purpose statement for his ministry on earth and our work in the expansion of his kingdom today. Demonstrations of our compassion may take on different forms depending upon the context in which ministry is given. "Then Jesus went about all the cities and villages, teaching in their synagogues, and proclaiming the good news of the kingdom, and curing every disease and every sickness. When he saw the crowds, he had compassion for them, because they were harassed and helpless, like sheep without a shepherd. Then he said to his disciples. 'The harvest is plentiful, but the laborers are few; therefore ask the Lord of the harvest to send out laborers into his harvest.'"[58]

Witness

The final words Jesus gave to the disciples define the scope of the witness Jesus intended the disciples and the church to have. Therefore, one aspect of our Kingdom Missiology involves being his witnesses.[59] This is the public declaration of the things that were seen and heard. Happily, we have eyewitness accounts of the core message. The foundational beliefs of our faith are founded on the testimony of eyewitnesses.[60]

God's Action

The entire Bible is a story of God's action[61] in redeeming his good creation damaged by sin. Beginning in Gen 3:15 we see a golden thread of God's redemptive acts,[62] first through

---

56. "This is why the Exodus event became the cornerstone of Israel's confession of faith: God took compassion on a band of slaves in Egypt and saved them." Bosch, "Reflections on Biblical Models of Mission," 180. Wright also notes, "The phrase 'Then you [or they] will know that I am YHWH' is virtually Ezekiel's signature—occurring some eighty times in his prophetic memoir . . . It means that the nations will come to the decisive and irrevocable knowledge that YHWH alone is the true and living God, unique in his identity, universal in his rule, and unchallenged in his power." Wright, *Kingdom of God*, 101.

57. Note the story of Jonah. God had compassion on Nineveh even when Jonah did not.

58. Matt 9:35–38. It should be noted in each case where Matthew uses the word compassion, the account begins with taking care of the immediate needs of the individual or group, Matt 14:14, feeding the multitude using five loaves and two fish; 15:32, feeding the multitude with a few loaves and fish; 18:27, forgiving the debt; 20:34, healing the blind.

59. Luke 24:44–48; Acts 1:8.

60. As an example, see 1 Cor 15:1–8 and note that the resurrected Christ was seen by more than five hundred eyewitnesses. This most central of all of our beliefs is founded on eyewitness accounts, many of whom were martyred for their faith. "It is no accident that all four Gospels link the beginning of the worldwide mission of the church explicitly with the resurrection . . . It was Easter that gave those first Christians certainty, but it was Pentecost that gave them boldness; only through the power of the Spirit did they become witnesses (Acts 1:8)." Bosch, "Reflections," 187. It should also be noted carefully that the phrase "according to the scriptures" is a clear reference to the Old Testament, the scriptures of Jesus' day.

61. "'Mission' is what God is doing *to* and *through* the Servant, not what the servant does." Bosch, "Reflections," 184.

62. "God created and ordered the universe; then man rebelled against God's order and the disorganizing

Abraham and his descendents, Israel, and then through the church, the new Israel. The witnesses were to bear witness to what God had done.[63] God's action in the lives of the disciples and church is in and through the ministry of the Holy Spirit. God expected Israel, and the church, to be witnesses of his mighty acts. An examination of the sermons in the Acts of the Apostles and other New Testament books reveal that the death-burial-resurrection of Jesus is the central message.

Missio Dei

Missio Dei refers to God's mission. We are participating in God's plan, not asking God to participate in ours. Bosch sets us on the right path when he writes, "In the new image mission is not primarily an activity of the church, but an attribute of God. God is a missionary God . . . To participate in mission is to participate in the movement of God's love toward people, since God is a fountain of sending love."[64] Since this goes to the very heart of God, it is not possible to go any deeper. This is the source of mission. When we are involved in mission we are mere participants in God's overarching mission. "The God who has *compassion* on the stranger, the widow, the orphan, and the poor in Israel is also the God who turns human categories upside down: he uses the weak, the suffering, and those of no consequence as his witnesses (*martyres*) in the world. Ultimately, however, mission remains God's *mission, missio Dei*, since he retains the initiative, creates *history*, and guides it toward fulfillment."[65]

Holism

As has been pointed out earlier, holistic ministry takes into account the whole of human needs: spiritual, psychological, political, social, and personal. Many people have not frequently encountered the poor, let alone desperate poverty, and would have no idea how important it is to meet the very real physical needs first, but Christ did and is our example in addressing many types of poverty—to the woman at the well he addressed her social salvation as she was stigmatized and an outcast, an immoral person. Jesus ignores the cultural rules of the day and speaks to her in public, something that simply wasn't done. He talks about water because that is the setting, the context, and the only thing they have in common. In other instances Jesus addressed the poverty of loneliness, money, food, blindness, and whatever enslaved the individual he was addressing at the time.

---

power of sin required the intervention of the creator-redeemer, the Lord of nature history. The first glimpse of God's glory appears in Gen 3:15." Strauss, "God's Promise," 192. The message of Gen 1–11 is obvious: humankind cannot solve its own problems.

63. Acts 4:20, "for we cannot keep from speaking about what we have seen and heard."

64. Bosch, *Transforming Mission*, 390.

65. Bosch, "Reflections," 187.

Incarnation

> And the Word became flesh and lived among us, and we have seen his glory, the glory as of a father's only son, full of grace and truth.[66]

These words recorded by John form the basis of incarnational ministry.[67] Wright appropriately says, "The incarnation of God in Christ brings two new factors into our theology of mission; the inaugurated presence of the kingdom of God and the incarnational model and principle itself."[68]

For our purposes here it is important to emphasize that the incarnational model is in concrete form in a specific context. Jesus came to first-century Palestine. What God did in Jesus, and the teaching of the kingdom, was to give people hope, giving *shalom* in the form of a kingdom, a physical entity. Missionaries go to specific places and particular people. As such they embody the presence of the kingdom of God by modeling ministry in the context in which they are called and serve. "The *context*, therefore, indicates where our emphasis ought to be and the *circumstances* dictate the way in which our witness has to be communicated."[69] The incarnation is never an abstract idea but always involves a ministry context. The particular circumstance will determine the best strategies to meet the real life needs and provide the basis for the starting point in ministry.

Transformation

How can we transform a world with such great need? Where do we start? As was pointed out by Glasser earlier, the goal and ultimate test of all our theology and strategies is, do they make disciples? The task seems overwhelming, but when we turn to the scriptures the message seems clear: transformation[70] through disciple-making is our urgent task.[71] The kind of transformation that takes place with Kingdom Missiology is as vast as humanity itself, slave owners are transformed into freedom fighters, drug addicts into counselors, oppressors into those who will enter the acts of solidarity side-by-side with those who are oppressed. In short, transformation, if it is truly biblical, must address all of human need.

---

66. John 1:14.

67. For a more complete description of the incarnational model in ministry, see Chapter 2 by Ashley Barker in this volume.

68. Wright, *Mission of God's People*, 42.

69. Bosch, *Witness*, 229.

70. "Biblical transformation as the process of restoration to God's intentions of all that was broken when humanity rebelled against God at the Fall. It is not the same as spiritual conversion, though it beings there. It is God's work. He calls his people to participate with him in it. This ongoing process will not be fully completed until Christ returns." Swanson and Williams, *To Transform*, 43.

71. "We believe that transformation of a city is predicated on our learning to read the Scriptures with new eyes and rediscovering the ancient message once again, learning what it means to be an agent of grace in our generation." Swanson and Williams, *To Transform*, 84.

CONCLUSION

Throughout this Introduction we have attempted to give the primary components of *Kingdom Missiology*. We started by throwing out the false dichotomy that has existed between social action and evangelism. We have shown that the biblical model is both/and, not either/or. Jesus had compassion on the poor, the hungry, the diseased, the oppressed; in short, those who were hurting. At the same time he came to seek and to save the lost. Kingdom Missiology must include all that Jesus did and taught. In this way we can make true disciples of the King.

Transformation takes place one person and one community at a time. It begins with an individual and moves through communities much like yeast leavens bread. That is what Jesus says the kingdom is, yeast, a mustard seed, small yet powerful, subversive at times, but with enough potential to take over a garden or a loaf of bread, a kitchen, a house, a neighborhood, a community, a city, even a world. It is the renewing of the mind at the street level.[72] Rather than viewing the enormous need that exists in the world today, it is far better to start by bringing *shalom* into the community that is immediately available to us. In that ministry context we can work toward a world made right, a world where all individuals and institutions, families, and people, regardless of their social standing, as well as the whole of creation, are joined together leading to the praise of the Lamb, who alone is worthy of our praise, and makes all things new.

It starts by taking action. Even imperfect action by those who don't have it all together helps. It is far better to be doing something than doing nothing. The Bible is full of examples of those who were used by God to bring change, who were not perfect, and many had glaring faults, but they were faithful, available, and teachable. As we demonstrate the *shalom* of God before those who do not yet know Him, they will be drawn to the life-changing river of God. The way we live, the purchases we make, the places where we shop, all give testimony to the fact that we are ambassadors for the King. Simplifying our lives so that we have more to share with those who don't have basic necessities is another essential step. Getting involved in a local urban mission as a volunteer, donating clothes to a shelter, giving food to a food bank, all help and get us involved at a very vital level.

Until the day comes when all things are finally restored and made whole, we serve because we represent the kingdom of God here and now. The new heaven and new earth will be a place where all that is wrong because of sin will be made right. But for now, we must be about the King's business.

> As the church, we have the opportunity to influence and transform our communities and our culture—not by being a critic of the culture, not by merely creating a vision of a different culture, but by embodying the change we would like to see and actually living out the kingdom message of Jesus. Lasting cultural change will happen only as believers create a more attractive and compelling picture of what life can be—living out what it means to put others above ourselves, valuing servanthood above power, doing acts of justice, loving mercy, and walking humbly with God.[73]

---

72. Rom 12:1–2.

73. Swanson and Williams, *To Transform*, 64.

1

Preach the Gospel or Feed the Hungry

A Flood of Misunderstanding[1]

by Doug Priest

I F YOU WANT TO start an argument, ask a group of involved church members this question: "Of all the ministries this church performs, which is the most important?" Stand back and watch the fireworks begin.

When I was a missionary kid growing up in Ethiopia, the government required the missionaries to establish and manage primary schools. These schools provided the only opportunity for the local children to receive an education. My father oversaw the expansion of the school, and one of the tasks was constructing outhouses for the students. This meant that funds given for missions were used to build toilets. Nobody had a problem with this use of his time and their mission dollar.

A few years ago I visited Ethiopia and one of the missionaries had an objective that year for constructing seven different latrines. There were no concerns with the use of mission money for such a mundane task as digging pit latrines.

I have walked in many urban areas of the world and smelled the stench of raw sewage flowing through concrete pipes open to the air above. If it is acceptable to use mission money to dig latrines in rural Ethiopia, cannot mission money be used to help with sewage problems in urban parts of the world? Can somebody who has a degree in engineering, urban planning, or sanitation put that education to use for God in expanding the kingdom in the urban centers of the world while using mission funds to do so?

What exactly is the primary ministry or mission of the church? How should the church balance the focus between word and deed? Is evangelism more important than social transformation? Should we preach the gospel or feed the hungry?

WORD AND DEED

Throughout its history the church has been actively involved in addressing the social problems of the world. During the Middle Ages, church members ministered to those suffering from the plague while many of the medical practitioners ran away. Later, the

---

1. Portions of this chapter first appeared in Priest, "Balancing," 2009.

abolishment of slavery came about because Christians stood up against this evil. Schools and hospitals all over the world were started by Christians. In country after country, it was Christians who reduced languages into writing, which led to the education of its citizens. Literacy, fostered by Bible translation and the desire to read the Bible, was a key component in the independence movement and the demise of colonialism.

In the eighteenth century John Howard, a strong believer, noted the horrible prison conditions and determined to change the system. The prison conditions at the time were despicable, housed in run-down filthy buildings. The inmates were surrounded with indecency, alcohol, and disease. Prisoners were mistreated at the least provocation. Howard gave his life and his personal fortune to remedy the conditions and was later personally thanked by the British House of Commons.

Florence Nightingale is regarded as the founder of modern nursing. She received her training at a Christian school, and her faith was deeply influenced by the evangelical revivals in England. The deeply religious Lord Shaftesbury helped to reform the working conditions for the common laborers.[2] His reforms cut the working hours in factories from sixteen to ten hours a day and abolished all but necessary work on Sundays. The church established orphanages, emancipated women, educated prisoners, and extolled temperance, all the while exalting Christ and extending his kingdom. Through the centuries, ministries of word and deed went hand in hand. They were seen as two sides of the same coin.

WORD OR DEED

But a century ago seminaries in Europe began promoting the rise of modernism and theological liberalism. Many Christians reacted, holding tenaciously to the biblical fundamentals of the past in the face of Higher Criticism.[3] When some began to openly question the authorship of various books of the Bible or the Virgin birth, others broke away and formed new associations of like-minded believers. One of the scandals of Christianity in the previous century was when, for reasons that were not valid then and certainly are not valid today, the church became polarized over the dichotomy of *evangelism vs. social action*. This false dichotomy became pronounced during the early decades of the last century. Churches separated themselves into camps that labeled one another as either "conservative" or "liberal." The liberals engaged in doing good deeds, termed *social action*, while the conservatives concentrated their efforts on evangelism, personal piety, and starting churches. Each group first offended and then later largely ignored the other.

The rift between liberal Christians and conservative Christians widened. As a result, denominations split along these lines. The mainline denominations generally adopted a more liberal agenda that included active response to the social ills of the day. The intellectual movement that sought to apply Christian ethics to social problems became known as the *Social Gospel*. The liberals talked about "salvation today." To them, salvation was characterized by peace, justice, alleviation of hunger, and the lack of poverty. The messy *here and now* became more important than the sweet *by and by*. In contrast, the conser-

2. Orr, *Evangelical Awakenings*, 38.

3. Higher Criticism is a form of literary analysis, studying the biblical texts to determine their authorship, origin, and meaning.

vatives described salvation as eternal life and the blessings that come with heaven. The liberals accused the conservatives of "being too heavenly minded to be any earthly good," while the conservatives berated the liberals for their "socialist agenda."

Conservative churches promoted new efforts of evangelism and planting new churches. Their focus became piety along with sharing the gospel widely so that all would have a chance at salvation. Crusade evangelism became commonplace. Books and articles were written discussing various methods of evangelism.

A growing focus on heaven and eternity meant there was less emphasis and desire to address social problems. By and large, Christians were forced to choose between *word or deed*, between faith or works. To put it bluntly, one could study the Bible, or one could serve in a soup kitchen at the rescue mission. Most conservative Christians chose Bible study. Unfortunately, the "church's lack of concern about social issues led many social activists in the 1960s and 1970s to think they had to leave the church to make a difference in the world"[4]

Through the first three quarters of the twentieth century, the ministry options of *word and deed* were like going to a closet and having to choose either a brown shirt or a turquoise shirt. Both are pieces of clothing, but they are completely different. To choose either evangelism or social transformation and exclude the other does violence to what the Bible clearly teaches and is therefore a sin against both God and humanity. Choice between *word or deed* should not be an option. Rogers reminds us that "to ignore the physical realities and implications of poverty, hunger, sorrow, and mistreatment in favor of a purely spiritualized ministry is to ignore God's compassion for the suffering of his human children."[5]

WORD OVER DEED

The Lausanne Congress on World Evangelization in 1974 marked a watershed event in the life of evangelical and conservative churches. As the conference was devoted to world evangelism, delegates from all over the world attended. The context of Christianity for many of the delegates from the Majority World included poverty, lack of food, minimal education, and environmental degradation. While the attendees from the West spoke of the priority of evangelism over social action, the delegates from the Majority World rose up *en masse*, wanting nothing to do with such a one-armed ministry. They noted that in the rich West, where needs for food, housing, employment, and clothing were largely met, it was easy to speak disparagingly of social action. But in their world, they could not afford an amputated gospel. To them, evangelism included such activities as feeding the hungry, addressing poverty and unjust structures, freeing the oppressed, and restoring sight to the blind.

For evangelical Christians, Lausanne was a wake-up call. The voices of the delegates from the Majority World were heard. From the Lausanne Congress onward, conservative Christian thinkers slowly began to break down the dichotomy of *word or deed* and began to see both were necessary to be true to the Bible and to the world situation. Samuel Escobar, mission theologian from Peru, reflects:

4. Sider, *Churches that Make a Difference*, 43.

5. Rogers, *Holistic Ministry*, 175.

> The missionary agenda in the Third World cannot avoid the issues linked to Christian mission and social transformation—issues such as human rights, the socio-political consequences of missionary action, the ideological use of the Christian message for political aims, and the religious sanction for contemporary forms of economic or cultural colonialism.[6]

One does not change one's opinion on deeply held theological positions overnight, and so a compromise in *word and deed* thinking was reached. Evangelicals or conservative Christians now understood that neither evangelism nor social action should be left off the ministry agenda. Both were necessary. They held that evangelism was *primary*, while ministries of social action were *secondary*. In community after community the church began to involve itself in social ministries as had earlier generations. The concept of meeting people's felt needs (secondary purpose) as a means of attracting them to Christ (primary purpose) became a prevailing ministry strategy.

Not only was *word* seen as *primary*, it was also seen as *priority*. Many believed the best way to change a society was to first introduce individuals to Christ. These people then, as they came to understand the implications of their faith, would naturally address social needs and society would benefit. Due to a trickle-down effect, it was believed, society would be transformed. As plausible as this strategy sounds, it usually worked only at the individual and immediate family level. Even with a growing Christianity around the world, the rich got richer while the poor got poorer. As Christians in the West dieted, Christians in the Majority World starved.

WORD WITH DEED

In his life, Jesus exemplified exactly the commandments of loving God and loving one's neighbor. Jesus' life was a balance between proclamation and demonstration, between *word and deed*. Jesus came into this world to provide atonement for sin. While he ministered to the poor, the marginalized, the oppressed, and the rejected, his message glorified God and brought salvation to the lost. His ministry included both word and deed. Rogers asks,

> Did Jesus feed everyone he taught? No. Did He heal everyone He encountered who needed healing? Probably not. Did He change the physical circumstances of everyone He encountered? No. Can we? No. But does that realization relieve us of the obligation to do what we can to help people when and where we can? It does not.[7]

No matter whether Jesus was cleansing the leper, feeding the crowd, releasing the oppressed, healing the sick, comforting the afflicted, or lifting up the downtrodden, his ministry brought material change to people's lives. Jesus came to bring good news to the poor (Luke 4:18). In his ministry, he showed that he had a preferential option for the poor. Jesus did not focus on those who had it all together. He went instead to those who could barely scrape it together.

Mission strategists today speak of *holistic mission* or *transformational development*. These terms represent the balanced ministry of Jesus. Holistic ministry sees people as physi-

---

6. Escobar, "Evangelical Missiology," 108.

7. Rogers, *Holistic Ministry*, 189.

cal, emotional, intellectual, and spiritual beings. People live in relationship to others. The gospel seeks to relate to people in the totality of their relationships and as whole people.

God cares about marginalized people, and holistic ministry includes demonstration as well as proclamation. Our ministry must be both in *word and deed*. Our outreach must be balanced. Our concern is not only about the material needs of the poor; it is about all the needs of people—whether physical, emotional, intellectual, social, spiritual—whatever needs they may have. Holistic ministry seeks to meet the needs of people who have been created in the image of God.

Combining *word and deed* brings together the spiritual and social realities of life, putting God at the center of human existence. Here is how Bryant Myers describes holistic ministry or transformational development:

> The Kingdom vision for a better human future is summarized by the idea of shalom: just, peaceful, harmonious, and enjoyable relationships with each other, ourselves, our environment, and God. This Kingdom vision is inclusive of the physical, social, mental, and spiritual manifestations of poverty, and so all are legitimate areas of focus that is truly Christian. Therefore, immunizing children, improving food security, and providing potable water can be a part of the Kingdom future if the community says they need to be. Reconciliation, peace-building, and enabling everyone to make their contribution is part of the emergence of the Kingdom of God in the community. Working to make social systems, and those who manage and share them, accountable to work for the well-being of all can be a part of moving toward the Kingdom. Stress counseling and simply listening and being with those whose poverty begins in the inner heart or broken spirit is Kingdom business. Whatever heals and restores body, mind, spirit and community can be part of the transformational development which is synonymous with advancing the Kingdom of God, and hence is our mission as we seek to promote wholeness.[8]

As Christians look at their communities and, indeed, at the world, we are confronted with a myriad of images demanding our attention-—tsunamis, abortion clinics, declining inner-city schools, Katrina-force hurricanes, starvation, HIV/AIDS, rampant poverty, racial prejudice, other religions, lack of prayer, shallow levels of commitment, and the large number of unbelievers. We must struggle to address these important needs.

In the Majority World, one half a billion people are living in absolute poverty, meaning they earn less than $1.25 per day. Three to four billion people in the world live on less than $2 a day. Eight-thousand people contract HIV/AIDS every day. One-third of the world is well fed, one-third is under-fed, and one-third is starving. The church wants to be involved and wants to be more externally focused. Every community, every context, has different needs crying out for attention.

Where do we begin? Picture a circle. At various stopping points of the circle are listed the specific needs of the community. In one area, the needs might be the rising divorce rate, the influx of internet pornography, the plight of the homeless, those without Christ, or the recent flood. Perhaps the obvious starting point on the circle is the most pressing need.

---

8. Myers, *Walking with the Poor*, 113.

How then do word and deed fit together? What is the correct relationship between the two? Christopher Wright suggests an answer as we examine the various points of need on our circle. He believes in the *ultimacy* of evangelism rather than the *primacy* of evangelism. He writes,

> Ultimately we must not rest content until we have included within our own missional response the wholeness of God's missional response to the human predicament—and that of course includes the good news of Christ . . . Mission may not always begin with evangelism. But mission that does not ultimately include declaring the Word and the name of Christ, and faith and obedience has not completed its task.[9]

Prioritizing between *word and deed* in ministry has varied over time. Choosing between evangelism *or* social action results in a truncated gospel. Evangelism as *primary* and social action as *secondary* has not measurably affected societal ills. Social action as *primary* has seen evangelism's decline in the face of so many pressing needs. But evangelism as *ultimate*—that is, ministry has not been completed unless evangelism has taken place—provides the appropriate and biblical balance. The gospel is not limited to evangelization or establishing church-planting movements. Rather, it is about transformation at both the personal and the societal level.

How do transformation and evangelism relate to one another? Some would say that transformation is the *consequence* of evangelism. As people come to know the Lord, they change their lives, and as more lives are changed, society can be changed. Others would say that as transformation occurs as a result of Christian ministry, people will respond positively and hence evangelism will occur. Transformation, then, would be a *bridge* to evangelism. Finally, some would say that transformation and evangelism should be *full partners*, with both taking place at the same time. Each influences the other, as the following examples from Kenya will show.

TRANSFORMATION IN THE SLUMS

Nairobi is the capital of Kenya. Sitting at an elevation of 5500 feet, not far from the equator, the city has drawn people from the rural areas of the country. Nairobi is home to five million people. Approximately 70 percent of those live in a series of slums that surround the city. There are ten different major slums in Nairobi. There are few schools in the slums. Unemployment is rampant. Up to 25% of the people living in these slums are HIV positive or have AIDS.

One of the slums is called Mathare Valley. It extends for about a mile and a half and is less than half a mile wide. The slum is home to nearly a million people who live on the slopes going down to the valley floor. The hills are not large, which means the people are crammed into very little space. The homes are shanties, most of which are one room or two at the most. Into these homemade shanties—most of which measure only ten by twelve feet—reside as many as five, ten, or even fifteen people. I visited the home of a single mother named Khadijah who had eighteen people living in her house. She has no

---

9. Wright, *Mission of God*, 318–19.

space, but simply cannot turn away people in need. So she just crams them in. They sleep on the floor and in three-tiered bunk beds. They sleep four deep.

Private landlords rent out a little space, and the people construct their shanties using scrounged wood and sheets of aluminum. Almost none of the shanties have running water. Instead there are a few spigots throughout Mathare Valley where water jugs can be taken and filled for a price. Some of the slum residents have run illegal wires so that there is some electricity in a few homes and shops.

What is noticeable about the homes in Mathare Valley is that there is no running water, and hence, no toilet facilities. There are a few public toilets in the area, but these are often locked up. To use these toilets costs money. It takes a family of five one-third of their daily income for each person to use the toilet just one time a day.

Money is at a premium because the average wage in Mathare Valley is one dollar a day. Most choose not to use that money to pay for toilet facilities. Instead, the children relieve themselves wherever they can. Any open space will do. Older children and adults want privacy, so the people of the slums of Kenya have invented a system they call "flying toilets." The people relieve themselves into plastic bags, tie a knot, and then fling the bags as far as they can. Many end up on the roofs of the shanties, many end up on the paths. As can be imagined, there are plastic bags everywhere, and the stench can be overpowering.

Along the valley floor is a small river. The poorest of the poor in Mathare Valley live the farthest down the hillsides, alongside of the river. At the very top of the hills are some cement buildings that are rented out by the room. Farther down are the corrugated tin shanties. All of the sewage runs downhill, so the closer to the valley floor, the more sewage flows from above.

One of the communities at the very bottom of Mathare Valley is called Madoya. Following training in community development, the dozen leaders of the community determined that their biggest needs were toilet facilities. They understand the health problems associated with open sewage. The plan they came up with was to construct six different toilets in Madoya, an area that has thousands of people and no toilets.

The facility would measure twenty feet by twenty-six feet. One side of the first floor had toilets for men, and the other side had toilets for women. There were also showers in the building. At the outside of the building would be clean water with which the people could clean themselves and also purchase water to carry to their homes. Several members of the group that was trained are Muslims. Yet the toilet facility was drawn to have two floors. The top floor was to be used as a church and a community meeting hall. The building was constructed. A church was started and within two years needed to find a larger facility as it had outgrown the space. Christ's call to the church is to not simply save souls but to transform communities in his name. Holistic ministry aims for "both spiritual renewal and social renewal, including institutional development, structural reform, and creation care."[10]

In the Nairobi slums I was introduced to an emaciated woman named Phanice who has five children. She came to Nairobi in 1992 and lived for eight years with her husband. He was a casual day worker, taking any job he could for the day. In 2000 they had to relocate due to lack of money. They had to move because her husband lost his casual job

---

10. Sider, *Churches*, 50.

of loading and unloading trucks. He lost his job because his strength was waning. In 2002 he died from AIDS.

Phanice contracted the virus from her husband. She was visited by a health worker and a minister in 2004. The minister prayed for her and the health worker secured AIDS medications for her. Phanice committed her life to Christ and has actively been involved in the church since then. In 2004 she attended a training session on Community Health Evangelism, a Christian strategy to help people live holistic lives. She learned the benefits of development as opposed to relief. She learned about using what resources she had to help herself. She learned that preventing diseases is as important as curing them. Following this training, Phanice formed a group of single mothers living with AIDS to support one another.

When I first met Phanice I saw how sick she was. The next time I saw her, two months later, she had deteriorated so much that I did not believe she would live much longer. On that trip Phanice was blessed by one of the preachers visiting with me who decided to sponsor her son, Collins, a thirteen year-old, who had passed his exams to get into high school. But Phanice had no means to pay the required school fees, so he was living with his mother, seemingly with no future. Today Collins and two of Phanice's other children are being sponsored so that their school fees are paid and they receive school uniforms, books, food, health care, and spiritual mentoring.

Today Phanice is alive. Because of her medications and her faith, she has gotten stronger and has been able to hold down a job. Her life has been changed physically and spiritually. She takes comfort in knowing that her children are in school learning, eating, and loving Jesus. She is at ease mentally. Phanice has a future. She is in control of her economic state and she loves God.

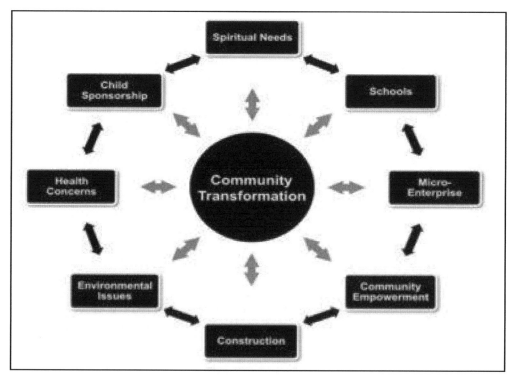

The diagram above shows the major components of need in Mathare Valley. There are upwards of 95,000 children in the valley who have no money or schools to attend. A high percentage of the people have no jobs, so loans to help them establish businesses is a priority. Empowered communities are better able to solve their own problems. The homes are shanties that provide little shelter from the elements, little privacy, and most have no electricity. There is little clean water available. Sanitation is an issue. Garbage sits on the ground with no collection. Disease is rampant. Spiritual needs abound.

Following Christopher Wright, as mentioned above, it does not matter which need is addressed first in ministry. Starving people need food. Children need education. Those suffering from AIDS need to be comforted. The unemployed need a livelihood. All need shelter, sanitation, and access to clean water. People need to be introduced to Jesus. Churches need to be started. "God wants to renew every area of human society, from moral choices to family relationships to neighborhood associations to community institutions to laws. Holistic ministries, therefore, confront sin and foster transformation at every level."[11]

POVERTY IS LINKED WITH JUSTICE

Recent works on poverty alleviation by Yunus,[12] Corbett and Fikkert,[13] and Greer and Smith[14] are exemplary of a growing trend toward sustainability instead of dependency. These authors all realize that any lasting attempt to address social issues must consider the root causes of the associated problems. While *relief* is needed for the short term, *development* is required for lasting change. Feeding a hungry child is crucially important, but unless the deeper issues of joblessness, unjust economic structures, political oppression, and lack of education are addressed, the child will become hungry again within a few hours. A lack of clean water may be directly related to deforestation, which may be caused by refugees who need to cut down the trees to warm themselves and cook their food. The refugees may be in their new location because a corrupt government was involved in ethnic genocide or used their limited resources for a needless war on a neighboring country rather than building up their own infrastructure.

The growing awareness of root causes has captured the mind of Christians who now realize that many social problems are due to injustice. In this decade a rising concern for justice is a hallmark of the Millennial generation. These youth understand that Christians throughout the world cannot benefit physically or spiritually unless they are free from what oppresses them. Youth today raise funds, write letters to their congressional leaders, advocate, march, pray, and work to change policies. They travel to Asia to make documentaries about sex trafficking, move into the inner city to live among the destitute, make contributions to fund microenterprise initiatives, and shoot free throws to raise money for the hungry. They also vote their conscience. They see the results of affluent consumerism

11. Ibid., 87.
12. Yunnus, *Banker to the Poor* and *Creating a World Without Poverty*.
13. Corbett and Fikkert, *When Helping Hurts*.
14. Greer and Smith, *The Poor Will Be Glad*.

and are saying emphatically, "Enough is enough!" They desire involvement and want to get their hands dirty. Gill writes, "A rising generation is calling for a more comprehensive "kingdom mission" that transforms the evil injustices and inequities of global society."[15] This generation is motivated to make a difference in the world by caring for the poor. They and their churches are using their resources to attack poverty.

> Never in our lifetime—perhaps not anytime in the last one hundred years—has the possibility of explosive growth in holistic ministry been so promising. . . We believe the next few decades could see an explosion of holistic ministry that will draw millions to personal faith in Christ, restore broken people to wholeness, and renew entire neighborhoods and societies.[16]

Build houses in the slums, bandage the wounded, pick up the trash in the park, and ensure that when all is said and done, the name of Christ has been proclaimed as both word and deed. Those who have been ministered to have now joined the family and are ministering to others.

May it then be said about us:

> Those Christians are the ones who run in when everyone else is running out. Those Christians are the ones who didn't give up on the crumbling inner cities. Those Christians are the ones who brought peace to Darfur. Those Christians are the ones who put an end to human trafficking. Those Christians are the ones who helped with the war on AIDS around the world. . . Those Christians are the ones that made me want to believe in God.[17]

---

15. Gill, "Reassessing the Frontiers," 21.

16. Sider, *Churches*, 11, 14.

17. Kinnaman and Lyons, *unchristian*, 233.

2

Enfleshing Hope:
Incarnational Approaches to Emulate

by Ashley Barker

INTRODUCTION

THE IDEA OF ENFLESHING or incarnating comes from the Latin *incarnatus* and literally means a "fleshing out," used as a metaphor for making real or effective.[1] In Christian theology Jesus is understood as the Incarnate One who, as the Word, "became flesh" and lived among us, John 1:14. Ross Langmead, in surveying different Christian traditions, identified three main uses of the term "incarnational" in mission and this definition is a starting point. These are:

1. following Jesus as the pattern for mission

2. participating in Christ's risen presence as the power for mission

3. joining God's cosmic mission of enfleshment in which God's self-embodying dynamic is evident from the beginning of creation.[2]

Enfleshing hope is a theological motif that builds on Langmead's definition and uses the centrality of hope as anticipating and beginning to experience the promises of God.

If one end of the incarnational spectrum sees no value at all for Christians in an incarnational approach, then the other end has a far more concrete and literal understanding of how crucially the Incarnation relates to Christians in mission. This can be seen in at least two ways.

First, Christ's Incarnation can be understood as a particular methodology that has specific steps that Christians can follow and apply in mission. This methodology is often raised in reaction to less credible, unenfleshed methodologies, such as attracting people out of poor neighborhoods to middle class churches, or visiting poor communities to make evangelistic raids only to return to nice, safe neighborhoods. John Perkins sums up

---

1. *The Free Dictionary*, http://www.thefreedictionary.com/incarnate, accessed August 10, 2010, s. v. "Incarnate."

2. Langmead, *The Word Made Flesh*, 8.

the common reaction to these kinds of methodologies in the following statement: "Jesus relocated. He didn't commute to earth one day a week and shoot back up to heaven. He left his throne and became one of us so that we might see the life God revealed in him."[3]

Incarnational mission here is often about pragmatic concerns and using the best methodologies possible and the methodology of the Incarnation is quickly cited as a justification. John Hayes, cites 1 Cor 9:20–23 as giving practical reasons for an incarnational methodology: "Living with and like the poor hastens language and culture learning, helps demonstrate that we are for real, and places us near the heartbeat of poor communities."[4] As another example, Dave Andrews provides five specific steps, developed with reference to Phil 2:4–8. They are:

- Step one—move into the locality

- Step two—remember our humanity

- Step three—empty ourselves

- Step four—serve others

- Step five—embrace suffering.[5]

Those who hold the incarnational position can differ in their opinions as to what specific steps and aims are involved in an incarnational methodology. What they have in common, however, is that they not only take seriously the idea of "following Jesus as a pattern for mission," to use Langmead's definition, but they also go further and make incarnational mission a specific methodology. They use the enfleshing metaphor based solely on the Incarnation of Christ and in a more literal way than other understandings we will consider. The provision of a variety of specific steps required for the methodology to be followed is another feature of this understanding, so it is possible to clearly assess whether a method is incarnational or not according to their definition.

Second, incarnational mission can be understood as a specific model to emulate or copy in mission strategy, more than simply a methodology to apply. A model in this sense is about using a demonstration to make logical future predictions. The Incarnational event then can be viewed as the true prototype for specific models of Christian mission today. Modelling after this event is not only about true discipleship of Christ, but also expects to result in lives being transformed just as Christ transformed lives, because it is the true mission of the church, too. These approaches can often fit within one of the three parts of Langmead's definition as "following Jesus as a pattern for mission," though there can be great diversity of opinion about what following this model means.[6] This can include models of devotion, contextualization, simple lifestyle, friendship evangelism, or social liberation. In fact, such a variety of understandings of what the specific model of Christ in mission is and how it should be copied today in slums makes it difficult to group

---

3. John Perkins, *With Justice For All*, 88.

4. Hayes, *Sub-merge*, 116.

5. Andrews, *Compassionate Community Work*, 31–32.

6. Langmead, *The Word Made Flesh*, 219–220.

these approaches together. As John Stott writes, however, what they have in common is the following assertion:

> Jesus did more than draw a vague parallel between his mission and ours. Deliberately and precisely he made his mission the model of ours, saying 'as the Father sent me, so I send you'. Therefore our understanding of the church's mission must be deduced from our understanding of the Son's. Why and how did the Father send the Son?[7]

The theological focus here is almost exclusively on the model of the Incarnation of Christ. Such an incarnational model is often weaker in identifying how the two other parts of Langmead's definitions relate to incarnational mission, if at all. Joining with the Creator's ongoing incarnational dynamic in creation and participating with the Sprit for empowerment in mission is not often an integral part of any specific part of an incarnational model of mission.[8]

In what sense can the Incarnation be understood as the specific method or model for Christians in mission today? What is the method or model the Incarnation provides for transformation? The following incarnational methodologies and models are examples of how this position can be seen in relationship to transforming lives and communities for Christ.

INCARNATION AS RELOCATION

Incarnational mission can be seen as a methodology of moving home to live and serve, as Jesus did, in another neighborhood. John's prologue is important as a basis for this methodology. Eugene Peterson paraphrases John 1:14 as "moving into the neighborhood"[9] because *skenoo* comes from a family of words which means to "pitch a tent," "encamp," "live," "dwell," "tabernacle."[10] Following Jesus into mission, therefore, is viewed as requiring a methodology of literally moving to live and make one's home in another place. Phil 2:5–7 is another key relocation passage. Jesus gave up the location of heaven to be born a human in a particular location on earth. Similarly, and as discussed above, Andrews and Perkins see the first step in an incarnational methodology as "moving into the neighborhood," not simply "commuting" or "visiting."[11] The Incarnational event can also mandate risking ourselves to physically go to the "other side of the road," like the Good Samaritan, Luke 10:25–37, or as in John's great commission, John 20:21, relocate as Jesus did.

In recent times, an incarnational methodology such as relocation has been especially advocated by Christians working and living among the poor. Relocation is often contrasted in frustration with methodologies used by Christian workers who commute from middle class suburbs into poor neighborhoods. The methodology Christians choose, it is argued, can undermine the message Christians preach. Dorothy Harris describes the early experiences of her colleagues where neighbors said that "Jesus can't live in the slums, but only

---

7. Stott, *Christian Mission*, 23.

8. Langmead, *The Word Made Flesh*, 219–228.

9. Peterson, *The Message*.

10. Gerhard Kittel, *Theological Dictionary of the New Testament*, 1040.

11. Andrews, *Compassionate Community Work*, 31–32.

in the nice big middle class churches." This raised up a commitment to prove otherwise and that Jesus can live in the slums. Harris noted that, "After ten years of church planting, community development, health care, non-formal education, income generation, etc., we are more convinced that the slums are not abandoned by the Father."[12] Perkins also sees Phil 2:5–8, as well as John 1:14, as a call to relocation in inner-city America: "He came and lived among us. He was called Emmanuel—God with us—the incarnation is the ultimate relocation."[13]

That incarnational mission requires the method of relocation can be a controversial view, especially among Christians who do not relocate. Michael Duncan, while living in a Manila slum with his family, raised this idea at the Lausanne Congress on World Evangelism in Manila in 1989, and faced strong opposition. "Should all missionaries who are working with the poor live in slums?" he was asked. "In the end I simply encouraged all missionaries to reread their Bibles and seek the Lord on the matter," but admitted that,

> I was upset over the fact that hundreds of missionaries were residing in some of the best residential areas of Manila while the majority of Manila's inhabitants were reduced to living in inhumane slums . . . They would have preferred it if I had simply said each to their call. But the intensity of feeling created over my answer suggested that I needed to explore this matter further.[14]

Duncan would go on to study and reflect further on the matter. After considering key texts and motivations for incarnational mission as relocation, he concluded that where Jesus focused his life and ministry implies Jesus' priorities and gives "textual help in terms of how to relocate and what is needed in relocation," though he also concluded that, "even though on the one hand scripture doesn't command us to relocate, scripture on the other hand is very much supportive and helpful in choosing this option. Relocation, therefore, is not solely a matter of personal choice and human effort."[15] Relocation and incarnational mission are still intrinsically tied together here.

Incarnational mission as a method takes up the idea of following Jesus, but often in a narrower and more literal sense than other views we will consider. As we shall see, there are limits to identifying with Jesus metaphorically in this way. Is where the Christ lived before his human birth in Bethlehem really analogous to a middle class neighborhood? Relocation can also neglect the other two parts of Langmead's definition of joining and participating with Christ, which do not necessarily fit with the one specific methodology of simply moving house.

INCARNATION AS CROSSING CULTURES

Incarnation can also be viewed in relationship to culture. As a method it can be understood as how a Christian worker joins a particular people group, seeking to become one

12. Harris, "Incarnation as a Journey in Relocation," 175.

13. Perkins, *With Justice for All*, 88.

14. Duncan, *Mission: The Incarnational Approach*, 2–3.

15. Duncan, *Mission*, 13.

of them or an insider. This method may or may not include relocation of home, but also draws heavily on Phil 2:5–7. Just as Jesus truly became a particular kind of human—a Galilean—to reach humanity, so too should Christians "have the same attitude as Christ" and identify with the community they want to reach. Former Bangkok slum worker Rob O'Callaghan writes that the philosophy of ministry of his organization commits them to an incarnational methodology but asks, "How are we to imitate God becoming human?" One of his answers is by identifying with the poor: "To serve the poor in the way of the Incarnation means being willing to embrace poverty. It might mean eating things that we would normally throw out as unfit. It might mean coming into contact with filth. It might mean jeopardizing our social standing."[16]

This use of incarnational mission as a methodology of identification is also evident in the writings of many emerging-church authors, such as Michael Frost and Alan Hirsch, who view incarnational mission as a specific methodology including identification. In their influential book, *The Shaping of Things to Come*, contrasts are made between *attractional* and *incarnational* methodologies. The attractional method is where the "church bids people to come and hear the gospel in the holy confines of the church and its community."[17] In contrast, the Incarnation provides a method going in the opposite direction, where Christians go out and identify with a people group: "The Incarnation provides us with the missional means by which the gospel can become a genuine part of a people group without damaging the innate cultural frameworks that provide that people group with a sense of meaning and history . . . Incarnational mission will mean that in reaching a people group we will need to identify with them in all ways possible without compromising the truth of the gospel itself."[18]

Whereas incarnational mission as a methodology of relocation mostly focuses on Christians moving downward to poorer neighborhoods, it is worth noting that incarnational mission can be viewed more broadly than just moving toward the poor. Hirsch and Frost contend that "The practice of incarnational identification with a group of people . . . should apply to all forms of genuine mission whatever the context. Not only because it 'works,' but because it somehow reflects that primal act of identification that was an intrinsic part of Christ's Incarnation."[19] The view of incarnational mission as a methodology can lead us to employ strategies of identification and service with a particular target group to further the kingdom of God among those people.

Whether such identification with those of another culture is possible needs further consideration. Most cross-cultural missionaries are aware that while they can do much to show that they love and stand beside those of another culture, they ultimately remain outsiders, or semi-insiders. They are never natives but are always in some ways strangers bringing gifts.[20] This is certainly true of those who move from a rich country to a poor slum and squatter neighborhood. Incarnational mission as methodology can lend itself

16. Rob O'Callaghan, 'What do we mean by "Incarnational Methodology?"', 6–8.

17. Frost and Hirsch, *The Shaping of Things to Come*, 41.

18. Ibid., 37–38.

19. Ibid., 38.

20. Gittins, *Gifts and Strangers*.

to participating with what God is doing within a culture, but to claim to be the same as people born into other cultures or sub-cultures is to claim more than Jesus did. He was born into one human culture of first century Palestine. Modern Christians who identify with a sub-culture not their own are not the same as Jesus at that point. There is potential for practical helpfulness in this kind of methodology, but there are also inadequacies that will be considered shortly.

A slightly less literal understanding of the Incarnation in relationship to culture focuses on Jesus as a model for contextualization. That God sent Jesus Christ to become a Jewish person can be seen as the model for all cross-cultural missionaries. Jesus spent over thirty years a part of the Jewish culture, playing a particular role in family and work, before his public ministry began. Cross-cultural Christian workers, it is argued, should not take the host culture they go to live among any less seriously than Jesus' model.

This understanding has been particularly important in helping Christians move away from colonial models of civilizing local cultures with European Christianity. Nevertheless, cultural arrogance, even racism, can still emerge today, especially in cross-cultural settings. Jesus' model of humility in crossing cultures is an antidote to this. Rob O'Callaghan makes the point: Jesus' Incarnation "reminds us that we cannot divorce our witness from the specific cultural context within which it takes place."[21]

Judith and Sherwood Lingenfelter are prominent advocates of Jesus as the model for cross-cultural ministry. Taking a Christian anthropologist's approach to incarnational mission, they develop a specific incarnational model of relating contextually.[22] Ideas of humility, a learning posture and "growing up" in a new setting can be a helpful description of what is required in adapting to new cultures. Often cross-cultural workers need to shed identities and limit differences that can be barriers to their new host culture. There are issues we will come to shortly when Christ's deity and pre-existence are identified with a new culture.

Todd Billings has some serious objections to this formulation of Christ. He believes that Jesus' ministry was unique and cannot be replicated by Christians today. He also raises one objection not yet considered: "The divine nature is not a 'culture' and we cannot (and should not) see ourselves as analogous to the pre-incarnate Word that then takes on humanity."[23] Since deity is not the same as culture, there are dangers in Christians identifying Christ as our model for crossing cultures. The Incarnation as a model for cross-cultural ministry has real limitations when applied like this, but as Billings argues, "We should identify with the culture so that our lives offer an intelligible witness to the one redeemer of peoples from all cultures, Jesus Christ. It is not enough to bear witness to Jesus as the model for crossing cultures. Jesus is much more than a model."[24]

At best, the model of the Incarnation for cross-cultural ministry can pick up one of three themes identified by Langmead in incarnational approaches. That is, "co-operating

21. O'Callaghan, "What do we Mean by 'Incarnational Methodology?'"
22. Lingenfelter and Lingenfelter, *Teaching Cross-Culturally*, 22.
23. Billings, "Incarnational Ministry."
24. Ibid.

with God's incarnational activity since creation"[25] because God is at work in a particular culture and Christians can join God in the ongoing transformation process is different from confusing divinity with culture. The limitations of this model lie in its potential to blur the uniqueness of Christ, to fail to see the differences between culture and divinity, or to set up Christian workers to try to do work which only the Divine can do. To identify cross-cultural mission as analogous with the Incarnational event is problematic and ultimately unhelpful in seeking the transformation of communities.

INCARNATION AS INFLUENCING OTHERS

The Incarnational event can be viewed as a classic methodology or model to see change in people and even see whole social movements emerge from among the host people group of a Christian worker.

First, particularly found in youth ministry circles, an incarnational approach to mission can be synonymous with following Jesus' model of personal influence via friendships. Jesus left heaven and focused his ministry on inviting twelve people to share life with him. That journey together influenced their lives, identity and destiny. Once these men became disciples of Jesus, they were then able to influence others to become Christ's disciples through the means of their personal relationships.

Andrew Root studied this approach to youth ministry.[26] He credits Young Life founder Jim Rayburn with creating a breakthrough in youth mission in America in the 1940s and 50s that has set the model for many contemporary youth ministry approaches.[27] Rather than expecting young people to come to church, or even the evangelistic crusades that many churches and youth organizations ran at the time, Young Life concentrated on developing influential relationships within high schools and would then invite students to events like Bible clubs. Rayburn soon discovered that if he could "accrue a currency of cool by incarnating himself within distinct youth culture," he could receive "cool capital from the most popular students' that would influence others."[28] Root observes that initially Rayburn did much of this kind of ministry intuitively. As Young Life perfected this approach and soon became a national and then international phenomenon, Rayburn began to reference the Incarnation as the model of relational influence for the gospel's sake:

> Using the incarnation as a pattern, an example of how ministry could be done, Rayburn positioned the incarnation as ministerial justification (rather than theological explication) of ministry. Because of this perspective, relational ministry to this day is infused with this understanding of the incarnational as solely a pattern for ministry.[29]

Real and relevant ways to connect with young people were found, but in a survey of youth ministers Root also discovered a darker side. A kind of cool, Christian ghetto

25. Langmead, *The Word Made Flesh*, 55.

26. Andrew Root, *Revisiting Relational Youth Ministry.*

27. Ibid., 50–53.

28. Ibid., 52–53.

29. Ibid., 53.

quickly emerged from following such a model. One where young people sometimes felt their friendships with leaders were a commodity. Root is particularly critical of those who don't see any intrinsic value in Christians sharing place unless it leads to church participation.[30] Seeking out relationships with vulnerable adolescents only as a means to get them to come to events and make Christian decisions is ethically problematic. Is the cost of this intentional friendship a young person's soul? Not only is this practice ethically dubious, young people and community residents can often smell a hidden agenda and withdraw.

Relational model imitation as incarnational mission has potential inadequacies around grace, creativity, and the ongoing incarnational work of God. There are, however, deeper questions. Not least is the question of whether incarnational mission is primarily a model to justify personal persuasive powers in friendship evangelism. Jesus of Nazareth did share life with his disciples and others in a way that can inform how Christians can relate to others, but what kind of model is Jesus in these relationships? This model of incarnational youth ministry outlined above claims to be based on how Jesus approached relationships, but when the Gospels are considered, few if any people with "cool currency" are found in Jesus' friendship circles. In fact, Jesus' closest friendships were with Galileans, fishermen, and Jewish tax collectors who were all among some of the most despised people of Palestine.[31] Further, rather than Jesus seeking to be paid back for his friendship by having friends join his group, Jesus commands his disciples to love others "expecting nothing in return."[32] When modern friendship evangelism aims to influence young people to join their in-groups via the currency of friendship, it faces a serious problem in justifying this on the basis of Jesus' model of sharing relationships. Jesus' life and teachings may well be useful as a pattern to help inspire new ways and models of just and compassionate relationships, but they are not coercive or exploitative. Root especially points to Langmead and Bonhoeffer to help develop a broader, more appropriate incarnational approach to youth ministry.[33] Sharing life "through the risen Christ," rather than striving to copy Christ's relationships as the right model, has particular relevance to Christians with neighbors. Incarnational mission needs to be more than a model of friendship evangelism. Incarnation viewed as one specific model of mission, but here we can simply say that incarnational mission needs to be more than a model of friendship evangelism.

Second, the Incarnation is the model of the ultimate movement initiator and instigator in slums. Jesus discipled the apostles and sent them out into the world to continue the movement, John 20:21. Following Jesus' way in the Incarnational event may include identification and relocation, but it can also be understood as a method of initiating Christian faith indigenized through a people movement. This view—often cited by emerging-church, house church, and church growth activists[34]—can especially be seen

30. Ibid., 62–80.

31. Matt 9:10–11, Mark 2:15–16, Luke 5:30.

32. Luke 14:7–17.

33. Root, *Revisiting Relational Youth Ministry*, 83.

34. See, for example, Hirsch, *The Forgotten Ways*, 190–216; Simson, *The Starfish Manifesto*; and Addison, *Movements that Change the World*.

in the writings and ministry of Viv Grigg in regard to slums. For example, drawing on John 17, Grigg outlines Jesus' incarnational strategy of discipleship as "a new sociological paradigm—a new small-group structure and a new pattern for birthing a movement. Based on these building blocks we can develop patterns for forming churches."[35] Referring to social change movements such as the rise of the Black Panthers and Pentecostalism, Grigg calls for Christian slum movements: "Movements grow from the communication of a positive and convinced faith. They tend to be absolutist in their beliefs, to have a strong esprit de corps, and tend to reject other groups because of it."[36] Yet such movements bring the possibility of transformation:

> The aim is not missions,
> Nor is it the planting of churches,
> The aim is not the multiplication of churches.
> The aim is to multiply fellowships
> In such harmony with the soul of a people
> That movements are established of disciples
> Who know this movement is Christ's answer
> To the cries of this people's heart.[37]

Grigg sees incarnational involvement as an indispensable part of a methodology of raising up such Christian movements in slums: "Is incarnation essential? For church planting, the leadership of the church in the slums must be incarnate in the community. The missionary, in order to train others in such pastoral work, must set the pattern of identification and model the incarnational lifestyle."[38] This methodology can call up images from all three dimensions of Langmead's definition. Church-planting movements can require Christians to follow, join, and participate with the risen Christ. Whether the claim that the Incarnation justifies this approach—or should be limited to this particular strategy or model—is defensible, however, it needs to be considered, along with other weaknesses that will be discussed regarding incarnational mission as a methodology in general.

INCARNATION AS SIMPLE LIFESTYLE

In a context where the increased wealth of Western missionaries is paired with the rise of urbanization where rich and poor can live side-by-side, affluence has been described as a barrier to real engagement with those facing urban poverty. Roger Greenway contends that when Christians keep accumulating possessions in front of poor people, "They are communicating a message about their values, priorities, and the deep affections of their hearts. And that message contradicts the gospel."[39] In the face of such challenges, the Incarnational event is drawn upon as a specific model for consumer lifestyle choices in

---

35. Grigg, *Cry of the Urban Poor*, 163.

36. Ibid., 218.

37. Ibid., 217.

38. Grigg, 'Sorry! The Frontier Moved,' 159.

39. Roger S. Greenway, 'Eighteen Barrels and Two Big Crates.'

mission among the poor. Paul's call to have the "same attitude as Christ"[40] is a mandate for an incarnational lifestyle because God became a poor person in Galilee for humanity's sake. Homeless, with "nowhere to lay his head,"[41] Jesus prioritized the needs of others above his own. His example calls Christians to be intentionally sacrificial and downwardly mobile rather than consumerist and upwardly mobile. As a model for living, Paul is often cited as "becoming all things to all people,"[42] in the way Jesus also modeled. Thus Christians are to reduce any socio-economic barriers that thwart their ability to relate to those facing poverty because that is what Jesus modelled.

The view of incarnational mission as a simple lifestyle model has been taken up by many contemporary Christian writers and activists,[43] but perhaps its best known and most controversial advocate is Jonathan Bonk. His book, *Missions and Money: Affluence as a Missionary Problem*, generated significant debate between Western and non-Western missionaries and church leaders. Central to Bonk's thesis is that affluence is a barrier that must intentionally be addressed by the inherently powerful Christian worker. Heb 4:15 is a key verse in an incarnational model for Bonk because Jesus is able "to sympathize with our weaknesses . . . tested, as we are, yet without sin." This view can be a call to follow Christ's lifestyle as a pattern that focuses on sustainability, generosity, and relationship, rather than hoarding resources. How, asks Bonk, can missionaries, who seem to be a group of people who do not have any needs, connect and identify with the needy poor and vice versa? Bonk argues that Christian workers can often model an inversion to the Incarnation depicted in Heb 4:15. If the missionary's lifestyle is dramatically different from the lifestyle of their neighbors then the medium of their lifestyle can undermine the message of the Christ who was poor but generous.[44]

Further, Bonk argues that the test for Christian fidelity in lifestyle and message is not the sincerity of intentions of the Christian worker, but what the receiving community actually understands the missionary's lifestyle to be saying. Bonk asserts: "By abandoning the Incarnation as a model for its own life and mission, the affluent church has assured its fundamental spiritual impotence."[45] Credibility and authority are undermined if a sacrificial lifestyle similar to that of Jesus is missing.[46] Bonk concludes that the communicators' lifestyles, not simply the words they say, is the key to sharing what the Incarnational event means. Words, even great words, can be easily dismissed, but a life "lived up close and personal" modeled on Jesus is hard, if not impossible to ignore. Paul's "all things to all people" then is a call to downward mobility.[47]

The lifestyle challenges raised by mission in slums are not issues only for Western missionaries in the developing world. The Thai Christian community in Bangkok, for

40. Phil 2:1–11.

41. Matthew 8:20.

42. 1 Cor 9:22.

43. See, Sider, *Rich Christians*, 2005.

44. Bonk, *Missions and Money*, 95.

45. Ibid., 95.

46. Ibid., 96.

47. Ibid., 61–64.

example, is predominantly wealthy, and so the gap between those living in Klong Toey slum and most Christians in Bangkok can be acute. It's one thing, for example, for a Thai Christian to drive a Mercedes into Klong Toey to share a Christmas message and then drive back home to a mansion. It is quite another to consider how the life and teachings of the Jesus who was born in Nazareth relate to the lifestyle of those both sharing and receiving the Christmas story. This incongruence between medium and message may be a major barrier to the transformation of slums in Bangkok.

Bonk is right to raise the growing gap between the messenger, the medium, and the message in slums. Whether the Incarnation needs to be used to justify responses or to reduce incarnational mission to a specific lifestyle model, however, needs further thought. Several problems exist, not the least of which is that many specifics of Jesus' core lifestyle model are impossible for a contemporary Christian to emulate in a slum or elsewhere. The way a first century, single Jewish male, with a vocation as an itinerant Rabbi, prophet, and Messiah lived cannot be repeated. Even if culture, dress, vocation, and gender roles are put to one side, how helpful would it really be for the transformation of an urban slum neighborhood if each Christian family took up Jesus' itinerant lifestyle and constantly moved around? Interestingly, even Jesus asked people not to follow his itinerant lifestyle model as exemplified by the healed demoniac, Mark 5:18–19. Jesus' unique mission required a specific lifestyle that was vastly different even from his contemporaries. Could it therefore be unhelpful for contemporary Christians, including contemporary Christian families, to live in slums using Jesus as their model for lifestyle? If incarnational mission is to be transformative in slums, it needs a broader definitional base than just what is or isn't part of Jesus' lifestyle model.

THE CHURCH AS CHRIST'S CONTINUING INCARNATION

Another view of incarnational mission understands the Incarnation to continue through the method of the institutional church. It rests on a literal reading of the metaphor of the body of Christ.[48] This view has become an important justification for the crucial role that local and denominational churches play in mission. Johann Adam Mohler wrote:

> The visible church . . . is the Son of God himself, everlastingly manifesting himself among men (and women) in a human form, perpetually renovated, and eternally young—the permanent incarnation of the same, as in Holy Writ, even the faithful as called the body of Christ.[49]

In general, Protestants have been keen to differentiate between any institutional church, the broader "people of God" and the even broader kingdom of God. Narrowing and blurring these demarcations in an effort to justify the paramount importance of the institutional local church as the primary manifestation of the continuing Incarnation is not uncommon. Many local church ministers feel all over the world in different ways: one aspect of their lives—the belonging to and leading of the local institution of their church—is actually being Christ incarnate. Given that a growing number of Westerners

48. Romans 12:4–5; 1 Corinthians 12:12, 27.
49. Mohler, *Symbolism; or, Exposition,* 333.

identify themselves as Christians but are not involved in any local church community, coupled with the fact that more aggressive Christian NGOs,[50] media ministries, and conferences now compete for Christian participation using more sophisticated means, the rhetoric of the local church as Christ incarnate is understandable. Warren, for example, writes that:

> The Bible calls the church 'the bride of Christ' and the 'body of Christ'. I can't imagine saying to Jesus, 'I accept you, but reject your body'. But we do this whenever we dismiss or demean or complain about the church.[51]

To identify the institutional local church as the sole, even ultimate, expression of the "body of Christ" is a common, but potentially problematic, use of the enfleshing metaphor in relationship to the Incarnation. Not the least of which is the potential problem of institutional abuse of power and organizational self-centeredness. Because few Christians feel comfortable saying "no" to Jesus, if Jesus is identified with an institution, then its survival can come above all else, whether it is right or wrong. This can especially be the case in slums where local churches among vulnerable people can often be run on authoritarian lines.

Any institution that claims to be Jesus Incarnate can also be in danger of idolatry, making itself Lord. At best, a high value on the local church institution can draw on Langmead's incarnational use of "following Jesus as a pattern in mission" in that Jesus of Nazareth lived and served in a committed community. Local pastors and missions are rightly concerned that in an increasingly individualized and consumer-driven society the call for more committed fellowship with other Christians is important. Langmead's notion of "participating with the risen Christ's continuing incarnation in the world" can be especially helpful in reinforcing this point, but note that this idea of Langmead's is a more modest calling than that of the church as the continuing Incarnation. It is dangerous for any institution to claim to be the literal Body of Christ simply because institutions are run by people who are at least partly flawed. The abuse of power that could be unleashed by adopting such a dangerous position could undermine the fidelity, credibility, and work of Jesus through a local group of believers.

ASSESSING INCARNATIONAL MISSION AS A SPECIFIC METHODOLOGY

Incarnational mission can be understood as a particular methodology or model. We can begin to further assess such approaches, as well as their strengths and weaknesses, doing so while giving special attention to slums.

Some Common Ground

The Incarnational event is used as a specific methodology, strategy, or model to emulate and so some common assumptions emerge. Potentially helpful and consistent with Langmead's definition, some aspects can also be at odds with a sustainable and helpful understanding of incarnational mission in slums.

---

50. NGO, Non-Government Organization.

51. Warren, *The Purpose Driven Life*, 132.

First, for this group an incarnational model or method cannot be an optional strategy in authentic Christian mission. Although some advocates of incarnational mission are exceptions in that they remain open to the possibility of other authentic strategies, (e.g., Duncan), these other methodologies are not considered to be consistent with God's methods. To remain "outside" and not to live among the people as "insiders," for example, is clearly non-incarnational. To use non-incarnational methods is not to do God's mission. Since some claim these methodologies have been employed by Jesus, they become mandatory for authentic mission because this is what God did in Jesus and what Christ passes onto Christians today.

Second, the Christian activist is the one who implements a specific methodology or model. Those committed to incarnational mission as method or model are seen primarily as those who are relocated—Christian activists who identify with a particular people group. Therefore, only those who have crossed cultures or moved geographically or are committed to implementing this specific strategy or model can be considered Christians doing incarnational mission, and those people who have not are not incarnational. It is clear, therefore, who is and is not doing God's mission by the methods or model they choose.

Third, the incarnational methodology or models have universal application. Methodologies of identification and relocation, for example, can be used in any people group, rich and poor alike.

Potential Strengths

A number of potential strengths can be seen in this way of drawing attention to the new challenges of urban mission.

First, a specific incarnational methodology can highlight the importance of locality in the new, globalized, urban world. Attention is drawn to the need for personal investment in a specific location for community transformation. We know from sociological researchers that urbanization has increased mobility and diluted the glue that holds communities together. The loss of proximity, belonging, and availability caused by increased mobility and commuting in particular has lessened the *social capital* a neighborhood draws on for its health and growth. Robert Putnam, for example, notes that for every ten minutes spent commuting, a person loses 10 percent of their social capital for others.[52] It is timely for the incarnational method of relocation to remind us that Christ was Jesus of Nazareth—a person who belonged to a particular place—and that Christian workers need to be the same in urban neighborhoods today. Commuting in and out of neighborhoods just to run programs fails to build the kind of social capital and connections that are required if transformation is to occur in slums.

Second, a specific methodology of incarnation highlights the importance of praxis in the urban world. Committing in challenging, tangible ways to serve people facing urban poverty has forced Christian workers to reflect on the orthopraxis required in community transformation, not just orthodoxy. In a time when adults want to keep all options open, specifically committing to identify with real people facing poverty in concrete ways reminds us of Jesus' call to love our neighbor as we love ourselves.

---

52. Putnam, *Bowling Alone*, 213.

Third, incarnation as a specific methodology has highlighted the importance of lifestyle priorities. The message and the lifestyle of the messenger are intertwined. This is a crucial issue in cities today where Christian workers can choose their neighborhoods and often choose some of the most comfortable.

Fourth, attention is drawn to following Christ's life and ministry priorities. Many models and methods of ministry today can be based more on marketing, public relations, and even popularity than on the priorities of Jesus. The attempt to center an approach on who Jesus is and what he did can unleash all kinds of creative and prophetic responses. This includes ministries in slums. However, such an emphasis does not need to be described as patterned or modelled after the Incarnation. A model can be better described as seeking to be centered on Jesus, who is still alive and working in a slum, rather than importing and copying exactly what Jesus did in first-century Palestine.

Fifth, as a specific model or method for ministry attention is drawn to Christ's sacrificial service. A willingness to sacrifice something for the sake of others is especially required by Christians serving in slums. If God in Jesus had not sacrificed for others, then it would be difficult to argue that Christians should as well. Again, whether this needs to be justified as copying the Incarnational model is debatable. Christians can, for example, be willing to sacrifice comforts because the same Jesus who died on the cross calls them to come and follow the risen Christ into the slums today.

Sixth, this specific ministry model draws attention to the very real socio-cultural barriers that often need to be overcome. God in Jesus Christ overcame barriers to ensure the salvation of the world. In that broad sense, to reach those living in slums does require the qualities of humility, compassion, and initiative that Jesus had. If God did not first love us, would Christians love others enough to move away from what is comfortable? Christians do need to step out in faith and cross barriers to reach slum residents. Again, whether this requires pointing to the Incarnation as a specific model for its justification is arguable.

Limitations and Weaknesses

The view that incarnational mission is a specific methodology or model for mission has limitations, which can be grouped into a number of objections. This does not mean that the methodologies proposed here have no value. They may actually be the best methods available to Christian workers. However, the claim that a specific methodology or model is the incarnational approach to mission has serious limitations.

First, is it legitimate to take a theological metaphor about Christ and use it literally to uphold one specific methodology or model as the way for Christians in mission? There are real problems with taking most theological metaphors too literally, and this is the case when the Incarnational event is seen as the Word becoming flesh. The metaphorical intention seems to be that God has become visible in human form, embodied among us. This is not analogous to what Christians can do today in slums. Specific strategies and actions can be helpful or even Christ-inspired, but they do not require legitimatizing as analogous to the Incarnation to be acknowledged as such.

Second, methodologies and models in slums need to differ from the Incarnational event. Jesus was not actually an outsider adult in the same way that adult cross-cultural workers are when they relocate. As a human Jesus was born a Jewish boy and grew up in that particular time, culture, and place. Jesus had very few cross-cultural ministry opportunities and was never immersed in or identified with an outside Gentile culture. Christians in slums often need to do things that Jesus of Nazareth did not need to do.

Third, can non-poor Christians really be the same as poor people? God in Jesus did become an insider to humanity in general and a poor community in particular, but no matter how hard non-poor Christians try to identity with those born into poverty, their advantages, connections and privileges as people growing up outside of poverty remain. Unable to recognize real differences from their neighbors, and Jesus, Christian workers can undermine their own credibility and effectiveness. This is because at the very least workers can be naïve as to the needs and starting points of their poor neighbors. At worst Christian workers can be judgmental, uncaring, and bitter toward neighbors who do not make the same choices they think they would in the same circumstances.

Fourth, can Christian workers' home culture be equated with heaven? Jesus' pre-existence is not the same as a Christian workers' original location. This is an important limitation to acknowledge in applying incarnation as methodology because if Christian workers want to see the "kingdom come on earth as in heaven," they need to avoid en-couraging conformity to their original lifestyle. Rather than liberating the poor to become the unique people God intended them to be in a given location or culture, Christian workers may unwittingly seek to colonize them. For example, I really like Melbourne, the city where I was born, but it is not heaven, nor the model for the Klong Toey slum to be conformed to.

Fifth, can the emphasis on Jesus' birth and life as the basis for the incarnational method and model downplay Jesus' ministry priorities and the work on the cross as an integral part of the Incarnation? Other than associations with the cost of the method-ology, there is very little discussion as to how the ministry, death, and resurrection of Jesus relates to the incarnational methodology. This can limit the scope and priorities of Christian mission as well as the uniqueness of Christ's sacrifice and resurrection. If a method of identification, for example, can be equally applied to the urban poor as well as to the urban rich, then Jesus' ministry priorities for the poor and for justice can be ignored. Jesus did minister to those who were rich and powerful, but did so from a place of solidarity with the poor. It was this solidarity with the poor that threatened the elite and caused Jesus to be killed. So, if defined as a multi-use methodology of identification for all classes and types of people, this could ignore the incarnational pinnacle of the cross and resurrection which resulted from Jesus' ministry priority for the poor.

Sixth, can these methods and models be considered the only authentic method of Christian mission? This is not only elitist, but also limits what strategies can be employed in some locations and contexts. This is especially the case in many "closed" slum and squatter neighborhoods where methods such as relocation and identification are not pos-sible for "outside" people. Sometimes the only mission strategies open to Christians to connect with people in these neighborhoods are more attractional or commuting strategies. Engaging these contexts can be far more dangerous than relocating into safer slum neighborhoods. Incarnational mission then cannot be limited to one strategy to be authentically Christian.

Seventh, can the model of the Incarnation really be imitated by all Christians? Jesus is limited and restrictive as a role model whether for a cross-cultural worker, lifestyle, friend, or devotee. The unique place Jesus has as fully human and fully God, not to mention the specifics of Jesus of Nazareth's life and ministry context, means that no Christian today can actually use Jesus as a specific model for themselves. This limitation is certainly relevant for life and ministry in a slum, which often requires aspects of life that Jesus of Nazareth did not experience. These can include spousal partnerships, families, a non-itinerant and stable home life, and the need to learn another language as an adult from a position of power, none of which Jesus actually had or did. Therefore if incarnational mission is the emulation of the model of the Incarnation, no one can actually do it.

Eighth, where is Christ now? The lack of emphasis on the Incarnation's resurrection is a significant loss. It is one thing to seek to follow the model of Jesus two thousand years ago, but quite another to join, participate, and follow what the living Jesus is doing today. Without the resurrection, Jesus' contemporary call to discipleship is severely restricted—it becomes only discipleship of a character in an old book. With the resurrection of Jesus, however, all kinds of new and creative initiatives are possible in slums today. To limit following Jesus to modelling themselves on what Jesus did in first-century Palestine limits what new things God can do in slums today.

Ninth, is following Jesus sustainable or even possible without the invitation, authority, and grace of the risen Christ? This objection also picks up the importance of the resurrection, for only the risen Christ can give to disciples "all authority in heaven and earth to go into all the world," Matt 28:18–19. This authority from Christ includes God's authority for life and ministry in slums. Without this authority, the slavish copying of Jesus can only be done in a Christian's own strength. Duty without Christ's grace ensures any enthusiasm and passion for life quickly grows cold. The empowerment of the Spirit and the joining with God's eschatological *finale* of creation are also often missing dimensions. The Incarnation as a specific ministry model to emulate, *without focusing on what the risen Jesus is currently doing*, is therefore simply not sustainable for even the most devoted Christian.

To live in a slum as a Christian is to be overwhelmed most days. This sense grows more intense as the scale, speed and complexity of suffering faced by multitudes of slum residents emerges not only across the world, but also in my neighbors' lives. As the focus turns to the incarnating God, however, an urgent and creative invitation right into the eye of a perfect storm of poverty also emerges. Active faith in such a God can be good news for all: those living in slums and those benefiting from them. Transformation is possible in slums through the incarnating God of hope. I pray this impulse helps generate in Christians a courageous sense of responsibility to focus our best resources on this phenomenon shaping our common future. As Abraham Heschel reminds us, 'Few are guilty, but all are responsible.'[53]

---

53. Heschel, *The Prophets*, 19.

3

The People of God and His Purpose

by Paul K. McAlister

OFTEN CHILDREN ARE RAISED in the church with disconnected images of Old Testament heroes. Sadly, it seems as though many throughout life never see the beauty, unity, and power of the grand narrative revealed by God. The Old Testament reveals God's magnificent calling of a people, who in turn will be the means of reaching all nations. Further, both testaments disclose God's purpose from creation to the new heavens and the new earth. The Old Testament leads to, and anticipates, the fuller revelation of the New Testament and ultimate fulfillment in Christ. The mission of God unifies and provides the hermeneutic to understand the purpose and character of God. Consider the words of Christopher Wright:

> In short, a missional hermeneutic proceeds from the assumption that the whole Bible renders to us the story of God's mission through God's people in their engagement with God's world for the sake of the whole of God's creation.[1]

THE BEGINNING POINT

Though often separated by many scholars from the remaining narrative of the Old Testament, Gen 1–11 is indispensable for the unveiling of the biblical worldview and recognition of the mission of God. These chapters disclose the setting and scope of God's redemptive purpose and also help to establish the unity of biblical thought. A first survey of the content of Gen 1–11 is our beginning point.

Genesis begins with the revelation of God's creation. The passage presents God's orderly creation and purpose. The passage presents the creation of a real world which is pronounced "good." There are immediate theological implications that disclose the uniqueness of the biblical account. God is not identified with his creation; he pre-existed all of creation. His creation is marked by many specific and identifiable features which make clear that the creation is real and not an illusion. Even statements of location in Gen 2 demonstrate that a real place is described. God creates in an orderly manner beginning with the division of his creation, then moves to inhabiting the creation. He creates the

---

1. Wright, *Mission of God*, 51.

flora and fauna before moving to the creatures. Quickly the scripture focuses upon the creation of people in his image. Even the earliest verses describing the creation of Adam make clear that God has given not merely blessing but purpose to Adam. The passage highlights that some of his creation demands cultivation and classification. From the outset humans are both the only members of his creation who are in his image, both male and female, and at the same time and they have responsibility to attend the remaining creation, both plants and animals. God called those created in his image as participants with Him in the work of attending to the rest of creation. Creation care is a part of the task given to humanity. There is implied a creation concern presented to Adam with management and stewardship implications.

The importance of humankind in the creation, while it is highly important, is not the whole story. Human identity is secured in the image of God. The value of the human is in relationship to the creation in the image of God, providing value and purpose. The value of humankind is a vital part of biblical thought. Discussion takes place endlessly concerning the nature and value of humans; this includes the difference between animals and humans, as well as what this means for value and ethical decisions. Humans are not simply the recipients of God's creational blessing; humans are a part of God's larger purpose which embraces all of creation. Having been created in the image of God, the value of people is given, as is a sense of purpose.

The magnificent presentation of God walking with Adam and Eve in the garden highlights the overwhelming blessing of a beautiful environment prepared for Adam and Eve, as well as the matchless privilege of relationship with God. Creation is the beginning of what becomes a grand narrative. The story begins in the initiative of God with power and purpose. God provides a garden of delight for Adam to dwell in and in which fellowship with God can be experienced. The beauty and wonder of his creation is clouded by the decision of the man and the woman to listen to the allure of Satan. God created people in his image with freedom. Instead of living in trust and dependence upon God; they sought to become like God themselves.[2] Their arrogance and presumptuousness shattered the glorious fellowship they shared with God.

The impact of the sin's presumptuousness is seen in virtually every dimension of personal, social, and physical existence.[3] Even the productivity of the soil is compromised. Yet, even here in the midst of the darkness, there is a gleam of light.[4] While things are frightening, it appears that the darkness will not have the final word.

The extent of the consequences of evil is seen in chapter 4 with the jealousy motivated murder of Abel by his brother. The consequence of the jealousy and anger within this murderous act not only meant death to Abel, but also, it led to guilt and estrangement. To leave in order to enter the land of Nod carries a deep loss of security and provides a sense of lost identity; the very word Nod means "wandering." Cain is doomed to settle down in a land of

2. Gen 3.
3. Gen 3:14–19.
4. Gen 3:15.

wandering. Instead of a garden his address has become somewhere east of Eden. This feeling of guilt, estrangement and lack of identity is everywhere experienced in this world.

The consequences continue to be revealed in the often neglected chapter 5. The chapter is seen by many as simply a genealogy. In fact, the chapter can be seen as a theological statement. At first glance, all that is seen is a list of people who lived a long time and then died. Perhaps that phrase, "and he died" is the key. These people lived a long time, then the text says, "and he died." This recurrent phrase is a sad refrain. The only light is in the account of Enoch who "walked with God," literally he walked back and forth with God.[5] This image of fellowship with God shows the heart of God. The text does not say that Enoch died as the others, it simply says that he was not because God took him!

In chapter six the arrogance of sin is dramatic. The presumptuousness led even to using people, taking anyone they chose. People where reduced to property. Issues of the contemporary world in cases of human slavery, trafficking, and the abuse of women echo these presumptuous realities. God judges those attitudes, and as the narrative continues God's judgment results. The flood is the result of the arrogant sin of chapter 6. Even here in the voice of God can be heard his redemptive intent for those who remained faithful.

The presumption of sin is seen again in societal proportions in Gen 11. Instead of dependence upon God and seeking identify in Him, they tried to build their own identity through their own technological efforts. They wished to make a name for themselves by building a city with a great tower. Instead of filling the earth,[6] they chose to resist being scattered. The result of the events on the plain of Shinar is seen in the division of languages. Clearly the table of nations in chapter 10 is the result of this arrogance and the division of languages is a result. They could no longer depend on their corporate arrogance to create and secure their identities or to be the source of their salvation. The implications of the separate languages have significance for reclaiming divided humanity through their own languages. All of these reflections from Gen 1–11 lead to the understanding of brokenness and the plight of humans. The brokenness of God's creation is in absolute need of healing and redemption. These chapters provide the unavoidable vision of lostness: spiritual, physical, creational, psychological, interpersonal, and social. God's original intent and his good creation stand in need of redemption.

To grasp the significance of the early chapters of Gen, one must consider the elements of worldview. Note the essential questions of worldview as described by Christopher Wright:

1. Where are we?

2. Who are we?

3. What's gone wrong?

4. What is the solution?[7]

---

5. Gen 5:24.

6. Gen 1:28.

7. Wright, *Mission of God*, 315–16.

It is very revealing to compare the material of Gen 1–11 to these questions and note that the elements of Genesis correspond to the central issues of worldview thinking. Worldview thinking includes not only what we think about, but how we think about those things. There are endless issues that can be described in worldview terms. Worldview thought forces us to think deeply about reality and purpose. These issues continue to plague current human existence. The struggle with failure and guilt, the quest for human value, the puzzlement over what is real, as well as the questions surrounding the meaningfulness of life torment human experience. At times efforts to describe faith are shallow and do not give us what is necessary to provide coherent and secure bases for understanding, meaning, and moral foundations. Many have difficulty standing against the onslaught of critical attack because they have no depth to their thought. The discussion of "Levels of Conversion" is a helpful analysis of the need for deeper worldview thinking.[8] Even efforts to reach people often target a very superficial understanding of conversion. Change is not simply a change in behavior, but in the way one views all reality from a Christian worldview. At base, a biblical worldview addresses the questions posed earlier and has implications that relate to understanding the nature of reality and truth as well as personal struggles with sin and guilt (national, international, and private). A biblical worldview addresses these major issues and provides unity of thought through God's mission purposes to find solutions.

THE EARLIER GREAT COMMISSION: GOD'S GLOBAL MANDATE

The missional nature of the biblical worldview is powerfully revealed in Gen 12:1–3. While many assume that the beginning point of missional thinking in Scripture is first seen in the great commission of Matt 28, the reality is that Gen 12 gives us insight into God's intent and mandate. There are other covenants, but they did not have a mandate to every people. God called Abram away from his home and people to go to a land that God would show him. The intent of this call to Abram is seen in Gen 12:1–3, and the promise or covenant is further seen in 15:1–21, and 17:1–27. Abram is told that he would not only be blessed, but would be a blessing to all nations, or clans (this does not imply political or national entities). This carries an imperative sense. Not only would Abram be blessed and have a great name, but he was mandated to be a blessing to all. The God of biblical revelation is not a tribal god. He is the God of all nations and his redemptive purpose is to be carried out through Abram and his people. The profound unity of scripture is seen in the reality of God's call of Abram against the background of hurt and cultural collapse.

---

8. Hiebert, *Transforming Worldviews*, 315–316. Hiebert states, "Conversion to Christ must encompass all three levels of culture: behavior and rituals, beliefs, and worldview. Christians should live differently because they are Christians. However, if their behavior is based primarily on their culture, it becomes dead tradition. Conversion must involve a transformation in beliefs, but if it is only a change of beliefs, it is false faith (Jas 2). Although conversion must include a change in behavior and beliefs, if the worldview is not transformed, in the long run the gospel is subverted and becomes captive to the local culture. That result is syncretistic Chrsto-paganism, which has the form but not the essence of Christianity. Christianity becomes a new magic and a new, more subtle form of idolatry. If behavioral change was the focus of early Protestantism, and changed beliefs the focus of the twentieth century, transforming worldviews must be central to church and mission in the twenty-first century."

Abram would leave his family and country to become the bearer of God's promise to all people through his descendants. There are ethical mandates to Abram as a part of his response to God's promise and these are extended to virtually all of the recipients of God's promise (18:19). This nature of God's promise to Abram restores hope for all people. The promise to Abram has, as many have called it, a top line and a bottom line. The top line is that Abram would be blessed and the bottom line is that the blessing was intended to be extended through Abram to all the clans or families of the earth. Many are content with accepting top line blessings without accepting God's mandate that through his people all peoples are to be blessed. From the beginning God's intent was global and his people are intended to be the instrument for achieving his purpose. The promise of God is closely associated with the nature of *covenant*. Covenant describes the nature of the relationship of God to his people and helps to understand how God will shape his people to be the vehicle of this blessing to all peoples.

There are more covenants throughout the Old Testament. They all share some sense of God's initiative, the content of his promise, and the required human response. There are some varied perspectives as well. The covenant with Noah in Gen 6:18–21, is universal in intent and demonstrates God's promise not to destroy the earth again as in the flood, but, also it demonstrates that God will preserve his creation in spite of continued misuse of the creation of God by many including those who claim his name.

The Exodus Covenant in Exod 19:3–6, 24 and Deuteronomy draws the covenant and global vision together. This covenant is clearly a national covenant. God identifies his people as recipients of his promise, but also identifies them as a "kingdom of priests." They will reflect God to the nations. The intension is centripetal. The distinctive nature of God's people is to draw the nations to their God. There is little in the Old Testament that could be called God sending his people to the nations centrifugal. The obvious exceptions are Jonah being sent to Nineveh, and Daniel's presence in a strange land. The text describes what took Daniel away, but makes it clear that what some intended for evil, God had planned for good. So, while it is clear that God has chosen a people for himself they were seen not as the sole intent, but rather they were to be his instrument to make Him known to the nations. Israel is redeemed from Egypt to be his special possession, the emphasis is not on location but upon what God's people would be called upon to do; they would be a kingdom of priests and a holy nation. It is important to recognize that the Exodus from slavery, or redemption, preceded the giving of the law. Keeping the law was not an initiative to earn redemption, but, rather a response to the gift that God had given. The people received his blessing, but that blessing included a call to holiness and purpose that they might be a light to the nations.

The covenant with David[9] is with the specific house of David. God's intent is to call all people to himself by means of the participation of his people Israel and now more clearly through one of David's line. This covenant was an ongoing covenant. The promise was that through the house of David the same ultimate goals seen in the Abrahamic

---

9. 2 Sam 7, 23:1–7.

covenant, God's intent for all nations would be realized.[10] Though this covenant is to the house of David, its intent is for the nations. David's rule was to be that of an example to his people to lead them to be responsive to the Father. This promise is carried out through David's line through the Son of David, Jesus. Jesus fulfills the promise against the reality that God's people had failed to keep the promise and to be a holy nation through whom all nations would come to God. The good news of God's redemptive purpose is that Jesus did provide the holiness and redemptive sacrifice needed to remove the barriers for people to come to the Father. The new covenant in Christ provides what the failure of the people of God could not provide. Christ is alone the faithful and suffering servant who takes away the sin of the world.

All of these covenants are built around God's concern for all of his creation. This is accomplished through creating a distinct people with a distinct purpose leading to the inclusion of the nations. The Christological fulfillment in the New Testament will be explored in a following chapter. The point which must be made is that the Old Testament is indeed revelation and presents the real validity of the faith of many. Those who did walk with God were embraced in his hope. As a people they failed, both by failing to live in holiness and failing to be the means by which others could come to know God. The people could not provide redemption, but one, who comes as the son of David, was faithful and victorious. Though the people fail and are not able to fulfill God's promise, Isaiah reveals that there is a faithful servant who remains righteous in contrast to the unfaithful servant who represents the nation.[11] The faithful servant who provides returns for the people by becoming the Passover Lamb who takes away the sin of the world,[12] with whom he identifies himself after the Last Supper.[13] God has promised a remnant that would return to Him, but that remnant has been reduced to the one faithful servant. He therefore provides himself as the sacrifice for all, and the means by which God carries out his missional purpose to redeem all of his creation. That redemption takes place only through the sacrifice and victory of the person of Jesus.

The fact that God has called his people to participate in his mission is manifested in the law, historical books, noting especially the covenants, wisdom literature, and the prophets. God's global purpose is evidenced in every part of the Scriptures. Note Ps 67 where both elements of blessing and purpose can be seen. The first verse of Ps 67 describes God's grace and blessing to his people. From verse 2, through the remainder of the Psalm, the focus is to make Him known to the nations. The first verse can be seen in many forms, on many pictures and Christian objects, but seldom is there attention to the majority of the Psalm. The blessing is for the purpose of making Him known. This makes an important point related to the ultimate purpose of God's mission. Mission does not exist exclusively for the purpose of blessing Israel. Mission exists to bring praise to God. The goal of mission is that every people, tongue, and nation should be gathered around the throne of God worshipping Him.

10. Note Ps 72:17, where the son of David is described as enduring forever and all nations will be blessed through him.

11. Isa 42:1–4; 50:4–9; 53:9.

12. Isa 53.

13. Luke 22:37.

The goal of mission is worship. Mission is not simply for the purpose of blessing humanity, but that through the mission of God all people have the opportunity to gather around his throne, not simply to find individual salvation, but to come together as a people of every tongue and nation to praise Him. God sought to create a people for himself and to work through his people to embrace the nations. This purpose has been seen again and again in Old Testament revelation, as well as in the further revelation in the New Testament.

The prophets also carry the global theme.[14] Here we are told that something would happen on that mountain, which will swallow up the covering that is over all people. The magnificent images of victory are all made possible as he destroys death forever. The promised victory is for all nations, and it is accomplished through God himself who will wipe away tears from all faces. The hurt, pain, and alienation of all people can be healed through the promise of God; again the all nations theme is underscoring his redemptive purpose.

The goal of God's mission is seen in the new heavens and new earth. The mission is not restricted to individuals, but in creating a new people, accomplished only in Christ; but there is more. This passage talks about a new heaven and a new earth, God seeks to redeem all of his lost creation.[15] The unity of biblical thought from the creation to the new creation is consistent. God seeks to redeem a fallen creation through his son, the faithful servant and holy one, the one who fulfills the promises and creates a new people whom he has redeemed and commissioned to reach out with that message to all peoples.

CONCLUSION

The Old Testament presents a consistent message. That God created this good world. He is the Creator and Lord of this creation and not to be identified with the creation. His creation is not evil by virtue of being matter. As a part of this creation, God created people with dignity and freedom. There is distinctive value in the image of God that separates human life from animal or vegetable life, but God's concern is not therefore exclusive to humans. He cares about all his creation and expects that his people would be stewards of that creation. Freedom became a stumbling block as Adam and Eve chose presumptuous arrogance and sinned. The ensuing destruction was like a plague that spread to all people and relationships. God's intent is to redeem fallen creation and this through his mission. He chose Abram and through him he wanted to bless the nations. His people failed to be the holy and the instrument through which the nations would know God. God did focus upon Israel, but that did not mean that they were exclusively the object of his blessing. He calls for holiness so that his people can reach or draw other nations. The historic failure leads to the understanding of his continuing purpose through Christ and his community. Mission is the mission of God, not human mission. Too often people are locked into finding their mission, or purpose, without seeing that Mission is God's and that the goal of his people is to find how they can fit into his mission. Only God can forgive and restore.

---

14. An example is found in Isa 25.

15. Isa 25:6–8; II Pet 3:13; Rev 21.

The biblical worldview provides recognition of the reality and goodness of God's creation. God cares about his fallen creation and seeks to redeem it. Biblical revelation deals with a real world lived out in real history with a real purpose. History is moving toward the redeemed new heaven and new earth of God's promise. His goal is to return his fallen creation to himself crowned by the return of the nations to his fellowship and worship. He created a people with purpose, his purpose. As an implication of the nations coming to him is the acknowledgment that truth transcends individuals or people groups. The message of God is cross-cultural; this implies a view of truth. There is no room for syncretism, universalism, or relativism. This truth is knowable through revelation in word and history. God has equipped his people to know him through the careful understanding of his Word. God has called a people to himself, not as sole recipients of his good news, but also as his instruments in the proclamation and exemplification of that good news. Scripture is a unity moving to God's ultimate purpose, the redemption of his creation. The Bible moves from creation to new creation and the mission of God structures that movement. The Bible cannot be understood in its intent without this missiological vision. The Bible is a grand narrative moving from creation to restoration, through the mission of God ultimately realized in the coming of Jesus in fulfillment of his promises. In the sense described, the Bible is a story, but unlike other stories this is reality and his people are participants in the story. His people called to moral holiness and, therefore purpose. He has blessed his people to be a blessing, so that all may join in eternal praise.

4

Missiological Reading of the New Testament

by Robert Kurka

This is the genealogy of Jesus Christ, the Messiah,
the son of David, the son of, Abraham[1]

O NE CAN GENERALLY ASSUME that these words will not be a part of most evangelical
churches' advent celebrations. Who in the twenty-first century really cares about a
list of hard-to-pronounce Hebrew names that come from the pages of the Old Testament?
Why not get right to the birth narrative itself, preferably Luke's, with its far more interesting human characters, e.g., Mary, Joseph, Elizabeth, Zechariah, and angels? Matthew's
initial chapter seems to be wasted and generally irrelevant space, unless one is reading it
within the framework of a missiological worldview.

Let us briefly rehearse the procedure and particular items that belong to this kingdom vision of reality. First, one does well to start a canonical reading of Scripture from
the very end, Revelation, that offers us a *grand finale* experience of three core images
that summarize the heart of Christian belief: (1) God and his salvation made available
in Christ; (2) the world's numerous and diverse peoples, who are united in; (3) eternal
worship of God.[2] These final biblical impressions serve to remind us that no matter how
many twists and turns there are in the biblical narrative, this is where the story ends and
what it is about. In fact, they direct us backwards in Scripture to a two-pronged plot, a
storyline that if one stays on course will not only direct us to these grand conclusions but
keep us on track with our purpose as the people of God. One only arrives at Rev 7 if we
read Scripture attentive to God's redemptive work in Jesus Christ and a desire to bring this
good news to every part of the globe. Jesus makes this two-fold narrative explicit in the
closing words to his disciples prior to his ascension in Luke 24:44–48. As Jesus identifies
these two themes as the message of the Old Testament, the Bible of his day, we are given
a wonderful interpretive instrument that unifies the first thirty-nine books to the twenty-

1. Matt 1:1, TNIV.
2. Rev 7: 9, 10.

seven books that will be added to the canon. This is the concept of promise-fulfillment; i.e., what God has *promised* in the Old Testament has indeed found its *fulfillment* in the person and work of Christ.[3] This end has a two-fold dimension, a present and future reality, as Jesus closes his discourse with these words: "You are witnesses to these things. I am going to send you what my Father has promised; but stay in the city until you have been clothed with power from high."[4]

While Jesus has *completed* the first of the two storyline themes, his followers *will participate* in completing the second. With the empowerment of the Holy Spirit, the church will carry, preach, and practice this good news to the nations. Since this, too, is the promise of God, and anchored in Christ, it will also be completed, as the scene in Revelation so poignantly affirms. It does not require much effort to see this Messiah-Mission motif played out in Luke's writings: his gospel largely narrates the first theme and his second book, Acts, quite clearly describes the early church's mission to the ends of the earth.[5] But so do the other three gospels, especially Matthew's, work which has generally been recognized as the most Jewish of the Jesus biographies, due to its extensive citation of the Old Testament.[6] Let's return to Matthew's messianic genealogy.

JESUS: THE PROMISED DAVIDIC KING OF THE JEWS AND GENTILES

Our preferred, missiological reading of the scriptural canon, from the end to the beginning, works quite well when reading the gospel of Matthew. The well-known missionary mandate, the great commission, (Matt 28:16–20), provides a fitting conclusion to a book that traces the royal lineage of Jesus back to King David and then another fourteen generations back to Abraham. The Davidic reference clearly establishes Jesus as the ultimate ruler of Israel, although this throne that will be established only after the latter's conquest of sin at the cross and tomb. Not surprisingly, Matthew, like his fellow evangelists, devotes a significant part of his gospel to the Passion Week in chapters 21–28. However, one is given advance warning that his coronation journey is going to be one of humiliation in his baptism by John, to fulfill all righteousness, and his subsequent encounter with Satan in which the devil challenges Jesus to establish his kingdom through the typical means of a king's success: tyrannical power, self-promotion, and arrogance.[7] When Jesus leaves the wilderness, he embarks on a three-year ministry that will credential him as David's messianic successor in a manner that defies human expectation but clearly fulfills what is written in the Scriptures.[8]

---

3 For a more extensive treatment of the promise-fulfillment theme, see Walter Kaiser, *Toward an Old Testament Theology*.

4. Luke 24:48–9 (TNIV).

5. Cf. Acts 1:8.

6. See the discussion on the Jewishness of Matthew in Keener, *Matthew*, 33–43.

7. Matt 4: 1–11.

8. Matthew frequently utilizes the concept of fulfillment to indicate that there is a general Christological content to an Old Testament saying or event, after all, Jesus is the *telos* of Scripture, 5:17–20, rather than what is often supposed by Christian readers: a very literal messianic prediction-come-true uttered by the Old Testament prophet that had little to do with his historical context. See Matt 1:23, 2:18, Isa 7:14, and Jer

Matthew, however, is not simply content in establishing the first theme of the Bible in his genealogy. He is clearly concerned with the second as Jesus is called the son of Abraham.[9] The reason for this familial connection becomes obvious from the words of the great commission, "make disciples of all nations." In Matthew's Greek text, *panta ta ethne* is a verbatim citation of God's promise to Abraham in Gen 18:18, in the Septuagint or LXX, that all the nations on the earth will be blessed through him.[10] This is a repetition of the original mandate given to Abram in Gen 12 which Jesus identified as the second great theme of the biblical story. Thus, our Lord's command to his disciples to be witnesses to all the earth is a not-so-surprising conclusion to the family tree of the ultimate Abrahamic son. Matthew has neatly book-ended Messiah and Mission with a commission and a seemingly boring family tree. The intervening chapters of this gospel, then, relate the completion of this twin story. And perhaps most surprising to readers expecting such an Old Testament-laced writing to tell the story of a Jewish King's ministry to and rejection by his people, is Matthew's attention to the second plotline, the mission to the nations.

THE GENTILE MISSION OF JESUS

We have been tipped off by Matthew's genealogy that the author is connecting with the blessing of Abraham. A more explicit signal is sent by five unusual characters named in this veritable cast of characters.[11] Among the list of Hebrew males, are five females, four of whom are formally Gentile, and the fifth, Mary, by virtue of her Galilean heritage, a Gentile in the estimation of the rabbinic establishment.[12] The implication is clear: Jesus is the Messiah of Jew and Gentile, men and women, and this surprising fact actually fulfills the Old Testament. Matthew continues his somewhat subtle missiology in chapter 2 as he, alone among the gospel writers, describes the vision, visit, and worship of pagan astrologers to the small child king, who in spite of their employ of Old Testament-forbidden divinization are nonetheless led to the world's savior.[13] This narrative brims with irony in that those who should have been at the forefront of adoring the Christ-child were either jealously planning his demise (Herod), or largely indifferent to their own Scriptures (chief priests and teachers of the law).[14] Furthermore, those who were earnest seekers of the truth were rewarded with the biblical revelation that directed them to Bethlehem,

---

31:35 as examples of this Christ-directed reading of the Old Testament.

9. Matt 1:1.

10. *Ethne* is largely understood to refer to "people groups," or tribal cultures rather than geographic nations. See Keener, *Matthew*, 401.

11. Tamar, Rahab, Ruth, "Uriah's wife," (Bathsheba), and Mary are included in this less-than-stellar family tree.

12. See Matthew's reference to Galilee "of the Gentiles," 4:15, that indicates how a Galilean such as Mary would be viewed in proper Jewish society. However, for Matthew this ethnic slur is actually a pointer to world-wide mission.

13. Matt 2:1–12. Cf. the Old Testament's denunciation of divinization, Deut 18:9–13; Isa 47:13, the kind practiced by the seeking magi.

14. See the discussion in Keener, *Matthew*, 66–68.

whereas those who possessed the divine words were condemned because they refused to heed them. Moreover, one has to surmise that the evangelist was not merely recording this incident to humiliate Herod and his religious counselors, or even the unbelieving Jews of his generation. Rather, it is highly likely that Matthew's Christian audience might have been showing a similar disdain for the pagans in this world, dismissing them as hopefully lost, while becoming spiritually complacent about the Christ themselves.[15]

The Gentile mission story weaves in and out of Matthew's gospel: the Capernaum centurion who elicits Jesus' statement that many Gentiles will take their place with the patriarchs in the kingdom of heaven, 8:5–13; the Canaanite woman, 15:21–28; the eschatological discourse's sign that the gospel will be preached to all nations, 24:14; and the reaction of the Roman centurion and his company at the crucifixion of Jesus, as they exclaim, "Surely he was the Son of God," 27:54. There are also a number of less obvious allusions to the worldwide mission of the disciples of Jesus: the angel's reason for the name, Jesus, "because he will save his people from their sins," 1:21, that anticipates a new people who will produce kingdom fruit, 21:43; the identification of Galilee as Galilee of the Gentiles, 4:15, which also becomes the sending point of the great commission; the news about Jesus spreading to foreign places, like Syria, 4:24; the reference to disciples as the earth's salt and the world's light, 5:13, 14; Jesus' apparent willingness to enter the homes of Gentiles, 8:7; and his cleansing of the Temple's outer Court of the Gentiles, 21:12–16, in which a fundamental statement of Yahweh's universal accessibility had become perverted in a way that precluded active Gentile participation in his worship.[16]

Thus, in some subtle and surprising ways, Matthew's very Jewish gospel becomes a paradigm, of the kind of missiological hermeneutic and worldview that Jesus sees in his reading of Scripture and John the Revelator so imaginatively captures at the end. Jesus has come into this world to save his people, who are increasingly identified as non-Jews throughout the gospel narrative. This fulfills God's promise to Abraham and defines the scope of the church's mission until the very end: to go to the ends of the world and preach the gospel. This mandate, as old as the Old Testament itself, will indeed succeed, since King Jesus has been given all authority, 28:18. This is kingdom language. Christ's followers are citizens of his kingdom, live within the rules of the kingdom, and preach a gospel that is of the kingdom, 24:14. Clearly the mission mandate, as well as the Messiah's work, itself cannot be understood without some understanding of the *Kingdom of God*.[17]

15. Ibid. Perhaps, there is a lesson in this narrative for 21st century believers who view their world's one billion Muslims as foes who are anathema to Jesus instead of monotheistic seekers who deserve to see *Allah* as he really is!

16. Cf. the discussion in Bosch, *Transforming Mission*, 61.

17. See the discussion of Kingdom Missiology and Shalom by Burris and Howells Douglas in the Introduction to this book.

UNLEASHING THE KINGDOM OF GOD

From that time on Jesus began to preach, "Repent for the kingdom of heaven has come near . . ." Jesus went throughout Galilee, teaching in their synagogues, proclaiming the good news of the kingdom, and healing every disease and sickness among the people."[18]

In Matthew's description of the beginnings of Jesus' ministry, one is introduced to an Old Testament notion, kingdom of God, or as Matthew prefers, kingdom of heaven, that can legitimately be termed, new to the New Testament. In the Old Testament, a future Day of the Lord is envisioned when the entire world recognizes Israel's divine king and bows down to him.[19] This day will be ushered in by an ultimate Davidic king who will bring peace, restoration of God's people, and a breath-taking reversal of the effects of the Fall.[20] It will be an age characterized by the eradication of sin, disease, death, and even the enmity of the animal kingdom.[21] God's Spirit will be poured out upon all humanity and they, in turn, will know him in the most intimate manner.[22] The injustices of this world will be righted, evil will cease to exist, and the Lord and his people will dwell together in unhindered fellowship. As Israel's national fortunes continued to dissipate in the Old Testament, this future hope became increasingly prominent in the preaching of her prophets.[23] Babylonian captivity, and subsequent domination by the prevailing world powers, only served to exacerbate Jewish longings for the in-breaking of Yahweh's promised kingdom, yet ironically in terms that often mirrored the nationalism and militarism of the hated Gentile rule.[24] Consequently, when the true deliverer, Jesus, did come, many among the Jews did not recognize the kingdom's presence, clothed as he was in *wisdom* rather than weaponry. Further compounding his humble coronation was the expectation that the promised peace and prosperity was to be immediately experienced upon the kingdom's arrival, a view of things that was not only held by the opponents of Jesus, priests, scribes, and Pharisees, but also by the godly John the Baptist. Indeed, John the Baptist, imprisoned himself, began to seriously doubt if the one whom he had reluctantly baptized and extolled as the "Lamb of God"[25] was indeed the "one who was to come."[26] Jesus' reply to the Baptist's inquiry, "the blind receive sight, the lame walk, those who have leprosy are cleansed, the deaf hear, the dead are raised and the good news is proclaimed to the poor," unequivocally declares that he is the coming king and his kingdom is present although there are still many who suffer from illness, material deprivation, injustice, and death, which will soon be the lot of John.[27] Herein lay the secret of the kingdom that was

---

18. Matt 4:17; 23–23, TNIV.
19. Glasser, "The Kingdom of God," 539–40.
20. Ibid., 540.
21. Cf. Isa 11:1–10.
22. Cf. Joel 2:28–32; Jer 31:31–34; and Ezek 36:26–7.
23. Glasser, "The Kingdom of God," 540.
24. Ibid., 540–41.
25. cf. John 1:29.
26. Matt 11:2–3.
27. Matt 11:4–5.

not readily apparent to the Old Testament writers: the kingdom of God would break into this world in *two* messianic advents.[28] The initial experience of God's salvific rule would be witnessed in the ministry of Jesus Christ and especially in his redemptive work at the cross and tomb. The Old Testament's kingdom promise of forgiveness of sin, peace, restoration, indwelling of the Spirit, ingathering of the nations, healing, empowerment of the marginalized, etc., was already being poured out in significant power and force in the earthly ministry of Jesus and subsequently, in that of his followers. This present but partial rule of Christ would be extended throughout the world until his second advent, providing a time of both substantial healing to the world and an opportunity to receive the gospel and be saved. Thus, the perfect kingdom expectation of the Old Testament would come to be, but only in this unexpected, *two-step* fashion.

There is another surprise to this kingdom that John the Baptist's anxious question raises and Jesus' reply explains. As the genuine kingdom of God is spread in this world, it is not going to be done in the political and often, militaristic ways that regimes are normally advanced. Christ's kingdom is going to be marked by miracles, certainly, but even more pointedly by humility, mercy, righteousness, integrity, peacemaking, forgiveness, and love of enemies.[29] These unworldly exhibitions of Christ's authority will not be often understood, for example John, or welcome in our world, note Jesus' opponents, and will bring a fair amount of persecution.[30] Indeed, the pages of church history are too often stained with a story of a concept of kingdom that far more resembles the rulers of the Gentiles than the dominion of Jesus. The rule of Christ is a constant struggle even for those who claim to know and follow him. Likewise, the past two-thousand years is also stained with the blood of innocent martyrs who have faithfully and courageously lived under the marching orders accomplished with sacrifice and mercy.[31] Nonetheless, the gospel of the kingdom has been extended to the corners of the globe because, in actuality, "all authority in heaven and on earth"[32] belongs to this king and his kind of kingdom rather than the perceived kingdoms of this world.

In short, the concept of the kingdom of God is integral to understanding the mission of Christ and his church. It reminds us of the *holistic* nature of the mission of God in Christ. God is redeeming and restoring every dimension of broken creation, especially people. The final, perfect restoration will not be experienced until Christ's return. This kingdom provides a paradigm for living, a Spirit-enabled existence, that views self, others, priorities, and success in ways that radically challenge cultural norms. In fact, this kingdom worldview is so unusual and difficult to maintain, that we have been given an additional twenty-seven books of biblical canon, the New Testament. As we have noted

28. Glasser, "The Kingdom of God," 540–41.

29. Cf. Matt 5:3–14; 43–48. See Stephen Westerholm's excellent study of Matthew' gospel as a Christian worldview instrument in his, *Understanding Matthew*.

30. Cf. Matt 10–12; 24:11.

31. Current estimates project that roughly 150,000 Christians are martyred each year. However, given current trends in governmental human rights abuses and militant religious movements, the number could swell to 600,000 by the year 2025. See Tallman, "Martyrdom," in *Evangelical Dictionary of World Mission*, 602.

32. Matt 28:18–20.

before, the New Testament is not so much a new message of salvation that differs from the Old, but rather an emphatic declaration that all of God's promises have been answered "yes" in Christ.[33] What is new is the unanticipated, two-fold nature of this fulfillment, as well as the distinctive, but utterly transformational mode of living that adopting this kingdom worldview brings. This new vision, in turn, demands that we see reality as defined in Christ's ministry, death, and resurrection. It demands that we see all the world's peoples as our neighbors. And this new worldview demands a new set of biblical books that will keep us practically grounded in these two advents of Christ and on task with his mission. At risk of sounding simplistic, this is what the books of the New Testament do. We will return to this notion shortly.

READING THE GOSPELS AND ACTS AS EXPOSITIONS OF ISAIAH

It has long been recognized that the Old Testament book of Isaiah was important in the ministry of Jesus and the church. One immediately thinks of the Servant Song chapter, Isa 52:13—53:12, when reading the Passion Week account, a remarkable prophetic vision of Jesus' sufferings ostensibly penned some seven centuries prior to that redemptive event. It is significant that when we read the Acts' account of the Ethiopian eunuch, and his desire to know who the prophet was talking about, that the Spirit directed Philip to approach the former's chariot-based Bible study.[34] After being brought into earshot of those familiar Isaianic words, "he was led like a sheep to the slaughter," and subsequently invited to interpret them, "Philip began with that very passage of Scripture and told him the good news about Jesus."[35] Certainly, it would be hard to equal this text in its moving description of the redemptive work of Jesus Christ. Isaiah 53 was most certainly a staple in the early church's preaching to the Jews, and continues to be a standard messianic prophecy in today's evangelical outreach and apologetics. But there is a use of Isaiah by the New Testament writers, especially the gospel writers, which has largely gone unnoticed until recently. This is specifically their use of the Isaiah's new exodus *storyline*, especially found in chapters 40–66.[36]

In this captivity-oriented section of his book, Isaiah offers some words of hope to a nation that despairs of its exile in Babylon. Yahweh will indeed honor his promises to the patriarchs and restore his people to the land, bringing not only the displaced Israelites to Zion but the Gentile rulers and their nations as well.[37] This exodus will be heralded by a voice calling in the wilderness, 40:3, who will prepare the way for God's Redeemer, the Servant. This messianic figure, who is also the perfect Davidic king, 9:6–7, will bring justice, righteousness, and light to the *nations*, 49:6, although his successful mission will ultimately cost him his life, 53:8. However, he will live again, and lead his people into

33. Cf. 2 Cor 1:20.

34. Acts 8:26–33.

35. Acts 8:26, 35.

36. This "New Exodus" theme is espoused by Rikki Watts in his study of Mark, Adrian Leske on Matthew, and by Mark Strauss and David Pao in their analyses of Luke-Acts. For a complete citation of their writings, see David Pao, *Acts and the Isaianic New Exodus*, 33–36.

37. Cf. Isa 54–56.

a restored land, specifically a new heaven and new earth, 66:22. Scholars have noted that Isaiah is describing this journey home in language reminiscent of the Exodus from Egypt.[38] The servant-messiah functions as a *Second Moses* who, unlike his predecessor, will actually proceed his people into the Promised Land, more like Joshua.[39] Thus, the final twenty-seven chapters of this prophetic book function as a future re-telling of an ultimate exodus from slavery to freedom, bringing to fulfillment the promise that God first enacted with Abraham.

Luke employs this Isaianic new exodus narrative in a fascinating manner. As with his fellow evangelists, he sees the words of Isa 40:3–5 fulfilled in the ministry of John the Baptist. However, in Acts, he picks up the *making way* theme in an ecclesiological sense; i.e., the Way is used as designation for the church.[40] David Pao's brilliant monograph suggests that this dual usage is a tip-off that Luke's two-part narrative is actually a continuous story of the new exodus; in fact, creatively told in reverse.[41] Pao notes that following the reference to John the Baptist, Luke next employs Isaiah in Jesus' visit to the synagogue in Nazareth where he picks up the scroll and reads the words from Isaiah 61:1–2.[42] These words of messianic restoration, coming at the end of the Old Testament book, envision the dramatic transformation that will take place in this world when the future kingdom of God breaks in. In typical New Testament fashion, Jesus associates these words with his present earthly ministry, drawing the ire of his hometown people when he dramatically pronounces that, "Today this scripture is fulfilled in your hearing."[43] From this glorified vision of the Messiah and the kingdom age, then, Luke begins to tell his version of the Isaianic Exodus story. His rendition will strangely move in a backwards direction as we follow the life and ministry of Jesus to his passion that the Lord explicitly connects to Isaiah 53.[44] In the Book of Acts, we encounter Isa 53 once more in the well-known Philip narrative, Isa 49:6 in reference to the apostolic mission to the nations, and conclude the reversed story in Acts 28 where Paul employs the words of Isaiah 6:9–10 to prophetically ground the gospel's rejection by the Jews.[45] If Pao is right in his analysis, Luke has given us a powerful, missiological reading of the Isaianic narrative. In the early stages of Jesus' ministry, we are told the future has arrived as the promised time of messianic deliverance has begun. By the end of the gospel, the servant songs have come firmly into view in the details of his gentle ministry, and then, his harsh passion. Subsequently, his post-death exaltation, Isa 52:13–15, is seen in the resurrection/ascension account at the end of Luke, only to be picked up again in the opening verses of Acts. The Isaianic mission of "light to the nations," Isa 49, is then identified with the Pauline mission that dominates the latter

38. Pao, *Acts and the Isianic New Exodus*, 51–59.

39. The success of the New Moses/Joshua's mission is witnessed to in Isa 52:13: "See, my servant will act wisely; he will be raised and lifted up and highly exalted."

40. Acts 9:1–2; 19:33–34; 22:3–5.

41. Pao, *Acts and the Isianic New Exodus*, 105–9.

42. Ibid., 108–9.

43. Luke 4:21.

44. Luke 22:37.

45. Acts 28:23–27.

half of Luke's second volume, as Gentiles increasingly receive the good news whereas the Jews resist it. The hardness of heart that God told Isaiah would characterize his people in response to the prophet's ministry, were prophetic of Israel's rejection of her messiah. These sobering words fortunately followed Isaiah's temple vision where he had been given a glimpse of God's awesome glory; thus, the prophet could be sustained in his difficult ministry. In like manner, the church had beheld the glory of Jesus and through the power of his Spirit, would extend his redemptive message to the nations in spite of intense Jewish opposition. Using the twin themes that Jesus has given us to understand the Scriptures, Luke has given us a masterful, two-volume reading of Isaiah's new exodus, if not the entire book itself. Thus, Luke-Acts becomes a missiological document in a most profound way, far eclipsing the typical readings that merely draw attention to the inclusiveness of the gospel, for example, Gentile author and audience, Adamic genealogy, prominence of women in Jesus' ministry, the Good Samaritan parable, and the thankfulness of the Samaritan leper.[46] For Luke, the mission of Jesus and his church are nothing short of a true exegesis of arguably the Old Testament's greatest theological treatise, Isaiah, albeit in the upside-down, or reversed, manner that one came to expect with the kingdom of God.

TASK LETTERS TO MISSIONARY CHURCHES

We have already suggested that this largest genre of New Testament writings, the epistles, need to be read in light of the church's commission to preach the gospel of the kingdom.[47] This entails seeing these as products of apostolic theologians who were concerned about keeping the people of God *on task*. These were letters written to real churches facing a plethora of challenges: religious, social and economic divisions, unstable homes, low morality, false teaching, occultism, unjust persecution, etc., that continually threatened a faithful presentation of the kingdom of God.[48] As seen in the case of the Corinthian correspondence, the pressures to conform to the wisdom of the age, can cause the church to depreciate the cross and become indifferent to the plight of their neighbors.[49] Satan is actively waging war upon the people of God, often times goading them to employ his ungodly weapons in their ostensibly, Christian endeavors.[50] While it is true that his defeat is assured, the devil and his minions are not in any mood to call off the onslaught, looking for every opportunity to subvert the church's witness to the nations.[51] In no small measure due to the diverse nature of satanic subterfuge, we have New Testament letters that

---

46. Cf. Luke 1:3; 3:23–38; 8:2–3; 10:25–37; 17:15–16.

47. cf. Matt 24:14.

48. Roger Hedlund, *The Mission of the Church in the World*, 221–22. Hedlund credits Fuller professor, Arthur Glasser, with the "task theologian" terminology and concept.

49. Cf. 1 Cor 1:18–25; 2 Cor 8:1–9; 9:6–15.

50. 2 Cor. 10:3–5. Also see Paul's discussion of "Christian weaponry" the "full armor of God" (largely adapted from Isa 11, 59) in Eph 6:11–17. God's Truth embodied in his people's righteous behavior is the most formidable weapon in this fundamentally spiritual struggle. The recognition of the true nature of the conflict as well as the necessary "spiritual weapons" is the by-product of a proper biblical, missiological, worldview.

51. Cf. Eph 6:12; 2 Cor 11:14; 1 Pet 5:8; Rev 12:9, 17.

exhibit a similar diversity in terms of issue, audience, and argument. Some epistles soar in exceptional theological exposition, e.g., Romans, while others seemed to be marked by a pointed practicality, such as James' uncomplicated definition of genuine religion as concern for orphans and widows and keeping oneself unpolluted from the world.[52] Sometimes, even the most gifted theologians seem a bit stumped at apparent contradictions that seem to arise among these treatises. Nonetheless, every one of these epistles are oriented to nurturing churches in a biblical worldview that would keep them focused on Christ and the kind of thought and action necessary to the expansion of his mission. While the specific details of the issues confronting the earliest churches might differ from our own, for example, eating meat that had been sacrificed to idols, the general, universal human themes, such as those noted above, confront the church of every age and culture.

THE ROMANS EPISTLE: THEOLOGY
IN THE SERVICE OF THE MISSION OF GOD

While Romans' great doctrinal exposition has served to cement Paul's reputation as early Christianity's preeminent theologian, it has also, through no fault of its own, tended to divert attention away from the apostle's primary calling, as a missionary of the gospel.[53] In short, what has too often been missed, or at least, minimized, is that Paul's immense theological arguments are placed in the service of the *mission of God*, an enterprise that interprets both his calling and also that of his Christian readers.[54]

Paul's letter to the church at Rome is book-ended by his missionary intentions. In the opening chapter, he explains to his readers why he has been prevented from visiting them personally. Such a mutually desired meeting has been preempted by his missionary activities among the other Gentiles.[55] As he moves to the conclusion of his epistle, the apostle becomes even more explicit about his absence as he stresses that "it has always been my ambition to preach the gospel where Christ was not known" rather than build on the work of someone else.[56] In fact, such a vision of "going to where no man has gone before," is what will finally bring about his long-awaited visit to the Roman church. Paul has planned a missionary journey to Spain which will bring him through Rome so that he can elicit their participation in this outreach.[57] Their willingness to partner with Paul in this venture, as well as pray for him in his impending visit to volatile Jerusalem, will be

---

52. Jas 1:27.

53. Hedlund, *The Mission of the Church in the World*, 217.

54. Schnabel approvingly notes the recent work of Mauro Pesce regarding the pastoral function of the Pauline epistles as the former discussed the ministry of consolidating the churches that these writings perform. In addition to Pesce's list of congregation-building contributions, use of Scripture, spiritual growth of believers, role of Christian prophecy, and an eschatological understanding of political power, Schnabel adds the needed missiological component necessary to a truly Christian, Pauline, worldview: the letters remind "the churches of the role of the congregation as a concrete representation of the 'words of life'... they offer to the world." Schnabel, *Early Christian Mission*, 1419. Also see Stephen Westerholm's fine study that approaches Paul's theology as formation of a Christian worldview in his *Understanding Paul*.

55. Rom 1: 13.

56. Rom 15:20.

57. Rom 15: 23–29.

effected in large measure by their receptiveness to the rich doctrinal exposition that flows between these chapters.

> I am not ashamed of the gospel because it is the power of God that brings salvation to everyone who believes first to the Jew then to the Gentile. For in the gospel the righteousness of God is revealed—a righteousness that is by faith from first to last, just as it is written, "The righteous will live by faith."[58]

Virtually every commentator will identify these words as the theme of the epistle but relatively few will frame them in light of Paul's invitation to join him in mission, a partnership that necessitates a missiological worldview. In short, Paul is correcting misunderstandings, apathy, or even embarrassment about the gospel, a constant challenge in any society that takes pride in its ability to achieve success. Members of the Roman church need to be reminded how truly dark the pagan world is and how little if any the unregenerate see of God's universally-accessible, general revelation.[59] Jewish believers also need to be reminded that apart from the gospel, they were not much better than the unenlightened Gentiles even though they had the "very words of God."[60] All human beings have sinned and fall short of God's glory, yet all can potentially be saved by faith in Jesus Christ, the gospel. [61] This faith in Christ was what actually saved Abraham, not some supposed works, and what in fact, saves all of his spiritual children, Jew and Gentile.[62] Thus, as a contemporary reader proceeds through the epistle's first four chapters he/she encounters a sharp challenge to any notion that our salvation is of our own achievement or that lost peoples can simply figure things out and live good, moral lives that please God. If we lose sight that it is the gospel that alone brings reconciliation and peace with God, we obviously lose any passion about extending it to the nations which in effect, is wishing a death sentence upon God's human creation.

If we recognize Romans as an instrument of worldview correction to a church that has gone off task, we can better appreciate Paul's eloquent discussion of sanctification, release from the law's condemnation, and eager expectation of future resurrection, even in creation, that dominate the arguments of chapters 6–8. In short, unholy lives are a repudiation of our baptism and a denial of the reality of the Spirit who has come to dwell in us and who wishes to use this divinely-empowered transformation as "exhibit A" to the nations. Such loss of kingdom vision not only diminishes our pursuit of present holiness but also our confidence in the future, especially in God's sovereign ability to work good

---

58. Rom 1:16–17, Hab. 2:4.

59. Rom 1:18–32.

60. Rom 2:17–24.

61. Rom 3:21–26.

62. Rom 4:1–24. While it is beyond the scope of this essay to specifically interact with Rom 5:12–21, the *locus classicus* of the doctrine of "Original Sin," it may do well to note that this difficult passage occurs at the end of Paul's discussion of the universal need for the gospel. Perhaps, rather than attempting to provide a theology on how sin was transmitted through the race, Paul is once again calling attention to our *common humanity*; i.e., all human beings are connected because of Adam and therefore deserve to hear the gospel of grace that has brought salvation to Paul's readers. Indifference to humanity's plight, or open disdain of those outside of Christ, subtly undermines the formation of a misssiological worldview.

in all things for those who love him.[63] For the believer, nothing can separate us from the love of God in Christ, unless we forfeit the grace of the gospel, as happened with the Jews of Paul's day that rejected their Messiah. In certainly the New Testament's most eloquent theology of mission, chapters 9–11, Paul calls attention to an inviolable truth: People are shown divine grace, which is located in the gospel of Christ, so that it can be extended to the, religiously Gentile world. God will accomplish this mission whether or not his people respond positively or negatively. In fact, the influx of non-Jews into the late first-century churches of Rome and elsewhere was not an unexpected event or aberration to the plan of God. While the unbelief of his kinsmen deeply pained the apostle, not to mention God, their decision to pursue their own righteousness ironically proved to be a primary vehicle for prompting Gentile faith in the gospel.[64] This present phenomenon, in Paul's day, was not all that difficult to predict by the Old Testament prophets as they lamented Israel's unrepentant idolatry and unholy lifestyle that in their day, had brought God scorn from the nations.[65] According to Paul, God was indeed fulfilling his promise to restore the nation, only this restored Israel was heavily populated by Gentiles who more readily understood that any standing with God was affected by the gospel. Paul is hoping that this mission theology will prevent Gentile believers from making the same error as the Jews; i.e., becoming arrogant in their salvation. Rather, they must see their gracious inclusion into the people as a privilege to be extended to the nations, particularly to the Jews, many of whom Paul anticipates will be saved prior to the return of Christ.[66] Connecting these two chapters to the eight that have preceded it, we can reasonably conclude that many of those Roman Christians who needed to be reminded of the power of the gospel were the same Gentile believers who considered themselves superior to their Jewish neighbors. This, in Rom 12:1–2, Paul offers an invitation, or more accurately a summons, to those who have heard his exposition of the gospel's salvation and obligation in doctrine and story: offer your bodies as living sacrifices. This is accomplished by refusing to adopt the false, graceless worldviews that our culture offers and being transformed by a kingdom worldview that reminds us of God's grace to his and his desire to extend it to others.[67] This Spirit and Word-facilitated renewal of mind will then enable us to practice the presence of the kingdom of God: in our estimation and treatment of other Christians, in our relationships to our neighbors, and in our civic duties.[68] Finally, it enables us to accept people who are different from us, and subsequently willingly participate in missionary endeavors that will take the gospel to them.[69]

---

63. Rom 8:18–37, 28.

64. Rom 11:11.

65. Paul strings together an impressive catena of Old Testament quotations that indict Israel for her unbelief: Hos 1:10; 2:23; Isa 1:9; 28:16; 10: 22–23; 52:7; 53:1, etc. In the case of this last text, the Fourth Servant Song, it is interesting to note that Paul is employing it in a missiological sense rather than its more generally understood Christological one, e.g., Acts 8:32–35.

66. Rom 11:11–16, 25.

67. Rom 12:1–2.

68. Cf. especially Rom 12:3–8; 14–20; 13:1–7.

69. Rom 15:1–13; 24–33.

From front to back, the Romans epistle is a missionary letter, offering its readers a detailed exposition on the nature of the gospel so that they in turn, would be reoriented to a missiological worldview and its demand to faithfully participate in the mission of God to the nations. This is not to denigrate its great theological content that has made it the centerpiece of orthodox doctrinal formulation throughout church history. Justification, sanctification, glorification, etc., are indispensible foundational beliefs that contribute to the church's spiritual depth and health and have historically called her to revival. More importantly to Paul, the task theologian, these great truths of the Faith are written in the service of the Mission of God, so that his people have their minds renewed and their hearts rekindled with love for the nations.

REVELATION: THE MISSION OF GOD ACCOMPLISHED

It is unfortunate that many Christians assume that John's Revelation is primarily about a cosmic war and the end of human history. The final book offers an inspiring *grand finale* vision of the certain completion of the divine mission and its stewardship by the faithful church. Even though God's people are engaged in what often seems to be a futile cosmic struggle, Christ's authority over heaven and earth will be brought to completion. Satan, the wicked, and death, itself will be permanently destroyed, and the resurrected saints drawn from "every tribe and language and people and nation" will eternally offer worship to the Lamb in a restored earth.[70] John's imaginative and sometimes dizzying array of images, serve to keep his readers Christologically-centered, ecclesiologically-invested, and doxologically-oriented in spite of their natural tendencies to view the world otherwise. In spite of initial impressions, the terrible occurrences of this earth are in reality servants of the redemptive mission of God.[71] Moreover, even though Satan's attacks are formidable and may result in physical suffering and death, his attempts to successfully deceive the nations will be in vain, prior to the second coming![72] *Contra* all appearances, the devil, himself, is actually bound through this entire church age, thus insuring that the gospel of the kingdom will be preached to every nation before the end comes. Perhaps the Johannine apocalypse is the perfect vehicle for communicating the missiological worldview that continually challenges us to walk by faith in God's promises rather than by our physical senses. Given that our normal perception is frequently way off in perceiving the expansion of the kingdom much less its values, it is with a touch of irony that the Revelator exhorts his readers to obey his message if they have "ears to hear." Clearly, such hearing is beyond the capabilities of persons bereft of divine revelation, or in the case of John's audience, continually ignoring it.[73] However, if the world-dulled believer can be stirred to re-open

70. Rev 20:7–11; 7:9–10, 22:1–5.

71. Rev 6:1–17. The Lamb opens the seals and invites the outpouring of these bleak occurrences. This reminds believers that although God is not the author of evil, he does co-op its power into means of judgment which hopefully will draw resistant humanity to his salvation.

72. Rev 20:1–3.

73. The apparent apathy and toxic self-deception of the book-end churches, Ephesus and Laodicea, Rev 2:1–7; 3:14–22. Only a renewed and growing missiological worldview can *save* these churches from terminal decay. The subsequent history of the Middle East suggests that while the Johannine generation may have

the door to the knocking Christ he can once again be renewed in vision and purpose and faithfully participate in the triumphal consummation of the mission of God.[74]

CONCLUSION

This essay was written to offer a missiological reading of the New Testament. One could reasonably expect that this purpose would yield an exegesis of Matthew's great commission, Matt 28:16–20, as well as some significant exposition of the book of Acts, describing how the early church became Jesus' witnesses to the ends of the earth with perhaps, some special attention paid to Paul's three missionary journeys and church-planting strategies. This would not have been a bad thing to do but it would have yielded a misleading conclusion. As we have approached the New Testament from its concluding *grand finale* in Rev 7 to its beginning words in Matthew's rendition of Jesus' genealogy, with some exposition on issues such as Gentile mission in a Jewish gospel, the surprising kingdom of God, the new Isaianic exodus, and task theology, we have hopefully seen that the New Testament is not so much a new salvific plan of God but rather the consummate exposition on the promises of God in the Old Testament, in this case, the fulfilled promises of God. In Jesus' view, the main narrative of the Hebrew Scriptures could be summarized in two themes: (1) his suffering, death, and resurrection that brought about the forgiveness of sins; and (2) this gospel message being proclaimed to the nations. The New Testament, then, declares an emphatic *amen* to both of these plotlines by calling attention to the finished work of Christ in his earthly ministry and to the guaranteed accomplishment of the second as the church, in the power of the Spirit, manifests the reconciling and restorative presence of the kingdom of God. While Christ's atoning work is a *fait accompli*, the missionary march of the people of God is an on-going work-in-progress, with every generation of Christian facing challenges that threaten to divert them from the task. While God's second promise will be fulfilled because it too, rests upon his power and not the efforts of his people, his desire is to reshape the worldview of his *ecclesia* so that we will joyfully partner with his redemptive mission. From the life of Christ, even his family tree, to the life in the new heavens and earth, we have been given a practical canon that keeps our vision clear and our path straight. No, God has not given us a New Testament in order to locate missionary flash-points, but rather a Spirit-breathed document that continually challenges us to read all of life's purpose from a missiological perspective. In Kevin Vanhoozer's words, we have been placed in a "divine drama," and the New Testament provides the "Easter to Second Coming" script that enables Christ's dramatists to perform their missionary role faithfully and convincingly.[75]

heard, their spiritual descendants lapsed back into this *Christo-myopic* condition.

74. Rev 3:20–22.

75. Cf. Vanhoozer, *The Drama of Doctrine.*

5

Teach Them to Obey All That I have Commanded

by Mark Moore

THE GREAT COMMISSION IS the process of making disciples of all ethnic groups. That much is straight forward. Equally obvious is the fact that the disciple-making process is divided by Jesus into two movements: baptizing and teaching.[1] What, pray tell, are we to teach?[2] The simple answer is: *everything Jesus commanded*. It is, of course, a bit more complicated than that. Below, we will attempt a more comprehensive and, hopefully, a more helpful answer. First, however, we need to clarify two caveats.

Caveat #1: Faith vs. Works OR Faithful Obedience. Some branches of Christian theology have drawn a sharp dichotomy between faith and works. Since we are saved by grace, works are relegated to a post-Christian response of love rather than integrated into the salvation process or demanded from a disciple. This is a false dichotomy that fails to account for the cultural values held by ancient Jews. For them, covenant loyalty was essential. Works in no way merited the covenant, but without them, Israel forfeited her covenant relationship with Yahweh. Faith was not something separate from works but was, in fact, expressed by them.

This is shown with striking clarity through the unlikely character of a prostitute named Rahab. Perhaps you will recall her story from Joshua 2, how she saved her family

---

1. Perrin, *The Resurrection*, 49, notes the massive significance of this moment. This is the first time the Apostles are commissioned to teach. That role had been Jesus' exclusive prerogative up to that point, Matt 23:8, cf. 4:23; 5:2; 7:2–29; 8:19; 9:11, 35; 10:24–25; 11:1; 12:38; 13:54; 17:24; 19:16; 21:23; 22:16, 24, 33, 36; 26:18, 55.

2. This question has been largely neglected. The interpretation of the great commission in general has received surprisingly short shrift in the history of Bible interpretation; cf. Davis, "'Teaching Them to Observe All That I have Commanded You': The History of the Interpretation of the 'great commission' and Implications for Marketplace Ministries," 65–80. To make matters worse, the content of this teaching is typically ignored by standard commentaries; e.g., France, *The Gospel of Matthew*; Hagner, *Matthew 14–28*; and Schnackenburg, *Matthäusevangelium 16, 21–28,20*. Ríos, *Comentario Biblica: San Mateo*, 335, offers nothing more than this devotional thought: "Estas cosas son las referentes a la doctrina de la salvación (en sus aspectos presente y futuro), al servicio y el testimonio cristianos, al evangelio en toda su purze y poder." Thomas, "The Great Commission: What to Teach," promises more, but his exclusive attention to the Sermon on the Mount hardly accounts for teaching "all things." Hendriksen, *Matthew*, 1002, offers a nice categorical summary when he suggests "all things" includes (a) Jesus' discourses, (b) parables, (c) "Precious 'sayings'", (d) Predictions and promises, (e) Various lessons, (f) Jesus' life experiences. Even so, the reader is left wanting for details.

by harboring the Hebrew spies in Jericho. She is remembered three times in the New Testament. She pops up first in the genealogy of Jesus as the great-great-grandmother of King David (not a bad start). Then she is mentioned in two consecutive books in the later part of the canon. Juxtaposed, these two Hebraic texts show how integrated faith and works were in the Middle-Eastern culture of the first century: "*By faith* Rahab the prostitute did not perish with those who were disobedient, because she had received the spies in peace."[3] "Likewise, was not Rahab the prostitute also *justified by works* when she welcomed the messengers and sent them out by another road?"[4] *Her act of hiding the spies was both faith and works.* How can this be? If we would simply translate the Greek word *pistis* as "faithfulness" rather than as merely "faith," it would remove the false dichotomy between them. Fidelity to Yahweh is essential to keeping covenant.

This caveat is critical. Jesus gave clear commands that we are to pass on to disciples. If they do not obey Jesus' commands, they are not his disciples. This is as true during the process of initiation as it is in the continued process of edification.[5] This in no way diminishes God's grace, nor does it augment it to merit our salvation. It simply and authentically portrays our appropriate response to God's grace as his covenant people.

Caveat #2: We don't know everything Jesus commanded. John put it this way in the last sentence of his epilogue: "But there are also many other things that Jesus did; if every one of them were written down, I suppose that the world itself could not contain the books that would be written," John 21:25. We simply do not have access to the complete record of Jesus' commands as did the apostles. Therefore, since the Spirit enabled them to recall the words of Jesus, John 14:26, we should tap into the book of Acts for a more complete record of the commands of Jesus and how they were implemented in a Christian context.

---

3. Heb 11:31.

4. Jas 2:25.

5. Jesus and the Apostles frequently attached salvation to specific "works." The following are imperatives connected with receiving or sustaining salvation: Repent, Luke 13:5; Acts 3:19; 17:30–31; Rev 2:16, 22; Call on Christ's name, Acts 22:16; cf. 2:21; Rom 10:13; Confess Christ, Matt 10:32–33/Mark 8:38; Rom 10:9–10; 1 John 2:23; cf. 1 Tim 6:12–13; Be baptized, Acts 2:38; 22:16; Obey Christ, John 3:36; Heb 5:9; 2 Thess 1:8; Heb 11:8; 1 John 5:1–3; Do Good Works, Matt 7:21–23; John 15:2; Acts 26:20; Rom 4:3–5; Jas 2:20–26; Live holy lives, 1 Cor 6:9–11; Gal 5:13–21; Eph 5:3–12; Heb 12:14; Forgive, Matt 6:14–15; 18:35; Jas 2:13; cf. Eph 4:32; Love, 1 John 3:10, 14; 4:7–21; Provide benevolence, Matt 25:31–46; 1 John 3:17; Provide for yourself and your dependents. 1 Tim 5:8; Eph 4:28–32; cf. 5:6; Remain faithful, John 15:6; 1 Cor 10:6–13; Col 1:22–23; Heb 3:6; 10:26–31, 36– 9; 12:25; 2 Pet 2:20–21; cf. Rev 2:10, 26; Save yourself, Acts 2:40; Phil 2:12; Guard your words, Matt 5:22–26; 12:36–37; 1 Tim 6:20–21; Jude 1:14–16; cf. Jas 3:6–12; Matt 7:15–20; 2 Pet 3:16; Guard your doctrine, Col 2:8, 18–9; 2 Tim 2:16–18; 2 Pet 3:16–17; 2 John 1:7–11.

The strategy of this essay will follow these two movements: First, we will list[6] the one hundred and ten commands[7] of Jesus under five dominant categories.[8] Second, we will cross-check these categories with the narrative history of Acts to see how the post-resurrection followers of the Messiah perpetuated and implemented his commands, drawing some practical pedagogical conclusions for missionaries who want to teach their new converts what it means to follow Jesus' commands.

Since we don't have anything close to a comprehensive list of Jesus' commands, it would be deceptive to teach disciples to follow this list of commands and leave it at that. What we are looking for is not a shopping list of tasks, but a template for priorities. What did Jesus feel strongly about? What were his talking points? What made him flush with anger or giddy, or passionate? These one hundred and ten, laid against the backdrop of Acts, should paint a fairly full picture of a life that imitates the Master. With such a template in hand, the Holy Spirit can apply, expand, focus, and cajole appropriately, so that the body of Christ can make Jesus famous to the ends of the earth.

ALL THE COMMANDS (CATEGORIZED)

All of what follows could be summarized by two Old Testament commands that arose in two separate conversations Jesus had with a couple of Rabbinic lawyers (Luke 10:25–28 and Matt 22:34–40/Mark 12:28–34): Love the one and only God, Deut 6:5, and love your "neighbors," Lev 19:18. Everything else is pretty much commentary, but what a beautiful commentary!

Following Jesus

1. Matt 4:17   Repent, for the kingdom of heaven has come near. Cf. Mark 1:15.

2. Matt 4:19   Follow me, and I will make you fish for people. Cf. Mark 1:17.

3. Matt 7:13   Enter through the narrow gate. Cf. Luke 13:24.

4. Matt 11:28   Come to me, . . . I will give you rest.

---

6. The list was generated by searching the "red letters" for (a) 2nd and 3rd person plural imperative verbs, (b) 2nd and 3rd person plural subjunctives and infinitives, particularly those prefaced with *mh*, and (c) contextual clues which suggest a command even though the grammar avoids imperative constructions [there are only three of these, all from John's gospel: John 3, being born again, and John 6, eating Jesus' flesh, and John 13, washing feet]. I have also ignored commands given to individuals (with the exception of the rich young ruler, whom I take as paradigmatic for all disciples at some level), commands given to the Pharisees concerning idiosyncratic Jewish practices, and commands given to the Apostles that are now obsolete (e.g., taking no bag for the journey [Luke 10:4], gathering fragments after feeding 5,000 [John 6:12], or staying awake while Jesus prayed [Mark 14:38]).

7. Others may come up with a different number depending on whether and how they combine commands which occur in a list (e.g., Matt 6:19–33), what they might include as allegorical commands (e.g. from parables), who they consider a paradigmatic disciple (e.g., Pharisees, Apostles, or specific individuals), and how liberal they are in granting imperative force from context apart from grammatical considerations.

8. Of these 110 commands, 67 are found in Matthew (which will receive priority since the theme verse for the essay comes from Matthew 28:20). Interestingly, 27 of the 110 arise from Matthew 5–7, the Sermon on the Mount. No other gospel text comes close to the concentration of Jesus' commands. Hence, for missiologists, this sermon must receive pride of place when teaching new converts the program and priorities of Jesus.

5. Matt 11:29   Take my yoke . . . learn from me.

6. Matt 16:24   Take up a cross and follow. Cf. Mark 8:34; Luke 9:23; 14:27.

7. Matt 22:21   Give to God the things that are God's. Cf. Mark 12:17; Luke 20:25.

8. Matt 23:8–10   Don't accept titles of honor.

9. Luke 10:20   Rejoice that your names are written in heaven.

10. Luke 17:7–10   Say, "We are unworthy servants . . . "

11. Luke 21:19   By your endurance you will gain your souls.

12. John 3:3–7   Be born from above. (implied command only).

13. John 6:53–58   Eat Jesus' flesh and drink his blood. (implied command).

14. John 7:37–8   Come to me and drink.

15. John 12:26   Whoever serves me must follow me (not an imperative verb).

16. John 20:22   Receive the Holy Spirit.

Believe and Abide

1. John 10:38   Believe the works I do.

2. John 12:35–36   Believe in the light. Cf. v. 46.

3. John 14:1   Do not let your hearts be troubled; believe in me. Cf. v. 27.

4. John 14:11   Believe me that I am in the Father.

5. John 15:4   Abide in me.

6. John 15:9   Abide in my love.

Listen to Jesus

1. Matt 13:3   Listen! A sower went out to sow.

2. Matt 13:18   Hear then the parable of the sower. Cf. Mark 4:3.

3. Matt 15:10   Listen and understand.

4. Matt 21:33   Listen to another parable.

5. Mark 4:24   Pay attention to what you hear.

6. Mark 7:14   Listen to me, . . . and understand.

7. Luke 8:18   Then pay attention how you listen.

8. Luke 9:44   Let these words sink into your ears.

9. Luke 18:6   Listen to what the unjust judge says . . .

10. John 15:20   Remember the word I said to you.

Eschatological Preparedness

1. Matt 24:6   Don't be alarmed at rumors of wars. Cf. Mark 13:7; Luke 21:9.

2. Matt 24:32   Learn the lesson of the fig tree. Cf. Mark 13:28; Luke 21:29–31.

3. Matt 24:42   Keep awake therefore . . . Lord is coming. Cf. Luke 21:34–36; Mark 13:32–37; Matt 25:13; Rev 2:25; 3:2–3.

4. Matt 24:43   But understand this. Cf. Luke 12:35–36, 39–40; Rev 2:10; 3:11.

5. Matt 24:44   Be ready. Cf. Luke 12:40; 21:34–36; Mark 13:35–37.

6. Mark 13:21   Don't chase rumors of false Messiahs. Cf. Matt 24:26.

7. Mark 13:23   Be alert (eschatologically). Cf. Mark 13:33, 35, 37.

8. John 16:33   Take courage; I have conquered the world!

Religious Piety

PRAYER

1. Matt 6:6   But whenever you pray, go to your inner room.

2. Matt 6:7–8   Don't pray like Gentiles do. (similar to Matt 6:1, piety for show).

3. Matt 6:9   Pray then in this way. Introduction to the Lord's Prayer; cf. Luke 11:2.

4. Matt 7:7   Ask, and it will be opened for you. Cf. Luke 11:9–13.

5. Mark 11:22   Have faith in God (concerning prayer and moving mountains).

6. Mark 11:24   Believe that whatever you ask will be yours.

7. Mark 11:25   Forgive others as part of your prayers. This also relates to prayer in the context of 11:22–24; cf. Luke 21:14, where it is found in an eschatological discourse.

8. John 15:7   Ask for whatever you wish.

9. John 16:24   Ask and you will receive.

OTHER PRACTICES

1. Matt 5:16   Let your light shine to the praise of the Father in heaven.

2. Matt 5:3–37   Do not swear (i.e., don't take oaths).

3. Matt 6:1–18   Beware of practicing piety to be seen by men: Alms, prayer, fasting.

4. Matt 6:5   And whenever you give alms, don't be like the hypocrites.

5. Matt 6:16–18   And whenever you fast don't disfigure your faces. Similar to Matt 6:1, practicing piety to be seen by men.

6. Matt 20:25–28   To be great you must be a servant. Cf. Mark 10:42–45.

7. Matt 26:26–28   Eat and drink the Lord's Supper. Cf. Mark 14:22; Luke 22:17–19.

8. Luke 11:35   Consider whether the light in you is not darkness.

9. John 4:24   Worship in spirit and truth.

MONEY

1. Matt 6:19–21   Do not store up treasures on earth. Cf. Luke 12:33.

2. Matt 6:25–32   Do not worry about your life. Cf. Luke 12:22–29.

3. Matt 6:26   Look at the birds of the air. Cf. Luke 12:24–25.

4. Matt 6:28   Consider the lilies of the field. Cf. Luke 12:27–28

5. Matt 6:33   Seek first the kingdom. Cf. Luke 12:29–31.

6. Matt 6:34   So do not worry about tomorrow.

7. Matt 19:21   Sell your possessions . . . come, follow me. Cf. Mark 10:21; Luke 18:22, 12:32–33.

8. Luke 12:15   Be on your guard against all kinds of greed.

9. Luke 16:9   Make friends with money for eternal homes.

10. John 6:27–29   Work for food that endures for eternal life. The work God demands is to believe in Jesus.

TREATMENT OF OTHERS

1. Matt 5:21–26   Come to terms with your adversary. Cf. Luke 12:57–59.

2. Matt 5:27–30   If your right . . . throw it away. Cf. 18:8–9; Mark 9:43–48.

3. Matt 5:38–42   Do not resist an evildoer. Cf. Luke 6:29–31.

4. Matt 5:44   Love your enemies . . . who persecute you. Cf. Luke 6:27–28, 35–36.

5. Matt 5:48   Be perfect, therefore, as your Father is perfect. Cf. Luke 6:36.

6. Matt 7:1   Do not judge. Cf. Luke 6:37; John 7:24.

7. Matt 7:5   First take the log out of your own eye.

8. Matt 7:6   Do not give pearls to pigs.

9. Matt 7:12   Do to others as you would have them do to you. Cf. Luke 6:31.

10. Matt 18:10–14   Do not despise children.

11. Matt 18:15–20   Confront a sinful brother. Cf. Luke 17:3.

12. Matt 19:6   Don't separate with divorce what God joined.

13. Matt 19:14   Let the little children come. Cf. Mark 10:14; Luke 18:16–17; Matt 18:3–5.

14. Matt 19:16–19   Keep the commandments. Cf. Mark 10:17–31; Luke 18:18–30; the portion of the Decalogue Jesus cited dealt with vertical relations.

15. Matt 22:37–39   You shall love . . . neighbor as yourself' Cf. Mark 12:28–34; Luke 10:25–38; Matt 19:19.

16. Matt 23:23–24   Pay tithes; more importantly, practice justice. Cf. Luke 11:42.

17. Mark 9:50   Have salt in yourselves and be at peace with one another.

18. Luke 6:37–38   Forgive, and you will be forgiven. Cf. Matt 6:14–15.

19. Luke 14:8–11   Do not sit in the place of honor.

20. Luke 14:12–14   Invite to your banquet those who cannot repay.

21. John 13:14–16   Wash one another's feet. (implied command).

22. John 15:12–17   Love one another as I have loved you.

PREACHING AND PERSECUTION

1. Matt 5:12   Rejoice and be glad (when persecuted); cf. Luke 6:22–23.

2. Matt 7:15–17   Beware of false prophets.

3. Matt 9:38   Ask the Lord of the harvest to send out laborers. Cf. Luke 10:2.

4. Matt 10:8   Cure the sick, . . . give without payment. Cf. Luke 10:9.

5. Matt 10:11   Find a worthy person to stay with. Cf. Mark 6:10–11; Luke 9:4–5; 10:5–7.

6. Matt 10:14–15   Shake dust from your feet. Cf. Mark 6:10–11.

7. Matt 10:16   Be wise as serpents and as innocent as doves.

8. Matt 10:23   When they persecute in one town, flee to the next.

9. Matt 10:27   What I say to you in secret, tell from the housetops. Cf. Mark 4:22.

10. Matt 10:26–28   Do not fear those who kill the body. Cf. Luke 12:4–7.

11. Matt 10:31   Do not fear. You are more valuable than many sparrows.

12. Matt 15:13–14   Leave blind guides alone.

13. Matt 16:6   Watch out, and . . . Pharisees and Sadducees. Cf. Mark 8:15.

14. Matt 22:9   Invite everyone into the wedding banquet.

15. Matt 24:4   Beware that no one leads you astray. Cf. Mark 13:5; Luke 21:8; Matt 24:26.

16. Matt 28:19   Go therefore and . . . of all nations. The final command in Matt 28:18–20 & in Mark 16:15, cf. Luke 24:47; see the contrast to Matt 10:6–7.

17. Mark 9:39   Don't hinder those promoting Jesus. Cf. Luke 9:50.

18. Mark 13:9   Beware of persecution.

19. Mark 13:11   Do not worry what to say when arrested. Cf. Matt 10:17–22; Luke 21:14–18.

20. John 15:18   If the world hates you, be aware that it hated me first.

CATEGORY 1: FOLLOWING JESUS

Far and away the largest category comprises commands about following Jesus. That makes sense. Being a disciple means, quite literally, following (or perhaps more authentically, *imitating*).[9] What makes this challenging, and for some disconcerting, is that the content of these commands are centered on a person, not on measurable ethical responses. There is surprisingly little in Jesus' commands concerning standard ethics. In a real sense, then, Matthew is a manual for discipleship, not a textbook for ethics.[10] There are no prohibitions against smoking or drinking, no harangue against abortion or homosexuality, no critique of harlots or gamblers. He simply says, "Come follow me" (Matt 4:19/Mark 1:17; cf. John 12:26) through a narrow gate, Matt 7:13/Luke 13:24, for a paradoxical combination of yoke and rest, Matt 11:28–29, all the while with a cross strapped to your back, Matt 16:24/Mark 8:34/Luke 9:23; Luke 14:27. It is a radical call to repentance, Matt 4:17/Mark 1:15, and absolute abdication of one's life to God, Matt 22:21/Mark 12:17/Luke 20:25; cf. Luke 17:7–10.[11]

In this process Jesus is the center, the sole means of getting to God. Never before or since has any sane person made so many and so radical self-referential (some could say egomaniacal) claims. He is the only one worthy of titles of honor, Matt 23:8–10, the bread we eat, John 6:53–58, and the water we drink, John 7:37–38. His very breath bestows the Spirit of God, John 20:22. The Apostle John frames it in the most deliberate language of *believing* in Jesus, John 10:38; 12:35–36, 46; 14:1, 11, 27, or *abiding* in him, John 15:4, 9. Jesus alleged that Christian ethics were about his person, not about legal or logical propositions. Hence, there is a surprisingly long list of references, permeating all levels of gospel traditions, ordering his followers to listen to his teachings in order to gain life: Matthew 13:3, 18; 15:10; 21:33; Mark 4:24; 7:14; Luke 8:18; 9:44; 18:6; John 15:20. The stakes are raised in the eschatological exhortations to be aware and alert, Matt 24:32; Mark 13:28; Luke 21:29–31; Matt 24:42–44; Mark 13:32–37; Luke 21:34–36; Matt 25:13; Mark 13:21, 23, 33, 35, 37; Luke 12:35–36, 39–40; John 16:33; Rev 2:10, 25; 3:2–3, 11.

9. Wilkins, *The Concept of Disciple*, is the definitive work on this word. He defines it as "learners" and "adherents" in particular opposition to Rengstorf's overemphasis of the Sophistic influence of Greek Philosophy, 415–61.

10. Teaching them to "keep the commandments" of Jesus is parallel language to Jesus' conversation with the Rich Young Ruler in Matt 19:17, also 5:17–20; 7:21–27; cf. Bruner, *Matthew: A Commentary*, Vol. 2, 825. This language is evocative of OT texts commanding fidelity to the very words of Yahweh, e.g. Exod 7:2; 29:35; Deut 4:2; cf. John 14:15; 15:10; 1 John 3:22–24; cf. Bonnard, *L'Évangile selon Saint Matthieu* , 419, and Gundry, *Matthew: A Commentary on His Handbook for a Mixed Church Under Persecution*, 597.

11. Many have placed this command in the financial category: "Give Caesar what is Caesar's and give to God what is God's." It has been used as an artificial prop to promote paying taxes to the secular government while still giving your heart to the Lord; e.g., Richardson, *The Political Christ*, 47, or Carmichael, *The Death of Jesus*, 127. A more authentic reading, followed here, is offered by Horsley, *Jesus and the Powers*, 4–5 and Myers, *Binding the Strong Man*, 31–12. Jesus was calling for Israel to extricate herself from the pagan economic system of Rome. Even possessing such an idolatrous coin that called Tiberius "Son of the divine Augustus" demonstrated complicity in a systematic rejection of God's sole rule over the nation. Jesus, in short, called for subversive political evasion of Rome's demand for socio-religious-political-economic fidelity; cf. Kee, "The Imperial Cult: The Unmasking of an Ideology," 120–21.

This first category comprises forty of the one hundred and ten commands. It places Jesus at the center of ethics and presents him as the sole source of salvation, wisdom, and rest. Teaching people to follow Jesus means that we introduce them to his person, works, and words.

CATEGORY 2: RELIGIOUS PIETY

There are eighteen commands about practicing piety; nine of them are about prayer. Jesus' heavy emphasis on this single spiritual discipline seems out of balance with modern practice, particularly the amount of time and attention it is given in corporate worship. We are commanded to pray in private, Matt 6:6, shunning the kind of vain repetition of pagans, Matt 6:7–8, because we are addressing an attentive Father, Matt 6:9, rather than a distant or disinterested deity. This fact enables us to pray for anything with absolute confidence that God will grant our requests in Jesus' name and according to his will, Matt 7:7; Luke 11:9–13; Mark 11:24–25; Luke 21:14; John 15:7; 16:24. Again, Jesus' emphasis on prayer is peppered through all layers of gospel traditions.

As for the other religious practices, there is a surprisingly singular emphasis, whether dealing with oaths, Matt 5:34–37, alms, Matt 6:5, fasting, Matt 6:16–18, tithes, Matt 23:23–24; Luke 11:42, or worship, John 4:24. Namely, Jesus demands sincerity and humility. He prohibits the use of religious practices for personal gain or self-aggrandizement. These are mechanisms for demonstrating trust in God's goodness as a father. He is capable not only of providing for our physical needs, but even for our social and psychological needs for recognition and/or affirmation.

CATEGORY 3, MONEY

There could hardly be a more difficult collection of teachings for Americans living in the lap of luxury. Invariably this train of teaching has been systematically allegorized, ignored, or relativized. If the most offensive teaching of Jesus to his fellow Jews was to carry a cross as a mechanism of Roman execution, surely following Jesus' financial principles would be equally painful for American Christians. Nevertheless, his commands are too prolific, too perpetual, and too pointed to easily ignore. They come at us from all angles. When we set up an IRA or 401k we have to consider, Matthew 6:19–21; Luke 12:33. When we nervously check our bank account or the Dow Jones ticker we have to contemplate Matthew 6:25–32; Luke 12:22–29. When we accept a promotion or take a job that invades our time and energy for ministry we have to confront Matthew 6:33 and Luke 12:29–31. We are commanded to set a guard against our greed, Luke 12:15, and vigilantly use our financial means to make friends for eternity, Luke 16:9. How? By giving to all who ask, Matt 5:42; Luke 6:30, and by selling our possessions then giving the proceeds to the poor, Matt 19:21; Mark 10:21; Luke 18:22, 12:32–33. For those of us who desire to, *"Work for food that endures for eternal life,"* John 6:27, Jesus' financial advice must include those toting disingenuous signs stating "Will work for food."

CATEGORY 4: TREATMENT OF OTHERS

The previous category of Christian financial principles is counterintuitive. Nonetheless, it does have an internal logic since most of us can readily see how infectious greed can be and how the pursuit of rampant wealth can cripple the spiritual moorings of a nation. This fourth category is equally challenging but without that same internal logic. In short, we are to die to self and live for the other. Problem: Most of us are pretty certain that "ourself" is the good guy and the other is evil, well, at least our enemies are. Nonetheless, Jesus commands us to love our enemy, Matt 5:44; Luke 6:27–28, 35–36. This is the most sociologically unique statement Jesus ever made—it cannot be found in any other ancient manuscript from any other Mediterranean culture! It is not only unprecedented, it would be considered traitorous. In the Middle East, to love an enemy was to endanger one's family. And if there is any question about what that might mean, Jesus clarified in the context: Do not resist evil persons; they can slap you in the face, force you to carry their bags, and sue you for all you have, Matt 5:38–42; Luke 6:29–31.[12] In fact, this is the only way to achieve the holistic mercy of God, Matt 5:48; Luke 6:36.[13] Since God loves indiscriminately, so too must we if we are to become "sons of God."

As if that is not difficult enough, we are banned from judging others, Matt 7:1; Luke 6:37; cf. John 7:24. Not only are we banned from beating an enemy, we can't condemn him![14] Even closer to home, we are to privately confront the errant brother and forgive him if he repents up to an outrageous four hundred and ninety times, Matt 18:15–20; Luke 17:3; cf. Luke 6:37–38; Matt 6:14–15. Surely that is part of the process of coming to terms with an adversary before it gets to court, Matt 5:21–26; Luke 12:57–59. And closer yet, within our own homes, we are commanded not to divorce a spouse with whom we are at odds, Matt 19:6.

At every level, our social relations are to be marked by peace-making efforts, Mark 9:50. This is what it means to be the salt of the earth. We serve our neighbors as we would ourselves, Matt 22:37–39; cf. Mark 12:28–34; Luke 10:25–38; Matt 19:19, and we serve our Christian comrades with the self-abnegation required in foot-washing, John 13:14–16. If we cannot accomplish that, we will never be prepared to love our brother with lethal sacrifice, John 15:12–17, as Jesus commanded.

---

12. Jesus' advice is actually quite clever. This kind of total self-abnegation shames the victimizer publically when you force him to strike on the left cheek with an open hand, to strip you naked before the judge, and drag you far from home as an indentured slave. Hence, public opinion turns against the evil one and the aggressor becomes offensive to the very populace he was trying to impress with his power. This kind of subversive pacifism is an effective social mechanism. Cf. Keener, *The Gospel of Matthew*, 199–205.

13. Matthew 5:48 says, "Be perfect." But *telios* does not mean "morally flawless." Rather, it implies "mature" or as I have translated it above "holistic." Our love must exceed the boundaries of our friends and family if we are to approach the standard Jesus commanded. And if it exceeds those narrow boundaries, then we will practically benefit those who attempt to harm us. Luke's phrase, "Be merciful, just as your Father is merciful," correctly clarifies Jesus' meaning.

14. Immediately following the prohibition on judging others (Matt 7:1) we are exhorted not to throw pearls to pigs or sacred offerings to dogs, Matt 7:6. Obviously, there is a time for critique of culture, confrontations of errant brothers, and a prophetic condemnation of social evils so long as it is bracketed by removing a log from your own eye, Matt 7:5, and treating others as you would be treated, Matt 7:12.

However, our practical peace-making must go beyond our peers whether friend or foe. Jesus commanded us to seek social justice for the powerless with whom we have neither issue nor interest. For the Master, mercy trumped tithes, sacrifices, and any other religious expressions of fidelity to Yahweh, Matt 9:13; 12:7; 23:23; Luke 11:42. This is epitomized in his commands to honor children, Matt 18:3–6; 10–14; 19:14; Mark 10:14; Luke 18:16–17,[15] in his unprecedented acceptance of women, in his openness to Gentiles, and in his revolutionary rules for social engagements. Specifically, his edicts of etiquette required the host to invite the poor to banquets rather than peers, Luke 14:12–14, and the guests to clamor for the ignoble positions around the table, Luke 14:8–11. All of this comes to a climax in Jesus' own vocation when he achieved greatness through the most humiliating execution, Mark 10:42–45, a socio-political methodology enjoined on his closest followers.

CATEGORY 5: PREACHING AND PERSECUTION

Matthew 28:18–20 is Jesus' great commission to make disciples of all ethnic groups.[16] This is hardly a new instinct for Jesus. Twice he told his disciples to pray for the Lord of the Harvest to send out laborers into the field, Matthew 9:38; Luke 10:2; or in parabolic language, to invite everyone to the wedding banquet, cf. Matt 22:9. Immediately following both prayers, Jesus commissioned the twelve apostles, Matt 10:6–7, and the Seventy Evangelists, Luke 10:3, to announce the arrival of the kingdom and to illustrate its substance with miraculous cures, Matt 10:8; Luke 10:9.[17] They were to find a "man of peace" who could broker their preaching in the village. They were to stay at his house for the duration of the visit, Matt 10:11; Mark 6:10–11; Luke 9:4–5; 10:5–7. They were then to fearlessly proclaim what Jesus taught them privately without fear for those who would molest them, Matt 10:26–28; Luke 12:4–7, because of their confidence in God's Fatherly love and protection, Matt 10:31.

This was particularly difficult for two reasons. First, much of the opposition came from the religious leaders they were raised to revere—the Pharisees and Sadducees, Matt 15:13–14; 16:6; Mark 8:15. In addition, there would be plenty of other false prophets also leading many astray, Matt 24:4; Mark 13:5; Luke 21:8; Matt 24:26. They were to be shunned—and here comes the tricky part—without hindering others outsiders who appeared to be promoting Jesus, Mark 9:39; Luke 9:50. The second reason it was difficult to preach Jesus' kingdom was the high probability of persecution, Mark 13:9; cf. Matt 10:26–28; Luke 12:4–7. After all, one can expect Jesus' disciples to be received and/or

---

15. In Jewish culture children were highly prized but often shunned in the "adult world." R. Dosa b. Harkinas said, "(1) Sleeping late in the morning, (2) drinking wine at noon, (3) chatting with children, and (4) attending the synagogues of the ignorant drive a man out of the world," *m. Abot* 3.10.

16. cf. Mark 16:15; Luke 24:47.

17. These early itinerant tours were clearly for Israel alone (Matt 10:4–6) when there would be no need for extra provisions, Matt 10:9–10; Luke 9:3. It is obvious, however, that Matthew intends these principles to be extrapolated to the final commission for he anachronistically records Jesus' promise of divine oratory when they stand before governors, kings, and Gentiles, Matt 10:18, which clearly only happened after the resurrection.

rejected as he was, John 15:18. At that point, the evangelists was to trust the Holy Spirit for the right words to preach, Mark 13:11; cf. Matt 10:17–22; Luke 21:14–18, shake the dust from their feet, Matt 10:14–15; Mark 6:10–11, head to the next town, Matt 10:23, all the while rejoicing, Matt 5:12. This complicated social setting, Jesus said, requires being both innocent and shrewd, Matt 7:15–17; 10:16.

IMPLEMENTATION OF THE COMMANDS INTO THE COMMISSION

These five categories of Jesus' commands build a fairly representative model of his emphases and priorities. That is not to say that others might not arrange them differently, give them different labels, or use a different bold font here and there. It is to assert, however, that as a whole, if one were to train a disciple to become competent in these five areas, they would live like Jesus and receive his commendation when he returns. In short: practicing these competencies fulfills Jesus' command in Matthew 28:20. Here is how that looked in the church of *Acts*, at least from Luke's perspective.

Following Jesus

Jesus' preaching was irreducibly egocentric. It was much more about who he was as a person than about a list of ethical principles. The apostolic preaching of Acts reflects this emphasis on the person of Jesus. From Peter's initial address at Pentecost, Acts 2, to Stephen's dying discourse, Acts 7, to Paul's legal defenses, Acts 24–26, they are about Jesus' identity as the risen Messiah. Of particular emphasis is the fact that Jesus is proved to be the prophesied Christ because of the bodily resurrection. This, therefore, must be our practice as we carry out Christ's commission. Our preaching is not about ethics, social issues, or current political policies. The model is clear: Preach the risen Christ with relentless tenacity. If we do that with the boldness promised by the Spirit, we will find our opponents describing us as the Sadducees described Peter and John, "These men have been with Jesus," Acts 4:13.

Religious Piety

The emphasis of Jesus on prayer is replicated in Acts. Though oaths, Acts 23:12, 14, 21, and fasting, Acts 13:2–3; 14:23; 27:9, are sparsely represented as well, prayer receives the lion's share of attention.[18] Given this emphasis, it is incredible that the Western church has so minimized prayer. Most of us give it a mere nod in our personal lives, in our corporate worship, and in our completion of the great commission. There could hardly be a greater disconnect with Jesus' praxis than our neglect of this critical discipline that he prized so highly and the early church practiced so fervently. Something has gone desperately wrong when it takes us ten times longer to voice the requests to one another than it does to bring them to the throne of God.

---

18. Acts 1:14, 24; 2:42; 3:4; 4:24, 31; 6:4, 6; 7:59; 8:15, 22, 24; 9:11, 40; 10:2, 4, 9, 30–31; 11:5; 12:5, 12; 13:3; 14:23; 16:13, 16, 25; 20:36; 21:5; 22:17; 27:29; 28:8.

Money

Jesus' commands on money could hardly be more challenging to the Western church. But they were no easier to the early church that had to grapple with the grinding poverty of the believing peasant class. It is likely that upwards of 90 percent of the first Christians were day-laborers that lived hand to mouth. This makes it extraordinary that twice the book of Acts records the economic egalitarian practice of the church, Acts 2:44–45; 4:32–35. They were practicing the same benevolence their Jewish forefathers were commanded, Deut 15:4, and for the same reason—God's reputation among the pagans was at stake in the believer's distribution of his wealth among the brothers. This was particularly important for the Galilean disciples who had left jobs and family networks to follow Jesus. It is entirely plausible that this original band of disciples lived with a shared community of goods since they had just witnessed the resurrection of Jesus, his ascension, and the Baptism of the Holy Spirit at Pentecost. They were living in extraordinary times that called for extraordinary measures of social cohesion. This is not so different than the practice of the Qumran community:[19] "Nor is there any one to be found among them who hath more than another; for it is a law among them, that those who come to them must let what they have be common to the whole order, insomuch that among them all there is no appearance of poverty, or excess of riches, but every one's possessions are intermingled with every other's possessions; and so there is, as it were, one patrimony among all the brethren."[20]

This communal lifestyle was nothing new for the inner band of Jesus' disciples. They lived like that long before Pentecost. They had been supported in part by a group of wealthy women, Luke 8:1–3, and shared their common purse with those in need, John 6:7; 12:6; 13:29.[21] Acts 2:42–47 and 4:32–35 have their roots in the praxis of Jesus himself that was perfectly at home in the patron/client system of the first-century world. It wasn't that every Christian sold what she or he had and lived in a commune. Rather, those with substantial means felt the spiritual obligation to provide for the economically despondent in their fictive family. We must model a new kind of society that models the kindness and self-sacrifice of our Savior. Those living in the modern West often have the most difficult time with, as well as the deepest responsibility for, imitating the radical economic sacrifice of the early church.

---

19. For a discussion on this sort of communalism, see Taylor, "The Community of Goods," 147–61; Bartchy, "Community of Goods in Acts" 309–18; Capper, "The Palestinian Cultural Context," vol. 4, 323–56; and Coppens, "La koinônia dans l'Église primitive," 116–21.

20. For further details see Johnson, "The Dead Sea Manual of Discipline," 129–42, 273–75. The only other group to practice this kind of communalism was the Pythagoreans (4th–3rd cen. bc): "At this time, then, the things belonging to each, that is, their possessions, were held in common, given to those disciples appointed for this purpose who were called 'politicians,' and experienced in household management and skilled in legislation" Iamblichus, *Vita Pythagoras* 17.72. See also, Josephus *J.W.* 2.8.3 §122; cf. 1QS 5.1–3; 9.3–11; Philo, *Hypothetica* 11.4–9; *Apology* 11.10–11.

21. This practice appears to have continued in the 2nd and 3rd centuries (cf. *Did.* 4.8; *Barn.* 9.8a). Though communalism has never been a universal practice of the church, benevolence has never been abandoned as an essential praxis for believers; cf. Hans-Joachim Kraus, "Actualität des 'urchristlichen Kommunismus,'" in *Freispruch und Freiheit*, 306–27.

Treatment of Others

Of all the five categories, this one has the least evidence of the early church imitating Jesus. Paul does shake dust off his feet on several occasions, Acts 13:51; 18:6; cf. 22:22–3. However, there is precious little to suggest that the church deliberately sought out the socially marginalized, "sinners," or children. There is a precious story in Acts 6:1–7 where widows were cared for. It was handled wisely, resulting in greater ministry, but honestly, it was a blemish on the early church. There is also, of course, a heavy emphasis on acceptance of Gentiles, beginning with the Samaritans, Acts 8:4–25, followed by the Ethiopian "God-fearer," Acts 8:26–40, and culminating in Cornelius's household being baptized, Acts 10:1–48. Nonetheless, each of these incidents was prompted by the Holy Spirit rather than the impetus of Christian compassion. Chapter 16 of Acts is the closest we come to a deliberate targeting of the undercarriage of society. Here Luke recounts three stories from Philippi where the gospel reached a woman, a slave, and a Gentile in apparent contradistinction to the common Jewish prayer, "God, I thank you that you did not make me a Gentile, a woman, or a slave."

Nonetheless, there are no stories of prostitutes, tax-collectors, outcasts or orphans we have come to expect from the ministry of Jesus. Happily, there has been a surge in modern missions toward social justice issues. Perhaps this is the only category in which the contemporary church outshines the early church. From micro-loans to women's literacy, from adoptions to exposing human trafficking, from clean water to AIDS research, Bible-believing Christians have robbed critics of much of their ammunition and opened millions of doors to preach the authentic gospel of Jesus Christ. If the gospel is not good news to the poor, it is not the good news of Jesus Christ.[22]

Preaching and Persecution

None of the previous categories come close to this fifth category for its fulfillment in Acts. There are twenty substantive Christian speeches in Acts: nine by Peter,[23] nine by Paul[24] and one each by Stephen, 7:2–53, and James, 15:13–21. Most of these speeches either lead to or stem from persecution of some sort. Peter and John were threatened, 4:16–22, followed by all the Twelve being arrested and beaten, barely saved by the intervention of Gamaliel, 5:17–42. Stephen didn't fare so well, being stoned under Saul's zealous eye, 7:54–8:1. Christians were systematically imprisoned and executed, 8:1–3, and evangelists like Philip were chased out of town, 8:4–5. James was beheaded, 12:2, and Peter escaped only through angelic intervention, 12:6–11. Of course Paul, the former persecutor, bore the brunt of the beatings. He had to escape from Damascus, 9:25, he was accosted by Bar Jesus, 13:8, run out of town both in Antioch, 13:50–51, and Iconium, 14:1–7, and finally

---

22. This has always been a strong emphasis among Catholic Liberation theologians; cf. Pimentel, "La Praxis de las Comunidades Cristianas al Comenzar un Nuevo Milenio: Una Lectura comunitaria y Actualizante de Hechos 2," 147–63. Bridel, "Espiritu Comunitario y Diaconia segun los Hechos de los Apóstoles 2, 42 y 4, 32," 301–08. Of course, this is also of concern to Mennonite scholars among others; cf. Reta Halteman Finger, "Cultural Attitudes in Western Christianity," 235–70.

23. Acts 1:16–22; 2:14–36; 3:12–26; 4:8–12; 5:29–32; 8:20–23; 10:34–43; 11:5–17; 15:7–11.

24. Acts 13:16–41; 14:15–17; 17:22–31; 20:18–35; 22:1–21; 24:10–21; 26:2–23; 27:21–26; 28:17–20.

stoned in Lystra, 14:19. In Philippi, he and Silas were beaten with rods and thrown into the dungeon in stocks, 16:22–24. The hooligans of Macedonia barely missed their mark in Thessalonica and again in Berea, 18:6–15. At last in Corinth, Paul gets a reprieve when the case against him is thrown out of court, 18:14, but it will not last long. In Ephesus he riled an estimated crowd of twenty-eight thousand, Acts 19:34–35, and in Jerusalem he instigated a riot in the Temple, 21:27–28. This resulted in five trials and years of imprisonment, Acts 22–28. Then there were the foiled plots against Paul, 9:23–24; 20:3, 19; 23:30, and the nasty shipwreck he had to endure, 27:39–44.[25]

As the contemporary church contemplates teaching everything Jesus commanded, we must include the bold proclamation of the risen Christ and the inevitable consequence of persecution. As our evangelistic effectiveness has risen, so has ugly and vicious opposition to believers. The Western church barely has a clue about the unprecedented evil against our brothers abroad or the unprecedented opportunity this affords for completing the great commission.

If you will allow, I would like to conclude this essay with a personal opinion gleaned from my friend Kevin Dooley. It appears to me that the great commission will be completed due to two current realities: Persecution and Economic Provision. The church in many countries is facing an aggression unparalleled even in the Roman Empire. Fact: More martyrs have been killed for their faith in the last one hundred years than in the entire history of the church prior. At the same time, there has been a meteoric rise in prosperity of the West which has no equal in the history of the world. Both of these may be from God. When the church of affluence recognizes the responsibility of that blessing, it could well fund the proclamation of the gospel to the ends of the earth by those ready to lay down their lives. We must realize that God never puts blessings in buckets but always in conduits. If God has lavishly blessed the church of America, it is not because he loves us but because he trusts us—he loves the *world*. If we become as sacrificial with our money, category #3, as our beleaguered brothers are with their lives, this generation could well experience the completion of the commission.

---

25. All this is not the half of Paul's sufferings. He himself records five lashings from the Jews, three shipwrecks, and two beatings with rods that Luke never mentions, cf. 2 Cor 11:24–25.

6

Surging Waters: Global Expansion
of the World Christian Movement[1]

by Stephen E. Burris

INTRODUCTION

BEGINNING WITH GEN 12:3 God communicates his central character as a missionary God. Since God is a missionary God, a review of the expansion of Christianity should reveal the church fulfilling God's purpose and plan.

First, an overview of the history of the church shows how God moves through his people, using both strength and weakness. At times surprising individuals have made major contributions to the expansion of the world Christian movement.

Second, the Holy Spirit empowers God's mission. In Acts we see the Holy Spirit as an initiator of the mission movement. Examples include how Philip brought the gospel to Gaza, Acts 8; how Peter was used to introduce the gospel to the Gentiles, Acts 10; the Holy Spirit led the Antioch church to "separate Saul and Barnabas," Acts 13; and at the conclusion of the Council of Jerusalem, Paul and Silas are told to go West, to Macedonia, to Europe, Acts. 15.[2]

Third, God's purpose is to reach all nations. Matt 28:19 has been called the great commission. In fact this is a restatement of the commission given to Abraham in Gen 12:1–3.[3] The Psalmist (67:2) reminds us that God "has made his way known upon the

---

1. Portions of this chapter appeared previously in the chapter entitled "God's Determined Purpose." Elliston and Burris, *Completing the Task*.

2. Robert, describing the significance of the Council of Jerusalem and the ultimate spread of Christianity outside of the Jewish boundaries writes, "The crucial decision to allow Greeks to become Christians and remain within their own cultural framework was a key that opened the future of Christianity to its global potential as a 'world' religion, rather than remaining a sect within Judaism." Robert, *Christian Mission*, 14. It should also be noted that as a result of the Council of Jerusalem the world view of the apostles and Jewish Christians underwent a change. Sanneh says, "Paul was determined that for those new Christians who were brought up as Hellenistic pagans, even the notion of adopting the lifestyle of very good, devout, observant Jewish believers should be rejected. In that reasoning, the new Christians are not just followers of Jesus; they are a new creation in the sense of their being baptized in him, of their being partakers in the redeeming life of Christ. They are, in fact, converts rather than just proselytes." Sanneh, *Disciples of All Nations*, 8.

3. "Salvation is not just a doctrine we believe in, or a condition we find ourselves in. *Salvation* is a *story*

---

earth, his saving power among all nations." Paul, Rom 16:26, declares the gospel is to be made known "to all nations, according to the command of the eternal God." Rev 5:9 and 7:9 give a glimpse into the throne room of heaven, a clear enough view to show representatives from every tribe and language and people and nation.

Fourth, God has ordained the church as the "body," "temple," "family," "people of God," to be the representation of God's love, the proclaimer of his kingdom among the nations, *laos tou theou* (people of God) going to *ta ethne* (the nations).[4]

One weakness in a study of history is cultural bias of the author.[5] Church history or other history written by a Western scholar will almost invariably show a Western bias. Much of the historical record readily available comes from the West. This bias leaves the impression that the early church grew out from Jerusalem to Judea to Samaria to the Roman Empire to Europe to England, the New World and so forth. The reality is Christianity went out from Jerusalem in virtually all directions.[6] A careful reading of the peoples present on Pentecost gives evidence of representatives from Africa and the Middle East. While the biblical and historical record shows a greater emphasis on the West, we should be aware that the expansion of the world Christian movement was global from the beginning. This expansion included similarities with the patterns of expansion in the West such as periods of advance followed by setbacks. Christianity may have found its strongest numerical strength in North Africa and Asia Minor.[7]

One example is the Parthians, also known as the Persians. Representatives of this people were present at Pentecost, Acts 2:9. Foster writes, "For nearly 500 years, from 240 BC to AD 225, the Parthians, whose first home had been south-east of the Caspian Sea,

---

we participate in – the story of what initiated through Abraham and accomplished through Christ." Wright, *Mission of God,* 72.

4. See Van Engen, *God's Missionary People,* and Burris, "The Biblical Basis."

5. Jenkins states that "For most of history, Christianity was a tri-continental religion, with powerful representation in Europe, Africa, and Asia, and this was true into the fourteenth century." Jenkins, *The Lost History of Chrisianity,* 3. Jenkins goes on to say "rediscovering the lost Christian worlds of Africa and Asia raises sobering questions about the nature of historical memory." Ibid., 4.

6. According to Robert, "The eastward spread of Christianity was so extensive that the fourth-century Persian Empire contained as high a percentage of Christians as the Roman, with a geographic spread from modern-day Iran to India. By the seventh century, Christians were living as far east as China and as far south as Nubia in Africa." Robert, *Christian Mission,* 8. Robert goes on to add, "according to Christian tradition, Jesus' disciples took the message from Jerusalem into new regions in which they were eventually martyred– Mark to Egypt, Thomas to India, Philip to Africa, and Peter to Rome." Ibid., 15. "By the time of Constantine, it is estimated that about 10 percent of the fifty million people of the Roman Empire were Christians." Bevans and Schroeder, *Constants in Context,* 83. Jenkins gives a larger perspective when he writes, "Founded in the Near East, Christianity for its first thousand years was stronger in Asia and North Africa than in Europe, and only after 1400 did Europe (and Europeanized North America) decisively become the Christian heartland." Jenkins, *The Next Christendom,* 19. Jenkins also reports that by the year 1,000 "Asia had 17 to 20 million Christians with a further 5 million in Africa . . . By this point, a reasonable estimate would suggest that Europe had some 25 to 30 million Christians, many whose faith was very notional indeed compared with the ancient churches of Asia and Africa . . . If raw numbers favored Europe, Asia could still properly claim the leadership of the Christian world." Jenkins, *Lost History,* 70.

7. See Latourette, *First Five Centuries,* 91.

ruled all the territory from Mesopotamia to the frontiers of India."[8] The written record supports a church being built as early as AD 135. Edessa[9] and Abiabene were key strongholds. Foster summarizes, "The Chronicle names seventeen sees (i.e., seats of a bishop's rule) which were established before the end of the Parthian period. Then follow these words: 'and there were bishops in other cities too.'"[10]

Another example comes from Africa. The Acts of the Apostles mentions representatives of peoples in Egypt and the parts of Libya belonging to Cyrene (Acts 2:10). We also have record of the Ethiopian eunuch and Philip recorded in Acts 8. Ethiopia claims to be the oldest continuing Christian country in the world.[11]

With this expanded perspective in mind, we turn to examine the expansion of the world Christian movement. This chapter examines the history of the church from Pentecost to approximately AD 1800 in three time periods. The division of these periods follows those suggested by Kenneth Scott Latourette in his massive seven-volume work, *The History of the Expansion of Christianity*. It also assumes nine theses proposed by Paul E. Pierson.[12]

It is not our intention to attempt in one chapter to give a comprehensive overview of eighteen centuries of expansion, but to identify a few important movements and key individuals within those movements.

PEOPLE'S MOVEMENT, 1—500 AD

There were only a few prominent missionaries during this period. One is Ulfilas[13] who in 350 became a missionary to the Goths and led a breakthrough to reach the barbarian tribal peoples. This breakthrough was the beginning of widespread evangelization.

8. Foster, *Church History I*, 92.

9. "By the end of the first century, as tradition contends, it is quite possible that there were indeed Christians in Asia from the Euphrates to India, and that Edessa, 'the blessed city,' has become the center of an early Asia Christianity so vigorous that it had already begun to penetrate eastward into the Persian Empire." Moffett, *A History of Christianity in Asia*, Vol. 1, 56. The region around Edessa was important in Jewish history as well. "Abraham's father died in Haron, only twenty-five miles from Edessa, and there Isaac found his wife Rebekah." Ibid., 46

10. Foster, *Church History I*, 95.

11. Ibid., 107.

12. Pierson *Dynamics of Christian Mission*, 4–5. Pierson provides helpful theses as a grid to look at such a vast amount of historical material covering the 1800 years included in this chapter. Pierson's thesis are: 1. That God's redemptive mission has been worked out in history through the normative use of two structures, 2. That the renewal of the church and its expansion are interlinked, 3. That renewal and expansion happen when the historical/contextual conditions are right, 4. That renewal and expansion are frequently triggered by a key person, 5. That renewal and expansion are often accompanied by theological breakthroughs, 6. That renewal and expansion are often accompanied by new spiritual dynamics or re-contextualized forms of spirituality, 7. That renewal and expansion are contagious in contexts where information is easily distributed, 8. That renewal and expansion are often seen to have been accompanied by new leadership patterns, 9. That renewal and expansion are often seen to have begun on the periphery of the ecclesiastical structures of the day.

13. Pierson writes about Ulfilas, "For forty years, from 341 until he died in 381, he was perhaps the only missionary beyond the frontiers of the Roman Empire." Pierson, *Dynamics*, 59. Gonzalez says Ulfilas, "invented a way to write the language of the Goths and translated the Bible into it." Gonzalez, *Story of Christianity*, 218.

Specifically, Ulfilas stressed the importance of presenting the gospel to the hearts of the people.[14] One way of accomplishing this was to speak the language of the people. Of his efforts Foster writes, "Ulfilas had grown up bilingual, so he knew what to do: take Greek letters to write Gothic sounds. And so he produced his Gothic Bible. It was the first book in the whole German family of languages, to which, later, English would belong."[15]

During this period, the movement was not led by missionaries, but by ordinary Christians moving from province to province, sometimes to escape persecution. Often this effort was outside the main-stream of church activity.[16] Soldiers became Christians and carried the good news to the outposts of the Empire. It would be a mistake, however, to confine the movement to the lower classes.[17] Justin Martyr is an example of the educated class accepting Christ. Clearly, Christianity had penetrated all social/economic classes, but the lower classes tended to dominate.

Persecution was an important factor in the expansion of Christianity.[18] Christians knew how to die nobly. Every Christian lived with the realization that at some point she or he might be killed. No church, however, was subjected to continuous persecution.[19]

In contrast to the general breakdown in society, the Christians demonstrated a new lifestyle. This lifestyle was characterized by Christian communities that demonstrated love and an emphasis on the family.[20] The Christians became known, even among their enemies, for their loving service and care for others, especially those in the church. More important than numbers were the character and quality of life the Christians demonstrated before a watching world.[21]

14. See Tucker, *From Jerusalem*, 35–38.

15. Foster, *Church History I*, 122.

16 Robert says, "growth takes place at the edges or borderlands of Christian areas, even as Christian heartlands experience decline." Robert, *Christian Mission*, 9.

17. Jenkins writes, "For all missionaries in that era, the ultimate dream was to convert a king or a ruling class, who would then bring the whole state into the church." Jenkins, *Lost History*, 68.

18. "Martyrdom had an enormous impact on shaping Christians' self-understanding and the depth of their commitment, in shifting public perception in favor of Christianity, and in attracting many non-Christians to take a closer look at these Christians who were willing to sacrifice so much for their faith." Bevans and Schroeder, *Constants in Context*, 86.

19. See Neill, *A History of Christian Missions*, 43.

20. Wright, *Mission of God*, 389. Wright emphasizes the ethical dimension of the Christian community as part of its witness to a watching world. "The message is plain. Christians are to be as visible to the nations by the quality of their moral lives as Israel had intended to be (but failed). And the purpose of that ethical visibility is ultimately to bring the nations to glorify God." Ibid., 389.

21. Sanneh, referring to Tertullian, writes, "the Christian view of community life offered a revealing contrast to the existing world . . . In their radical obedience to God rather than in their compliance with prevailing mores, Tertullian challenges, Christians became responsible and productive members of society, an argument Augustine of Hippo (d. 430) defended with great eloquence two centuries later. A running theme in Tertullian's discussion, as well as Augustine's is the idea that Christians are not a secret society, that their beliefs and rituals are open to public scrutiny, that membership and duties in the fellowship are voluntary, that religious office is not for sale, that believers practice mutual aid, and a common fund existed to help the poor and needy." Sanneh, *Disciples*, 15. Wright, describing Israel, writes, "So the nations were in principle invited not only to watch all the wonderful things God did for Israel, they were also supposed to be able to see the responsive righteousness of Israel living within the terns of the covenant. In other words, Israel's visibility to the nations was meant to be not merely historically remarkable but radically and ethically

Rapid Expansion of the Movement

Evidence suggests the apostle Thomas carried the gospel to India during the first century.[22] We have evidence that the church was planted in Ethiopia from 325 AD.[23] Patrick expanded Christianity's movement into Ireland. Other countries and regions were introduced to the gospel during this first period.[24]

Why has Christianity endured? Latourette suggests six reasons why Christianity has expanded and stood in spite of incredible obstacles, including, "The endorsement of Constantine … the disintegration of society . . . the organization which it developed . . . Its inclusiveness . . . Christianity was both transigent and flexible . . . Christianity supplied what the Greco-Roman world was asking of religion and philosophy and it did it better than any of its competitors."[25]

By the end of the first three centuries, in spite of the fact that Christianity was not officially recognized, all the main areas of the Roman Empire had an active Christian witness.[26]

In the year 311 Emperor Constantine issued the Edict of Toleration. At this time about 10 percent of the population of the Roman Empire was Christian. That the church was growing in spite of persecution is evidenced by the fact that in 250 AD the church at Rome had 30,000 members.[27]

A new situation existed after Constantine. The church was in culture, but the penetration was both ways. As both Pierson and Neill point out, this growth provided new opportunities to penetrate culture with the gospel, but it also opened the way for new temptations and dangers of cultural penetration of the church.[28] "With a new freedom, the Church was able to go out into the world; at the same time, a new and dangerous fashion, the world entered into the church."[29]

Shortly after the Edict of Toleration, persecution began in Persia. This persecution had its roots in what Foster describes as foreign policy. "In foreign policy, the Persians recognized the Romans as successors to the Greeks, i.e., as Persia's traditional enemy. So there began in 325 four centuries of Persian-Roman strife: disputed territory, frontier raids, invasion, [and] war."[30]

---

challenging." Wright, *Mission of God,* 470.

22. Moffett gives strong support to the Apostle Thomas as the founder of the church in India. "The general consensus of local Indian traditions is that Thomas came first to south India, not to Punjab of King Gundaphar . . . the date was A.D. 50 or 52. He founded seven churches." Moffett, *History of Christianity,* 34.

23. Elliston, "An Ethnohistory of Ethiopia."

24. As an example, Moffett reports on the growth of the church across Asia. "In less than two hundred years after the death of Christ, Syrian Christians were beginning to carry the faith not just across the Asian borders of Rome, and not into Persia alone, but out across the continent toward the steppes of the Central Asiatic nomads and the edges of the Hindu Kush." Moffett, *History of Christianity,* 80.

25. Latourette, *First Five Centuries,* 163–65.

26. Ibid., 100.

27. Ibid., 95.

28. Pierson, *Dynamics,* xxx.

29. Neill, *A History,* 47.

30. Foster, *Church History I.* 97.

The Christians in Persia were vulnerable after Constantine because they were now suspected of belonging to the religion favored by the Romans. This situation was created as a Roman Emperor openly demonstrated his pleasure with the large numbers of Christians in Persia. The reaction of the Persian authorities was predictable. The obvious question was whose side are the Christians on, Rome's or Persia's? The most surprising aspect is the length of time it took the Persian authorities to begin the persecution.[31]

Importance of Church Leaders

Several important church leaders emerged during this period. The first was Justin Martyr. Justin Martyr's most enduring contributions include his *Apologies* and *Dialogue with Trypho*. In contrast to the immorality associated with some religious rites, he stated that the *Logos* was made flesh in order to free individuals from evil. In his *Dialogue with Trypho* Justin places Christianity in the stream of Jewish thought, and its successor.

Tertullian, as another influential leader, formulated what came to be known as the Trinity formula. In the process he maintained the Messianic character of the Son and his atoning work on the cross.

Origen was a third important leader. As part of the school in Alexandria, he insisted on scholarship in the church. He believed that knowledge contributed to the understanding of truth that culminated in theology. Some consider Origen as the greatest scholar in the history of the church.

Augustine impacts Christianity to this very day. Augustine was a champion of the doctrine of grace. His *Confessions* and *The City of God* are considered among the world's great books. In *The City of God*[32] Augustine contrasted two cities, the church and the world, and showed how they were in opposition to each other. He suggested that events work out for the good of the church. Following Rom 8:28, Augustine showed what the world considers to be bad can be used by God for good. Foster notes, "The teaching of the *City of God* is that the Church, on pilgrimage through history, is that which gives meaning to history, and that the end of its pilgrimage is *beyond* history, the church Triumphant."[33]

Neill lists several human factors that contributed to the spread of Christianity during this first period, a period he notes as miraculous. "First and foremost we must reckon with the burning conviction by such a great number of the earliest Christians were pos-

---

31. Ibid. 97–98. Jenkins writes, "Once Rome became Christian, the link with that foreign government made life difficult for Christians living under the rule of the rival superpower of the time . . . The Persians responded by executing hundreds of Bishops and Clergy in a persecution at least as murderous as anything ever inflicted by Pagan Rome in the fourth century, the Persians killed sixteen thousand Christian believers in a forty-year period." Jenkins *Lost History,* 57. Moffett reports "One estimate is that as many as 190,000 Persian Christians died in the terror. It was worse than anything suffered in the West under Rome, yet the number of apostasies seemed to be fewer in Persia than in the West, which is a remarkable tribute to the steady courage of Asia's early Christians." Moffett, *History of Christianity*, 145. Moffett also adds that "the primary cause of the persecution was political. When Rome became Christian, its old enemy Persia turned anti-Christian." Ibid., 137. See also Foster, *Church History I*, 99.

32. "in Augustine's vision it was not the city of Rome—known instructively to its contemporaries as the Eternal City–that was the center stage of history, but the 'city' of God in which no age or society had closer or more distant affinity or nearness, or enjoyed greater or lesser advantage, than any other." Sanneh, *Disciples*, 53.

33. Foster, *Church History I.* 129.

sessed . . . unshakable assurance that in face of every obstacle men can be won and must be won for Christ, which was the mainspring of the whole enterprise . . . Thirdly, the new Christian communities commended themselves by the evident purity of their lives . . . finally, we must consider the effect of the persecution of the Christians on popular opinion about them."[34]

Latourette summarizes this period, "By the year 500, as we have seen, the overwhelming majority of the population of the Roman Empire were calling themselves Christian and the faith had begun to be carried beyond the borders of the realm."[35]

MIDDLE AGES, 500—1500 AD

This period has been labeled the "Dark Ages" because of the fall of the old civilization known as Rome. Additionally, a new foe, Islam, would also appear and threaten the Empire and the church. Latourette summarizes the problem as both internal and external. "The Roman Empire suffered from both internal weaknesses and external pressures. We have already noted that the weaknesses in part ante-dated the coming of Christianity, that they were for a time allayed by the imperial system inaugurated by Augustus Caesar, but that from the end of the second century they began again to be apparent, were aggravated, and multiplied. The external pressures were by invaders who took advantage of the internal decay to overrun most of the Empire."[36]

Breakup of the Empire

Two important invasions usher in this period and help bring about the fall of Rome. The first, in 410 AD, was by the Visigoths. The second, in 455 AD, was by the Vandals. The church appeared to gain ground, however. Some historians give credit to Leo I, also known as Leo the Great. He centralized the government of the Western church and had influence on the Eastern church. Under Leo and his successors, the church was the most stable institution and provided security during a time when the Roman Empire was breaking up.

ISLAM

The setback initiated by Islam is the greatest in the history of the church.[37] Not only did large areas convert to Islam, but the very advance of Christianity in other regions was

---

34. Neill, *History*, 39–42.

35. Latourette, *History of Christianity*, 236. Latourette gives a sobering note, however, "in this victory of Christianity was also something of defeat. The victory had been accompanied by compromise, compromise with the world which had crucified Jesus, compromise often made so half-consciously or unconsciously that it was all the more serious a peril to the Gospel." Ibid., 108.

36. Ibid., 270.

37. "It is worth noting as a significant weakness in the early Christian missions in Arabia that the major areas of Christian strength on the eve of the rise of Islam were all foreign dominated . . . The Christian faith retained a foreign tinge in the Arabian Peninsula. Nowhere was it able to establish an authentic Arabic base. It had not yet even translated the Scriptures into Arabic." Moffett, *History of Christianity*, 281.

threatened by surrounding the Christian strongholds. As a result many countries were permanently lost, including the Christian strongholds in Syria, Palestine, and North Africa.[38]

Islam enjoyed two periods of great success. The first was in the seventh and eighth centuries when the Arabs controlled Arabia,[39] Syria, Mesopotamia, Persia, Palestine, Egypt, North Africa and the Iberian Peninsula. The second was at the end of the thirteenth and the beginning of the fourteenth century when the Mongols of Chinese Turkestan adopted Islam. This effectively shut off the peoples east of the Euphrates to Christianity.[40] While attempts to regain what was lost to the Muslims were launched, most notably the Crusades, in most areas the loss was permanent.

MONGOLS

Christianity appears to have faded from China about 900. The Nestorian version of Christianity had spread out across Central Asia and by 635 Christianity had reached China.[41] Beginning at this point and continuing until about 900, China was probably the wealthiest and most civilized empire in the world.[42]

38. Foster, *Church History II*, 11–12. Scholars have made a strong case that the loss of North Africa to Islam was a result of the church that was established. "The North African church based in Carthage had at its height been one of the most powerful and influential in the whole of Christianity, yet very soon after the Muslims took Carthage in 698, that church vanished almost totally . . . Probably, most African Christians simply fled, rather than being killed or expelled." Jenkins, *Lost History*, 102. The population in North Africa was primarily made up of Romans, Carthaginians, and Berbers. When the Muslims conquered the region the Romans and Carthaginians left. The Berbers made up the primary population. Jenkins goes on to point out, "Where the African church failed was in not carrying Christianity beyond the Romanized inhabitants of the cities and the great estates, and not sinking roots into the world of the native peoples." Pierson writes, "It appears the church in North Africa was identified with the more elitist Romans and Romanized populations, less so with the Carthaginians, and even less with the Berbers. There were three primary people groups in North Africa. The Romans were the last colonists who had come to dominate under the Roman Empire. The Carthaginians were in the middle. They had come from Phoenicia, founded Carthage, and dominated the Berbers. The Berbers were the indigenous people, the lowest stratum of society." Pierson, *Dynamics*, 91. The native peoples were the Berbers, for the most part. In short, the failure of the North African church was that it never became indigenous. It is also noteworthy that the largest surviving church in North Africa is in Egypt, also known as the Coptic Church. "It is important to note that it [Coptic Church] had the Bible in its vernacular language." Pierson, *Dynamics*, 92.

39. "Though now the peninsula [Arabia] is one of the least Christian areas on the surface of the globe, for a time before the Islamic conquest three of the largest Arab kingdoms were Christian." Moffett, *History of Christianity*, 273. Moffett gives a graphic description of the conquest of the region by the Muslims, "up from the southern desert like a sandstorm came a deadlier peril than either Constantinople or Persia had faced in centuries. The armies of the Arabs in a dazzling burst of conquest brought Eastern Rome to its knees and simply absorbed Persia as the desert sucks up water." Ibid., 254.

40. Latourette, *Thousand Years of Uncertainty*, 288.

41. "The earliest formal mission can be dated to 635, when missionaries reached the Chinese imperial capital of Ch'ang-an, establishing a mission that endured for over two hundred years." Jenkins, *Lost History*, 64–65. Moffett confirms "In the year of the edict of toleration, 638, the first Christian church was built in China at the capital of Ch'ang-an, the largest city in the world." Moffett, *History of Christianity*, 293. Jenkins goes on to give an important missiological principle when he writes, "by the sixth century, Christian missionaries were reaching into the heart of Asia, and from the very beginning they recognized the need for vernacular scriptures, inventing alphabets where necessary." Jenkins, *Lost History*, 62–63.

42. Neill, *A History*, 95.

Monasticism was very influential in China. A significant difference is obvious in this form of monasticism, however.[43] Unlike Europe where the monk was likely the most highly educated, and perhaps one of few literate individuals, in China the monks lived among a highly civilized population and in competition with other religious systems, most notably Buddhism.

When the Mongols appeared, an important change took place in the way missionaries conducted their work. The Mongols were nomads. If the missionaries were to evangelize these peoples, they would need to adopt a nomadic way of life as well.

Genghis Khan,[44] considered by many to be one of the most remarkable conquerors in history, set out to invade China in 1211. On a positive side, he decreed that deference be shown to all religions.[45] Foster reports that under Kublai Khan the Mongol Empire was the "widest that the world had ever known, stretching from the China Sea westward to the river Danube, and from the Ural Mountains south to the Himalayas."[46]

Christianity missed an incredibly important opportunity during this period. Kublai Khan,[47] Genghis Kahn's grandson, requested that the Pope send a hundred missionaries. "In response Pope Gregory X sent two Dominican Friars, who travelled with Marco Polo, but turned back before reaching China."[48]

Not all was lost, however. One notable breakthrough came through the efforts of a Franciscan missionary. By 1294 John of Monte Corvino, perhaps the first missionary to reach China, arrived in Khanbalik (Beijing). He was allowed to build a church, and by 1305 he claimed to have baptized 6,000 persons. The report of John's success provided motivation to send additional missionaries to China.[49]

Summarizing this important period Foster writes of what might have been if the Pope had sent a hundred missionaries. "If it had happened, Christianity would have been reinvigorated by this mission-of-help, and might have spread from Mongols and other non-Chinese peoples to the Chinese themselves and so have survived in China. It might have even spread to the Mongols of central Asia, before Babar led them over the Himalayas

---

43. In the Eastern church "the ideal Christian was not only celibate, but must also rejected as far as possible any form of material comfort, including food beyond what was absolutely necessary to keep the person alive." Jenkins, *Lost History*, 111.

44. "Genghis Kahn (d. 1227) and at least two of his sons married Nestorian women. The powerful Nestorian princess Sarkaktani Beki (d. 1252), the wife of his youngest son, became mother of the Great Khan of the Mongols (Kublai Khan, d. 1294), and emperor of China, and an emperor of Persia." Robert, *Christian Mission*, 28.

45. Neill, *History*, 120.

46. Foster, *Church History II*, 80.

47. See Latourette, *A Short History of the Far East*, 132–3. See also, Latourette, *The Chinese Their History and Culture*, 209–13.

48. Foster, *Church History II*, 80.

49. Ibid., 80. See also Moffett, *History of Christianity*, 456–59. Gonzalez notes, "The Franciscan John of Montecorvino visited Persia, Ethiopia, and India, and in 1294, after a journey of three years, arrived in Cambaluc–now Beijing. In a few years, he had made several thousand converts. The pope then made him archbishop of Cambaluc, and sent seven other Franciscans to serve under him as bishops." Gonzalez, *Story of Christianity*, 306. See also Neill, *History*, 105–6.

in 1526 to found the kingdom in Hindustan, and permanently plant their religion there. The history of all Asia might have been different."[50]

CRUSADES

The Crusades were not primarily for the spread of Christianity or for regaining the peoples lost to Islam.[51] Pope Urban II stated the objective as rescuing the holy places in Palestine, defending Christians in the East, and pushing back the Islamic conquest.[52]

The purposes of the Crusades were only partially fulfilled. One negative result was the growth of bitter feelings between the Muslims and Christians. These feelings exist to the present day.[53] Not all was negative, however. For the first time the Crusades attempted to bring Christians together to act in a cause. Also, they opened the routes to the East.[54]

CELTIC MISSIONARIES

The great contribution of the Celtic monastic movement is evidenced in its fervent missionary activity and its commitment to learning. The Celtic church was unique. The center was the monastery. In spite of the Episcopal nature of the Irish church, the abbot was clearly the key leader, not the bishop.[55] Two individuals stand out as a key to understanding the movement and its contribution to the advance of the church.

At the age of 40 Patrick decided to return to Ireland.[56] During the next 30 years he organized 200 churches, and is credited with 100,000 converts. He contributed to the organized structure of the churches on Northern Ireland and to some degree he helped

50. Foster, *Church History II*, 171.

51. Pierson lists several reasons for the Crusades "The medieval definition of a true Christian was one who had been baptized into the right ecclesiastical institution in Western Europe–the Roman Church–and was relatively obedient to that Church . . . Medieval theology taught there were two kinds of penalties for sins: eternal and temporal. Jesus had paid the eternal penalties, but payment of the temporal penalties was still up to each person. Either one paid through acts of penance done in this life, or he or she paid afterwards in the flames of purgatory … Throughout the middle ages, people made pilgrimages to special shrines where they often venerated relics of the saints. It was believed there were enough pieces of the 'true cross' scattered throughout Europe to make ten crosses . . . The Church taught that the veneration of such relics would reduce one's time in purgatory . . . Naturally, a pilgrimage to the Holy Land was the greatest of all acts of penance." Pierson *Dynamics,* 302–3.

52. Latourette, *Thousand Years of Uncertainty*, 317.

53. "The Crusades left a trail of bitterness across the relations between Christians and Muslims that remains as a living factor in the world situation to the present day. To Muslims the West is the great aggressor. Nearly 900 years ago it deliberately entered into that role in the name of Christ, and today it finds it extremely difficult to change the image of itself that still remains in the Muslim mind . . . To Westerners it may appear that the Crusades happened a very long time ago; the Crusaders have slept well in their tombs in quiet English churches. The Far East has a different time scale; to every Muslim in the Mediterranean lands the Crusades are an event of yesterday, and the wounds are ready at any moment to break out afresh." Neill, *A History,* 97–98. See also Moffett, *History of Christianity*, 386–91, and Latourette, *History of Christianity*, 408–14.

54. Foster, *Church History II*, 76–77

55. Neill, *A History*, 57.

56. For a good brief introduction to the life of Patrick see Pierson, *Dynamics*, 70–74; Neill, *History*, 49–50; Robert, *Christian Mission*, 143–59; Walls, *Missionary Movement*, 38–42.

establish relationships with churches on mainland Europe. One important characteristic of the monasteries during this period was their missionary achievement.[57]

Columba settled on the tiny island of Iona and built a very simple monastery.[58] According to Latourette, Columba spent his time with study, prayer, writing, fasting, and watching. Describing the monastery Latourette says, "It was more in the nature of a centre in which missionaries could be trained and from which they could conveniently be sent forth."[59] Columba was involved in the training of Celtic missionaries. He also made frequent missionary journeys to Scotland.

ROMAN MISSIONARIES

Pope Gregory the Great was instrumental in bringing the English church into fellowship with Rome. He worked to set up dioceses similar to the pattern on the European continent. England, in turn, sent out missionaries to the European mainland, particularly to Holland and Germany. While these orders were founded for the purpose of expanding Christianity. While several orders were organized for the purpose of teaching, others were formed for missionary purposes. Creative ideas were employed to enlist the laity in missions. The most widespread was the Society for the Propagation of the Faith. Boniface stands out during this period of advance.

Many consider Boniface,[60] also known as Winfrith, the greatest missionary of this period.[61] He planned and calculated, strategized that the gospel should be preached to those still considered barbarous people.[62] Boniface was also instrumental in developing rules and practices of penitential discipline.[63]

Reflecting on the status of the expansion at this point Foster writes,

> 1. The conversion of northern Europe was almost completed by about 1000. 2. The first answer to the challenge of Islam was offered about 1100. The answer was neither decisive nor fully Christian, but at least western Christendom had sufficiently emerged

57. "When Patrick returned to Ireland from England he initiated the remarkable *Celtic* missionary movement that would continue for centuries, and which would be the source of missionary zeal and learning. His spiritual descendants moved from Ireland to Scotland, then to England, across the channel to the low countries, and finally into central Germany. They were later instrumental in the conversion of Scandinavia. They combined a deep love of learning, spiritual discipline and missionary zeal. As a result, Ireland became literate for the first time in Patrick's generation. The great monastery at Fulda, founded in the 8th century by St. Boniface from this tradition, became the main center of learning for much of Germany." Winter and Hawthorne, *Perspectives* 280.

58. Tucker, *From Jerusalem*, 40–42.

59. Latourette, *Thousand Years of Uncertainty*, 53.

60. Tucker, *From Jerusalem*, 46–49.

61. Latourette recounts an interesting story in the life of Boniface, "At Geismar, in the presence of a large number of hostile pagans, he began cutting down an ancient oak which was sacred to the god Thor. Before he had quite felled the tree a powerful blast of wind completed the demolition and the hoary giant, crashing, broke into four fragments. The pagan bystanders were convinced of the power of the new faith and from the timber Boniface erected an oratory to St. Peter." Latourette, *History of Christianity*, 348. For a more detailed description of the work and contribution of Boniface see, Neill, *A History*, 61–66; Pierson, *Dynamics*, 83–85; Dawson, *Religion and the Rise of Western Culture*, 59–60.

62. Neill, *A History*, 74.

63. Ibid., 77.

from the Dark Ages to feel that it could do something about the Muslim menace. 3. The Friars found a more excellent way, soon after 1200. Better than the Crusades, this movement of renewed Christian zeal came to express itself in mission in North Africa and the east. 4. The challenge given to win the Mongol rulers of Asia, just before 1300, seems to have been one of the biggest missionary opportunities of all time.[64]

REFORMATION/PIETISTIC MOVEMENT: 1500—1800 AD

Several advances are noteworthy during this third period. As in the previous two sections, individuals tended to lead the way, and often outside the mainstream of the church's activities.

Francis Xavier

Xavier is considered by many to be one of the best known Roman Catholic missionaries and one of the most successful missionaries in history. At the heart of his missionary activity Xavier taught followers three important documents: The Ten Commandments–Morals; The Lord's Prayer–Devotion; The Apostle's Creed–Doctrine.[65]

Neill writes concerning an incident early in Xavier's life: "To a passionate but disciplined nature, profound devotion, and an eager longing for the salvation of souls, Xavier added the wide outlook of the statesman and the capacity of the strategist for organization on a large scale. He went to India in 1542, not as an ordinary missionary but as the representative of the king of Portugal, armed with considerable powers, and with the right to correspond directly with the king."[66]

Matthew Ricci

Ricci was largely responsible for pioneering the Jesuit mission work in China. Early he realized that in order to gain a foothold for Christianity he needed to gain the favor and friendship of the ruling classes. He was able to accomplish this goal through several means. "Indeed, it was through their scientific knowledge and mechanical skill, especially in the realm of mathematics, the making of maps, and the regulation of the calendar, that the Jesuits were henceforth to acquire and to hold most of that respect which assured to them and to missionaries of other orders whatever opportunity was theirs to propagate the faith in the Middle Kingdom."[67]

Ricci's methods bear a surprising contemporary perspective.[68] He adopted the dress of a Confucian scholar and attempted to contextualize his message and the worship to fit the Chinese milieu whenever possible.[69] This approach was not lost on those he sought to

64. Foster, *Beginning from Jerusalem*, 52.

65. See Tucker, *From Jerusalem*, 59–63.

66. Neill, *History*, 148.

67. Latourette, *Three Centuries of Advance*, 340.

68. Robert writes, "Matteo Ricci (d. 1610) settled in China in 1583, lived as a Confucian scholar, translated Chinese classics, and wrote important philosophical works that bridged Christianity and Confucianism." Robert, *Christian Mission,* 39; See also Tucker, *From Jerusalem*, 63–66.

69. "Ricci was faced with the thorny problem of finding Chinese equivalents for Christian terms, and

influence. "He had become Chinese in dress, manners, and speech, and had won friends among the officials by his wide knowledge, so different from their wholly literary education.[70] Of this strategy Latourette writes, "Thus he rendered it possible for one reared in the Confucian tradition to become a Christian without being disloyal to two institutions esteemed by the Chinese as basic. Ricci was, in other words, endeavoring to meet the solid opposition offered by the structure of Chinese life by maintaining that Christianity was not antagonistic either to the family or the state, and that it was congenial to much in the Classics. Ricci wished, too, to adapt for Christian uses the pagoda, prominent in the Chinese landscape, and to have the form of Christian worship as nearly Chinese as possible."[71] Ricci enjoyed great success. He established a mission in the capital and had access to the very center of the Empire and to those in authority.

Robert De Nobili

Using a similar strategy to that of Ricci, Nobili believed that if the higher classes were brought to Christ the common peoples would follow. This contextualized strategy included the following elements: "So far as he could do so, without what he believed to be compromise of essential Christian principles and practices, he adopted Indian methods and customs and accommodated himself to Indian prejudices. He lived like an Indian holy man or *sannyasi*, and later, more like an Indian *guru*, or teacher. He adopted the vegetarian diet deemed by the Hindus consistent with the religious profession and employed a Brahmin cook. In conformity with the custom of the Indians, he admitted only Brahmins to his meals, although he would eat with other missionaries."[72]

He was criticized for the use of these methods, primarily from other missionaries. Nobili's methods were successful. He baptized more than a thousand adults each year.[73] While he concentrated on the Brahmin class, the majority of the Christians were from the lower classes.

---

of deciding how far ancient Chinese custom was reconcilable with Christian principle. From the start he had inclined to the later view of Francis Xavier–that in dealing with a great and ancient civilization it is necessary to proceed with great circumspection and respect. His travels had made him well acquainted with the Chinese suspicion of everything foreign; if Christianity was to be acceptable to the Chinese, it must be made as little foreign as possible. It was very easy to announce the principle, to apply it in detail was difficult beyond imagination." Neill, *History*, 149. Latourette writes, "Ricci, after prolonged study, took the moderate position, deciding that the cities in honour of Confucius and family had only a civil significance and that Christians could engage in them in so far as the laws of the Empire required. He would trust the Chinese Christians to decide eventually what they could and could not do, and he hoped that the Catholic practices concerning burial and honouring the dead would gradually supplant those of the older China." Latourette, *History of Christian Missions in China*, 134. See also Latourette, *History of Christianity*, 939–40; Latourette, *The Chinese Their History and Culture*, 236–37.

70. Foster, *Beginning From Jerusalem*, 88.

71. Latourette, *Three Centuries of Advance*, 341.

72. Ibid., 260. Pierson states, "He taught that converts did not have to break their caste rules unless these rules involved idolatry. Certainly, he believed that later on there would be unity in the Church, but he felt that as an evangelistic strategy, he had to identify totally with that cultural group in order to win them." Pierson, *Dynamics*, 174. See also Neill, *A History*, 156–59.

73. Latourette, *Three Centuries of Advance*, 261–2. Robert also reports that Nobili "wrote works in Tamil, Sanskrit, and Telegu." Robert, *Christian Mission*, 39.

Reformers and Missions

Not much missionary activity took place in the early years of the Reformation. Foster cites two reasons why the church was slow to respond. "First, the Reformation affected the small weak countries of northern Europe, still concerned about their own independence, rather than the great powers reaching out over the world for trade and empire . . . Second, in most countries Protestants had to struggle so long in self-defense against Roman Catholics in power that they grew accustomed to an attitude of self-regarding."[74]

One notable exception was the Moravians.[75] In its early years this movement was composed of refugees. Nicolas Ludwig, Count of Zinzendorf, provided a place for these refugees to settle at Herrnhut. Ludwig was a Pietist and had been educated at the University of Halle. Several factors make this group unique. "Herrnhut developed its form of pietism, with a deep devotion to the crucified Redeemer and an intense and strenuous demand for total surrender and consecration to his will. Under the leadership of Zinzendorf this small church was seized with a missionary passion which has never left it. The Moravians have tended to go to the most remote, unfavorable, and neglected parts of the surface of the earth. Many of the missionaries have been quite simple people, peasants and artisans; their aim has been to live the Gospel, and so to commend it to those who have never heard it."[76]

The beginning point for missionary activity was in 1732 and the Greenland mission. Foster reports that "this small denomination has maintained the highest standard of missionary giving in Christendom."[77]

The influence of the Moravians is seen in other areas besides missionary activity.[78] John Wesley was greatly influenced by his contact with this group. They also contributed to worship through a distinct liturgy and hymnology.[79] Others, such as Spencer, Franke, Ziegenbalk, Plutchau, and Christian David[80] also contributed, but space does not allow a summary of their activities. It is sufficient to suggest that Pietism leading to the Great

---

74. Foster, *Beginning from Jerusalem*, 74.

75. According to Pierson, the Moravians "were a small remnant of the *Unitas Fratrum*, the spiritual descendents of John Huss, and probably of Peter Waldo. The group had survived as an underground church through the sixteenth and seventeenth centuries, despite persecution . . . in a period of twenty-eight years, the Moravians sent missionaries to twenty-eight countries. One of every thirteen or so persons in the community went elsewhere as missionaries." Pierson, *Dynamics*, 189–91.

76. Neill, *History*, 237.

77. Foster, *To All Nations*, 19.

78. "They decided to send missionaries to the Caribbean after their leader, Count Zinzendorf (d. 1760), met a former African slave in Denmark named Anthony Ulrich. Ulrich asked Zinzendorf to send messengers of the gospel to his relatives still in slavery. Moravians moved in small groups to live in places where oppressed, non-Christian peoples needed their support–to black slaves in the Caribbean, American Indians in North America, and the Khosian in South Africa. Despite their persecution by slave owners, the Moravians evangelization of West Indian slaves showed the slaves' humanity and potential for peace and reconciliation in a post-slavery society. British abolitionists thus used the Moravian work as proof that slavery could be abolished without bloodshed." Robert, *Christian Mission*, 44–45.

79. Latourette, *History of Christianity*, 897.

80. For a general survey of the work of this remarkable group see Tucker, *From Jerusalem*, 67–82.

Awakening had great impact on the missionary activities of the church at the close of this period.[81]

The Roman Catholic mission efforts of this period were not terribly creative. The missionaries, for the most part, came from the monastic orders, most of which had developed in Medieval Europe. Most of the gains in membership came as a result of inclusion of tribes or castes incorporated as European dominance spread out over the rapidly expanding colonial lands.[82]

CONCLUSION

Throughout the history of the expansion of Christianity four missiological principles emerge. The first is the church and school work together. Missionaries were more often than not at the forefront of education, literacy, translation and other activities that brought learning along with the gospel. As the church expanded, schools opened centering on the particular needs of the people. In cases like Ricci's education was used as a strategy to open doors of opportunity.

The second principle is getting the Bible in the language of the people. From the earliest periods putting the Bible in the language of the people, or the heart language, has been evident. We have only noted a few examples, but the history of the expansion of the Christian movement is full of translation activity, beginning from about the middle of the third century AD.

The third principle is that preaching is aimed at conversion and on the needs of people. The incarnational model is clearly evident. Ricci and Nobili both underscore the importance of contextualizing the gospel message. While this is commonly accepted today, these pioneers, as well as others, were instinctively applying high level missiology.

And, finally, an indigenous ministry is developed as soon as possible. Missionaries realized the importance of leadership development. This along with the emphasis on education helped to secure the gains, often beyond the life and work of the missionary or mission.

While the history of the expansion of Christianity is a story of advances and setbacks, we can clearly see that in every age key individuals appeared who understood that God is a missionary God and attempted to expand Christian influence. Often our picture has been distorted since we haven't seen the entire landscape clearly. While Christianity might be experiencing setbacks in the West, often in those places out of the spotlight, such as China or India, fresh and exciting new developments were taking place.

81. See Randall, *Great Awakenings* for a more complete description of how this movement influenced the Great Awakening.

82. It is outside the scope of this chapter to analyze the factors that led to global exploration by the European powers, it is interesting to note, "as the Near East fell into the control of militant Islamic states, so Western European nations had an ever-greater incentive to find alternative trade routes commonly by exploiting the oceans." Jenkins, *Lost History,* 145.

7

Opening the Floodgates:
From Everywhere to Everywhere[1]

by Stephen E. Burris

BACKGROUND

THOMAS KUHN IN HIS landmark work, *The Structure of Scientific Revolutions*, provides a helpful model in understanding the development of the modern mission period. Kuhn suggests that change is often caused by a "paradigm shift." A paradigm is an accepted model or pattern that provides understanding in a particular situation or within a given set of circumstances. In this way Kuhn talks about the conceptual transformation that takes place during a paradigm shift. A conceptual shift also produces a shift in practice.[2] Kuhn, writing about science, maintains that paradigms have two basic characteristics. "Their achievement was sufficiently unprecedented to attract an enduring group of adherents away from competing modes of scientific activity. Simultaneously, it was sufficiently open-ended to leave all sorts of problems for the redefined group of practitioners to resolve.[3]

This chapter describes the paradigm shifts that have occurred during the approximately 220 years of the "modern missions" period. It builds on Ralph Winter's groundbreaking work "Four Men, Three Eras, Two Transitions: Modern Missions."[4] In light of Kuhn's model, it is helpful to see Winter's three eras as paradigms. Each paradigm was produced by a shift that not only changed the focus of mission work, but also helped clarify the unfinished task of world evangelization. Each paradigm shift sought to touch regions untouched by previous missionary activity. The impact of a shift of this magnitude is described by Kuhn, "That is why a new theory, however special its range of applications, is seldom or never just an increment to what is already known. Its assimilation requires

1. Portions of this chapter appeared previously in the chapter entitled, "Modern Waves of Expansion," Elliston and Burris, *Completing the Task*, 93–113.

2. Kraft gives three principles involved in paradigm shifts. 1) A change is initiated whenever a person or group adopts a new perspective to which a commitment is made. 2) The new information received led to new interpretation. 3) A very important factor to consider in advocating change is the strength of the commitment to the previous assumption or behavior. Kraft, *Worldview for Christian Witness*, 344.

3. Kuhn, *The Structure of Scientific Revolutions*, 10. See also Bosch, *Transforming Mission*, 181–89.

4. Winter and Hawthorne, *Perspectives*, 253–61.

the reconstruction of prior theory and the re-evaluation of prior fact, an intrinsically revolutionary process that is seldom completed by a single man and never overnight."[5]

Each era also produced a paradigm shift within the sending church. In the first era the understanding focused on continents. In the second era countries located in the interior of the continents began to dominate. In the third era "unreached peoples"[6] or socio-linguistic distinctions were the center of attention. Today, a fourth era, Kingdom Missiology, is present as the globalization and urbanization issues come into focus as we consider strategies for fulfilling world evangelization.

Similarities appear in each era as well. Education, for example, is present in each era. The development of local leaders has been a key to the expansion of the world Christian movement throughout history. Bible translation is another example. Bible translation, while highlighted in the third era, was present in the other paradigms. Translation is still a priority in the current paradigm, Kingdom Missiology. A third example is Winter's four stages of mission activity present in each era. Winter lists the stages of mission activity as:

Stage 1: A Pioneer stage. First contact with a people group.

Stage 2: A Paternal stage. Expatriates train national leadership.

Stage 3: A Partnership stage. National leaders work as equals with expatriates.

Stage 4: A Participation stage. Expatriates are no longer equal partners, but only participate by invitation.[7]

Other examples could also be cited. It should be carefully noted that although there are numerous similarities between the various eras, there are also distinct differences. Each paradigm produced a "conceptual transformation" resulting in a practice shift. It is the review of this shift that we now turn our attention.

FIRST ERA: FOCUS ON THE COASTLANDS[8]

William Carey[9] challenged the popular notion that world evangelization was not binding on the church of his day. In fact the Reformers said very little about the evangelization

---

5. Kuhn, *Structure of Scientific Revolutions*, 7.

6. Pocock et al, define unreached peoples (hidden peoples which is an older term used after the Lausanne Conference of 1974) as "People groups that currently have no access to the gospel. They are 'hidden' not in the sense that they are invisible but in the sense that there is no way, given current conditions, that they could hear the gospel in their own language in a way that makes sense to them." Pocock, *Changing Face of World Missions*, 15.

7. Winter and Hawthorne, *Perspectives*, 256.

8. It is easier to pinpoint the beginning of an era in general terms than it is to define the conclusion of an era. In fact, even though we have been in the Third Era for many years there continues to be a substantial amount of First Era and Second Era type mission work taking place today even as we are now in the fourth era. For that reason we tend to use general dates. A good overview is found on page 265 of *Perspectives*, 3rd ed. where Winter shows the First Era beginning about 1800, the Second Era beginning about 1865, and the Third Era beginning about 1935. It is well worth the effort to study this chart in detail as it places the modern mission enterprise in a larger perspective.

9. For a more complete discussion of this first era of mission activity see Pierson, *Dynamics of Christian Mission*, 199–206, Moffett, *History of Christianity*, Vol. II, 253–84, and Tucker, *From Jerusalem*, 114–21.

of the world. Stephen Neill cites Johann Gerhard, the dean of Westminster, who proposed that "the command of Christ to preach the Gospel to all the world ceased with the apostles: in their day the offer of salvation had been made to all the nations; there was no need for the offer to be made a second time to those who had already refused it."[10] Carey challenged the church to use "means" for the conversion of the heathen.[11] This position was in direct opposition to the paradigm of the day that can be summarized as follows: "the conversion of the heathen would be the Lord's own work in his own time, and that nothing could be done by men to hasten it."[12]

Carey was not the first Protestant missionary. The Moravians[13] are a notable example of others who were seriously involved in missionary activity before Carey. However, the involvement of the English-speaking world is usually attributed to Carey, as is the development of mission structures as the "means" to make possible the carrying out of the mission task. The English-speaking world would account for the predominant number of missionaries and also the majority of the funding for modern missions. This pattern remained true for about 180 years.

This paradigm was greatly influenced by a rising awareness of geography. Carey was significantly influenced by Captain Cook's writings. The Great Awakening had significant impact as well.[14]

Winter identifies two structures at work within the church. These structures are evident from the New Testament period to the present. The first is the church structure itself that Winter calls a "modality." The second is what is popularly known today as a "parachurch" structure, "apostolic band," or what Winter calls a "sodality."[15] These sodalities were voluntary organizations organized for a specific purpose. In Carey's case the "means" became a missionary structure[16] or sodality. Stephen Neill calls this the great age of societies. "In many cases the Protestant Churches as such were unable or unwilling themselves to take up the cause of missions. This was left to the voluntary societies, dependent on the initiative of consecrated individuals, and relying for financial support on the voluntary gifts of interested Christians."[17] In this era most of the sodalities were connected to denominations.

The paradigm shift Carey introduced focused on the geographical continents. Carey was able to form a sodality for the purpose of using "means" for the conversion of the heathen. As a result, Carey and his family left for India under the umbrella of the Baptist

---

10. Neill, *A History of Christian Missions*, 222.

11. For a complete understanding of Carey's appeal see *An Enquiry*.

12. Neill, *History of Christian Missions*, 261.

13. For a more complete discussion of the Moravians and the contribution that this remarkable group made to missions see Pierson, *Dynamics*, 189–95, and Tucker, *From Jerusalem*, 69–82. For an overview of the impact the Moravians had on slavery see Robert, *Christian Mission*, 101–103. For a discussion of the impact the Moravians had on John Wesley see Gonzalez, *Story of Christianity*, Vol. 2, 208–16.

14. For additional information see Orr, *Eager Feet, Light of the Nations,* and *Flaming Tongue*. Also refer to Randall, *Great Awakening*.

15. Winter and Hawthorne, *Perspectives*, 244–53. See also Walls, *Missionary Movement*, 241–54.

16. See Bevans and Schroeder, *Constants in Context*, 210–12.

17. Neill, *History of Christian Missions*, 252.

Missionary Society. Soon other sodalities in Europe and North America were formed for the purpose of world evangelization. Carey's work produced within Protestant leaders an awareness that they needed to understand the process of world evangelization. The result was a paradigm shift resulting in a church awakened to the unfinished task of world evangelization.

SECOND ERA: FOCUS ON THE INTERIORS

Hudson Taylor[18] challenged the church to think of the unfinished task in more specific ways, to go beyond the paradigm produced by Carey and others. Geography was also an important ingredient in this era as Taylor, like Carey, spent time studying maps. Taylor ushered in a new paradigm in mission activity as he challenged the church to consider the interiors of the continents. During Taylor's day a notion was circulating that the job of world evangelization was nearing completion. After all, the church was planted on every continent and so by definition the church had gone into "all the world." Taylor raised the church's awareness of the still large areas known as the inland regions that still did not have the gospel or the church. Taylor was interested in reaching the interior provinces, particularly in China. This also produced a new wave of mission practice across Asia and Africa.

The paradigm shift produced by Taylor included several characteristics. First Taylor located the headquarters for his mission in China rather than with the sending church. While following the shift introduced by Carey of organizing a sodality, Taylor believed that those closest to the work and most intimately involved were in the best position to make decisions regarding the direction and future of the work. Second, he believed in the faith principle regarding the support of the work. This principle ushered in what is now known as "faith missions." Taylor believed that "God's work, done God's way, will never lack for God's supply." While sodalities were already present, Taylor produced a new inter-denominational type of mission. Third, he allowed married women[19] as full partners with their husbands and single women to be involved in the work. Fourth, the missionaries would wear the dress of the local people, in Taylor's case a Chinese Mandarin scholar, and identify with the local people whenever and however possible. Fifth, the primary aim of the mission was evangelism. Sixth, opportunity of service was provided for those of little formal education.

18. For a more complete treatment of Hudson Taylor and the mission activity in China during this era see Moffett, *History of Christianity*, Vol. II, 463–501, and Winter and Hawthorne, *Perspectives*, 271–74. Tucker gives an excellent overview of Taylor in *From Jerusalem,* 173–88. For a discussion of the methods used by Taylor and the China Inland Mission, CIM, (today Overseas Mission Fellowship or OMF) see Pierson, *Dynamics*, 243–45, where Pierson notes that Taylor ushered in a new paradigm that no longer depended on a single denomination to fund and populate the mission society. Pierson notes that the CIM accepted members from different traditions. Ibid., 244. See also Winter and Hawthorne, *Perspectives*, 319–26.

19. For a treatment of the role of women in missions see Robert, *Christian Mission*, 114–41. See Sanneh, *Disciples of All Nations*, 259–63. Pierson, *Dynamics*, 251–59. Clouse, *Two Kingdoms*, 506–7, and Moffett, *History of Christianity,* Vol, II. 437–42. See also Robert, "American Women in Mission" *Modern Mission Era.* Smith, *Women in Mission.* Tucker, *Guardians of the Great Commission.* Robert, *Gospel Barriers, Gender Barriers.*

A key in this era was the Student Volunteer Movement.[20] This movement, the largest student movement in history, provided the personnel and the funding during this second era. John R. Mott[21] was a key leader. This movement produced 100,000 commitments from students with about 20,000 students going to the field while 80,000 stayed behind to pray and support those who went out.[22]

THIRD ERA: FOCUS ON THE UNREACHED PEOPLES

The third era was influenced by both geography and culture. A relatively new discipline, anthropology, became influential in this era. This paradigm highlighted linguistic and cultural differences.[23] While Bible translation[24] work had been going on for some time and was a prominent component of William Carey's work, as well as many others, a heightened awareness of the place of linguistic and cultural differences is present in this era.

The new field of psychology was also having an impact on the Western mind. Specifically what some have called the "self-centered self" began to emerge. One effect of this was the movement in Western thought toward the individual. This created the tendency in the West to interpret from an individualistic perspective. Yet, the majority of the world continues to be group oriented.

Two individuals served as a catalyst in this third era. Cameron Townsend[25] went to Guatemala in the 1930s to distribute the Bible. He noticed that the majority of the people did not speak Spanish. Townsend became aware of the linguistic distinctions that separated peoples. As a result of Townsend's efforts, Wycliffe Bible Translators was born.

20. For a more complete treatment of the impact of student movements see Pierson, *Dynamics*, 246–49, Tucker, *From Jerusalem*, 261—86, Showalter, *End of a Crusade*, and Wallstrom, *The Creation of a Student Movement*.

21. See Pierson, *Dynamics*, 247–248, and Hopkins, *John R. Mott*.

22. See Wallstrom, *The Creation*. Stanley, *World Missions Conference*, Ross, *Edinburgh 2010*.

23. Hiebert, describing the discipline of missiology writes, "The central question of missiology is: how can the gospel of Jesus Christ be incarnated in human contexts so that the people understand and believe, societies are transformed, and the kingdom of God is made manifest on earth as it is in heaven? . . . Missiology seeks to integrate four bodies of data into a single discipline: theology, anthropology, Scripture, and church history. . . missiology is an integrative discipline drawing on four sets of theories and findings to answer its central question." Hiebert, *Gospel in Human Contexts*, 33. Hiebert states further that "missiology is a discipline that asks the critical question: how should we work to communicate the gospel to people in their historical and sociocultural contexts so that they understand and believe, and so that the gospel becomes a power that transforms individuals and societies to become followers of Christ who manifest his kingdom on earth?" Hiebert, *Gospel*, 161. Tippett defines Missiology as "the academic discipline or science which researches, records and applies data relating to the biblical origin, the history, including the use of documentary materials, the anthropological principles and techniques and the theological base of the Christian mission. The theory, methodology and data bank are particularly directed towards: 1) the processes by which the Christian message is communicated, 2) the encounters brought about by its proclamation to non-Christians, 3) the planting of the Church and organization of congregations, the incorporation of converts into those congregations, and the growth and relevance of their structures and fellowship, internally to maturity, externally in outreach as the Body of Christ in local situations and beyond, in a variety of culture patterns." Tippett, *Introduction to Missiology*, xiii.

24. For a thorough treatment of the importance of Bible translation see Sanneh, *Translating the Message*. See also Walls, *Missionary Movement*, 2–42. See also Chapter 16 in this volume by Greg Pruett.

25. See Tucker, *From Jerusalem*, 350–58, 363–64. See also Winter and Hawthorne, *Perspectives*, 327–28.

Donald A. McGavran[26] focused on cultural distinctions and similarities. In India, with its caste system, McGavran noticed the cultural differences in the nearly 3,000 subgroups.[27] McGavran called these groups homogeneous units. "The homogeneous unit is simply a section of society in which all the members have some characteristic in common."[28] McGavran suggested that the key to discipling a homogeneous unit was within that unit. In leading peoples to become Christian, the church must aim to win individuals in their corporate life. The steady goal must be the Christianization of *the entire fabric which is the people*, or large enough parts of it that the social life of the individual is not destroyed.[29] On another occasion McGavran said it this way, "Men like to become Christians without crossing racial, linguistic, or class barriers."[30]

During this third era, homogeneous units have popularly been called "people groups." In this paradigm a new way of looking at the world is present. The common missiological focus is not continents or countries but unreached peoples, wherever they are found. In this sense to speak of an "unreached people" generally means to speak of a tribe, clan, extended family or close-knit community, and generally in a rural or tribal context.

Several additional characteristics are present in this paradigm. The first is the rise of "Majority World"[31] missions. World evangelization is becoming less of a Western activity.[32] Traditional mission fields such as Korea, Philippines, Japan, China, and many others are now sending missionaries.

---

26. See Tucker, *From Jerusalem*, 475–79. See also Winter and Hawthorne, *Perspectives*, 335–46. See also Kraft, *SWM/SIS at Forty*, especially Chapter 1, "Donald A. McGavran," 3–25, Chapter 4, "The McGavran Era I: The Founders," 69–88, and Chapter 5, "The McGavran Era II: Completing the Six," 89–118.

27. See McGavran, *Bridges of God*.

28. McGavran, *Understanding Church Growth*, 85. For a more complete discussion of the homogeneous unit principle see Wagner, *Our Kind of People* and Burris, "The Biblical Basis."

29. McGavran, *Bridges of God*, 16.

30. McGavran, *Understanding Church Growth*, 198.

31. Majority World is an attempt to see the world in proportion and acknowledge the growing number of missionaries and mission agencies outside of the West. A more recent term "Global South" may better communicate the internationalization present in current mission activity. Pocock et al., define Majority World as "That part of the world's population living outside Europe and North America. Terms such as non-Western, third world, two-thirds world, developing nations, and undeveloped nations have been used to designate such areas and peoples. No single term has been accepted by all, and all such terms have a negative political, economic, and social connotation. By using the term *Majority World* we simply recognize that the peoples living outside Europe and North America constitute the largest demographic block in the world." Pocock, *Changing Face of Missions*, 16.

32. Sanneh, describing the missionary conference in Edinburgh in 1910, notes, "In 1910 Europe was still the powerhouse of Christianity, not yet even dimly aware of the religion's worldwide appeal. Accordingly, only 17 of the more than 1,200 delegates came from the Third World: 8 from India, 4 from Japan, 3 from China, 1 from Burma, and 1 from Korea. There was not a single delegate from Africa. What no one at the time knew was that Edinburgh 1910 would be the last time that the Western missionary movement would hold center stage, not because the religion would decline, but because expansion of the church would exceed anything the leaders could have dreamed of . . . The most visionary of missionary statesmen had not the vaguest intimation that they were at a historical fault line and that Christianity would soon embark on its course to become a more widespread and diverse religion than at any other time in its history. It would be the era of unprecedented missionary surge." Sanneh, *Disciples*, 272. See also Wallstrom, *The Creation*, and Stanley, *World Missionary Conference*.

A second characteristic is the rise of new nations, beginning with Pakistan and India in 1947.[33] This has resulted in the collapse of the colonial apparatus so prominent during the first and second eras of modern missions.[34]

Another characteristic is the rise of independent churches. This is the result of the four stages, listed earlier in this chapter, at work during the past 200 years, and the successful completion, in many cases, of those steps. The work of evangelization has resulted in churches across the Majority World moving from the Pioneer Stage to the Paternal Stage to the Partnership Stage to the Participation Stage. This is the reason most missionaries went out in the first place, to plant an "indigenous church."[35]

The unreached peoples paradigm of this third era may still be helpful in this time of urbanization. While McGavran's original definition of homogeneous units is general enough to include the paradigm shift or perhaps the new application of the third era paradigm to the cities that we have been experiencing, it has often been applied narrowly to families or clans, and usually in a rural setting. However, in order for the unreached peoples' characteristic of the third era to be helpful in this day of urbanization, resistance to a narrow definition is necessary. It is at this point that a dynamic tension has caused a rethinking that leads to adjustment in this paradigm. The question that must be answered today is: where are the frontiers?[36] As we have moved into the fourth era we must rethink the task at hand.

FOURTH ERA: FOCUS ON THE CITIES

In the twenty-first century two ideas are in focus. The first is the internationalization of the Christian movement. Today, two-thirds or more of the Christian population live in Africa, Asia, and Latin America. The West, Europe, and North America primarily—while dominating the first two eras and most of the third era—will not dominate as we move forward. This change requires a redefinition of missions. For over 200 years missions has been synonymous with the Western church sending out missionaries to the Majority World. Today, this definition is no longer appropriate. A new definition setting forth the twin tasks of communicating the gospel and forming the church must be emphasized. In other words, the church is in the mission business.[37]

---

33. "The great era of imperial collapse began when the British withdrew from India and Pakistan in 1947, and the Dutch recognized Indonesian sovereignty in 1949 . . . In sub-Saharan Africa, the decisive phase began with the independence of Ghana in 1957 and proceeded rapidly over the next decade." Jenkins, *Next Christendom*, 63.

34. For a more complete discussion see Winter, *Twenty-Five Unbelievable Years*.

35. An indigenous church is "A church that fits well into a local culture. Traditionally, this is defined in terms of three "self's": self-governing (not dependent on outside agencies to make decisions), self-financing (not needing outside funding to carry on its work), and self-propagating (able to evangelize effectively within its own culture). More recently, self-theologizing (the ability of a church to develop its own theological understandings from Scripture)–has been added to the criteria." Pocock, *Changing Face*, 15.

36. See Greenway and Monsma, *Cities: Missions' New Frontiers*. See also Howells Douglas, "Facing the Challenge of the Urban Frontiers," Gill, "Reassessing the Frontiers," and Grigg, "Sorry! The Frontier Moved."

37. Wright states that "Missional is simply an adjective denoting something that is related to or characterized by mission, or has the qualities, attributes or dynamics of mission." Wright, *Mission of God*, 24. He

A second focus is urbanization. The mass migration to the cities of the world has been underway for some time, particularly since the 1950s. Evangelical missions have been slow to meet the challenge of the shift in population to the cities. Social concerns such as crime, disease, illiteracy, poverty, among other problems, are clearly present in virtually all urban centers. However, as Paul Hiebert suggests, "Cities also offer tremendous opportunity. They are the centers for world communication, and the source from which ideas spread to the countryside. One reason for the rapid spread of early Christianity was its movement through the cities. We desperately need to look more closely at modern urban dynamics in order to understand how change takes place, and then to apply these insights to today's mission planning."[38] Hiebert goes on to ask important questions, "This rapid urbanization of the world raises many questions for those concerned with church growth. What is the societal structure of a city and how does this structure influence communication and decision making? How do changes take place in the highly mobile and varied city society?"[39]

The answers to these questions will suggest strategies appropriate for this era of modern missions. Likely these strategies will continue to account for the unreached people's paradigm, but increasingly strategies targeting the city, holistic missions, will be added. These new strategies will consider societal structures that are unique to the urban milieu, and not just clans, families, and people.

A fundamental question is what types of societal structures are present in the city. Unlike the beginning of the third era that centered on families, clans, or people groups, the urbanization process has created new webs of relationships. Harvie Conn suggests that these webs "are more and more defined in terms of macrostructural social classes, the social groups structured around wealth, power and prestige."[40] Relational webs are organized on a more voluntary basis. People groupings are only one of the distinctions and, therefore, one way of establishing the church among those in the city. Networks and geographical groupings are also important ways to reach the previously unreached. In an urban setting the use of media becomes an important tool, for example. When considering the city Conn writes,

> In the city, however, family networks are only one method of socialization among many. Personal relationships and a sense of belonging can be created out of commonly shared residential territory (a neighborhood). You build relationships with the mechanic who lives next door, the barber down the street, your child's teacher in the house on the corner. Vocation can bring non-neighbors together. You socialize with your fellow factory workers, the teachers in the same school where you work,

goes on to say "*Jesus himself* provided the hermeneutical coherence within which all disciples must read these texts, that is, in the light of the story that leads *up to* Christ (messianic reading) and the story that leads *on from* Christ (missional reading). That is the story that flows from the mind and purpose of God in all the Scriptures for all the nations. That is a missional hermeneutic of the whole Bible." Ibid., 41. Wright summarizes missional in this way, "a missional hermeneutic proceeds from the assumption that *the whole Bible renders to us the story of God's mission through God's people in their engagement with God's world for the sake of the whole of God's creation.*" Ibid., 51.

38. Winter and Hawthorne, *Perspectives*, 422–28.

39. Ibid., 428.

40. Conn, *Clarified Vision*, 17.

the woman selling apples in the stall next to yours in the market. The city spawns such networks in much larger array than the village and rural cultures. *People create an identity from a plural set of groups.*[41] (Emphasis mine)

There is also the growing influence and participation of Majority World missions.[42] This subject is the focus of the next chapter, so we will only give a brief overview in order to place it in its historical context. Larry Pate, writing in 1990, said,

> This establishes the fact that the Two-Thirds World Protestant missions movement has assumed a major portion of the church's responsibility for world evangelism. As of the end of 1990, Two-Thirds World missionaries comprised 35.6 percent of the total Protestant missionary force in the world! These missionaries are not mere statistics. They are living, suffering, struggling, sacrificing, witnessing, and often very effective cross-cultural missionaries, who very well may make a greater impact than their counterparts from the Western world . . . If both the Western missionary force and the Two-Thirds World missionary force continue to grow at their current rates, the majority of the world's Protestant missionaries will be from the non-Western world by the year 2000. The number of Two-Thirds World missionaries would overtake the number of Western missionaries some time in 1998."[43]

The following table lists the number of missionaries sent and received by continent in 2010 and demonstrates the accuracy of Pate's prediction.[44]

Missionary exchange, 2010

Received by

Sent from	Africa	Asia	Europe	L.America	N.America	Oceania	Global
Africa	17,000	400	2,000	200	1,800	100	20,700
Asia	700	38,400	3,600	1,300	2,300	800	47,100
Europe	21,600	13,000	54,700	36,000	4,000	3,500	132,800
Latin America	1,000	1,000	5,000	24,000	27,100	300	58,400
Northern America	53,100	5,700	24,000	40,200	5,100	6,900	135,000
Oceania	300	700	700	300	700	3,300	6,000
Global total	93,700	59,200	90,000	102,000	40,200	14,900	400,000

© Edinburgh University Press, 2009

As the above table indicates, there are now 132,200 cross-cultural missionaries sent from the Majority World, or Global South. In fact, the traditional West of Europe and North America currently receives 130,200 cross-cultural missionaries.

---

41. Ibid., 197.

42. Winter and Hawthorne, *Perspectives*, 369–75.

43. Ibid., D-233–34. Developments over the past twenty years have shown that Pate was absolutely correct in 1990. For example, there are now about 4,000 Majority World mission agencies.

44. Johnson, *Atlas of Global Christianity*, 263.

Another factor is the rise of creative strategies such as tent-making ministries, non-resident missions, and other ways of entering restricted access countries.[45] Ruth Siemens defines tentmakers as "mission-committed Christians, who, like Paul, support themselves in secular work, as they engage in cross-cultural ministry on the job and in their free time."[46] Siemens goes on to give six practical reasons for tent-making: "Tentmakers can gain entry into restricted access countries . . . 2. Tentmakers can serve in needy open countries . . . 3. Tentmakers help solve the problem of the cost of missions . . . 4. Tentmakers help solve the problem of personnel . . . 5. Tentmakers are ideal workers for emerging mission agencies . . . 6. The international job market itself is an argument for tent making because it does not exist by accident, but by God's design."[47] Examples include teachers, engineers, medical and business persons, and others.

A further characteristic is the availability and use of technology. Technology provides unprecedented opportunity for world evangelization but also raises serious questions.[48] To what extent should a mission be involved in the use of technology? What does it mean to be "human" in a technological age? What is the risk of technology altering the message? What contextual considerations affect our choice among various technologies? Charles Kraft's emphasis on "receptor-oriented" approaches may hold a key to the answers to these and other questions.[49]

C. Peter Wagner has written describing another characteristic, Post-Denominational Churches. Wagner defines this term as, "A generic term that covers the rapidly expanding segment of Christianity including independent charismatic churches, house churches in China and elsewhere, African independent churches, apostolic networks, urban megachurches (charismatic and non-charismatic), central "mother" churches surrounded by numbers of satellite churches, and others. These churches are characterized by indigenous leadership, contemporary worship, concert prayer, power ministries and mutual affiliation based on spiritual rather than legal and bureaucratic ties."[50] Wagner states that these churches are "by far, the most rapidly growing segment of Christianity on all six continents."[51]

---

45. See Pocock, *Changing Face*, 209–44.

46. Winter and Hawthorne, *Perspectives* D–246.

47. Ibid., D–246.

48. "Appropriate technologies are those that can be used in a given context because they rely on locally available and affordable materials rather than on the ongoing resources or presence of outsiders." Pocock, *Changing Face*, 12. See also chapter 11, "The Impact of New Technologies: Life in the Virtual World." In Pocock, *Changing Face*, 299–320.

49. Kraft writes, "While participating in the society around Him, Jesus was receptor-oriented. He knew what communication specialists have pointed out that it is the receptors who decide the meanings of whatever we do in our attempts to communicate with them. His primary concern was that those who heard and watched Him have a decent chance to understand and do something about His messages. To that end He both lived as they lived and spoke a language (indeed, the disrespected Galilean language of His receptors) that they could understand. Furthermore, He used cultural forms (e.g., parables, healings) that would be familiar and attractive to His audiences." Kraft, *Worldview*, 466–67.

50. Wagner, *Ministries Today*, 50.

51. Ibid., 49.

Christian community development, also known as holistic mission,[52] is also a characteristic in this paradigm.[53] Balance will likely be the key in the future as it has been in the past. This is not an either/or situation, evangelism and church planting vs. Christian community development—holistic mission, but a both/and approach. The church must be aware of and give a Christian response to the growing disparity between rich and poor, basic social services such as food, shelter, health care, education, social witness, and a variety of other issues we might lump under the term "social action." The church must demonstrate the kingdom of God, *shalom*, to the people and structures of the city. This is Kingdom Missiology.

ISSUES FOR THE FUTURE

The future calls for a new model of mission activity that seriously considers the current global trends. Paul Pierson suggests a beginning point for a new model.[54] This model incorporates the elements of a Kingdom Missiology paradigm.

A New Model of Missions[55]

First, the church must be the base—not return to earlier autonomy of the missionary organization or structures. This is a return to the New Testament pattern.[56] Antioch sent out Paul and his missionary band. Paul was given a great deal of latitude in deciding the where and how of the work. Paul remained accountable to Antioch, however.

Second, the "base" cannot be the end of mission; mission is not "inter-church aid." The mission station approach that dominated the first and second eras often produced a limited response to the gospel. And, it was based on a colonialization model.[57] Sanneh correctly points out, "As it developed, the European impulse of colonization was driven as much by the strategic need to circumvent Islam as it was by economic interests, and any considerations of faithfulness to the church's teachings were secondary to calculations of political advantage and monopoly rights."[58]

52. "Holistic mission: Mission that takes into account the whole of human needs: spiritual, social, and personal. Holistic mission includes both evangelism and church planting as well as development and social transformation." Pocock, *Changing Face*, 15.

53. Doug Priest treats this subject in more detail in chapter 1 of this book.

54. Pierson, *Dynamics*. 315–20.

55. See the Introduction to this book for a more complete description of Kingdom Missiology.

56. Roland Allen, *Missionary Methods*, and Michael Green, *Evangelism in the Early Church*, are two classic studies on this subject. Schnabel, *Paul the Missionary*, is a more recent comprehensive study.

57. See Sanneh, "The civil pattern of New World religious naturalization was repeated in many places across the world, and its cumulative effect drew Europe out of its intellectual isolation. When it succeeded in breaking free of crown control, the Western missionary movement in both its Catholic and Protestant forms carried the intellectual seeds that transformed Christianity into a world religion, though the mental habits of Christianity as Christendom, of Christianity as political kingdom or as cultural domain, concealed from people the force of that fact. The changes following Columbus's New World explorations were soon reflected in new geographical maps of the world, but the mental maps remained unaltered for many centuries afterward. Globalization meant then, as it has tended to mean now, the corralling of the world's resources by dominant powers, and traversing the globe for that purpose." Sanneh, *Disciples*, 94.

58. Ibid., 106.

Third, the end of mission: "That the world might believe." In the twenty-first century a new affirmation to reaching the whole world with the whole gospel is in order. "And this gospel of the kingdom will be preached in the whole world as a testimony to all nations, and then the end will come" (Matt 24:14). In some places the nations will include families, tribes, and clans. In other situations, especially in urban settings, the nations will include webs of relationships.

Spiritual Power

An examination of the discrepancy existing between our theological interpretation and validated field experiences concerning spiritual power is overdue.[59] This danger is often present both in historical settings such as seen in Palestine at the time of Christ and in contemporary cultures influenced by a Western worldview. We need to keep an open discussion on the theological presuppositions governing our beliefs of what God can or will do. Documented examples of God demonstrating his power in miraculous ways create a tension with a "closed" theology. A clear exegesis and reexamination of all of the relevant, not just our favorite, passages is necessary.

At least two issues demand our careful attention. One concerns our view of the biblical text and the other concerns our experience. We hold a high view of Scripture. At the same time, how do we make sense of the biblical text, as we have been taught from a Western perspective, and honestly account for undeniable experience? The problem is further complicated as Kraft explains. "In spite of our suspicions of the validity of experience as a measure of truth, we accept as fact very little that does not fit our experiences."[60] Every person's interpretations are closely connected to her/his experiences, or lack of experience, and therefore contribute to this tension. The often pointed to dichotomy between Scripture and experience is a "red herring." Scripture is interpreted in terms of and related to experience and experience to Scripture. Yes, we can go too far–experience without Scripture. Without balance we not only risk missing the truth of the gospel but may also miss what God is actively accomplishing in the world today.

Mission Tension

An urgent issue requiring immediate attention is the tension that exists between missionaries who are operating under one paradigm or another, often in proximity. Transitions are seldom easy. This is especially true today as several of the paradigms may be simultaneously present in the same geographical location. Kuhn understood this and referred to paradigm shifts as revolutions. Kuhn suggests that, "When, in the development of a natural science, an individual or group first produces a synthesis able to attract most of the next generation's practitioners, the older schools gradually disappear."[61] This trend is

---

59. For a needed and healthy balance to the subject of power encounter see Pocock, *Changing Face*, 183–208.

60. Kraft, *Christianity With Power*, 44.

61. Kuhn, *Structure*, 18.

also evident in missions.[62] The primary point of tension is that the old may be held on to for a longer period of time even though the new is proving to be a more helpful paradigm. This has been the case in every era of modern missions and is evident in the current transition from the unreached peoples to the urban paradigm.

Two additional factors contribute to mission tension. First, paradigms are human contructs. We devise paradigms as an attempt to understand and explain. We look at situations and circumstances and try to bring meaning. Therefore more than one paradigm may exist at any given time, and they often overlap. This is the basis for tension on the field and in the sending church. Secondly, God has made himself known but we do not exhaustively know him. There is room for reasonable people to disagree. God's plan is the same, however. Even in our desire to know God's plan and be involved in what God is doing, our interpretation is fallible. Attempts to complete the task of world evangelization are not exempted from this problem.

Steps to Reduce Tension

Building on Harry Larson's suggestions, the following five steps may provide a means of reducing tension in the mission community.[63] Missionaries, mission agencies, and supporting churches will do well to seriously consider the implications of these five steps.

First, continue to support and honor the veteran missionaries who are working at a different task. Great care should be exercised in our communication. In our enthusiasm we should not make those who have labored long and hard in the difficult places of the world to feel that they are unfaithful, irresponsible, or out of touch. Those involved in a different type of work may not be working at a less strategic task, and they may be exactly where God has called them to work. However, this is not an excuse to be out of touch with current strategies or to the nature of new paradigms of mission practice. The missionary, mission executive, and supporting church continually need to stay current with mission

---

62. One example is the recapture of the emphasis on "holistic missions." This paradigm will cause tension in some regions of the world and among missiologists. Rather than dismiss this paradigm as the old tension of evangelism vs. social action that came out of "liberalism" of a century ago, we need to rethink God's mission to the whole world. Wright gives helpful insight into holistic missions when he writes, ""Where do we start? The language of the "priority of evangelism" implies that the only proper starting point must always be evangelistic proclamation. . . . But the difficulty with this is that (1) it is not always possible or desirable in the immediate situation, and (2) it does not even reflect the actual practice of Jesus. . . *But ultimately* we must not rest content until we have included within our missional response the wholeness of *God's* missional response to the human predicament and that of course includes the good news of Christ, the cross and resurrection, the forgiveness of sin, the gift of eternal life that is offered to men and women through our witness to the gospel and the hope of God's new creation . . . Mission may not always begin with evangelism. But mission that does not ultimately *include* declaring the Word and the name of Christ, the call to repentance, and faith and obedience has not completed its task. It is defective mission, not holistic mission." *Mission of God*, 318–19. Wright gives a helpful balance when he states, "*The ultimacy of evangelism and the nonultimacy of death.* And within that biblical holism the necessity of sensitive evangelism is clear and nonnegotiable. I put it as the final item on the list, decidedly not because it is the last thing we need to do but because it is the ultimate thing, the thing that holds all the other imperative responses together within a truly Christian worldview in which death is *not* the ultimate thing." Ibid., 439.

63. Larson, "Eras, Pioneers, and Transitions," 23–25.

trends. This serves to alert when paradigms are changing. In this way the missionary can evaluate the local work in light of current missiological developments.

Second, educate concerning the nature of the task. We need to be involved in a variety of mission tasks. Given the circumstances at the local level, the task may well be different from one field to another, particularly comparing a rural and urban situation. The "strategic mix" is critical. The sending church should not be placed in a position of choosing between one type of activity or another without careful analysis of the local situation. With this field analysis in hand, the sending church can assist in the development of strategies that make sense in the local context. The more evangelization has moved forward, the more necessary it has been to carefully define targets, so as not to waste effort. The church has often been slow to grasp the new paradigms of mission activity. The tendency has been to hold onto the old ways too long.

Third, allocate new resources and missionary personnel to the most strategic task. Given the local circumstances this may involve emphasis from each of the eras in modern missions. However, we should quickly note that a "church" may look different in the various contexts into which it is planted.[64] For example, a church may be four or five people meeting in secret, a group of fifteen or twenty meeting in a home or under a tree, or a group that meets in a "traditional" church building.

Fourth, share a new vision with present missionaries. Many need to re-tool in order to be informed concerning new methods and strategies. In some cases a broader base is needed. In other cases a different paradigm is needed. This will likely include a variety of approaches including additional formal training, as well as a mix of informal training such as seminars and conferences, and reading in current missiological books.

Fifth, maintain a strategic balance among different types of missionary work. This may be the key in the reduction of tension. In partnership with the missionary, the sending church should intentionally consider what goals and plans ought to be implemented. This will serve as the overall "grid" through which decisions can be filtered as to their strategic importance. Key questions may include: 1) Are we praying and seeking God's guidance regarding our missions program? 2) Are we satisfied with the "strategic mix" in our missions program? 3) Where should we allocate *new* resources?

CONCLUSION

Wagner suggests that missions has come "full circle" (Acts 11:19–13:3). By following the pattern in the book of Acts, Wagner suggests that the circle consists of the following major phases.

- 90° Mission to go, evangelize, and plant churches

- 180° Fruit, church is planted

- 270° Church gains autonomy

- 360° New church gives birth to a mission Antioch[65]

64. In this context we are describing the church as the *ekklesia*, the called-out ones, rather than looking at the place of meeting or the building, or lack of building. This is an emphasis on the function of the church, Acts 2:42, 46, 47, rather than the location or physical surroundings.

65. Pierson, "Historical Development," 89.

Have we come full circle? Roland Allen suggests, "St. Paul's theory of evangelizing a province was not to preach in every place himself, but to establish centres of Christian life in two or three important places from which the knowledge might spread into the country round. This is important, not as showing that he preferred to preach in a capital rather than in a provincial town or in a village, but because he intended his congregation to become at once a centre of light."[66]

In the current paradigm that focuses on urban centers, it would appear that we have indeed come full circle. And a renewed study of the methods used in the Acts of the Apostles is in order. Much remains to be learned regarding the strategic choices to be made. This includes strategic points and identification of webs of relationships within those strategic points.

The Holy Spirit has always raised up individuals and movements that help articulate a new paradigm and thereby clarify the remaining task of world evangelization. As we move forward, it is critical that the church recognize the global nature of the missionary enterprise—become involved in more clearly defining the remaining task in order to complete the task of discipling the nations that our Lord commissioned us to do.

66. Allen, *Missionary Methods,* 12.

8

Upon Closer Examination: Status of World Christianity

by Todd M. Johnson and Gina A. Bellofatto

To UNDERSTAND THE STATUS of global Christianity and world evangelization at the beginning of the twenty-first century, it is important to first reflect on the previous two centuries. Eminent church historian Kenneth Scott Latourette described the nineteenth century as a "great century"[1] for Christianity, a time of significant global advancement for the religion, initially through missionary activity but also (somewhat regrettably) on the wings of European imperialism.[2] At the turn of the twentieth century, Christian leaders were full of optimism for what they anticipated would be a time of great strides for the church, a century of peace—a "Christian Century," as the eponymous magazine put it. The advancement of Christianity was to go hand in hand with the "civilization" of the remotest parts of the world. Human beings would no longer exploit one another, being too advanced and educated to continue in the "primitive" activities and beliefs of less civilized times.

In 1910, evangelical Protestant leaders gathered in Scotland for the Edinburgh World Missionary Conference, which encouraged Christians to engage in purposeful missionary work around the world. The "fundamental conviction" of the conference was that "the good news of Jesus Christ can take root in every culture across the world and produce fruit in church and society everywhere."[3] The vision of the conference was firmly planted in a Western-dominated picture of global Christianity. The delegates included 500 Britons and 500 Americans, with a comparatively small continental European representation (170). A mere 17 delegates were included from "younger" churches in India, China, and Japan. No delegates came from Africa, Latin America, the Roman Catholic Church, or Orthodox churches. To the Europeans and Americans gathered, this seemed like quite the diverse crowd, but in hindsight the limitations of the gathering are obvious.[4]

---

1. Defined as 1815–1914 in Latourette, *History of Christianity,* 1063.

2. See Stanley, *Missions, Nationalism, and the End of Empire*; Dana Robert, *Christian Mission.*

3. Ross, "Edinburgh 1910: A Defining Moment," in *Atlas of Global Christianity,* xvi–xvii. For a thorough overview of the 1910 Edinburgh World Missionary Conference, see Stanley, *World Missionary Conference.*

4. Ibid., xvi.

In addition to their prominence in the Christian world, Western powers exerted dominance in science and technology throughout much of the twentieth century. Daniel Jeyaraj notes that "Unprecedented Western discoveries in science, technology, medicine, information communication, dissemination of knowledge, and transportation predicted not only progress and prosperity for all peoples, but also the end of poverty and other miseries. People hoped for a mutual sharing of the earth's resources. They anticipated equal access to knowledge, opportunities, not just global markets and politics."[5]

The optimism of the early twentieth century was crushed by war and conflict, starting with World War I in 1914, which began the severe decline of hope through a number of traumatic and deadly events, including the Bolshevik Revolution, the rise of Adolf Hitler, World War II, the horrors of the Holocaust, fears of Communism, Mao Zedong in China, and Pol Pot in Cambodia. More people worldwide were killed in warfare in the twentieth century than in the previous four centuries combined.[6]

RELIGIOUS CHANGE IN THE TWENTIETH CENTURY

The twentieth century was also a tumultuous time for religion. In general, the world in 2010 was less religious than it was in 1910. In 1910, nearly the entire world claimed adherence to some form of religious belief. By 2010, however, 11.6 percent of the world's population was either atheist or agnostic. The reasons for this are twofold: the rise of Communism worldwide, and the phenomenon of secularization, particularly in the global North.[7] At the same time, there have been a number of other significant changes in religious adherence both globally and regionally.

---

5. Daniel Jeyaraj, "The Re-emergence of Global Christianity, 1910–2010," in *Atlas of Global Christianity*, Johnson and Ross, 54–55.

6. Conquest, *Reflections on a Ravaged Century.*

7. Johnson and Ross, *Atlas of Global Christianity*, 6. But note that the percentage of atheists and agnostics has declined since the collapse of Communism in the former Soviet Union. Here, "global North" is defined in geopolitical terms by five current United Nations regions (comprising 53 countries): Eastern Europe (including Russia), Northern Europe, Southern Europe, Western Europe, and Northern America. The United Nations definition also includes Australia and New Zealand.

TABLE 1. WORLD RELIGIONS BY ADHERENTS, 1910 AND 2010

Religion	Adherents 1910	percent 1910	Adherents 2010	percent 2010	100-year 1910–2010 percent p.a.	10-year 2000–10 percent p.a.
Christians	611,810,000	34.8	2,269,200,000	32.9	1.32	1.31
Muslims	221,749,000	12.6	1,533,733,000	22.2	1.95	1.83
Hindus	223,383,000	12.7	949,875,000	13.8	1.46	1.46
Agnostics	3,369,000	0.2	665,134,000	9.6	5.43	-0.01
Chinese folk-religionists	390,504,000	22.2	465,384,000	6.7	0.18	0.69
Buddhists	138,064,000	7.9	463,517,000	6.7	1.22	1.02
Ethno-religionists	135,074,000	7.7	265,808,000	3.9	0.68	1.25
Atheists	243,000	0.0	137,316,000	2.0	6.54	-0.19
New religionists	6,865,000	0.4	63,084,000	0.9	2.24	0.28
Sikhs	3,232,000	0.2	23,927,000	0.3	2.02	1.54
Jews	13,193,000	0.8	14,761,000	0.2	0.11	0.72
Spiritists	324,000	0.0	13,700,000	0.2	3.82	0.94
Daoists	437,000	0.0	8,429,000	0.1	3.00	1.73
Baha'is	225,000	0.0	7,299,000	0.1	3.54	1.72
Confucianists	760,000	0.0	6,449,000	0.1	2.16	0.36
Jains	1,446,000	0.1	5,316,000	0.1	1.31	1.53
Shintoists	7,613,000	0.4	2,761,000	0.0	-1.01	0.09
Zoroastrians	119,000	0.0	197,000	0.0	0.51	0.74
Total population	1,758,412,000	100.0	6,895,889,000	100.0	1.38	1.20

Source: *World Religion Database*, Brill, July 2011.

First, Africa has experienced a profound religious transformation over the past 100 years. The number of Christians on the continent has increased dramatically, growing from 11.7 million (9.4 percent) in 1910 to 495 million (48 percent) by 2010. This represents a 100-year growth rate of 3.82 percent per year, almost twice that of the population as a whole (2.14 percent). Muslims also grew from nearly 40 million in 1910 (32 percent) to 418 million (40.5 percent) by 2010. While the number of tribal religionists increased from 72 million to 107 million over the hundred years, they declined as a percentage of Africa's population from 58 percent in 1910 to only 10 percent by 2010. Also surprising has been the rise in the number of African agnostics (0.0 percent to 0.5 percent), who reside largely in major urban areas.

Second, despite changes, Asia has continued to be the most religiously diverse major area of the world. In 1910 over 50 percent of Asia's population was Chinese folk-religionist or Buddhist; today, these two religions together total only 22 percent. As expected, eth-noreligions declined from 5.6 percent of the population in 1910 to 3.7 percent in 2010. These declines were countered by remarkable gains by Muslims (16.6 percent to 26 percent) and Christians (2.4 percent to 8.5 percent). However, both agnostics (0.0 percent to 11.8 percent) and atheists (0.0 percent to 2.8 percent) picked up most of the losses, especially in China. The growth of the nonreligious in Asia was truly unprecedented, growing at an average rate of 10 percent every year over the entire 100-year period. Despite this, there are still more religious communities in Asia than anywhere else in the world. South Korea in particular has five religions over 10 percent of the population; Vietnam, North Korea, and Singapore each have four.[8]

Third, migration is increasing religious and ethnic diversity around the world. Two hundred million people are on the move today—both voluntarily and by force—carrying with them their cultural and religious backgrounds. At least 720 million people live outside of their culture's main country, facing the challenges of retaining their culture and heritage while being immersed in another. Almost half of these are Christians—often religious minorities who faced persecution in their home countries—representing about 16 percent of all Christians worldwide. Muslims, Hindus, and Buddhists also live outside of their historic homelands in large numbers—often facing misconceptions and preconceived notions about their beliefs and traditions. Ian Goldin points out that never have so many people been on the move, and never have they been so unwelcome![9]

Fourth, it is important to consider the contextual relationship language has with religion. Perhaps against conventional wisdom, the top five mother tongues of Islam are Bengali, Urdu, Western Panjabi, Turkish, and Javanese; these languages represent over a quarter of all Muslims worldwide.[10] For Hindus it is perhaps more intuitive that the top five spoken languages are all from India, the historic home of the religion: Hindi, Bengali, Telugu, Marathi, and Tamil. For Buddhists the top five most-spoken languages are Mandarin Chinese, Japanese, Vietnamese, Burmese, and Thai. For agnostics the top language is Mandarin, the second English, and the other three are other Chinese languages; German and Korean (representing North Korea) are not far behind.

Recent changes in global Christianity are easily seen when looking at the languages with the most Christian speakers in 2010. While Northern languages predominated in 1910 (although Spanish and Portuguese represent Latin American Christians as well

8. Ibid., 32. South Korea's five religions over 10 percent of the population are Buddhism, Christianity, Confucianism, ethnoreligions, and New Religions. Vietnam's four religions with over 10 percent of the population each are agnosticism, Buddhism, ethnoreligions, and New Religions; North Korea's are agnosticism, atheism, ethnoreligions, and New Religions; and Singapore's are Buddhism, Chinese folk-religion, Christianity, and Islam.

9. Goldin, *Exceptional People*.

10. Johnson and Ross, *Atlas of Global Christianity*, 215. Arabic does not show up on the top five mother tongue list because of its various dialects; for example, Egyptian Arabic and Moroccan Arabic are considered two different languages. If Arabic were to be considered a single language, however, it would be the largest mother tongue of Islam.

as European ones), in 2010 the 10 largest languages are from both the North *and* the South.[11] Spanish moved to the top of the list around 1980 as Latin America, already heavily Christian in 1910, had much higher birth rates than Northern America and Europe. Similarly, Portuguese moved to third due to high Christian birth rates in Brazil. Chinese and Tagalog are newcomers to the top 10 largest Christian languages, representing the growth of Christianity in Asia.

TRENDS WITHIN GLOBAL CHRISTIANITY

Christianity's Shift to the Global South

In the contexts of religious transformation, religious diversity, and language, one can now consider demographic trends both within global Christianity and outside of global Christianity. The most significant trend within global Christianity is that, demographically, Christianity has shifted dramatically to the South. This shift has been documented by many scholars as a groundbreaking process affecting not only all religions worldwide, but how Christianity itself is practiced as a global phenomenon.[12] Looking at the graph below of global Christian percentage, it appears at first glance there has been little change in the status of global Christianity over the past 100 years. Over the course of the twentieth century and already into the twenty-first, Christians have continued to make up approximately one-third of the world's population. However, this sustained percentage masks dramatic changes in the geographical make-up of global Christianity—a process of both North-South and East-West movement stretching back to the earliest days of Christianity that is far from inconsequential.

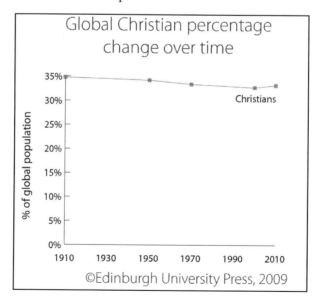

11. Here, "global South" refers to Asia, Africa, and Latin America.

12. See Jenkins, *Next Christendom* and *New Faces of Christianity*; Robert, *Christian Mission*; Noll, *New Shape of World Christianity*.

The shift of Christianity to the global South is most clearly illustrated by the drastic changes in Christian percentages by continent between 1910 and 2010. In 1910 the majority of Christians worldwide resided in the global North, with only small representations in Oceania, Africa, and Asia; in 1910, 66 percent of all Christians lived in Europe. By 2010 Europe's claim on Christianity had dropped to only 25.6 percent. Conversely, less than 2 percent of all Christians lived in Africa in 1910, which skyrocketed to almost 22 percent by 2010. The global North contained over 80 percent of all Christians in 1910, falling to under 40 percent by 2010.

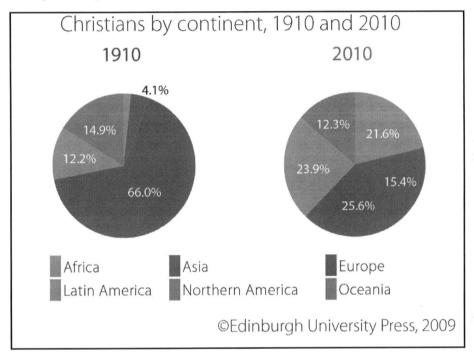

These remarkable geographic changes in Christianity also reflect serious differences between the worldviews of "Northern" and "Southern" Christians. In many ways Christianity has shifted to the global South demographically, but not culturally. This is a legitimate concern for Christians around the globe. Compared to most other religious traditions, Christianity has been generally accepting of scriptural, liturgical, and cultural translation throughout its history, with the translation process of the Christian message going back nearly to its inception. Christianity is the only world religion for which the primary source documents are in a different language than that of the founder (the New Testament is in Greek, while Jesus spoke Aramaic).[13] Cultural and linguistic translatability are some of Christianity's greatest strengths; strengths that, in light of its recent demographic shift, ought to be seen more readily in the diverse communities of Christians worldwide. The kind of cultural translatability needed today is similar to that seen when first-century Christianity moved out of its original Jewish setting.[14]

13. See Walls, *Cross-Cultural Process*.

14. For a thorough examination of this process, see Wilson, *Our Father Abraham*.

The shift of Christianity to the global South has the potential to open up new possibilities for the life and health of Christianity around the world. It has been argued that the way of life in the global South actually aligns more closely with the circumstances of biblical authors and events.[15] African and Asian societies in particular have much in common with the biblical context, including the newness of the Christian faith and its minority status among religions. Philip Jenkins states, "In Africa particularly, Christians have long been excited by the obvious cultural parallels that exist between their own societies and those of the Hebrew Old Testament, especially the world of the patriarchs."[16] If the global South's worldview is actually closer to the one espoused by Jesus and His followers, what does this mean for the Western-dominated history of Christianity? It is true that Western Christians have picked up habits and beliefs along the way that are now considered normative in Christianity, but do not necessarily line up with the biblical narrative. One example of this is experiences of healing, which are central to the validity of the apostles' message and testament to the presence and power of the Holy Spirit. Western Christianity has by and large pushed miraculous healing and spiritual explanations for everyday events to the periphery of Christian thought, preferring scientific theorizing and other secular values and beliefs. However, healing and spiritual explanations for happenings in daily life are fundamental to the worldviews of many Christians in Asia and Africa.[17]

Christian missionaries from the global North took the Gospel to the "ends of the earth"—regardless of their motivations—providing an initial spark that helped to make Christianity a worldwide phenomenon (although most of the evangelism was done by local converts). Unfortunately, in this process, Western Christianity was imposed on other cultures, giving the impression that Christianity was a Western religion, despite its translatability. Moonjang Lee notes, "The subsequent globalisation of the image of Western Christianity poses a problem for non-Western Christianity. Though we talk about a post-Christian West and a post-Western Christianity, the prevailing forms of Christianity in most parts of the non-Western world are still dominated by Western influences."[18] In addition, the transition of Christian leadership from North to South has been anything but smooth. At the onset of World War II, missionaries around the world were forced to abandon their posts with little notice, handing power over to native leaders who did not receive adequate, if any, training. Funding dried up, leaving huge infrastructure issues for fledging Christian communities around the world.[19]

In addition, the shift of Christianity to the global South is widening the gap between theology in the academy and theology in the congregations.[20] One key trend in the academy is the growth of "identity theologies." The twentieth century experienced the emergence of liberation theology in Latin America, which effectively encouraged the

15. See Jenkins, *New Faces of Christianity*. This includes the Old Testament, which speaks directly to local conditions especially in Africa, 42.

16. Ibid., 45.

17. Ibid., 184–185.

18. Lee, "Future of Global Christianity," in *Atlas of Global Christianity*, 104–105.

19. Jeyaraj, "Re-emergence of Global Christianity," 54.

20. Markham, "Theology," in *Blackwell Companion to the Study of Religion*, Segal, 208–209.

development of other identity theologies such as black theology, womanist theology, and Hispanic/Latino theology. However, despite the fact that many of the new Christians in the global South belong to such identity groupings, these progressive principles do not adequately reflect what is happening theologically in the congregations, who are generally more concerned with presenting a "consistent witness to the nature of God and of God's relation with the world" than with the implications of God on a particular identity or subject.[21] The demographic shift of Christianity is only positive if it is accompanied by theological reflection from fresh cultural perspectives of more recent members of the global church. Fortunately, many excellent examples of indigenous Christianity around the world are available to aid in this process.[22]

A unique way of illustrating the shift of global Christianity is to map its statistical center of gravity over the past 2,000 years (shown below). The statistical center of gravity is the point on the globe at which there are equal numbers of Christians to the North, South, East, and West. Mapping the center begins at the birth of Christianity in Jerusalem in AD 33 (the year of Christ's crucifixion). With the missionary activities of the early Christians and the growth of Christianity throughout the Roman Empire, the center of gravity creeps northwards, peaking in the year 1500 in Budapest. At this point, Roman Catholics arrive in the Americas, continuing to pull the center of gravity westward, through the Iberian Peninsula. Protestant and Anglican missions worldwide begin in earnest around 1800, although in 1900, 80 percent of all Christians are still Northern. By 1970, however, the churches are critically declining in Europe while mushrooming in Africa and Asia. As a result, in 2010 the Christian center of gravity was around Tessalit, Mali (northeast Mali). This 100-year shift is by far the most dramatic in Christian history. If current growth and decline patterns persist, it is likely that the center of gravity will continue to move southward with the growth of Christianity in the global South and contraction in the global North.

21. Ibid., 204–205.

22. Examples are often most apparent in art and music. See a wide variety of artistic works published at the Overseas Ministries Study Center (www.omsc.org). For a fine compendium on Christian worship from around the world, see Farhadian, *Christian Worship Worldwide.*

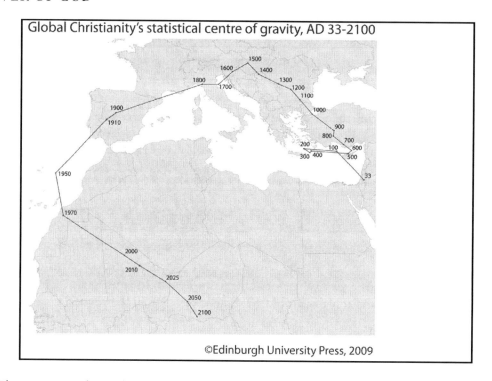

Global Christianity's statistical centre of gravity, AD 33-2100

©Edinburgh University Press, 2009

The recent southern shift of Christianity should be placed within the context of its entire history. Christians in the global South were in the majority for the first 900 years of Christian history. This includes the churches recorded in the New Testament that were planted by biblical figures in Jerusalem and Asia Minor. From this perspective, European domination of global Christianity can be seen as a more recent phase, now passed. Beginning in 1981, Southern Christians were, once again, in the majority.

It is clear that Christianity in 1910 was largely a Western phenomenon, including a strong European Roman Catholic presence in Latin America, where few church leaders were actually Latin Americans. By mapping the same phenomenon by province 100 years later, it is clear that the global situation has changed. The most dramatic difference between these two dates is in Africa—less than 10 percent Christian in 1910 but nearly 50 percent Christian in 2010, with sub-Saharan Africa well over 70 percent Christian.

Another way of viewing the southern shift of Christianity is through the countries with the most Christians in 1910 and 2010 (see below). In 1910, nine out of the top ten countries were in the global North, with Brazil as the only exception (placed at number nine). The list looks profoundly different in 2010; Brazil has moved to the number two spot, and is joined by six other countries in the global South: China, Mexico, the Philippines, Nigeria, Democratic Republic of the Congo, and India. The only Northern countries that remain are the USA, Russia [3, down from 2 in 1910], and Germany [10, down from 3 in 1910]. The fastest growth over the past 100 years and over the past ten years has all been in the global South (over the past 100 years, the fastest Christian growth was in Burkina Faso, Chad, Nepal, Burundi, and Rwanda. Over the past ten years, the countries include Afghanistan, Cambodia, Burkina Faso, Mongolia, and Timor). The United States is an extraordinary case, as it continued to have the most Christians over the course of the century. The number of Christians in the United States has grown dramatically, despite persistent discussions about secularization and defection in the global North. The United States will likely continue to be listed as the country with the most Christians even in 2050 due largely to the high numbers of Christian immigrants who arrive in the country, both legally and illegally.

Largest Population of Christians

1910	Christians	2010	Christians
1 USA	84,800,000	USA	257,311,000
2 Russia	65,757,000	Brazil	180,932,000
3 Germany	45,755,000	Russia	115,120,000
4 France	40,894,000	China	115,009,000
5 Britain	39,298,000	Mexico	105,583,000
6 Italy	35,330,000	Philippines	83,151,000
7 Ukraine	29,904,000	Nigeria	72,302,000
8 Poland	22,102,000	DR Congo	65,803,000
9 Brazil	21,576,000	India	58,367,000
10 Spain	20,357,000	Germany	58,123,000

©Edinburgh University Press, 2009

Divisions Within Global Christianity

Another trend within global Christianity is the increasing number of Christian denominations in the world. There are now over 41,000 Christian denominations that range in size from millions to less than one hundred members.[23] Moonjang Lee opines that "Christianity has become too fragmented. Existing in a fragmented world, churches fail to show a united front. There are so many divisions within Christianity that it is an intriguing task to clarify a Christian identity."[24] Early Christianity was far from monolithic, of course; the issue of sectarianism in Christianity goes back to the very beginnings of the religion, when converts included Hellenized and non-Hellenized Jews, Galilean and Palestinian Jews, and Roman citizens and non-Roman citizens, among others.[25] Today, the vast majority of denominations are located in the Independent (over 27,000) and Protestant (nearly 11,000) traditions. If current trends continue, by 2025 there could be 55,000 denominations.

Christian denominations are often less attached to language and ethnicity than are some other world religions. The six major traditions (Anglican, Roman Catholic, Independent, Marginal, Orthodox, and Protestant) are globally pervasive and ethnically

---

23. See the *World Christian Database* for a complete listing of Christian denominations in every country of the world.

24. Lee, "Future of global Christianity," 104.

25. Wilson, *Our Father Abraham*, 43–44.

diverse. Nonetheless, there are correspondences between geography and those traditions. For example, many Orthodox churches are tied to ethnic lines in Europe (Greek Orthodox and Russian Orthodox, among others).[26] The Lutheran church (Protestant) is supported by the state in many Nordic countries (though in many cases this is just a formality for births, marriages, and deaths). Independent churches, many of which are found in Africa, are the fastest-growing Christian tradition.

Christian Renewal Worldwide

A further trend inside global Christianity is the appearance of unprecedented renewal movements occurring globally within all traditions. There are many forms of renewal within global Christianity, including Evangelical movements, liturgical renewal, Bible-study fellowships, and house church movements. These movements are in no way limited to Protestant and Independent churches; one of the largest renewal movements worldwide is the Catholic Charismatics.[27] One of the most visible and well-known movements is the Pentecostal/Charismatic renewal, described by Julie Ma and Allan Anderson as "one of the most significant forms of Christianity in the twentieth century . . . In less than a century Pentecostal, Charismatic and associated movements have become a major new force in world Christianity."[28]

Pentecostalism was already emerging in various locations around the world in the early 1900s, when the outlook for the new century was bright.[29] Though hardly recognized as a global movement, by 1910 Pentecostalism was already operating in 40 countries worldwide. It would have been unthinkable that this seemingly insignificant movement would help shape Christianity into a largely non-Western phenomenon by the end of the century.[30] Several characteristics of the movement helped catapult it onto the world stage. Pentecostalism's stress on the spiritual realm very much aligns with the worldviews of the global South, where spiritual and emotional experiences weigh heavily on daily life. The lively music found in Pentecostal worship sessions mimics Southerners' exuberance of musical expression. In addition, the movement's holistic spirituality—belief that not only is personal identity intimately connected to spirituality, but that one experiences a mystical connection to the Earth and cosmos through that spirituality—actively promotes the ideals of Spirit-filled holy life.

The numbers of Christians involved in various kinds of renewal movements include 300 million Evangelicals (uppercase "E," enumerated with a structural definition

---

26. See Garrard and Garrard, *Russian Orthodoxy Resurgent*, 8.

27. Latin-rite Catholic renewalists stand at over 133 million members. Other large groupings of renewalists include Baptistic-Pentecostal (77 million), Chinese Charismatic (76 million), African Independent Pentecostal (26 million), and Brazilian/Portuguese Pentecostal (17 million). Almost 23 percent of Catholics are renewalists, 3 percent of Anglicans, 51 percent of Independents, 1 percent of Orthodox, and 22 percent of Protestants. See Johnson and Ross, *Atlas of Global Christianity*, 102.

28. Ma and Anderson, "Pentecostals (Renewalists), 1910–2010," in *Atlas of Global Christianity*, 100–101.

29. Anderson, *Introduction to Pentecostalism*, 35–38.

30. Ibid., 100.

provided by the *World Christian Encyclopedia*[31]), 600 million Pentecostals, 700 million Great Commission Christians,[32] and 500 million evangelicals (lowercase "e," enumerated with a theological definition used by *Operation World*).[33] The locus of Christian renewal is clearly in the global South, where the majority of its practitioners live and where it is growing the fastest. Some of the countries with the fastest 100-year growth rates for renewalists include Brazil, the Philippines, Democratic Republic of the Congo, Mexico, and Colombia. The top countries with the highest ten-year growth rates include more representation from Asia: Laos, Afghanistan, Cambodia, and Bangladesh. Eighteen countries have a majority (over 50 percent) renewalist presence among their Christians. The largest population of renewalists worldwide in both 1910 and 2010 were in the global South—South Africa in 1910 and China in 2010 (though note that the United States remained in the number three spot in both years). The United States is the only Northern country on the list of highest percentage of renewalists worldwide in 2010, with countries in Africa largely dominating the list.

Inequality of Resource Distribution

Finally, the unequal distribution of Christian resources worldwide is another notable ongoing reality within global Christianity. In comparing each continent's percentage of all Christians versus its portion of all Christian wealth, it is easy to see the huge disparity in resources. Even though the global South (Asia, Africa, Latin America) now contains the majority of the world's Christians, the majority of Christian financial resources still remain in the global North. Asia, Africa, and Latin America combined have less than 20 percent of Christian wealth; Northern America and Europe have about 40 percent each.[34] Christians in the South represent 60 percent of all Christians worldwide but receive only about 17 percent of all Christian income. This puts churches in the global South at a critical disadvantage in supporting their ministry staff, home missions, foreign missions,

---

31. The structural definition of "Evangelicals" (capital "E") consists of all affiliated church members self-identifying as Evangelicals. Christians are also considered Evangelicals when they are members of an Evangelical church, congregation, or denomination. Characteristics of Evangelicals include personalized religion (being "born again"), dependence on the Bible as the Word of God, and regular preaching and/or evangelism.

32. The term "Great Commission Christians" is equivalent to "evangelical" (lowercase "e"). An evangelical (lowercase "e") is any church member who believes in or embraces seven key components: (1) centered on the person of Jesus; (2) obedient to Christ's Great Commission; (3) committed to the Gospel as set forth in the Bible; (4) day-to-day personal witness to Christ; (5) involved in organized methods of evangelism; (6) involved in Christ's mission in the world; and (7) working towards Christ's second coming and final Advent. The term "Great Commission Christians" is prominent in the conversation about global evangelicalism, *Atlas of Global Christianity*.

33. In the most recent edition of Mandryk, *Operation World*, the usage of the term is described as "very close but not identical" to Bebbington's usage in *Evangelicalism in Modern Britain*. The "Bebbington Quadrilateral" includes four characteristics: crucicentrism, conversionism, Biblicism, and activism. Therefore, *Operation World* defines evangelicals as affiliated church members who adhere to the four qualities above. This generally means grounded belief in the crucified Christ, an experience of a personal conversion, theological foundation in the Bible as the Word of God, and active missionary evangelism or preaching of the gospel.

34. Johnson and Ross, *Atlas of Global Christianity*, 297.

and overall holistic ministry goals of their organizations. As global Christianity continues to move southward, the global church will be forced to develop new and creative ways to encourage global sharing and responsible giving and spending.

TRENDS OUTSIDE GLOBAL CHRISTIANITY

Secularization

A current trend affecting not only global Christianity, but also religion as a whole, is secularization; the term is defined by Alan Aldridge as "the process by which sectors of society and culture are removed from the domination of religious institutions and symbols."[35] Although predicted to die out by the twenty-first century, religion in some ways has experienced a significant revival. Evelyn Bush states that if "the secularization theory reached its pinnacle in studies of the world system, it has also been increasingly rejected by sociologists of religion who argue that religion is not in inevitable decline and that it can actually co-exist with modernization quite comfortably."[36] Although the secularization theory has largely been debunked, it is still a consistent challenge to religious faith and a contemporary issue in religious demography. One example of this is the European churches and their leaders who have "lost their once dominant position in contemporary Europe," resulting in the continued decline of church attendance.[37]

Simultaneous to the shift of Christianity to the South has been the decline of Christianity in the North. Two primary reasons for this decline are the rise of Communism during the twentieth century and the continued influence of secularization. Communism had its greatest impact on Christian defections between 1910 and 1970. By 1970, nearly 15 percent of the global population was agnostic, and 5 percent atheist. This trend had its origins in the Russian Revolution and eventually enveloped much of Eastern Europe. The most drastic nonreligious changes occurred after 1950 in North Korea and China, though other countries already influenced by the Soviet Union were also affected, including Kazakhstan, Uzbekistan, and Ukraine. Agnostic growth due to secularization has continued in Western countries (United States, Britain, France, Germany). Low birth rates in many Eastern European countries caused agnosticism's share to decline more recently.[38] But today, most of the world's nonreligious live in Asia, particularly China, Japan, and North Korea.

Whether secularization is still a viable explanation of religious decline worldwide continues to be a popular topic in the sociology of religion. In the twentieth century, many theorists held the basic assumption that religion reached its pinnacle of influence in the early modern period (1500–1800) and was not able to exert such powerful—or any—influence in the later modern period (1800–1945). Many declared that religiosity was on the decline and would be virtually nonexistent in the twenty-first century, but this did

35. Aldridge, *Religion in the Contemporary World*, 77.

36. Bush, "Measuring Religion in Global Civil Society," *Social Forces*, 1,648.

37. Halman and Draulans, "How Secular is Europe?" *British Journal of Sociology*, 263.

38. Johnson and Ross, *Atlas of Global Christianity*, 28.

not come to pass.[39] Although Western European countries in particular have undergone dramatic secularization, the collapse of Communism has meant new opportunities for religion to make a comeback in Europe.[40] In addition, secular substitutions for religion did not fare well in the twentieth century, and their demise provided opportunity for religious revival.[41] Globally, religion is on the rise and secularization has, for the moment, been kept at bay.

Reaching the World for Christ

By one measure, 46 percent of the world's population was evangelized in 1910.[42] This increased to 70.7 percent in 2010. There are, however, significant continental and regional variations. For example, Africa was roughly 20 percent evangelized in 1910; in 2010 the figure was 75 percent. But within Africa, the south is over 90 percent evangelized while large portions of north Africa are predominantly Muslim with few Christians. Asia (with millions of Muslims, Buddhists, Hindus, and agnostics) still remains the continent with the least access to the Gospel, whether churches, Bible translation or personal witness. Asia remains the least-evangelized major area in 2010, with only 58 percent evangelization (up from 18 percent in 1910). Ironically, regions that received the gospel first from the early church (Western Asia, North Africa) are today less than 50 percent evangelized.

One might have the impression that the remedy to this problem is more evangelistic activity. But, in sheer quantity, there is already enough evangelism in the world today for every person to hear a one-hour presentation of the Gospel every other day all year long. This amounts to over 1,136 billion hours of evangelism generated by Christians every year, ranging from personal witnessing to television and radio broadcasting. When broken down by United Nations regions, it is easily seen once again that Asia and Northern Africa have the lowest amounts of evangelism but the largest non-Christian populations.

With so many Christians and so many evangelism hours available worldwide, why are there still huge unevangelized populations? The staggering reality is that most Christian outreach never reaches non-Christians—over 85 percent of all Christian evangelism is aimed at other Christians.[43] This highlights a crucial problem in the attitudes and activities of Christians worldwide: there is little interaction with people of other faiths. One explanation for this reality is the unanticipated success of Christian missions in the twentieth century; missionary personnel overseas are working among Christians—as support staff for indigenous churches and ministries. But this may be changing, as new churches in the global South are surprisingly mission-focused; when the tide of emigration shifted after World War II, formerly colonized peoples were increasingly brought into the former

39. This story is recounted in the chapter titled "Secularization, RIP," *Acts of Faith*.

40. Dark, "Large-Scale Religious Change and World Politics," in *Religion and International Relations*, 50–82.

41. Aldridge, *Religion in the Contemporary World*, 83.

42. An evangelized person is defined as "an individual who has had adequate opportunity or opportunities to hear the gospel and to respond to it, whether he responds positively or negatively." See Johnson and Ross, *Atlas of Global Christianity*, 326.

43. Johnson and Ross, *Atlas of Global Christianity*, 318.

colonizers' kingdoms. New movements and conferences were convened that highlighted themes such as evangelization of Asia by Asians, and how to make the transition from receiver to initiator of the Gospel.[44]

With over two billion Christians spread throughout the world, one might think that a significant number of non-Christians would have personal contact with a Christian. Recent research reveals, however, that as many as 86 percent of all Muslims, Hindus, and Buddhists do not personally know a Christian.[45] Contact typically takes place in majority-Christian countries with small populations of other religionists; in these places it is easy for a Buddhist, for example, to know a Christian, since he or she is surrounded by Christians. Muslims, Hindus, and Buddhists living in countries with small Christian populations have fairly low interaction. This includes much of North Africa and Asia, not coincidentally regions that typically have restricted religious freedom. It is too large a task to leave reaching the world's religionists for the missionary enterprise only. Local churches and organizations in majority-Christian countries need to take the initiative to educate their congregations about the other world religions, engage in interreligious dialogue, and give people of other faiths the opportunity to consider Jesus. A recent survey by the Pew Forum on Religion And Public Life found that evangelicals are less knowledgeable about world religions than are atheists, Jews, or Mormons. Evangelicals answered 18 out of 32 questions about world religions accurately while atheists/agnostics, Jews, and Mormons answered more than 20 of 32 correctly.[46] This illustrates that the church faces a monumental task in order to reach other religionists for Christ, a task that begins with the education of Christians.

Counterintuitively, research has also revealed that Muslims, Buddhists, and Hindus are quite responsive to the Gospel.[47] Of the one hundred most responsive people groups over 1 million in size, 22 are tribal (9 percent of the total by population), 31 are Hindu (48 percent), 31 are Muslim (25 percent), and four are Buddhist (9 percent). The five most responsive of these are the Jinyu of China (Buddhist), the Khandeshi of India (tribal), the Southern Pathan of Afghanistan (Muslim), the Magadhi Bihari of India (Hindu), and the Maitili of India (Hindu). This means that the most responsive groups appear to be in the least-Christian areas.

GLOBAL TRENDS AND CHRISTIAN UNITY

What do these trends mean for Christian unity? Christianity has shifted to the global South, and in the process has further fragmented into more denominations. Christian resources are unevenly distributed, and Christians are out of contact with members of other religions. These trends put Christians in a profoundly different context than 100

44. Robert, "Missionaries Sent and Received, worldwide, 1910–2010," in *Atlas of Global Christianity*, 258–259.

45. Johnson and Ross, *Atlas of Global Christianity*, 316.

46. Pew Forum on Religion & Public Life, "U.S. Religious Knowledge Survey." See Appendix A for survey methodology.

47. See "Georesponse," in *World Christian Trends*, 771–778.

years ago. Two areas have been identified for brief consideration here, namely (1) theology and (2) contact with adherents of other religions.

Theological Implications

In recent centuries, Northern scholars wrote the dominant theologies of Christianity, but new theological reflections by Southern Christians will likely chart the future of discussions about Christian unity. To some extent this has already begun, as seen in the rise of liberation theology in Latin America, *minjung* theology in South Korea, and black theology in the United States. Theological education in the church will continue to reflect regional differences in order to produce the kinds of spiritual leaders necessary for the twenty-first century,[48] leaders who will be willing to work out these theologies from the global South and see what they can tell us about how normative Christianity should look. While the reflections of Northerners were largely shaped by the political and ecclesiastic structures of Christendom, Southern Christians are writing from the context of religious and ecclesiastical diversity.

Contact with other Religionists

For 100 years the majority of Christian growth has been taking place not in the traditionally Christian countries of the North, but in both non-Christian and newly Christian lands in the South. As a result, Muslims and Christians are now in proximity in countries such as Nigeria, Sudan, Indonesia, and the Philippines. The same is true of Hindus and Christians in India and of Buddhists and Christians in Southeast Asia. Some see inevitable conflict in the future between adherents of different religions, especially with global Christianity. It has been argued that probable conflict lies on two levels, the level of international politics and at the grassroots level.[49] However, too much attention has perhaps been given to the potential for clashing between Christians and other religionists, particularly Muslims. Many adherents of the world's religions are living together as neighbors, co-workers, and friends as a result of migration and globalization. Migrants may build bridges across cultures, rather than serve as instigators of "clashes of civilization." Religious identity works differently than ethnic nationality; as Peggy Levitt states, "religion lends itself particularly well to expressions of transnational belonging."[50]

This trajectory has given Christians around the globe a new opportunity to show hospitality to non-Christian neighbors and to take a genuine interest in their religions and cultures. With Muslims and Christians accounting for 55 percent of the world's population (and expected to rise dramatically by 2050), it is especially important for members of each tradition to make a concerted effort to build friendships and talk to each other for the sake of restoring relationships and obtaining mutual understanding. In order to gain mutual understanding between the two religions, adherents will need both factual

48. Lee, "Future of Global Christianity," 105.
49. Ibid.
50. Levitt, "Redefining the Boundaries of Belonging," in *Everyday Religion*: 103–120.

knowledge and, as Catherine Cornille states, "some degree of empathic resonance with the other;" sadly, the latter is rarely, if ever, perfectly realized.[51]

CONCLUSION

The southern shift of Christian demographics over the past 100 years represents a new chapter in the world Christian movement. This trend has major implications for all other areas outlined in this survey, including theology, mission, evangelism, and secularization. It is certain that Christianity can no longer draw on a dominant Northern theological, cultural, linguistic, or political framework for Christian unity. Neither can the future be seen exclusively through the perspectives of Southern Christianity. The world Christian movement today is truly global in the context of ever-increasing diversity, however difficult actually achieving unity might be. The unanswered question for Christians from both the North and South is how well they will respond to this new reality, and what new tools need to be developed and taught in order to live effectively as a unified whole. At the same time, outreach to other religionists will go forward in the completely new context of global Christianity, where the Gospel can no longer be perceived as a Western phenomenon.

---

51. Cornille, *The Im-Possibility of Interreligious Dialogue*, 212.

9

Anthropology and Missions:
Learning to Understand the Sea of Humanity

by Doug Priest

Fᴿᴏᴍ ᴛɪᴍᴇ ɪᴍᴍᴇᴍᴏʀɪᴀʟ ᴘᴇᴏᴘʟᴇ have traveled from one region to another and have noted that there are differences between groups of people. Many of these travelers kept notes or penned journals describing the customs of those with whom they came into contact. Western exploration and then trading trips often included a scribe who was to chronicle the journey. Their records included observations of the people and places visited. Artifacts were collected, which made their way into private and museum collections.

In the 1800s, scholars began to compile and compare this wealth of information, and the discipline of anthropology came into being. Anthropology is the study of humankind (*anthropo* = human; *logy* = study). Anthropologists are interested in how people act, what they do, how they organize themselves, and what they think. Anthropology covers a broad field, one of the broadest of any academic discipline. Anthropologists study people. They study a people's origins, their past, their present, and their future. Wherever people are found throughout the world, anthropology is concerned with them. Paris and Howell write that "Anthropology is fundamentally about people, how they see the world, and why they do what they do."[1]

Studying human civilizations from the past involves the sub-discipline of anthropology called *archaeology*. Studying the origins of humankind, including evolution and comparison of physical types, is termed *physical anthropology*. When we examine the languages of the world, we utilize *linguistics*, another sub-discipline in anthropology. When our desire is to understand groups of people in the present and in the recent past, then the area of the discipline is termed *cultural anthropology*. These four sub-disciplines together, then, constitute the academic discipline of anthropology.[2]

---

1. Howell and Paris, *Introducing Cultural Anthropology*, Kindle e-book, location 3331–32.

2. Some say that another sub-discipline of anthropology is *applied anthropology*, that is, using anthropology to address current concerns. The validity of applied anthropology has been called into question by some because it supposedly takes the objectivity out of the study, i.e., Whose agenda determines what is a problem, and who gets to decide which solutions should be applied to the problem? When missiology, the study of missions, uses anthropological insights and practices to help it achieve its specific aims, then missiology is

Because of its breadth of scope, anthropology is interdisciplinary. While other disciplines tend to compartmentalize humans by examining such features as history or language or science or psychology, anthropology is integrative in looking at the whole spectrum. It takes an integrative and holistic view of humankind; it is "centered on diversity, culture, and human difference."[3]

Often the term *ethno* (*ethno* = a group of people; *ethne* = nations or people groups) is placed in front of another word to indicate that the study is being done among other groups of people. When we study the medical practices of a group of mountain dwellers from the Andes, it is termed *ethnomedicine*. If we wish to know about the native plants used for food in the rain forest, the term *ethnobotany* is used. *Ethnohistory* helps us to better understand groups of people from earlier times and *ethnotheology* informs us in the developing and understanding of theology in other cultures. Studying the thought patterns of other people—how people make sense of the world—is called *ethnosemantics*.[4]

It is clear from this brief description of anthropology that the discipline has tremendous alignment with the church's God-given mission. We represent a people-focused God who sent his Son to save people. We do not want to be like the presidential candidate from the northern part of our country who journeyed to the Southwest to campaign. He stopped at a Texas border town and was given some tamales to eat. The tamales were each wrapped in a corn husk which is to be removed prior to eating. However, the candidate was unaware of this and proceeded to eat the tamale with the husk intact, much to the chagrin and embarrassment of his hosts. Needless to say, even though he claimed the tamales were very good, his effort to show the people how much he cared for them was somewhat muted. Anthropology helps Christians understand and communicate clearly God's love to people different than we are.

Christians have the greatest message in the world. Our desire is to share the good news of Jesus Christ with all people. God created the world so that his creation can love him in return. He sent his Son to reconcile the world to himself. We want to do everything in our power to ensure that the gospel message is clearly communicated and clearly understood.

CULTURAL ANTHROPOLOGY

Well over fifty years ago, Bible translation consultant and missionary anthropologist Eugene Nida stated that cultural anthropology is concerned primarily with three questions: 1) What makes a culture click? 2) What makes a particular member of society act

---

a form of applied anthropology. Hiebert writes, "In recent years the moral responsibilities of scholars have become matters of academic debate. Anthropologists traditionally study a non-Western community, earn their degrees, and acquire tenured faculty positions in universities, but give little back to the community in exchange for what it has given them. There is a growing awareness that anthropologists have moral obligations to help the people who help them. Today applied anthropologists have begun to make significant contributions to development projects." Hiebert, *Transforming Worldviews*, 262.

3. Howell and Paris, *Introducing*, Kindle e-book, location 3223–24.

4. The list goes on and on, for example, *ethnolinguistics*, *ethnomusicology*, and *ethnoscience*. All of these terms refer to specific types of study across cultures.

the way he does? and 3) what are the factors involved in the culture's stability or change?[5] Cultural anthropology seeks a total understanding of a group of people. One of its goals is to see how a society solves its needs, whether they be biological, spiritual, cultural, or psychological. Grunlan and Mayers assert that "the basic premise of anthropology is that there are principles or 'laws' that underlie all human behavior. The goal of anthropology is to discover these 'laws.'"[6]

Culture Defined

One of the key contributions of anthropology was the development of the idea of *culture*. In 1871 Edward Burnett Tylor, Oxford professor considered to be the father of modern anthropology, defined culture as "that complex whole which includes knowledge, belief, art, morals, law, custom, and any other capabilities and habits acquired by man as a member of society."[7] The term made its way into American anthropology, being introduced by Franz Boas and his student A. L. Kroeber. By culture they meant "the patterns of learned beliefs and behavior that order human activities."[8] Howell and Paris, in their recently published volume, define culture as "the total way of life of a group of people that is learned, adaptive, shared, and integrated."[9] They go on to elaborate, "A key concern . . . is the relationship between society (the large-scale organization of social life) and culture (the ideas, symbols, and interpretations people have around the world."[10]

The simplest definition that I have used for culture is "all that a people do and think."[11]

Let us examine that definition, phrase by phrase. *All* refers to those practices and customs—the totality of activities—which people do. It refers to child-rearing activities, socialization techniques, learning, eating, playing, re-creating, and establishing boundaries. It involves the construction of shelter, moving from one place to another, creating tools and art, studying, and mortuary practices. "All" means "all encompassing." Whatever people do is a part of their culture.

A people refers to a group of individuals, people who see themselves as different than other people. They usually reside in a given area, often speak the same language, and share customs and beliefs with others in their group. They may dress similarly, eat the same types of food (or avoid the same types of food). These individuals know that there is a linkage between themselves and others in their group. They define themselves as "us" as opposed to "them," generally people from a different culture. Luzbetak says, "Culture is conceived as a way of life of a social group, not of an individual as such. It is the way a society copes with its physical, social, and ideational environment . . . Culture is a society's

---

5. Nida, *Customs and Cultures*, 27.

6. Grunlan and Mayers, *Cultural Anthropology*, 34.

7. Tylor, *The Origins of Culture*, 1.

8. Hiebert, *Transforming Worldviews*, 26.

9. Howell and Paris, *Introducing Cultural Anthropology*, Kindle e-book, location 535–36.

10. Ibid 3113–14.

11. Priest, *Doing Theology*, 68. See also Kraft, *Anthropology for Christian Witness*, 4.

regularized or standardized design for living. *Society* can be defined as a permanently organized aggregate of persons sharing a common way of life and group consciousness."[12]

Historically peoples bound themselves into groups primarily upon the basis of geography and language. Society and culture are related to one another. In a society the people are organized—there is a social structure. The society's learned and shared way of life is its culture. Today, with half of the population of the world residing in urban centers, the distinctive marks of geography and language are no longer so important as in the past. Today people, especially urban people, move in and out of groups with ease. Their group may be related to their vocation for part of the day. Later, their group may be those with whom they eat their lunch or with whom they exercise. On the weekend their group may be their extended family and those with whom they worship. Or perhaps they feel a sense of unity based upon a hobby or a loyalty to an athletic team or an alma mater. Globalization and the options of movement provided by transportation have served to break down many former barriers.

Do, as noted earlier, refers to the actions of a people. How are the actions carried out? One boy quenches his thirst by downing a cold soda while his sister meets the same need by drinking iced tea. However, many people from Singapore consider it unhealthy to use ice in their drinks. Anthropologists try to not only discern and elaborate the variations in behavior but also try to understand why people do the things they do.

What a people *think* forms an important component of culture. How a people organizes reality in its mind and how it organizes information into categories is learned. Culture in this sense provides a mental map. At the core of every culture is its worldview. The worldview contains the central assumptions, allegiances, and values to which a society or culture commits itself. Worldview guides behavior and gives a society perspectives on all areas of life.[13] One person believes "the sun rises in the East and sets in the West," while another one says that the earth rotates on a daily basis. In Singapore the people believed red to be an auspicious color, while white was the color worn by the family members at funerals. In Indonesia at one restaurant I saw a caged bin of cobras, available to those who wished to eat snake for dinner. To me, the thought of eating snake was unfathomable.

Differences in worldview account for much cultural miscommunication and misunderstanding. The worldview differences also provide humorous illustrations. A summer intern from California, Steve, was visiting me in Tanzania. One evening for dinner we had invited a Tanzanian-born Indian named Bipin to have dinner with us. I asked Steve to help me prepare dinner by opening a can of meat. When some time had gone by, I asked him, "Hey, where's that meat?" He came into the living room and sheepishly replied that he was having a hard time using the can-opener because, as he put it, "In our kitchen at home we have an electric can-opener and I've never used a hand-operated can-opener." Bipin's eyes got wide. He was flabbergasted. "You mean you don't know how to use a can-opener? How else do you open a can? And you mean to tell me that in America they have electric can-openers? Why?" In Bipin's worldview there was no category for an electric

12. Luzbetak, *The Church and Cultures,* 111.

13. Two recently published books by missionary anthropologists provide an in-depth discussion of worldview. See Kraft, 2008, and Hiebert, 2008.

can-opener, nor for an adult who did not know how to use such a simple gadget as a hand-operated can-opener.

Characteristics of Culture

Anthropologists who have studied cultures all over the world have helped us to see that all cultures have some characteristics in common. A culture is shared by a group of people. A society is a group of people that holds some ideas and ways of doing things in common. They are tied together by their commonalities and see themselves as distinct from others who do not share the same ideas and practices. The ideas and practices of a society—its culture—are learned by its members. Babies are not born with this knowledge, they learn it over time, a process called *enculturation*. They learn their culture as they grow up in their culture.

As language is an important component of culture, it is informative to see how children learn language. Children begin making different sounds and learn very early that they have a certain control over people by uttering specific sounds—da-da, mama, papa, baba. They observe the magic of these sounds when their parents smile, believing they have been personally addressed by the child. In time the children begin to mimic sounds they hear. They learn to put words together to make sentences. They learn from being corrected, "No Johnnie, that is a shell, not a fish." Within a few short years, the child is fluent without ever taking a grammar test.

Culture describes the totality of the learning, thinking, and doing of a group of people. Haviland explains that "culture is a set of shared ideas, values, and standards of behavior; it is the common denominator that makes the actions of individuals intelligible to the group."[14] Not everyone in the group will know everything about the culture. The various roles in a culture call for different learning or specialization. Age and sex differences require specific knowledge. The child may not need to know how to solve chemical equations, and the aged parent may not know how to use the newest iPad. Culture is a generalization, a code, a mental map, a construction of reality, a total design for living. While not all hold everything in common, all do hold enough in common so as to be received and accepted as members of the culture. The farmer, scientist, and socialite may attend the same worship service, being tied together by common practices and religious beliefs.

Cultures are integrated and provide people with a way to order their lives. The practices, customs, and traits fit together as a system. If one part of a culture changes, the ramifications are often felt throughout the entire culture because cultural practices are interrelated. The extent to which the pieces fit together properly helps to explain the health of a culture. When the pieces fit together, the culture functions smoothly. When the pieces do not fit together, there is dysfunction and the culture breaks down. The less the pieces fit, the less healthy a culture. In times, there may be very little integration in a culture, and the culture ceases to exist.

14. Haviland, *Cultural Anthropology*, 14.

Cultures, however, are hearty and the members of the culture can see where there is dysfunction and can address it. The culture can be changed. People are adaptable and people change. In the early 1980s only a few rural Maasai spoke English. On recent visits to Kenya it seemed that there were few Maasai who did not speak English. Thirty years ago the Maasai learned of events in Kenya and beyond from those who visited town and by listening to shortwave radios. Today many Maasai have cell phones and are in constant contact with people all over the world. Culture is dynamic. Every culture changes or it dies.

A culture must be able to meet the basic needs of its members. All people have basic needs to be met—physical, social, safety, health, intimacy—and different cultures meet these needs in different ways. One needs to be sheltered from the environment. In the rainforest, this might mean living in tree houses. In the Arctic, at one time it meant living in igloos. The traditional Maasai construct homes with branches covered with cow manure. Culture meets the basic biological needs, as well as the social and psychological needs of the people. Cultures provide a means for "the production and distribution of the goods and services necessary for life."[15]

Cultures are complex. Early anthropologists were proponents of social evolution and believed that peoples could be defined as either barbarian, primitive, or civilized. These anthropologists' definitions of a civilized culture were, of course, their own. They thought that some cultures were simple. While some cultures may be more complex than others, no culture is simple. As Kraft points out, "No matter how simple their technology and material culture may be, their ways of living, their customs, their perceptions of and responses to the reality around them are patterned in a complex way that often defies the attempts of outsiders to learn or even to understand them."[16]

He goes on to note two final characteristics of culture. First there is "conscious (or explicit) culture and unconscious (or implicit) culture. Conscious culture includes the ways of behaving and thinking that people are aware of and usually can see and explain. Unconscious culture . . . consists of those patterns of behaving and thinking that lie below the level of a people's consciousness." Secondly, there is ideal culture and there is actual culture.[17] Ideal culture refers to the way a people believe and desire their culture to be. Actual culture is the way culture really is, noting what people actually say and do.

Ethnocentrism and Cultural Relativism

We live in a globalized world. We can easily travel and visit other cultures, and through the media we have instant access to seeing the ways that people live around the world. When we are confronted with other cultures, we come face to face with practices we do not understand. Generally, we tend to evaluate customs that are different from our own based upon our own values. It is easy for us to misunderstand and even be critical of another culture's practices simply because they are different from our own. To judge another culture based on one's own cultural values is called *ethnocentrism*, literally meaning one's own culture is central while all others are peripheral. Ethnocentrism sees the world

15. Ibid., 20.

16. Kraft, *Culture, Communication and Christianity,* 53–54.

17. Ibid., 58.

in terms of one's own culture. Because we learn our culture unconsciously, we assume it is the only correct way of ordering life. Though it is a natural reaction, one must guard against ethnocentrism.

The summer Steve visited me in Tanzania we drove from the airport in Dar Es Salaam to our rented house in Morogoro. Along the way Steve observed hundreds and hundreds of people walking alongside the road. He commented to me, "Don't these people have anything to do?" What he meant was that in America most people don't walk along the road. They drive their cars. Only a small percentage of people in Tanzania owned their own vehicles, so to get to work or the store or to visit their friends, they had to walk. Steve assumed that because so many people were walking along the road, most people in Tanzania did not work. He thought they had nothing to do. In fact, all of those people had something to do.

A few minutes later Steve asked me, "Where do people work out?" Steve was on his college basketball team, and working out in a gym was a daily activity for him. He assumed Tanzanians would work out as well. Most Tanzanians did not work out; they did not need to, as they walked everywhere they went, many times, miles a day. They dug their own gardens, they cared for their own animals. Of course some Tanzanians involved in sports did work out, but few Tanzanians worked out for health reasons.

Instead of evaluating a culture's practices based on one's own culture, we should evaluate a culture's practices on how well those practices measure up to the culture's own ideals. *Cultural relativism* means we try to understand cultural activities in light of how well the activities meet the needs of the culture. "Cultures can only be understood relative to the historical, ecological, and social context in which they developed."[18] We should try to understand the culture's reasons behind a specific practice.

A visitor in our country on the Fourth of July would see many people enjoying fireworks. The visitor could make observations: 1) shooting off fireworks is dangerous because actual fires can be started and sometime people have accidents lighting firecrackers; 2) shooting off fireworks is a waste of money; 3) Americans have nothing better to do than to sit around waiting until sunset when they could be doing something more beneficial with their time. Each of these observations may contain some measure of truth, but they miss the important point of those fireworks being linked with America's day of independence and our concept of freedom that we celebrate annually. The visitor would likely miss the sense of pride, tradition, and bonding with fellow Americans that the custom provides. The best way to understand fireworks on the Fourth of July is how the custom is understood by Americans.

What does cultural relativism say to the Christian who lives in another culture? In addition to how a culture evaluates its own practices, so too does the Bible provide standards for evaluation. Christians must be careful that they do not mistake Western practices for biblical practices. The best approach in evaluating and applying biblical standards is to work together with the local believers in determining whether a cultural practice meets biblical standards, a process called *contextualization*.[19]

18. Howell and Paris, *Introducing Cultural Anthropology*, Kindle e-book locations 445–46.

19. An excellent treatment of contextualization is found in Hiebert, *Anthropological Reflections*, 75–92.

Cultural Institutions or Systems

Anthropologists are fond of describing a culture in terms of its various institutions or systems. These are often diagrammed as a pie chart, with each system of the culture representing a piece of pie. Some of the systems they identify are the kinship system, the technological system, the economic system, the political system, and the religious system. At the center of the pie, overlapping all the systems is the culture's worldview, described earlier.

Such a model of culture is helpful in that it provides a way to understand the culture. In each system are customs and behaviors that can be examined in light of the system. But the same customs and behaviors can also carry over into another system. A simple sacrifice, for example, can be examined in light of the social structure (who provided the animal to whom and why?), the economic system (is the animal repayment for a debt, a gift, or was it purchased?), the political system (is the animal a peace offering between warring tribes or families?) and the religious system (is there a special class of people who perform the sacrifice, or, to whom is the sacrifice offered?).

In addition, it is often the researcher who provides the outline that labels the systems (the pieces of the pie). The people being observed may have their own way of understanding the reality of their culture that may or may not see the difference between, say, the political and the economic system. An understanding of the cultural institutions and systems using common categories does have the benefit of making cross-cultural comparisons.

ANTHROPOLOGY AND CHRISTIAN MISSION

Missionaries leave their home culture to minister in another culture. To effectively serve in another culture, missionaries must immerse themselves in the new culture. They need to understand the new culture so that their communication of the gospel will be understood. Like a sponge, missionaries need to soak up the new culture, observing strange customs, hearing new words, and participating in new activities. Understanding other people's customs requires knowing what other people think. Missionaries must appreciate the point of view of those from the new culture. Anthropology provides the tools to gain cross-cultural understanding. In theological terms, "we view human beings as the apex of God's creative work. Hence, we see anthropology as a discipline that helps us to better understand the central object of God's creation."[20]

Even before leaving for a new culture, missionaries should spend time studying the published anthropological research of the group to whom they will minister. There are few people groups that have not been studied by anthropologists, and reading their material will help the missionary to gain an initial awareness of the group's history, customs, belief system, social structure, values, kinship, residence patterns, economy, and use of leisure time.

Upon arrival, the missionary will need to devote considerable attention to language and culture learning. Studying the culture is aided by anthropological techniques such as

20. Grunlan and Mayers, *Cultural Anthropology*, xiii.

interviewing and participant observation. Collecting myths, proverbs, and stories can be invaluable in understanding the worldview of the people. Keeping a daily log of observations and writing down new vocabulary strengthens cultural awareness.

One of the projects I undertook when living with the Maasai in Kenya and Tanzania was to make notes on their material culture, those physical objects that the Maasai use or create in their daily life. I learned of a dozen types of wooden sticks which were used to mark ceremonial events, to keep the sheep in a herd, to be thrown at wild animals, or to be held as symbols of status. I noted dozens of uses for leather, which led me into exploring how hides were used for bedding, in rituals, as ceremonial clothing, and even in children's riddles. Gleaning such information was a demonstration to the people that I took them seriously and wanted to learn from them. Some of this learning could then be used as sermon illustrations and as a means to explore other aspects of the Maasai culture. For example, studying hides naturally led into how the Maasai described their cattle in terms of color, markings, horn shapes, and brands. As a group to whom cattle represent wealth and livelihood, they were only too happy to speak with me about their most prized possession.

Anthropology can help the missionary adjust to the culture with a minimum of culture shock. The discipline provides guidance on understanding how cultures change and how new belief systems can be incorporated. Anthropology helps the missionary answer key questions: what makes this people tick, and why do they do what they do, information any missionary needs to know.[21]

As the church is planted, anthropology provides guidance so that the church is not a carbon copy of the missionary's home culture, but one that is relevant and fits the context of the new culture. Howell and Paris provide good guidance when they write, "those who feel called to cross cultural boundaries in sharing their faith need to understand how symbols, myths, rituals, and other practices of religion work together to help people believe. Communicating meaningfully with others requires an understanding of one's own beliefs and practices. Being able to speak to the deep concerns in someone's life involves an understanding of how the symbols and practices of various faiths seek to answer those questions."[22]

CONCLUSION

Our model for mission practice should be Jesus Christ, who left Heaven and came to earth in the form of a human being. In fact, he was so human that few recognized Him to be God Incarnate. "Being born in human likeness and being found in human form, he humbled himself and became obedient to the point of death."[23] In the Incarnation we see Jesus identifying with a particular culture, living as one of them, participating in their rituals, being a member of a family, and having a job. In the period of his ministry we

---

21. In the next chapter, we will demonstrate the use of anthropological theory in the study of a particular aspect of a culture, its symbols and rituals.

22. Howell and Paris, *Introducing Cultural Anthropology*, Kindle e-book, locations 2682–83.

23. Phil 2:7–8.

see Jesus crossing cultural barriers as he interacted with Samaritans and Romans. Many became believers based on Christ's Incarnational witness.

The discipline of anthropology can offer much guidance in our efforts to be Incarnational witnesses for our Lord. Whiteman asks, "So, what does it mean to be Incarnational in our approach to cultural differences?" He then goes on to answer his own question:

It frequently means at least the following eight practices:

1. We start with people where they are, embedded in their culture and this frequently requires downward mobility on our part.

2. We take their culture seriously, for this is the context in which life has meaning for them.

3. We approach them as learners, as children, anxious to see the world from their perspective.

4. We are forced to be humble, for in their world of culture we have not yet learned the acquired knowledge to interpret experience and generate social behavior.

5. We must lay aside our own cultural ethnocentrism, our positions of prestige and power.

6. We will be very vulnerable; our defenses will have to go, and we'll have to rely more on the Holy Spirit than our own knowledge and experience.

7. We make every effort to identify with people where they are, by living among them, loving them, and learning from them.

8. We discover, from the inside, how Christ is the Answer to the questions they ask, and to their needs that they feel.[24]

As we obey our Lord's command to make disciples of all people—or all people groups— let us utilize every tool available to us to accomplish that purpose. In order to love our neighbor we must first understand our neighbor. The discipline of anthropology, being the study of humankind, provides much help in this calling.

---

24. Whiteman, *Anthropology and Mission*, 33–34.

10

Using Anthropology to Understand Ritual and Symbol

by Doug Priest

W E WERE MOVING ALONG the trail, single file, most of us on our own mules. It was 1967 and as a missionary kid on break from the boarding school, I was allowed to tag along on an evangelistic trip to a new set of villages in the Wollega Province of Ethiopia. Our destination that day took us through high mountain passes toward the lowlands. In our group were several Oromo evangelists and my father. We were going to spend several nights at the invitation of the local leader in the area. It was an opportunity for the gospel to make headway among the animistic Oromo.

All of a sudden the lead mule shied, and the rider was thrown to the ground, to the amusement of the rest of the group. We stopped for a break, and I learned that the mule had shied at that particular point because of a large tree beside the trail believed to be sacred. We were told that the Oromo offered sacrifices at the site of the tree, called an *adbar*. An evangelist pointed to a clay bowl which was set in the juncture of a large limb and the trunk. He said, "In the bowl is the blood from a sheep which has been sacrificed to the spirits, *ayana* or *sheitani*." I recoiled like the mule before me.

A dozen years later I am back in Africa as a missionary learning the language and culture of the Maasai people of Kenya and Tanzania. My wife and I are living in the house of Imeyu, one of four wives of a Maasai man who is allowing us to rent this house while we study. One morning we wake to some strange sounds. As we step into the entry area of the house, we see that the sounds are coming from a sheep being hung by the neck in the doorway of the house. I ask the young men present about the occasion and they respond, "It is because Imeyu has had her baby. She needs to drink blood and eat meat to recover her strength. We Maasai always sacrifice a sheep in thanksgiving to God at the birth of a child."

Another dozen years pass, and we are now living in Singapore. Each day as I walk to the bus stop, I pass through a housing estate with numerous high-rise apartment buildings. The sidewalk takes me past many family altars dedicated to the ancestral spirits of the Chinese inhabitants. Almost every day I see incense being offered up to the ancestors, and often bits of food are left at the altar as sacrifices.

On a trip to Indonesia I saw dozens of sheep tethered in the middle of the sprawling urban center of Surabaya on the island of Java, a city of three million people. The sheep have been brought into town to be purchased by the city dwellers and offered as sacrifices. The occasion is the Muslim holiday known as *Hari Raya Haji*, a festival marking the end of the yearly pilgrimage.

My experiences of seeing sacrificial rituals are not unusual. These, and many others like them, lead me to agree with Don Richardson that "after acknowledgement of God's existence, Creation, and the rebellion and fall of man, sacrifice is the most common component of folk religions worldwide."[1]

After my rude awakening that morning in Kenya to the sounds of a sheep struggling for life, I determined I was going to try to understand the practice of sacrifice among the Maasai. I wanted to learn what the anthropologists who study ritual and symbol said about the act of sacrifice. This chapter is the result and serves as a case study in examining practices of another culture. We deliberately leave aside any comments about how this research could be put to use among the Maasai. The focus of this chapter is research methodology, not application.

RITUAL AND SYMBOL THEORY

Since sacrifice, after prayer, may be the most widespread religious ritual, much has been written about the act. Sacrifices continue to be offered by many peoples even to this day.

Definition of Terms

Fortes used the term "ritual" to refer to "any customary spoken and/or acted out pattern of behavior recognized by the actors as directed towards or referring to the supernatural."[2] Turner's definition of ritual is very similar: "prescribed formal behavior for occasions not given over to technological routine, having reference to beliefs in mystical (or non-empirical) beings or powers."[3]

Two limitations from these definitions should be noted. First, ritual is a form of drama. While the analogy is useful, in Western dramas the performers know what the outcome of the drama will be. They are participating in an art form. Rituals in other cultural contexts are more often attempts to mirror reality. Secondly, both Turner and Fortes follow the common distinction between the sacred and the profane in that they see ritual as having to do with the supernatural. The heavy smoker who lights up after every meal is practicing a habit, not performing a ritual.

The basic meaning of a symbol is that which stands for something else. Beattie, quoting Radcliffe-Brown, states that "whatever has meaning is a symbol, the meaning being whatever is expressed by the symbol."[4] Firth said that "the essence of symbolism lies in the recognition of one thing as standing for another, the relation between them normally being that of concrete to abstract, particular to general."[5]

1. Richardson, *Eternity in Their Hearts*, 155.
2. Fortes, "Anthropologists and Theologians," ix.
3. Turner, *Drums of Affliction*, 15.
4. Beattie, *Other Cultures*, 69.
5. Firth, *Symbols, Public and Private*, 15.

If ritual means action directed to the supernatural, and a symbol is that which stands for something else, then the two concepts can be related to one another. Ritual is a symbolic form of behavior of either an individual or a group of people that is meaningful to them. It "is a way through which a society experiences and expresses its symbolic understanding of life and conveys it to succeeding generations."[6] The most basic relation is that ritual is symbolic action in relation to sacred objects.[7]

Properties of Rituals and Symbols

Communicating through the use of symbols is universally practiced. One may say, "Look, a dog," when referring to the appropriate four-legged creature. Communicating by actions is seen in that when a man puts his arm around a woman's waist many people assume that he loves her. Thought communication is seen when non-verbalized prayer shows devotion to God. Communicating symbolically is one way of communicating personal and social values.

Anthropologists have listed the various properties of symbols. Edward Sapir mentioned four: 1) a symbol may contain many meanings; 2) economy of reference which means that the symbolic linkage is easily seen—as with a country's flag; 3) the predominance of emotional quality in symbols; and 4) associational linkages with the unconscious.[8]

Turner agrees with Sapir that a symbol may convey many meanings. He noted the meanings of a symbol are interconnected by having analogous qualities or being associated together in thought. The symbol of Christian baptism, for example, conveys numerous meanings—acceptance into the Church, forgiveness of sins, cleansing from impurity, reception of the Spirit. Turner also noted that symbols are polarized in that they refer to the social or moral order on one hand, and the natural or physiological on the other. He termed these poles "ideological" and "sensory."[9]

There are both dominant and secondary symbols in any ritual. Dominant symbols are the basic unit of ritual—the Cross on top of the church building, the water of the baptismal service, the ox of the sacrifice. Secondary symbols—the words of the song on the screen, the prayer at the baptismal service, the knife which is used in killing the sacrifice—derive their importance in relation to the dominant symbol. Dominant symbols deal with values and help in determining the flow of the ritual.

Firth pointed out that symbols have both a public and a private domain. The public character of symbols is studied by anthropologists, while psychologists are more interested in private symbols. Public symbols are characteristic of groups and are the symbolism of collectivity. They can be seen in myth, ritual, and social structure. Private symbols are

6. Swantz, *Ritual and Symbol*, 44.

7. Firth, *Symbols*, 301.

8. In Turner, *Forest of Symbols*, 29.

9. Ibid., 28.

not often shared by the whole group. They represent personal interests and are manifested in dreams, hallucinations, or prophetic revelations.[10]

Symbols and rituals have the attribute of efficacy. They are believed to work, to result in what the community or individual desires. Proper adherence to a ritual form will result in the desired aim. Rainmaking rituals are a prime example. Through symbolism, what was once profane—the everyday products used in the rainmaking ritual—become sacred or imbued with power. They are believed to bring rain. In time, in the people's mind, they do bring rain.

Symbols often have a timeless quality about themselves. They can be detached from the present to stand for either the past or for the future.[11] Conversely, rituals and symbols can be changed. They are adaptive, as well as persistent. New meanings can be given to old symbols. The basketball player's jersey is retired and now rests in the Hall of Fame as a symbol of her past greatness. New ritual practices can be adopted by a society as a means of expressing new values.

Ritual, Symbol, and Worldview

Symbol and ritual are vehicles of communication. They say something in a way different from ordinary language and behavior. Symbols present forms of expression, knowledge, and control. They are "the only means of expressing value; the main instruments of thought, the only regulators of experience."[12] What then is the nature of such communication?

Every society has its own way of apprehending the world. It has its own ideas about nature, humankind, and the supernatural. Such concepts have been termed a society's worldview. Kraft defines worldview as "the totality of the culturally structured images and assumptions (including value and commitment or allegiance assumptions) in terms of which a people both perceive and respond to reality."[13]

Symbol and ritual are related to worldview in that they enforce the categories through which a people perceive reality. Ritual is a way of acting out and experiencing the symbolic understanding of reality. Elderly men do not participate in the rites of Cub Scouts. Humans find their place in this reality by placing themselves in the system of symbols. When individuals participate in rituals they become part of such reality. Ritual and symbol are attempts to mirror reality or to mirror a particular worldview. As Shorter notes, "Symbolism is the only satisfactory way of expressing and communicating the experience of ultimate reality or, indeed, of making the whole of the reality intelligible to ourselves."[14]

Participation in ritual creates a unity in experience because rituals are used to assert a hierarchy and order to reality. They help affirm the "value of the symbolic patterning of the universe."[15] Through rituals, humans express relationships to their environment and

---

10. Firth, *Symbols*, 207.

11. Ibid., 22.

12. Douglas, *Natural Symbols*, 60.

13. Kraft, *Worldview for Christian Witness*, 12.

14. Shorter, *African Culture and the Christian Church*, 50.

15. Douglas, *Implicit Meanings*, 102.

their fellow beings. The rituals correspond to the people's total view of life. Ritual systems present a coherent system of thought.[16] The symbolic lines and boundaries in ritual are reflective of the boundaries which organize experience and society.[17] In many countries men sit on one side of the church auditorium and women sit on the other. Among the Maasai, women do not participate with the men in a meat-roast.

A people's worldview not only helps them order their experience, it is used to reflect the values of a society. Rituals help a people express their moral qualities and values. As rituals are performed, they serve to enculturate such values. Turner says that "Personality is shaped at the forge of ritual."[18] Many ritual values are laden with emotion. People find emotional satisfaction in ritual. A mother cries at the wedding ceremony of her daughter.

Rituals and symbols are used to promote cultural unity. Rituals play an important part in maintaining the balance of the society. They ensure a secure place for the individual within the context of the group. Potentially divisive elements in society are held in check through ritual. Ritual helps maintain the proper social order. Ritual can provide an integrative force in society. Douglas says that ritual exercises a "constraining effect on the social behavior."[19]

One of the ways that society deals with conflict is to have conflict resolution as a function of ritual. Ritual works to heal broken social relationships and attempts to resolve conflicting social principles. Turner says that the conflicts of a society are the same as those dramatized and symbolized in ritual. Because "people are deeply concerned emotionally about such conflicts, they are moved when they see them ritually portrayed. And when they are ritually resolved, they feel an emotional 'catharsis.'"[20] Family peace is often achieved between siblings at the funeral of their parent. However, Gluckman says pointedly that rituals do not solve societal conflicts because such conflicts are part of the fabric of social life. But ritual does tend to mask the conflict by promoting truces and affording temporary reconciliation.[21]

A final function of symbol and ritual is that they help a people to bring that which is invisible into clarity, to make the unknown known. Beliefs, ideas, values, and sentiments are made known in ritual. A symbol is like a light or a landmark. Through ritual and symbol the unpredictable becomes predictable and the abstract becomes concrete.[22]

Ritual and Symbol in Relation to Social Structure

There is a direct correlation between ritual and social reality. In ritual action the social structure and social systems can be observed. Swantz notes this relation when she says that "the symbols which a society uses reflect in a profound way something of the very

16. Ibid., 67.

17. Ibid., 73.

18. Turner, *Forest*, 143.

19. Douglas, *Natural Symbols*, 42.

20. Turner, *Drums*, 238–39.

21. Gluckman, "Les Rites de Passage," 46.

22. Fortes, "Anthropologists," ix.

essence of the people who form the society."[23] It is through the use of symbols and in ritual that the nature of a society can be seen. Rituals present "moments in the unending stream of developing and declining relationships between individuals and groups."[24]

Douglas suggests the following chain: communication depends on symbols; symbols depend on structure; structure comes from social order.[25] The religious communication that takes place through symbols in religion, then, depends on a structure that is related to the very social structure of the society. The understanding of such symbols of necessity includes an understanding of the social structure.

SACRIFICE AS A SYMBOLIC RITUAL

We shall take our definition of sacrifice from that enunciated by Hubert and Mauss in a key anthropological work on the subject over a century ago. They wrote concerning sacrifice: "This procedure consists in establishing a means of communication between sacred and profane worlds through the mediation of a victim, that is, of a thing that in the course of the ceremony is destroyed."[26] I would further add that sacrifices most generally consist of an animal victim. The key components of sacrifice, then, are: 1) communication with the sacred arising from the world of the profane; 2) the communication enhanced through an animal victim; and 3) the death of that victim.

The literature, both in theology and anthropology, has given rise to many theories to explain sacrifice. The reason for such a multitude of diverse theories is because the act in itself is complex. Every society has one or more purposes for offering a sacrifice. The ritual must therefore be studied first in its own particular context if we are to understand it. And it is here that general theorizing breaks down. For example, just because sacrifice in many of the biblical periods was to purify from sin, one cannot postulate, as do many theologians, that all sacrifice in the Bible was to remove sin. Nor can we assume that because in some parts of Latin America sacrifices are offered to human-made gods, that all sacrifices today should be seen as gifts to idols. The practice is too widespread and varied to assume there is only one reason for sacrifice.

Beattie pinpoints the most interesting problem in sacrifice as being "that of understanding sacrifice from the point of view of the participants, as far as this is possible. What do they see as its purpose, and what are the categories, the ways of thinking about reality, which are implicit . . . in their view of the matter?"[27]

Another difficult problem for the anthropologist is just how to distinguish between slaughtering and sacrifice, slaughtering being defined as the slaying of the victim, but without recourse to the supernatural. Are both the same? Are they different? And if they are different, how are the two practices differentiated? Much of the meat eaten by Muslims on a daily basis has to have been slaughtered by another Muslim who enjoins the cutting

23. Swantz, *Ritual and Symbol*, 28.

24. Turner, *Revelation and Divination*, 30.

25. Douglas, *Natural Symbols*, 60.

26. Hubert and Mauss, *Sacrifice*, 97.

27. Beattie, "On Understanding Sacrifice," 36.

of the throat with a prayer to God. I define this everyday occurrence as a sacrifice because as a ritual it is a repetitive behavior that is directed toward the supernatural.

Functions of Sacrifice

Before proceeding to discuss anthropological theories of sacrifice, it will be helpful to list the different functions of sacrifice as listed by anthropologists on the basis of their observations. Beattie suggests three general functions of the rite: 1) sacrifice provides a dramatic performance for its practitioners and witnesses; 2) it provides a catharsis in that it is often thought of as a way of eliminating evil; and 3) sacrifice provides a social event that has social consequences.[28] Evans-Pritchard lists a total of fourteen meanings of sacrifice as practiced by the Nuer people of Sudan: communion, gift, apotropaic rite, bargain, exchange, ransom, elimination, expulsion, purification, expiation, propitiation, substitution, abnegation, and homage.[29]

Another function of many sacrifices is the desire for gain. A person undergoes a loss—such as that of an animal victim—so that he or she may receive gain. The person hopes to gain something by making a vicarious sacrifice of himself or herself.[30] There seems to be an element of either demand or persuasion on the part of the participant. The gain may be material gain or receiving something intangible, such as the respect of others. Or the gain may be from the deity as in protection or forgiveness. But not all sacrifices involve a desire for gain, as Bourdillon notes, "A calculation of material gain may be an element in religious sacrifice, but it is not always present. Particularly when sacrifice is a group or community affair, questions of cost and gain can be completely overshadowed by cosmological meanings of corporate ritual symbolism."[31]

An Anthropological Theory of Sacrifice

Social anthropologists view sacrifice in its various settings and contexts with an aim to better understand humans and their society. These rituals, as dramatic symbols, serve to express the beliefs and values of people.

AN ANTHROPOLOGICAL TREATMENT OF SACRIFICE: HUBERT AND MAUSS

Hubert and Mauss wrote one of the earlier books on the subject of sacrifice. They analyzed the stages of the act. The ritual must be surrounded with a religious atmosphere which is accomplished through the use of religious agents. The one who offers the sacrifice, the victim, the area, the instruments, and the participants must all be consecrated so that they may move from the realm of the profane to the sacred. The reason for this consecration is that that man and the god can come into contact with one another.[32] The religious act

---

28. Ibid., 35–36.

29. Evans-Pritchard, *Nuer Religion*, 282.

30. Beattie, "On Understanding Sacrifice," 30.

31. Bourdillon, *Sacrifice*, 12.

32. Hubert and Mauss, *Sacrifice*, 9–11.

must be accomplished with a religious mind and atmosphere that continues throughout the entire rite.

The next stage of the rite is the death of the victim. The divine principle or power that resides in the animal is its only link with the profane world. In its death, this link is severed. In the immolation, the religiosity of the victim passes to the one who does the killing. The sacrificial animal is then eaten and it is in the eating that the contact between the sacred and the profane is accomplished.

After eating the animal the participants exit the sacred area. "In reality, the religious atmosphere of the sacrifice is abandoned."[33] In many sacrifices there is a changed state that occurs. The one for whom the sacrifice was offered has regained a state of grace, acquired divine power, and eradicated the evil to which he or she was prey.[34] Such a changed state is often accomplished with a name change, which essentially gives expression to the change.

Nilotic Illustrations

We now proceed in our discussion of sacrifice as a symbolic ritual with illustrations from three Nilotic tribes—the Mandari, Nuer, and Dinka—all from the southern Sudan. As pastoral Nilotic tribes, they share many similarities with the Nilotic Maasai of Kenya and Tanzania. Jean Buxton[35] writes about the Mandari, E. E. Evans-Pritchard about the Nuer,[36] and Godfrey Lienhardt discusses the Dinka.[37]

MANDARI

The Mandari offer sacrifices, not to the Creator, but to his agents. They say, "You do not offer back to Creator what he has already."[38] The sacrifices offered are the animals of the Mandari herds, which to a certain extent, represent the people. A bull gives the herd its identity and potency, and can only be sacrificed in the rite for male impotence. Neutered animals are sacrificed for ordinary purposes: sickness, burial, and funerary rites. Fertile cows are not sacrificed—they are too scarce. When goats and sheep are sacrificed, the same rules apply.

Sacrifices take place as treatment for those suffering mental illness, when a chief is buried, following the burial of most people, as an appeasement to the ghosts, at simple dedications, to cause rain, and to purify from sin. Pollution and sin are not the same thing to the Mandari. Pollutions are erased by cleansings or disposal of the polluted material. Such acts do not involve confession, do not require elaborate rituals, nor do they result in sickness. Sin, on the other hand, pollutes the sinner. Sins require public confession. Sin is committing an offense or a wrong. Sickness is the result of sin. A form of purification

33. Ibid., 46.

34. Ibid., 62.

35. Buxton, *Religion and Healing in Mandari*.

36. Evans-Pritchard, *Nuer Religion*.

37. Lienhardt, *Divinity and Experience*.

38. Buxton, *Religion and Healing*, 29.

from sin is sacrifice. The goal of such a sacrifice is to "secure the maximum protection for an individual by placing him under the direct care of the Creator."[39]

Funerary sacrifices highlight the fact that a change has taken place; they are a typical rite of passage which dramatizes the fact that death is unnatural and, therefore, caused by someone or something. Vengeance must be extracted. The community must react with violence against the death. A following or second sacrifice shows that the dead person is now incorporated with the ancestors and life comes back to normal.

The rain sacrifices of this tribe illuminate the prevailing Mandari worldview. The people state that "no one makes rain. It is the Creator who sends it, and it will fall when he decides."[40] The rains are a gift from God, and they fall during the wet season. The Mandari see rain as being of two types—universal and specific. The universal rain comes from the Creator and it is outside the control of man. But the specific rain can be controlled. The specific rain is territorial, not rain for the entire land of the Mandari. Each territory is responsible for its own rain. It cannot come if there is sin or trouble in the area. Such troubles could be ritual offenses, quarreling, disrespect for the elders, and breeches of prescribed behavior. These wrong-doings must be resolved before rain sacrifices are performed lest they be ineffective.

When the specific rains are late and the community suffers, much thought goes into finding the solutions to the late rains. Hidden wrongs exist, and these are brought forward to be confessed and righted. When isolated showers arrive, they raise the hope that the community has been purified. Soon the full territorial rain comes. The people cease to speculate about the initial failure of the rains, the troubles and breeches are forgotten. The primary objective of the sacrificial rain rites is to bring about change at the physical level—to bring the needed specific rain. This differs from the sacrificial rites of purification, which seek to affect inward moral changes so that spiritual healing takes place.

NUER

The Nuer are a cattle herding society. Their environment is harsh. The herds have to forage over large areas to have enough to eat. Most of the people's livelihood comes from the cows. The Nuer do not kill their animals for food except in dire necessity or when custom demands it. When cows are killed, they are killed as a sacrifice. "Nuer surrender in sacrifice the most precious thing they possess."[41] God and spirits receive sacrifices. Prayer and sacrifice are ways of communicating with God. But the sacrifices, even if offered to spirits, are offered to God as the spirits proceed from God. Ghosts do not have sacrifices offered to them.

There are many occasions of sacrifice: when there is sickness, at the birth of a child, when a wife is barren, at times of initiation, when sin has been committed, at marriage, at funerals and mortuary ceremonies, at rituals honoring the spirits of the dead father, after homicides, at the settlement of feuds, prior to war, when there is no rain, at the time of

---

39. Ibid., 186.
40. Ibid., 349.
41. Evans-Pritchard, *Nuer Religion*, 248.

famine, when lightning strikes someone, and prior to large-scale fishing expeditions. It is easy to see that sacrifice is the "most typical and expressive act of Nuer religion."[42]

A function of some sacrifices is to wipe out sins and faults. The sinner's transgression is blotted out by the sacrifice. Sin is "a spiritual state which can only be changed by sacrifice; and not even sacrifice is sufficient by itself to change it, only sacrifice which carries with it the will and desire of the sinner."[43] Sickness is the result of sin. So if a serious sin has been committed, a sacrifice is made before the oncoming sickness appears.

Cattle are the primary sacrifice of the Nuer. Though they serve as a focus of the removal of sin, "there is no evidence at all that cattle are venerated or in themselves are in any way regarded as guardian spirits."[44] The Nuer see an equivalence between themselves and their cattle. They are substituted for one another in sacrifice. Cattle are important to the Nuer for salvation, because in sacrifice social relationships are sanctified, and sickness and sin are done away with. Cattle are a dominant symbol.

Evans-Pritchard divides Nuer sacrifice into *collective* and *individual* or personal sacrifice. The former accompany social activities such as birth, initiation, marriage, and mortuary rites. They are offered on behalf of social groups. They serve to confirm that a new relationship has been established, and are usually festive occasions. Individual sacrifices prevent danger and involve the idea of expiation. They are the most common Nuer sacrifices. They are offered to God to remove sin.

The actions of both collective and individual sacrifice are similar. Four stages are gone through in these sacrificial rituals: presentation, consecration, invocation, and immolation. Each stage has its own individual rites which accompany it.

For the Nuer, sacrifices are gifts offered to the deity. The gift must be a life or something which stands for life. A gift is a symbol and may have many meanings. The general idea surrounding personal sacrifice is substitution—the life of a beast being given in exchange for the life of a person. But Evans-Pritchard notes that it would be wrong to simply sum up these personal sacrifices under a single theory or term. Collective sacrifices do not contain the notion of substitution, but these sacrifices "are least important to an understanding of Nuer religion."[45]

Dinka

For the Dinka, the sacrifice of their animals, which are considered perfect victims, is the central religious act. Sacrifices, as well as prayers, are made to God, to spirits, and to clan divinities. In such acts these beings are "asked to come near to men and help them."[46] In sacrifice, human beings and divinity are brought into communion with one another. A relationship with divinity is maintained by the dedication and sacrifice of beasts to it.

---

42. Ibid., 197.
43. Ibid., 191.
44. Ibid., 249.
45. Ibid., 285.
46. Lienhardt, *Divinity and Experience*, 38.

Dinka sacrifices meet many needs: healing; giving people security; promoting fertility; providing purification; freeing one from an oath; and signifying the passing of one human state to another. Sacrifices are also offered for rain.

Some of the overt symbolism in Dinka sacrificial practices comes from the colors of the sacrificial animals. Sacrifices offered to the divinity, *Deng*, should be pied with bold markings of black and white. These colors are fitting in that they reflect thundery skies. A white stripe on a cow's belly is reminiscent of lightning. Other symbolic props include the shrine where the sacrifice takes place and the spear with which the animal is killed. Because the sacrifice brings vitality to the people, things associated with sacrifices are perceived as having inherent power.

A feature of all Dinka sacrifices is invocation directed to God or the lesser divinities. The phrases used in these rites are said repeatedly by the one officiating and the participants. The invocations contain the elements of statement, supplication, and honor rendered. All three elements are intermingled in the ritual of sacrifice.

The Dinka herd is a microcosm of the homestead, and thus of the larger community, and people say that "the people are put together as a bull is put together." When the beast is sacrificed its various parts are divided up among the various groups within the kinship system. When the whole animal is divided, it "corresponds to the unitary solidarity of human beings in their common relationship to the divine, while the divisions of the flesh correspond to the social differentiation of the persons and the groups taking part."[47] If the cow is representative of society, then the sacrifice of the cow reflects the communal nature of Dinka society. The sacrifice is made on behalf of the community. It is primarily a social event.

The sacrificial ox is made the object of the hostility of the group. Through their oral rites and killing, the Dinka act out a drama in which the weakening victim as it dies makes the community strong. The weaknesses of the people are transferred to the ox. His death is substituted for the death of the people. They become strong as a result of the sacrifice. The community is spared and strengthened. Sacrifice is a human drama of life and death for the Dinka. Lienhardt summarizes the sacrificial theory of the Dinka as he sees it:

> The sacrificial rite is first and foremost an act of victimization. A strong and active beast is rendered weak and passive so that the burden of human passion may be transferred to it. It suffers vicariously for those whom sacrifice is made, and men, thus symbolically freed from the agents which image their sufferings, and corporately associated with each other ... proclaim themselves creatures who [have] prevailed [and] received the gift of life.[48]

Summary of Nilotic Sacrificial Practices

The three authors point out several factors in their discussion of sacrifice among these Nilotic tribes: 1) cattle are a symbol, perhaps the dominant symbol, in pastoral societies; 2) when a pastoral tribe sacrifices a cow, it offers up its most prized possession; 3) the

47. Ibid., 234.
48. Ibid., 251.

sacrifices have a variety of functions; 4) no single explanation encompasses all of the varied meanings of the act for the people; and 5) the sacrifices fall into two categories—thanksgiving and purification.

CONCLUSION

As the discipline that studies all that a people do and say, anthropology has much to contribute to understanding people from other cultures. In this chapter we have tried to demonstrate the value of anthropological theory in understanding a cultural practice—sacrifice. We limited our focus to library materials. We have not discussed the other steps that would be needed to understand this practice in its cultural setting—such steps as learning the language, studying the social structure, participant observation over time, interviewing, developing a vocabulary concerning rituals and symbols, cataloging the props used in the practice, comparing related rituals, and developing theories.[49] All of these steps need to be undertaken so that one will have a better chance of understanding the practice as the people see it rather than from the perspective of the outside observer.

Any person who wants to interact with and understand those from another culture, whether on a short-term mission trip or as a long-term resident, should have some awareness of the discipline of anthropology. Paul wrote, "To the Jews, I became as a Jew, in order to win Jews. To those under the law I became as one under the law . . . To the weak I became weak, so that I might win the weak. I have become all things to all people that I might by all means save some."[50] That should be our attitude as well.

49. The author has attempted this sort of study regarding the sacrificial practices of the Maasai. See Priest, *Doing Theology with the Maasai.*

50. 1 Cor 9:20–22.

11

Rethinking Mission Strategy
to Lead Others to the Streams of Life

by Doug Priest

SHOULD A MISSIONARY RESIDE among the people they are trying to reach? I have a couple of missionary friends whose ministry focus is the urban poor—people who live in terrible slum conditions in huge cities. Both families are loved, accepted, and respected by the people among whom they minister. One family lives in Bangkok, Thailand. They have a wonderful ministry involving outreach through a community center, microfinance, sports ministry, and evangelism. This couple lives in the middle of the slum, in the same type of house their neighbors have. They have suffered from the same diseases that affect their neighbors and they are careful about fire since fire can wipe out an entire area of the slum in minutes.

The other family ministers in the slums of Nairobi, Kenya. Their holistic ministry includes establishing private schools since there are not nearly enough schools for the children. They minister to HIV/AIDS sufferers, run a microfinance program, train leaders, operate a health clinic, and advocate for community development, such as sanitation projects. This family lives away from the slums in a modern home in a part of town where other foreigners live.

Each of these families, if asked, would agree that their missionary strategy involves a decision about where they choose to live. Each would provide credible reasons for their choice. One family would speak of the importance of total identification and immersion into the culture of the slum. The other family would speak of the need to have a daily break from the horrible slum conditions and a place for their high school children who attend an international school to call home. They would also say that those living in the slums all want to escape the slums and would not be able to understand why someone who did not have to live in the slums would choose to do so. Neither missionary family would be critical of the other, even though their strategy regarding housing differs significantly.

WHAT IS MISSIONARY STRATEGY?

Missionary strategy refers to what missionaries do and how they do it. Missionary strategy is based on the belief that what missionaries do, and how they do it, can affect the outcome of their work. While firmly accepting God's providence, sovereignty, and the role of the Holy Spirit in conversion and enlightenment, missionaries believe that *how* they fulfill their calling has a bearing on *how* their message will be received.

Surprisingly, not all missionaries have focused on developing a strategy. Dayton and Fraser write, "All over the world we have visited missionaries who seem to be in the business of doing, rather than in the business of getting things done. They appear not to have any strategy as to why they are there and what God intends to do because they are there."[1] This is not as it should be since, as Christians, "we have a tremendous advantage in considering strategy. Because we have the word of God, a source of ultimate values and absolutes, we can most appropriately develop grand strategies . . . We can rest in the confidence that God's Will will be done. Our role is to cooperate with him in bringing his Kingdom to fruition."[2]

It is smart to understand strategy. A strategy is a means to accomplish an objective. It is the framework or approach that determines how a problem will be solved or a goal will be reached. Each year all professional American football teams have the ultimate objective of winning the Super Bowl. Each team has its own strategy of how to get to the Super Bowl. Some teams place less emphasis on winning their pre-season games than do other teams. In the pre-season these teams experiment with a variety of rookies in a variety of positions. Their regular starters play only a few series before being pulled from the game. Some teams emphasize passing rather than running, and they draft accordingly. Other teams believe that a strong defense will win the Super Bowl. All coaches have a roadmap to help them get to the Super Bowl. Like a map, there are a variety of routes that they can follow, and if they feel they are not moving in the direction needed to win, they reevaluate and make the necessary changes.

Since it is important to have a strategy, let us turn our attention to the components of a strategy, types of strategies, and levels of strategy.

Components of a Strategy

Strategic planning has long been a mainstay of secular and Christian institutions. In strategic planning, the plan is developed, the plan is executed, and then the plan is reviewed. The basic components of a strategic plan include gaining an understanding of the current situation. If the strategic planning is done for an organization, an internal analysis of the organization is coupled with an external analysis of factors where the plan is to be carried out. Another approach is the SWOT analysis where strengths, weaknesses, opportunities, and threats are analyzed.

1. Dayton and Fraser, *Planning Strategies for World Evangelization*, 20.
2. Ibid., 19.

Next the vision, the mission, and the values of the organization are determined. Objectives are written and action plans developed to accomplish the objectives. The plan is then implemented.

The important step of evaluation must be a key component in developing a strategy. Evaluation must be an ongoing process in addition to when the project comes to a close. Evaluation leads to additional planning, changing of objectives, and corrections and adjustments in continued implementation. Accountability to God, to the church, to supporters and prayer partners demands that evaluation take place. Avoiding accountability is avoiding stewardship.

The entire process of determining a missionary strategy involves much time in prayer and utter reliance upon the Holy Spirit. We listen for God's direction. We ask, "What is God doing in the world and how can we be involved?" We seek confirmation from the church. The outcomes of missionaries strategy are not a tribute to our human wisdom but to God's grace and for His glory. We plan our action relying on the Lord to determine our steps and outcomes. Engel and Dryness correctly state:

> In recognition that God alone must take the strategic initiative, the people of God will assume enlightened responsibility for stewardship that is ensured by strategic thinking, proper management of resources and ongoing evaluation. Strategic thinking is a valid endeavor for Christians. It is a corporate process that takes human initiative and rational processes seriously. Nevertheless, it is to be activated and empowered only through divine counsel. In other words, we respond to the call and leading of God. Rational thinking is infused with prayer and scriptural reflection.[3]

Types of Strategies

Dayton and Fraser speak of four types of strategies to achieve a goal.[4] The *Standard Solution Strategy* determines a way of doing things and the uses for that approach regardless of the situation. Use of a common media all over the world, such as *The Jesus Film*, is an example of a Standard Solution Strategy. The strategy assumes that all people will get the message regardless of where it is shown.

The *Being in the Way Strategy* believes that planning is unnecessary. People do not need to plan for the future because God will lead. The missionary who says, "I am called to Japan and I will wait upon the Lord to guide me in everything I do once I get there. I will be His pawn. There is no need for me to plan" is an example of this strategy.

The third strategy is termed the *Plan So Far Strategy*. In this strategy, the missionary does indeed do some initial planning to begin the work, but believes that God will do the rest. Youth groups who go to Tijuana, Mexico, to build a home for those in the slums believe that God will use them once they are there, in ways they cannot know ahead of time, so there is no need to plan on anything other than building the house.

Finally, there is the *Unique Solution Strategy*, which assumes that every situation is different and, therefore, every situation requires a special strategy. It is a pragmatic

---

3. Engel and Dyrness, *Changing the Mind of Missions*, 181.

4. Dayton and Fraser, *Planning Strategies*, 17–18.

approach that believes for every problem there is a unique solution because standard solutions will not work.

Strategies are unique; they are not repetitive. If the inoculation of children to prevent measles is the goal, in America that may be accomplished through making the inoculations a requirement to get into elementary school. In Ethiopia, this may take place by going from home to home to ensure that each child is vaccinated. In another country, children may be enticed into getting inoculated by the promise of a treat. In each case the goal is achieved, but the strategies are all unique.

Levels of Strategy

In addition to types of strategies, there are three levels of strategy: 1) the grand strategy; 2) the intermediate strategy; and 3) the short-range strategy.[5] These levels can be illustrated from the country of Ethiopia. Christian Missionary Fellowship (hereafter CMF) sent her first missionaries to Ethiopia in 1963. The *grand strategy* was to locate an area of the country that had not had a previous Christian presence and to establish a church-planting movement there.

The *intermediate strategy* included a host of key activities. Meetings were held with the international mission community in the capital city of Addis Ababa. This group informed CMF that one particular area of the country south of the Blue Nile River in Wollega Province among the Oromo people had no church presence, save for a few Ethiopian Orthodox Church buildings. Research trips by vehicle and mule were undertaken to this area; government officials were visited; the initial missionary family was joined by new missionary families who went to language school; there were many prayer meetings; official permission was secured; supplies were purchased and trucked out to the area. Residence was established in 1965.

Upon arrival to the remote area, the missionary constructed a house for his family, established an elementary school and a clinic as requested by the government and made as a condition for residence in the area. An airstrip was cut out of the forest so that there could be contact during the rainy season when the roads were not passable.

The initial *short-range strategy* involved hiring Ethiopian Christians to teach at the elementary school. These teachers would share their faith as appropriate with the children in the community. On evenings and weekends, the teachers and the missionary would visit villages to get acquainted with the parents of the students and to begin sharing the gospel.

The newer missionaries followed the same short-term strategy in other locations in the region—one thirty miles away from the first location, another fifty miles away. As people heard the gospel and wanted to become Christians, churches were established, even in the face of persecution.

Once churches had been established, the short-term strategy changed to include an emphasis on training leaders. Missionaries began to specialize in leadership development. Materials were produced and courses for leaders were established.

5. Ibid., 313.

By 1977, there were thousands of Oromo Christians and many churches had been established. At that time a Communist takeover of the country occurred and Ethiopia became a Marxist nation. The grand strategy of establishing a church planting movement among the Oromo did not change, but the short-range strategy involving the missionaries had to once again change. To encourage the churches and to foster evangelistic efforts, contextual Christian radio programs were produced from another country for the next decade. Hundreds of thousands of Oromo listened to *The Joy Program*.

Politics once again changed and CMF missionaries once again returned to live with the Oromo. The membership of the churches had increased, there were seasoned leaders, and so the short-range strategy now became one of serving and assisting the national church.

In summary, the components of a strategy include developing, executing, and evaluating a plan to determine success. The process is based upon the vision, mission, and values of the organization, and in Christian organizations, all planning is bathed in prayer, seeking the guidance of the Spirit throughout the process. Strategic plans have a temporal dimension. We have long-range objectives, mid-range objectives, and short-range objectives. Missionary strategies have both a general and a specific focus.

We will now examine some specific well-known missionary strategies, using as our data base case studies from Tanzania, Indonesia, and Kenya, areas where I have been personally involved in ministry and the development of missionary strategy.

THE INCARNATIONAL STRATEGY

My family went to Africa as missionaries in 1978. I was a firm believer in the homogeneous unit principle, which indicated that people like to become Christians without having to cross barriers, whether cultural, racial, economic, class, or caste.[6] We were going to work with the Maasai, a semi-nomadic tribe living in East Africa. Our focus was the Maasai, with little concern for other tribal groups. Our mission team knew the importance of learning the Maasai language, and we were exemplary in this task. Two of our team had college degrees in anthropology, and most of us had taken graduate courses in that discipline. We studied the Maasai culture in depth. Some of us kept copious notes about traditional Maasai culture and engaged in credible anthropological research, which was later published. We chose to live in or next to Maasai villages rather than in the cities. Our goal was to know the Maasai inside and out—at least the Maasai that lived away from the towns and cities.

The Maasai of Kenya in those days were divided between the majority who chose to live in the traditional villages and those who had been educated in Kenyan schools and lived in the urban centers of Kenya. My bias was definitely with the traditional or rural Maasai. I am ashamed to admit that I was suspicious of the educated Maasai for abandoning their culture. Though academically I knew full well the dangers of romanticizing a people, I was guilty of just that. The educated Maasai wore Western clothes, spoke in Swahili rather than Maasai, and some even looked down on their traditional brothers and

6. McGavran, *Understanding Church Growth*, 223.

sisters. I remember once when an educated Maasai pastor refused to drink a cup of tea in a Maasai village because a fly had landed on his cup. My disgust at such an insult was deep, and confirmed for me that we missionaries were right in our appeal to the traditional Maasai. When another educated Maasai once asked me why I so wanted to "keep the Maasai in their backward state," I bristled and could not even comprehend how such a question could be asked.

Against this backdrop, our family went to Tanzania in 1984 to initiate a work with a Maasai-speaking group there.[7] Using our mission's Kenya work as our model, we sought to locate out in "the bush" where the Maasai speakers were rather than in town where the rest of the missionaries lived. After all, we already spoke Maasai.

When Tanzania became an independent nation in the 1960s, she chose a different path than Kenya. In Kenya the national language was English, which was taught in all the schools. It was easy to get around in Kenya knowing only English. When we were with the Maasai in Kenya (who did not speak English), we spoke to them in Maasai. And since we were not working with other groups, we reasoned that it really did not matter that we did not know Swahili.

Tanzania chose to make Swahili the national language. The majority of the people in the country spoke Swahili rather than English. With the Maasai this presented no problem—we just talked to them in Maasai. However, we were not able to converse with most of the people of Tanzania. Years later I realized that our unwillingness to learn anything but the barest minimum of Swahili was an affront to the Tanzanians who were proud that they spoke "pure Swahili," rather than the "illegitimate form" which was spoken in Kenya.

When new missionaries came to Tanzania to join us, following our Kenya example, they began to learn the Maasai language. Now not only did I, the experienced missionary, not speak Swahili, I encouraged my fellow missionaries to follow my lead rather than the example of other missionaries in Tanzania who opted to begin with Swahili.

We had another strategic value which separated us from many missionaries living in East Africa. Our desire was not to build church buildings until we had a congregation of believers to help in the task with their labor and with their financial backing. Other missions often constructed church buildings in an area when there were just a handful of believers. The missionaries usually paid for the entire building. We felt such an approach was a denial of a major tenet of the "indigenous theory"—self support.

While there were other factors involved, our correct mission strategy in Tanzania landed us in hot water. To the local government officials we were just too unbelievable. "Do not missionaries live in town? Yet you live in this miserable place." (And it was not an attractive place, especially during the rainy season when we would be stuck for weeks on end due to impassable mud). "Do not other missionaries learn Swahili? Yet you do not know Swahili even though it is our national language. You even insult us by speaking in Maasai to these people in front of us, and we do not know what you are saying." (Since these conversations were in English, and the Maasai present did not speak English, I in-

---

7. The Maasai speak the Maa language, as do the Baraguyu of Tanzania, groups with whom the author lived.

terpreted for them). "Do not other missionaries build churches? Where is your church? Why do you choose this backward Maasai people to work with rather than a more advanced group? Our conclusion is that you are not missionaries. You are surely here for some other reason."

Our carefully crafted missiology, honed in seminary and practiced with admirable results in Kenya, did not work in Tanzania. Under government pressure, we all left Tanzania wondering where we had gone wrong. We had followed the textbooks to the best of our abilities. Who could have guessed that following the LAMP[8] method of language learning and other incarnational approaches would get us into trouble?

Proven missionary strategy is only as good as where God last honored it. It is incorrect to assume that missionary principles which work in one area will automatically work in another. Not only do we need contextual theologies,[9] we also need contextual strategies.

THE INDIGENOUS THEORY STRATEGY

Let us now travel to Indonesia where missionaries from CMF arrived in 1979. They went as partners with a group of missionaries from the same church background in America. Some of the missionaries went to Indonesia after mission experience in Ethiopia. This is important to note, because the work in Ethiopia was with rural farmers who all spoke the Oromo language.

Indonesia in the 1970s was primarily an agricultural country. Four-fifths of her huge population lived in rural villages. It was among these villagers that a rapid turning to the Gospel had taken place between 1965 and 1971. According to Willis, during that time two million Javanese were baptized.[10]

The missionaries already at work on the island of Java were pursuing a strategy common to most other missionaries in Java at that time. They lived in the cities and itinerated to the nearby villages. The target group was almost exclusively the receptive Javanese farmers. Such a strategy fit in very well with the Ethiopian-experienced missionaries who had practiced much of the same thing before coming to Indonesia. These missionaries learned the Javanese language as well as Bahasa Indonesian, the national language. Their approach was contextual—they identified with the villages as much as possible. Some of the missionaries moved out to the villages and became villagers themselves in their attempts to evangelize and plant churches.

While I cannot vouch for this supposition, I imagine that many of the missionaries of Java during the late 1970s were helped in forming their mission strategy by reading a contemporary book by Avery Willis.[11] The author lists various methodologies that contributed to the amazing growth of the church in Indonesia. Factors he stressed included:

8. The LAMP method of language learning encourages learning language as a child does, conversationally rather than in a classroom. See Brewster and Brewster, *Language Acquisition*.

9. The term "contextual theology" derives from the notion that a people, drawing upon the Bible and the involvement of the Holy Spirit as well as church history, should develop their own theology rather than adopting it wholesale from others.

10. Willis, *Indonesian Revival*, 1977, xv.

11. Ibid.

acculturation that allowed Christians to remain Javanese; emphasis on responsive groups; nurturing of people movements; and planting of hundreds of new congregations. He then went on to list methods that hindered growth: neglect of Javanese culture; restriction of spontaneous expansion; lack in training local leadership; and miscalculation of opportunities.

When it came to suggestions for the future work on the island of Java, Willis noted:

> The worldwide trend toward urbanization is influencing the direction Indonesian society is moving. Yet, over 80 percent of Indonesia's people still live in rural areas, and the majority will probably continue to live there for the remainder of this century. Therefore, the Javanese churches cannot allow their emphasis to center only in urban areas. They must continue to go to rural areas, where the Javanese people live in greatest numbers, and where they are most responsive.[12]

I became CMF's Asia Coordinator in 1989, and on my first trip to Indonesia, I saw many of the things that Willis was talking about. I recall being taken for a ride up to a rural mountain area and told to look at all of the villages—dozens of them—and not a one with a church. Having lived in Ethiopia, Kenya, and Tanzania in rural areas, I was quick to agree that this is where we ought to concentrate our missionary efforts.

But as I began to visit Indonesia more often, as I read and studied and began to ask questions, I came to a different conclusion. I felt that our missionaries, like many of the other missionaries of Indonesia of the 1970s, had two prominent values that guided their mission strategy. One was the value of concentrating on the rural villages, and the second was to uphold the indigenous theory, with its goal of establishing self-supporting, self-governing, and self-propagating churches, termed the "three-selves."

The indigenous theory with these "three-selves" goes back to mission executives Henry Venn and Rufus Anderson, who proposed the theory 150 years ago. Venn was the general secretary of the Church Missionary Society based in London, and Anderson was the foreign secretary of the American Board of Commissioners of Foreign Missions. Remember that the England and America of the mid-19th century were vastly different places than those countries are today. The rest of the world where this theory was to be carried out was also a much different place than it is today.

In the 1990s (and probably even in the 1970s) these two strategic values of starting indigenous churches and doing so among the rural Javanese were basically mutually exclusive. One cannot start self-supporting, self-governing, and self-propagating churches in the villages of Java. Oh, yes, churches could be started in the villages—we had started some twenty-five—but not a one was self-supporting.

With the ever-increasing disparity between the "haves" and the "have-nots," I question whether there can be self-supporting churches in most of the developing world. What developing nation currently gets by on its own without securing loans from the International Monetary Fund, World Bank, or donor nations? If governments with access to all the resources of the entire nation must have outside assistance, why should we Westerners expect that the churches in such countries can (or worse, *must*) be self-

---

12. Ibid., 205.

supporting? Is that not highly paternalistic? It is not surprising that primarily the "haves" have promoted the "three-selves" model, not the "have-nots."

If churches in the developing nations cannot be self-supporting in terms of finances, should they be self-governing? Christian donors want to be able to make some suggestions in how the funds are used. Is not *partnership* a better strategy than the old *indigenous theory* model? What about self-propagating? Many churches in the developing world plant churches. But there are also many churches that need some financial assistance as they attempt to carry out the evangelistic mandate. Partnership is a better alternative. This is not to say that there should be no effort to plant churches among the rural Javanese. Not at all. But in carrying out such a plan, we should not hold tenaciously to the Western standards of self-support, self-government, and self-propagation.

It is possible to have churches in the developing world that are indigenous churches in the sense of the "three-selves." This I found to be true in Indonesia. But these churches were not rural churches made up of peasant farmers. Rather, they were urban churches, largely made up of members of the middle-class. Many of these churches have never received funds from others. They have paid their own way from the start. Many of them have never had a foreign missionary working with them, save for an outsider being asked to offer the occasional seminar. These churches are self-governing. They have rapidly planted daughter churches throughout Indonesia, including the rural areas.

Avery Willis could not foresee back in the 1970s the coming changes that make his strategic suggestions outdated today. In the last thirty years in Indonesia there has been a tremendous move toward urbanization. People are flocking to Indonesia's cities. Students who finish their schooling are reluctant to return to village life. Opportunities do not abound there. They prefer life in the city. Some Indonesians have gone so far as to say that the villages today are the homes of only the very young and the very old. A smaller percentage of the population tills the soil each year. Access to these rural villages has been severely restricted. Westerners must be invited to come into the villages. Such invitations are hard to come by. Without an official invitation, they are not welcome.

Indonesia has embarked on a process of Islamization that curtails missionary freedom much more than in the past. Each year there are fewer missionaries in Indonesia, hence, there is less opportunity for concentrating on the rural Javanese as Willis espoused.

Modernization is rapidly displacing traditional Javanese culture in Indonesia. The winds of change are blowing, and contextual churches in Java today are not defined by the use of the Javanese language, Javanese melodies, and Javanese instruments. Contextual churches in the Indonesian cities look quite a lot like churches in cities in many other parts of the world. I was amazed as I traveled from city to city in Asia, sat in Sunday services and heard the same choruses over and over again, each time in yet another language. But the song was the same, it was Western, and the instruments that accompanied the song used the same forms of amplification.

THE CHE STRATEGY

Community Health Evangelism (CHE) began as a strategy to assist communities in a comprehensive health program in the name of Christ. Overall health has spiritual, psychological, social, and physical dimensions, and CHE is designed to address each of these dimensions. The approach is related theoretically to Asset Based Community Development (ABCD), a program developed at Northwestern University in Evanston, Illinois. The website for the ABCD Institute at the university notes that this strategy is:

> at the center of a large and growing movement that considers local assets as the primary building blocks of sustainable community development. Building on the skills of local residents, the power of local associations, and the supporting functions of local institutions, asset-based community development draws upon existing community strengths to build stronger, more sustainable communities for the future.[13]

CHE differs from the more common macro-approaches to poverty, such as the programs initiated by the World Bank, the International Monetary Fund, and most government programs. These approaches are "top-down," while CHE and ABCD are grassroots "bottom-up" programs that originate with the community members themselves. History has shown that, in general, top-down approaches have failed and have not proven to be sustainable.[14]

CHE concentrates on meeting priority needs keenly felt by the community through simple, sustainable community projects. Good health is broadly defined and can involve projects in health education, agriculture, literacy, sanitation, nutrition, immunization, clean water, maternal care, employment, medical treatment, care for babies, and prevention of disease. The possibility for projects, especially in areas of poverty, is endless, and all projects are undertaken in the name of Christ.

The CHE strategy involves finding a leader in a community and asking if he or she is interested in receiving training to help the community to develop. If the leader agrees, the leader is asked to find other leaders in the community and invite them to come for a period of training. The training covers the basics of the CHE development philosophy and how to initiate a program. Evangelism is emphasized. The leaders discuss their community, noting its problems and noting the assets that the community has available to them locally. After the training, a CHE committee is formed.

The committee is encouraged to select a seed-project that they can undertake on their own, one which has a good chance of success. The building of a hospital would not be a good seed project if the community was in an urban slum. The community would not have the funds to construct the hospital or have the means to keep it running without outside resources. But a slum community could undertake a seed-project like draining stagnant water pools as a means of preventing the hatching of mosquitoes. In so doing, the community could reduce the incidence of malaria.

13. http://www.abcdinstitute.org/.

14. The top-down approach is highlighted by Sachs, 2005, and is to be contrasted by the grass-roots approach of Easterly, 2006.

As the committee works together on the seed-project, and as the project succeeds, the community begins to see that it can solve its own problems, that it has assets to achieve sustainable development. Other projects are initiated, based upon the community's expressed needs. More and more projects are undertaken, and as success is achieved and the community gains confidence, outsiders such as churches and mission agencies can be encouraged to participate and partner with the community in providing needed resources. Since CHE is a Christian approach to community development, the spiritual component is emphasized, and many become believers. When other communities see these positive changes, they want the same thing to take place in their community, so the cycle is repeated, community after community. Empowerment and sustainability are key features of the CHE strategy. It is important to note that it is not the foreign missionary or short-term visitor who determines which CHE projects should be undertaken and which needs should be met, a common mistake of many missionary and church mission strategies.

Kangemi is the name of a slum in Nairobi, Kenya. A CHE program was initiated in the slum, and after the initial period of training, the group was encouraged to assess the issues facing them as a community. They were then asked to select one of the problems as a seed-project.[15]

Running through the slum was a small river, and the nearest bridge to cross from one side of the slum to another was a mile away. During the dry season the river was easy to cross from one side to the other via a log. But in the rainy season, the river became a torrent. The log became slippery due to the mud and the rain, and every year children fell off the log and drowned. The CHE group determined that they would build a suitable bridge to cross the river. Assignments were made. Some on the committee were sent to scour the slum for lumber. Some were sent to the officials to secure permission to build the bridge. Others were sent to find nails and tools. Various tribes living in the slums—at times antagonistic toward one another—saw the need and came together for a common purpose. The materials were assembled, a day was selected, and the construction began.

Soon the bridge over the river was completed. Though not a strong bridge, a small vehicle was able to drive across the bridge. The community had come together to mutually tackle what they all saw was a problem. They celebrated their success with singing, dancing, and praying. When the government saw the initiative that the community had undertaken, they came into the slum and constructed a secure bridge using steel and concrete.

We have highlighted three commonly used missionary strategies: 1) the incarnational strategy of developing close ties with a specific people group; 2) the indigenous "three-selves" strategy in a rural setting; and 3) the CHE strategy among the urban poor. Each of these strategies differs from the others, and we have tried to show how successful strategies must fit the local context, noting how the foisting of one strategy into a different context often causes problems. We now turn to an important, but often unrealized, disclaimer.

15. This incident is recounted in Priest, *Get Your Hands Dirty*, 128–30.

STRATEGY DOES NOT ENSURE SUCCESS

A key assumption behind the formulation of missionary strategy is that this effort will have some bearing on the success of the missionary endeavor. Missionary strategy could lead one to assume that with the correct strategy the kingdom will advance. If ingdom advancement does not occur, it would seem, then there was an error in the strategy planning process—mistakes were made that can be corrected so that the desired growth will take place. Samuel Escobar labels this sort of thinking as "managerial missiology."[16] He notes that a pragmatic approach to missions "demands a closed view of the world, in which the tough questions cannot be asked because they cannot be reduced to a linear management-by-objectives process." Escobar goes on to add that such an approach "has no theological or pastoral resources to cope with the suffering and persecution involved many times in mission, because it is geared to provide methodologies for a guaranteed success."[17]

There is a dilemma in missionary strategy that we must acknowledge. Failure to plan is a plan for failure. None of us desires failure in our mission efforts. However, "the best laid plans of mice and men often go awry." (Steinbeck) While it is correct to note that we can make strategic decisions that will result in achieving the desired outcomes, it is equally correct that strategy formulation does not take into account some spiritual factors over which we have little control. The best strategy, determined only after careful study of the local context may not lead to that for which we hope. All the more reason to bathe our efforts in strategy formulation in humility and prayer.

A MISSIONARY STRATEGY FOR TODAY

Missionary strategies need to be thoughtfully considered and regularly evaluated. Those strategies God blesses in one setting may be a hindrance in another. While we may agree on the desired outcomes—making disciples, feeding the hungry, praying without ceasing, caring for widows and orphans, etc.—we need not agree on the methods used to achieve these ends. There are no universal missionary strategies. In determining what to do, and how to do it, missionaries would do well to consider these critical questions. Stewardship demands no less.

- Does the proposed strategy enhance localized efforts and initiatives that infiltrate all segments of society?

- Will local churches in both the sending country and the field of ministry assume their central role in the world mission of Jesus Christ?

- Does the envisioned strategy encompass the full Gospel of the Kingdom in which there is no dichotomy between evangelism and social transformation?

- Is the strategy based on the totality of the great commission, so that disciples are taught and motivated to follow all that Christ modeled and proclaimed?

16. Escobar, "Evangelical Missiology," 109.
17. Ibid., 110.

- Is the strategy grounded in prayer and fasting, seeking the will of God as he reveals where he wants us to join him in his work in the world?

- Is proper stewardship being demonstrated by strategic thinking undertaken in a commitment to be true co-laborers with God?

- Does the initiative foster collaboration and partnership?[18]

In the following chapters you will have an opportunity to read about mission efforts in many cultural settings. Different strategies for advancing the kingdom of God—church planting, Bible translation, community transformation, incarnational evangelism in the inner city—will be highlighted. As you read, keep these seven critical questions in mind.

18. Engel and Dyrness, *Changing the Mind*, 182–3.

12

Only the Street Knows Your Name

by Kendi Howells Douglas

INTRODUCTION

STANDING ON THE ROOF of a tall building top of the dormitory belonging to G.O. Ministries in Santiago, Dominican Republic, I was waiting for my students to wake up and assemble for breakfast. As I drank my coffee and looked over the barrio and waited, I watched as Isaias Gabriel—the graduate with whom we were working—walked from his house about a half mile away through the five or six streets to the dorm where he would join us for breakfast. I watched as he stopped over six times and stood in various doorways with people, some of whom were hung-over from the night before, or exhausted from selling themselves for enough money to feed their children, or wired from big drug deals that had gone down. It didn't matter. He stopped and chatted with them, he joked and listened and shared a glimpse of hope, a smile, a hug, a handshake, or a cup of coffee and invited them to church, to a street baseball game, or to a rap concert he was planning. I smiled and wished I would have recorded that walk to show my urban ministry class. I would have entitled it, "This is how the work of transforming lives gets done in the inner city: one relationship at a time."

But make no mistake—this is tough, messy, disappointing, slow, and hard work. It is not to be idealized romantically, and it is dangerous and taxing. It is not for everyone. Isaias grew up in that neighborhood and knows everyone. They trust him and he knows the ins and outs of how that particular city works. He knows the social stratification and the intricacies of the gangs and drug and crime rings. This is not something an outsider can look at, package and teach in a formulaic way to everyone hoping to work in the inner city. But it is in observing and listening to practitioners of inner city mission presence today that I have begun to see that neat programs and tidy strategies built out of idealizations of hope for the city are killing the work in inner cities; creating stress when the reality of the city doesn't live up to the expectations, and leading to early burnout and abandonment. Bonhoeffer said aptly, though not specifically addressing the inner city, "Those who love their dream of a Christian community more than the Christian community itself become destroyers of that Christian community even though their personal intentions may be ever so honest, earnest, and sacrificial."[1] And that certainly seems to be the case today in inner cities around the world as there are many who love the idea of "inner city" programs. And yet something isn't working. This chapter is an attempt to recount the history of the inner city dilemma as far as social and ecclesiastical involvement is concerned, and an attempt to learn general attitudes from people who currently live and work there in order to understand more about our hope for the future of Christian presence in inner cities.

The following chapter discusses the growing field of Urban Mission Studies and Strategies as the world becomes more and more urban and is, as Greenway and Monsma have put it, "Missions' New Frontier."[2] Why then, a separate chapter on inner city missions? The "inner city" differs from the general category of "urban" in that generally urban is defined, (though there are many definitions) as comprising one or more central places and the adjacent densely surrounding territory that together have a minimum of 50,000 people.[3] In addition "urban" connotes the idea of a wide range of socio-economic levels and ethnicities represented.

Inner city specifically indicates an older part of a city, densely populated and usually deteriorating, inhabited mainly by poor (often minority) groups and specialized populations that fall through the urban cracks, including homeless, drug addicts, mentally ill, prostitutes and gang members. (See Fig. 1 below.)[4] Various terms other than inner city are more familiar to those outside of the U.S., including slums, favelas, shanty towns, barrios, and ghettos. While some of the conditions described in this chapter pertaining to inner cities may mirror the conditions present in slums etc. . . . there are obvious differences in building structures, plumbing, protection, sewage treatment, government aid, access to fresh water, electricity, and the land itself. This chapter's focus is on (mostly Western) inner cities, and in no way is an attempt to address the worldwide growing slum issues.

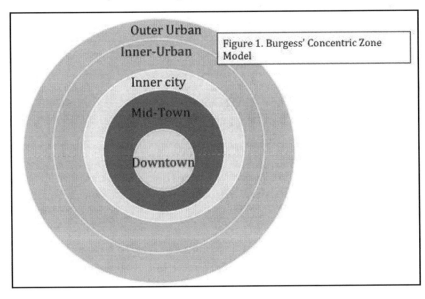

Outer Urban

Inner-Urban

Figure 1. Burgess' Concentric Zone Model

Inner city

Mid-Town

Downtown

---

1. Bonhoeffer, *Life Together*, 36.

2. Greenway and Monsma, *Cities: Missions' New Frontier*, xi.

3. United States Government, Census Bureau.

4. Burgess, *Growth of the City*, 85.

CURRENT STATE OF INNER CITIES AND HOW WE GOT HERE

As we have defined inner city and have shown its location in most city models, we now need to address how and why the inner city has come to inherit most problems of urban areas and, also, historically what has been the typical Christian response to such issues. In order to think about the future we must visit the past and understand how we got here. A bit of history is needed, and then we will examine the current issues continuing to plague specifically this central area of most U.S. cities. We will look to an age-old "motif" of mission that is evidenced both in Scripture and from people working in these areas from all over the world.

Major urbanization patterns in the United States, including the substantial migration to the suburbs following WWII are important to understand the current situation. The U.S. population in general was overwhelmingly rural for many years, as Table 1 indicates.[5]

Year	Percent	Year	Percent
1800	6.1	1910	45.7
1810	7.3	1920	51.2
1820	7.2	1930	56.2
1830	8.8	1940	56.5
1840	10.8	1950	59.0
1850	15.3	1960	69.9
1860	19.8	1970	73.5
1870	25.7	1980	73.7
1880	28.2	1990	73.9
1900	39.7	2010	79.21

Table 1: Urban Population in U.S. Cities

Cities in colonial America were simple in their intent: to have a small village center that could accommodate all of the area farmers for an occasional meeting, commerce, and security.[6] Many churches were pleased to meet those simple needs, and thus the model for many years in the early history of the United States reflected this.

5. United States Census, 2010 TABLE 1: Percent of Urban Population, United States, 180 010.

6. Conn, *American City and the Evangelical Church*, 17.

THE MOVE FROM RURAL TO URBAN AMERICA

With the mechanization of agriculture, much more land could be tilled and cared for by one person. With urban industrialization, people began to migrate to the cities for work, and millions more migrated to America from other countries. Conn and Ortiz refer to this as "The Third Great Wave: The Industrial City."[7] They note that transportation technology expanded to meet demands, and the cities, increasingly serviced by the railroads, exploded in growth. "In the one hundred years between 1790 and 1890, the total U.S. population grew sixteen-fold, but urban population increased 139 times."[8] The "first churches" and city churches generally grew. Many "first churches" began to feel comfortable in their prominent downtown positions, since the downtown areas of the country were the hub of activity and economic flurry at this time. Jones and Wilson document the role of the "first churches" in *What's Ahead for Old First Church*:

> "In some places First Church was also used for community concerts because it had the only auditorium large enough to hold them. A counseling ministry has also been a tradition at Old First … The traditional role of Old First can be described by the terms *quality, prestige*, and *leadership*. Quality was found in the church program, in worship services, and in the facilities. Prestige came from being associated with a large, strong institution, some of whose members held important positions in the community. Such an institution is looked to for leadership in both denominational and civic affairs."[9]

Economic boom times generally did not last, and America suffered depressions in 1873 and 1893. With the great labor strife in 1877 conditions worsened. In the cities, water and sewer systems were not able to handle the overcrowded conditions. In many urban neighborhoods, poverty was immense, exacerbated by air and water pollution. Norris Magnuson comments,

> During the decades following the Civil War the United States rapidly shifted from rural and agricultural social and economic order to urban-industrial status. Other factors, like the increasing tide of city-bound immigration from southern and eastern Europe, intensified the poverty and attendant miseries spawned by this transition. A small but increasing number of American Protestants responded to the plight of the urban poor with what came to be known as the social gospel, and Roman Catholicism, generally closer to immigrant and laboring classes similarly adjusted its emphasis.[10]

The impact of these conditions then eventually led to the formation of many Christian agencies, which focused on the devastating conditions and the unequal distribution of the nation's wealth. Sydney Ahlstrom describes four such types of agencies:

> "There were four very diverse but yet distinctly innovative forms of urban concern that became important during the postwar period though they all had earlier

7. Conn and Ortiz, *Urban Ministry*, 48.

8. Ibid., 50.

9. Jones and Wilson, *What's Ahead For Old First Church?*, 3–4. (Emphasis theirs.)

10. Magnuson, *Salvation in the Slums*, 1.

origins. The best known of these is the Social Gospel movement. The other three are more clearly related to problems of evangelism. Least heralded were the slum-oriented efforts of the Salvation Army, its offshoot, the Volunteers of America, and a diverse group of rescue missions, many of which were founded by Holiness and Pentecostal sects. Far more extraordinary in their special adaptation to city needs were the Young Men's and Women's Christian Associations."[11]

Many books outlining these problems began to make their way into the hands of Protestant readers, and church leaders sought solutions. *Our Country,* written by Josiah Strong in 1885, was one of many books which alerted Christians to their responsibilities to the social problems and conditions.[12]

Christian leaders concerned with these issues began to organize and to publish their ideas and convictions. Donald Gorrell writes, "Beneath the ebb and flow of these tides of political and spiritual unrest ran an undercurrent that provided stability and continuity for social Christianity during this period. The long evolution of social-gospel thought provided ballast during unsettling storms, and its presence became evident in new statements of basic concepts by leaders of the movement."[13]

RISE OF THE SOCIAL GOSPEL

This activism gave birth to the Social Gospel movement which served to renew city churches' interest and participation in dealing with the crisis at hand. Robert Handy states that the Social Gospel movement, though complex and dynamic, can be summarized in these points:

- A conviction that the social principles of the historical Jesus could serve as reliable guides for both the individual and social life of any age.

- Central to Christ's teachings was a stress on the immanence of God, the goodness and worth of human beings, and the coming of the kingdom of God on earth.

- At the very heart of the gospel was the message of the kingdom, and the church was seen as having the key to the kingdom.

- Through the efforts of people of good will the kingdom of God would soon become a reality, bringing with it social harmony and eliminating social injustices.[14]

The background and impact of the Social Gospel movement are important to this study because in many ways they marked the division of liberal Christianity (stereotyped as being involved in city work) and conservative Christianity (stereotyped as not being involved in cities although many were) that to some extent still exists today. This seems to have been and continues to be one of the deterring factors as to why many churches have not been active in inner city work. According to Ahlstrom, "The Social Gospel must be understood as a transi-

---

11. Ahlstrom, *Religious History of the American People,* 742.

12. Brauer, *Westminster Dictionary of Church History,* 776.

13. Gorrell, *Age of Social Responsibility,* 124.

14. Handy, *Social Gospel in America 1870—1920,* 10.

tory phase of Christian social thought. It was a sub-movement within religious liberalism, with a certain view of man [sic] and history governing its rationale."[15]

The Social Gospel movement came to public attention about 1890 with the founding of several journals and periodicals which called the churches to social action. In fact the term "Social Gospel" comes from the title of one such publication, the periodical *The Social Gospel* which was begun by the Christian Commonwealth Colony in 1897. Prior to that some Christians concerned with social issues were called Christian Socialists or referred to as members of the Social Christianity Movement.[16]

By the early 1900s the influence of the Social Gospel Movement was evident in all major U.S. denominations. Kenneth Bailey in his study of twentieth century Protestantism wrote, "Hence between the turn of the century and World War I, the Protestant groups underwent significant changes in programs and outlook. Absorbed at the turn of the century in evangelism and little mindful of social needs beyond blue laws and prohibition, the churches emerged during the next fifteen years as advocates of social justice, proclaiming the Christian obligation to fashion Christ's kingdom on earth."[17]

The Social Gospel movement developed effective interdenominational agencies, the most influential of which was the Federal Council of Churches, organized in 1908. Two of the most prominent and influential leaders were Walter Rauschenbusch (1861–1918) and Washington Gladden (1836-1918), whose names would become inextricably tied with the Social Gospel movement.

The call for renewal or for the restoration of the way things were intended to be in the early church, as evidenced in the thought and writing of the leaders of the Social Gospel movement, opened the eyes of many. Compassionate Christians involved in the Social Gospel movement chose to believe that emphasis only on the future aspect of the kingdom of God fell short of its full understanding, responsibility and glory, then worked within their churches to change that. One of the first documents drafted by the "Brotherhood of the Kingdom" stated: "The Spirit of God is moving men [sic] in our generation toward a better understanding of the idea of the kingdom of God on Earth. Obeying the thought of our Master, and trusting in the power and guidance of the Spirit, we form ourselves into a Brotherhood of the Kingdom, in order to re-establish this idea in the thought of the church, and to assist in its practical realization in the world."[18]

The history of the Social Gospel movement is important to this study for several reasons. It is instructive to see what Christians concerned with urban issues did to change the conditions and future of cities. The impact of the movement is still felt today, as it is credited with having contributed in part to the civil rights movement, the development of the World Council of Churches, antiwar movements, and Evangelicals for Social Action. "Though a minority movement, the Social Gospel was very influential. It has been called America's leading contribution to Christian thought."[19] It is important to know what the

---

15. Ahlstrom, *Religious History of the American People*, 786.

16. Brauer, *Westminster Dictionary of Church History*, 777.

17. Bailey, *Southern White Protestantism in the Twentieth Century*, 17.

18. White and Hopkins, *Social Gospel*, 73.

19. Brauer, *Westminster Dictionary of Church History*, 777.

conservative or fundamentalist reaction to this movement was in order to understand some of the apparent hesitation churches still have today in participating in alleviating some of the negative social issues that affect the city.

FROM THE CITY TO THE SUBURBS: 1945-2000

Following World War II, the suburbs grew rapidly as thousands of veterans returned from war, and a series of technological advances in transportation enabled urban dwellers to commute longer distances than was previously practical. This in turn influenced the Federal Housing Administration to make mass housing outside of the cities affordable as never before. The National Defense Highways Act of 1950 ensured easy access to jobs and shopping in the city and homes in the suburbs.[20] Conn and Ortiz note the exodus from city to suburb: "Repelled by urban growth and decay associated with industrialization, the wealthy upper classes were the first to follow the ideology 'we keep to ourselves' out to the commuting suburbs. By the beginning of the twentieth century, with the expansion of public transportation, those with white-collar positions could begin to follow the trolley tracks through urban fragmentation to the suburban dream. With the help of Henry Ford and the private automobile, the working classes would eventually follow also."[21]

Initially city churches did not feel much of an impact, as members who had moved to the new suburbs continued to drive to church. However, as Robert Fishman observes, "It did not take long for suburbia to reshape the whole modern metropolis. Suburbia succeeded too well. It became what even the greatest advocates of suburban growth never desired—a new form of city."[22] The shopping mall was introduced and many businesses, including banks, gas stations, hospitals, and restaurants, moved to suburban locations in order to enjoy the steady stream of business. People now could live in affordable housing outside of the city and do all of their shopping, banking, fueling, and everything else they needed to do without entering the city at all, except for big sporting and cultural events.

It didn't take long for churches to follow the trend. According to Harvie Conn,

> By the middle of the 1920s more than 15 million persons were residing in the fringe neighborhoods of the city. Slowed down by a depression and a world war, the great push continued after 1945. By 1955, approximately 1,200,000 Americans were moving to the suburbs annually. And scholars were predicting that 85 percent of city growth during the 1960s and 1970s would be suburban. The churches followed, giving primary attention to their suburban expansion. The amount spent on new churches (i.e., church buildings) rose steadily, the bulk of it concentrated on the suburbs. Between 1946 and 1960, money spent on church building moved from $76 million to $1 billion, 1.6 billion.[23]

The "First Churches" that chose to remain in the city, which for so long had held prominent positions downtown, were unprepared for the demographic transformation

---

20. Bakke, *Urban Christian*, 29.

21. Conn and Ortiz, *Urban Ministry*, 70.

22. Fishman, *Bourgeois Utopias*, xi.

23. Conn, *The American City and the Evangelical Church*, 97.

that occurred as thousands of African Americans arrived (especially in northern cities) seeking economic opportunity during what historians call the Second Great Migration.[24] Heather Thompson states: "Clearly the Second Great Migration had completely upset the social and political status quo of the urban North and, as a result, cities like Detroit were racially polarized and crisis-ridden."[25]

Members of the churches were moving in large numbers out to the suburbs, often leaving behind large homes. During the ten-year period 1950-1960, central city populations in the largest 25 Standard Metropolitan Statistical Areas increased by 3 percent while the suburban populations increased by well over 60 percent.[26] As people moved out of the city their houses in the older neighborhoods depreciated and were often divided into apartments and multiple dwelling units, which meant a lower level of income was needed to live downtown. This in turn attracted more immigrants, transients, students and other people of lower economic levels, many of whom were black.[27] The churches continued to lose members, and while some did open their doors to their new black and Hispanic neighbors, many did not. Between 1960 and 1973, seven out of ten "First Churches" reported losing significant amounts of members, and many closed completely.[28]

According to Bakke and Roberts, intense racial discrimination and consistent racial clashes and conflicts in Northern cities affected city churches immensely. "Wave after wave of blacks migrated to the North in an attempt to escape the harsh reality of oppression. In most cities the relations between the newcomers and the native whites were fraught with conflicts. The whites' reaction in most cases was that of either outright hostility or mild suspicion, followed by a move on their part to the suburbs."[29]

And so the "white elephant" syndrome (the abandonment of the large, often white, "First Churches" in downtown areas for new church buildings in the suburbs) and "white flight" occurred in thousands of cities across the country.[30] According to Bakke and Roberts, "Old Firsts have now come upon hard times. Their once thriving memberships became depleted when countless members chased the 'American Dream' to the outer fringes of the suburbs. The large magnificent edifices, so imposing in their grandeur in an earlier time, now appear forlorn as row upon row of empty pews give mute testimony to faded glory . . ."[31]

Bickford notes two theories regarding the white flight phenomenon. The first is the "pull" hypothesis which asserts that the combination of affordable housing and highway and mall development in the suburbs created an "intrinsic lure," which pulled thousands of households out from the cities to the amenities of the suburbs. The second is the "push" theory, which suggests that changing social conditions in the central cities due to an in-

24. Thompson, "The Fight for Freedom on the Streets and Shopfloors of Postwar Detroit," 3.

25. Ibid., 3.

26. Bickford, "White Flight," 1.

27. Ibid., 1.

28. Jones, *What's Ahead For Old First Church?*, 1.

29. Bakke and Roberts, *Expanded Mission of City Center Churches*, 16.

30. Ibid., 47.

31. Ibid., 16.

flux of minorities served as a catalyst for white people to move to the suburbs to "achieve a more homogeneous lifestyle."[32] It is probably reasonable to assert that both theories apply, depending to some extent on each context and individual. Whether it was pull or push, millions left the cities, increasingly attributing negative characteristics to cities.[33]

While this exodus during the 1950s, 1960s, and 1970s was not the first period in which people attributed negative factors to the city, this period did exacerbate the negative stereotype of the city and of the people who dwelled there. Pollution, costly property, overcrowded dwellings, fear of crime and many other factors seemed to cement, for many churches, the decision to flee. Suburban Americans became more and more individualistic and private.[34]

Many significant sociological, economic, and psychological changes took place in the cities as the period of white flight occurred.

SOCIOLOGICAL CHANGES

In the various stages of this progression, the rapid growth of the cities brought increased crime, poverty, and other problems associated with over-population. The growth of suburbia resulted in thousands of abandoned buildings in downtown areas all over the U. S. Many resources once available within walking distance moved miles away to the edge of town. In many urban neighborhoods, the sense of community changed forever. People left in cities harbored feelings of resentment towards those who moved out and took with them banks, fair-priced grocery stores, hospitals, and churches.[35] "The city becomes the land of those left behind—the poor, the under-employed, the ethnic outsider. The conditions they inherit are economic decline, physical decay and social disintegration."[36]

ECONOMIC CHANGES

Along with the sociological changes came quite real economic changes. With the shift towards the suburbs, new superhighways were built to accommodate the commute, and soon many city businesses relocated all along the highways. Rutgers University History Professor Robert Fishman noted, "These new cities [suburbia] contain along the superhighways all the specialized functions of a great metropolis—Industry, shopping malls, hospitals, universities, cultural centers, and parks."[37] These developments eventually left millions of unskilled people struggling economically, miles away from their jobs or the possibility of future employment.

32. Bickford, "White Flight," 2.

33. Bakke and Roberts, *Expanded Mission*, 33.

34. Bellah, *Habits of the Heart*, 26.

35. Hadaway, "Church Growth and Decline in a Southern City," 373.

36. Conn and Ortiz, *Urban Ministry*, 70.

37. Fishman, *Bourgeois Utopias*, 7.

PSYCHOLOGICAL CHANGES

The psychological impacts of the shift from a rural paradigm to an urban and then suburban one are significant. DuBose speculates that the psychological effect on the inhabitants of America's cities was profound as people watched businesses, families, and churches' boarded up buildings in what was previously a thriving community and flee.[38] In some places immigrants and refugees are pouring into cities where they often have little help in acclimating to their new home. Gentrification and disinvestment are also important economic issues that have been a cause of psychological pain as well. Often revitalization in the form of substantial reinvestment in the end means displacement of current residents.[39] As rental property is purchased and torn down and upscale living units or commercial property replace it, the tenants of the low-cost housing are often left homeless with negative psychological as well as economic consequences.[40]

This despair felt by many left behind in inner cities can be summed up well by Brian, a homeless man in Louisville, KY, who was befriended by one of my students interning at a homeless shelter in the summer. My student, Spencer, spent a lot of time talking with Brian, a 45-year-old street person who said, "You know what I want to be when I grow up? "Free and utterly free." Socially, economically, psychologically, physically free. A privilege many outside the inner city areas of the world enjoy and take for granted.

So, for many influential writers who have seen the transformation of cities from places of hope to places of despair, "The city scene was backdrop for frightening experiences, personal defeat, icy intellectualism, heartless commercialism, miserable poverty, crime and sin, smoke and noise, dusk and loneliness."[41] Especially disconcerting from a missiological perspective, however, is that this negative perception of the city continues to affect many churches and ministries decision to not work in inner cities today.

FROM A MODEL TO A MOTIF

So what can be done? It seems as though this is a pretty grim picture—a sketchy past as far as effective involvement in the inner cities by churches, including elements of racism, classism, fear of perceived theological compromise, neglect, and the projections that the world is quickly becoming more urban. Clearly we need new models, a new strategy for effective presence in the inner cities of the world. However, in researching urban church strategies for over fifteen years, I have come to appreciate those practitioners who are boldly saying it's time to stop looking at cookie-cutter programs and strategies, and just be present in the urban areas to build on what is there, and be OK with it being unique to the particular urban context you find yourself in.

Bart Campolo, Claude Marie Barbour, Ash Barker, and many others are saying to those in the suburbs, "Come join us and get to know the people in your neighborhood, discover their felt needs and go from there." Echo what Mother Teresa said decades ago

---

38. Dubose, *How Churches Grow in an Urban World*, 19.

39. Wetzel, "What is Gentrification?" 2.

40. Christensen, *City Streets, City People*, 35.

41. White and White, *Intellectual Versus the City*, 37.

when people asked to help her in India: "Find your own Calcutta"—which means more than just, "Work where you are," but also, "Do what makes sense where you are."[42] It was Barker who said recently, "Perhaps it is time to think of urban work in terms of motif, not model,"[43] meaning looking at what works in various contexts on its own terms, and as it is found to have a biblical precedent in principle; not as prescription, but description of the love, time, and patience needed for this work.

Campolo, a past president of Mission Year, a national Christian service program that recruits young adults to serve in teams that live and work in inner city neighborhoods, states the *modus operandi* of that organization in these terms:

> Imagine an inner city neighborhood. The houses are old and worn out. The streets are dirty. Noise is everywhere; traffic, rap music, laughter, arguments, kids. Lots and lots of kids. Now imagine a houseful of young people living in that neighborhood as disciples of Jesus. People who seek out their neighbors. Listen to their needs, and pray for them over and over. People who work hard to make things better. People who stay long enough to become good friends. Imagine those young people living simply, setting aside material comforts for the sake of spiritual growth and loving relationships. Imagine a house becoming a haven, a safe and accepting place where people see the gospel lived out, alive and available to all. Imagine each individual in that house getting up early each day to listen to God, then going out into that neighborhood to do what God says. Church involvement. Community service. Neighborhood outreach. Hours and hours of voluntary hard work. Do not forget these young people are eager to grow and to learn. Imagine them discussing good books, integrating their faith with real life issues, learning how to get along with one another under all kinds of pressure, and embracing the values of the kingdom of God.[44]

Ash Barker echoes this motif in the organization he founded to work in the slums of the world, Urban Neighbors of Hope (UNOH), stating that what we need to understand is that everything we know about mission will have to change in the light of the urban situation. Traditional mission strategies are just ineffective, so intentional communities of small, adaptive, innovative, healthy Christian teams with no desire or compulsion to prescribe to anyone else's "this is how it is done universally," but rather focusing on the felt needs of their own unique community are what we are looking at. Programs don't work, another institution for urban strategies is not needed, but true presence is what changes urban understanding.[45]

It is what Claude Marie Barbour has been saying for decades—what she calls "mission-in-reverse,"[46] as what is effective in our current urban world. Learning from the people in the urban community, by living among them and understanding firsthand what the felt needs are, finding God at work and joining God there. This is what works and will

---

42. Muggeridge, *Something Beautiful for God*, 62.

43. Barker, Urban Workshop.

44. Campolo, *Kingdom Works*, 17-18.

45. Barker, Urban Workshop.

46. Barbour, "Seeking Justice and Shalom in the City," 299.

work in the unique and vast inner cities today, as another group of students can attest to as we worked in the inner city St. Louis, MO, one summer.

St. Louis in July is hot and humid. Most of the crowded apartments in the area where we worked had no air-conditioning and were unbearably hot. It was a high crime, minority populated area, and many of the working adults left children home locked up in their apartments all day. The centrally located park became a necessary refuge for the children, as there was a large fountain and sprinkler structure for the kids to play and cool off in. But a few gangs had recently met there and broken glass, and the city didn't want kids to step on glass so they cut off the water. My students and I, with the help of the local minister, cleaned out the area and called to get the water back on. Now if I had heard about this from the air-conditioned comfort of the suburbs I would have likely thought, "Well that's a nice extra thing to have for the kids, but there are other more important things to focus on first I would think." But being there in the hot summer placed this effort on a different priority list, one that cannot easily be explained to an outsider. It was important to community, to mental and physical health, and overall quality of life that makes little to no sense outside of the context. I can't explain the triumph these kids experienced as we had gathered many of them together to walk around the park and pray until the officials gave in and turned the water back on. It was as though they had received a gold medal at the Olympics. A little triumph, in the scheme of global urban mission maybe, but a huge one for those kids on that day in that place.

Another example from that same summer was a ministry in which we participated, which again from the outside seems so strange. Once a week a local Christian cook volunteers his time and gathers resources and cooks a hot meal for some of the city's homeless people. While there are literally hundreds of services available to the homeless and inner city population of St. Louis, this man has noticed a particular population who has fallen through the cracks. They are either too mentally ill to fill out the necessary paperwork some shelters require or for one reason or another choose to shy away from established organizations. So this man drives a van full of food, clothes, shoes, and blankets to the same park every Friday and hands out hundreds of meals. When we drove into the area where he served, I observed a newly gentrified area, complete with the cliché coffee shop, bookstore, candle store, and other hip places for those with money to gather. It was well-lit and clean. I wondered why in the world we would go there. Strangely, but not uniquely in cities, just one block away was my answer. One block from the gentrified strip were the displaced, the homeless who saw the van and recognized it as the meal van, and like a scene from a Broadway musical where the "scenery" suddenly comes to life before your eyes, a hundred or so homeless people came crawling out from under park benches, stoops, entryways, and lined up at the van. They told us stories and would tell us if they needed shoes or clothes, and we would write it down and tell them we would bring it next week. It was not efficient, very organized, or high-tech, but needs were met. My students stayed for hours talking one-on-one with many of St. Louis's homeless population who were, if seen at all, typically viewed as scenery or a problem. How do you make a model from that? That won't work everywhere. But one man in one inner city is helping in that specific way.

This taps into a motif I believe we find throughout scripture. Didn't Jesus himself meet these kinds of needs on his way to fulfilling his ultimate mission here on earth? Didn't he have plenty to say about something small becoming something huge? Sometimes he healed, sometimes he rebuked, sometimes he spoke plainly, sometimes in more cryptic messages, sometimes he met the felt and expressed need, and sometimes he met the deep and unexpressed spiritual need; the point being, there were a variety of "models" that cannot be replicated but one motif that can guide us in our various contexts.

There are those who have picked up on this motif throughout history and actually an ancient model of missions that Catholic mission communities have practiced for centuries. Their model involves simple things such as presence, hospitality,[47] integrating faith and work, and other very "simple" and ancient practices. Rodney Stark, in his book *The Rise of Christianity,* credits the rapid and expansive growth of Christianity to these very practices carried out by the early church; not programs, models, or strategies put forth by people removed from the conditions of the urban dweller safely tucked away in a suburban board room; Christians simply lived out faith shoulder to shoulder with those who lived there.

To some, the story of Isaias at the beginning of this chapter or any of the stories portrayed here may sound too simplistic, or romantic . . . perhaps all of this sounds that way. How could having coffee with people and chatting possibly lead to community transformation? Through these relationships and by having a finger on the pulse of what the needs are in his community, Isaias was able to develop a very popular tournament of *vitilla*.[48] The teams were made up of gang members, drug dealers, and pimps, and the tournament was taken very seriously. There were trophies and over 100 young street *vitilla* players involved. Some of these young men have since joined Isaias' church and become active in his rap music ministry and urban youth event held annually called *Cristo Urbano*, In fact one of the island's most influential former drug dealers is currently the drummer in his worship band.

Transformation at the street level

I don't know of any program exported from the U.S. that could have had such an outcome in his neighborhood. Relying on the Holy Spirit and asking God to open windows over coffee and baseball has changed lives. The lives of countless young people in Santiago have taken a dramatic 180 degree turn. Playing ball with a bottle cap is not a prescription—It likely wouldn't work anywhere like that in the United States, and so we can't market it and use it as an easy formulaic answer to solve the issue of inner city problems. At this point some become frustrated and allow the tendency to be jaded and critical and to say there must be more of an explanation for this phenomena. How does a game transform lives? It can't be. Barker addresses this cynicism in this way, "When we downplay this type of

47. For an excellent treatment of Hospitality as mission modality see Christine Pohl's, *Making Room: Recovering Hospitality as a Christian Tradition.*

48. *Vitilla* is baseball played with large cap from water bottles popular in the streets of Santiago and around various countries of Latin America where standard equipment is not available because of lack of financial resources.

power we rip people off and we discredit these types of experiences for the poor."[49] The reality is that hanging out, playing street ball, and building relationships that led to discipleship IS changing the island and simple endeavors similar to that are changing hundreds of cities and urban areas around the world. Giving hope to hopeless. Like simply talking to a woman at a well.

The gift of hope cannot be undervalued, Mother Teresa warned "Never deprive someone of hope – it may be all they have."[50] Hope for change is the beginning of making change.

Returning to the homeless in Louisville, we see hope as one of the men said goodbye to Spencer as the summer internship was concluding. One man shook Spencer's hand and hoped out loud, saying what may sound funny to us, but nonetheless poignant. His parting words, "Hey hopefully, I will see you on Jeopardy someday," were a sweet sentiment and a compliment for Spencer who understood the man's heart in these words and knew that he had made a friend.

One relationship at a time

Doing the hard work. Growing hope and sharing the good news of the present kingdom, I think that is work of the inner city presently and in the near future. The simplicity and freedom is maybe what makes it such a challenge, but at the same time such an exciting opportunity for authentic ministry today.

49. Barker, Urban Workshop.

50. Muggeridge, *Something Beautiful for God*, 63.

13

Urban Ministry: The River of God Makes the City Glad

by Linda Whitmer

INTRODUCTION

EMILY HAD BEEN SELLING her little crocheted cloths on the street for two years when I met her. I had already spent all the money I had in my purse to buy bread and milk for several boys who lived on the street when I saw her. As Emily approached, I knew she was one of the thousands who lived in the high-density suburbs of the town in which we lived. I politely said, "No, thank you," as she offered to sell me one of her cloths, and started to return to my conversation with the boys. Something was different with Emily, though. I noticed tears welling up in her eyes as she turned to move on.

Emily and her husband had lived together with their children in a two-room house wedged in-between thousands of others in the "slums of hope"[1] in Gweru, Zimbabwe. They, like many others, had migrated to town to find work because there was no way for them to dig out a living in the drought-stricken rural areas. Emily was diabetic and quickly going blind when her husband had left her. "I have had enough of having a sickly wife," he said. Emily never saw him again. Now she had six children to feed, no money, was living in a slum, and had no one to help. When I asked her, "Why are you crying?" she said, "You were my last hope. We have no food and haven't eaten in days. The streets are empty, and I was turning back to go home and just die with my children."

Needless to say, I put her in my truck and we went to my home. Emily was ushered straight in to eat the first meal she had had in quite some time. While Emily ate, we gathered what the family would need for eating over the next month from our supplies. Her first comment about the food was, "I can't eat while my children go hungry." When we showed her the store of food we were preparing to take to her little shanty, the next question on her lips were the beginning of an eternal change, "Why?" Over the next few

---

1. The term "slums of hope" was coined as a descriptive term referring to the hope with which people arrive to the place with, and the hope with which the settlement is often ordained by the governmental powers of the area. Stokes, "A Theory of Slums." 187–97.

days, we told her about Jesus' love for her, introduced her to a loving faith community, and watched as she grew to love Jesus.

All over the world, people are moving to the city in record numbers. Since the time of Cain's move to a city (Gen 4:17), people have migrated to the city for many reasons—to escape poverty, to look for work, to seek better healthcare or better education, to escape violence, or simply to look for the bright lights and excitement hoped for in the city. Today, however, we are seeing an unprecedented rush to urbanization. While there is a tremendous strain on resources in the way of basic infrastructure and public services of the city, the real impact is on the people themselves. Too often, when we speak of urbanization and the people who are flocking to the cities, we are speaking of poverty and need. Some say that by the year 2050, three billion, half of the world's population, will live in slums. churches, missionaries, and mission organizations all over the world are waking anew to the frontier of urban evangelization and care of urban ministry.

Not everyone in the city lives in poverty. The strategies and trends for reaching the suburban and middle-class of the world are not addressed here. In this chapter, we will examine the changing frontier of urban ministry and how the shifting urban world is being addressed by the church and her people.

OUR CHANGING URBAN STATE

In 2008, according to a United Nations Populations Fund report,[2] for the first time in the history of the world, urban populations have exceeded the rural populations of the planet. No longer do the majority of the people in the world live in rural areas, drawing their resources from rural life. Now, for many, the connections to the rural life and its resources, family connections, and sense of belonging have been severed.

Populations of the world's cities and their growth rates are staggering. While actual figures vary according to source and usually vary because of where actual boundary lines are drawn for the extent of the city, growth rates are similar. Cities are large and growing larger. The figures below include not only the metro area, but also the recognized populations within the neighboring communities, which also depend on the city infrastructure and resources.

1. Tokyo, Japan—32,450,000

2. Seóul, South Korea—20,550,000

3. Mexico City, Mexico—20,450,000

4. New York City, USA—19,750,000

5. Mumbai, India—19,200,000

6. Jakarta, Indonesia—18,900,000

7. Sáo Paulo, Brazil—18,850,000

8. Delhi, India—18,680,000

2. "2007 State of World Population (UNFPA) and World Population Prospects: The 2005 Revision."

9. Osaka/Kobe, Japan—17,350,000

10. Shanghai, China—16,650,000 [3]

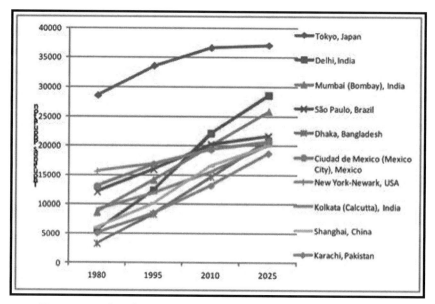

Figure 1: Top 10 Populated Cities in 1980 and Urban Expansion Projected to 2025[4]

The growth of mega-cities is staggering; however, this simply illustrates the same trends seen in smaller cities. More people live in smaller cities than in the mega-cities, and in many nations the smaller or medium-sized cities are growing at a rate even faster than the mega-cities.[5] When we examine the growth of the mega-cities, and think of the same thing happening to smaller cities at an increased rate of speed, the challenges become apparent. How can so many new people be incorporated successfully into the city system in such a short amount of time?

If we break the growth rate down into a chart by major regions, the trends for the world are clearly visible. By 2025, there will be more people in the urban setting than in rural areas throughout every area in the world.

3. http://www.worldatlas.com/citypops.htm.

4. Adapted from "World Urbanization Prospects: The 2009 Revision, United Nations Department of Economic and Social Affairs/Population Division."

5. Monsma and Greenway, *Cities: Missions New Frontier*, 20.

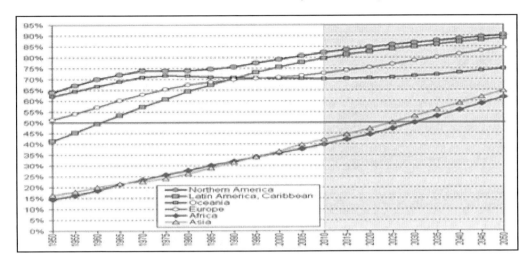

World Urbanization Prospects, the 2009 Revision

Figure 2: Urban population by major geographical area
(in percent of total population)[1]

The sheer masses of people present who are not a part of the city system and natural city growth contribute to a host of problems as people try to survive:

- poverty
- gangs
- crime
- homelessness
- injustice
- immigration issues
- sex trafficking
- slavery
- drug addiction
- alcoholism
- family breakdown, and
- complete marginalization—of the individual, of the family, of the ethnic group.

Urban ministry must address all of these issues, along with the deep spiritual need of the lost, in order to be successful and relevant in today's urban world—in a way that makes sense to the marginalized people of the cities. "Love your neighbor" (Mark 12:33) takes on a whole new meaning in the city.

OUR CHANGING URBAN MINISTRY

Compassion shown toward those in need has been a hallmark of God's people from the time of the early church until today. God built directly into the cultural system of his chosen people a system to take care of those around them, to show compassion for the lost, and to show love—even when it is not convenient. Urban ministry has been called a ministry of inconvenience. That is a true description, but it is a ministry we cannot ignore.

Old Testament

Even before the first century church days, the Old Testament was filled with reminders and laws regarding what the response should be toward the poor, the alien in the land, and the widow and orphans–those marginalized in society. Walter Kaiser informs us that there are "over a dozen Hebrew words for the 'poor' and almost three hundred instances in the Old Testament where they are mentioned."[6] God saw the poor in Old Testament times, and made provisions for their care and uplifting. Significant pockets of poverty as we see in our cities today surely sadden his heart. Hardening one's heart against someone that is poor is a sin against God (Deut 15:7–11), and he who oppresses the poor shows contempt for his Maker (Prov 14:21, 31).

The Old Testament Law required the poor and strangers should be allowed to have the corners of fields, the gleanings of fallow fields, and the gleanings of leftovers (Lev 19:9–10; 23:22; Deut 24:19–22; Judg 8:2; Ruth 2:6, 8, 9; Isa 17:5–6; Jer 49:9; Mic 7:1). By law, those who could not help themselves were to be provided for in a way that helped to uphold their dignity and physical needs.

Marginalization and oppression of the poor is common in the city today. The unscrupulous rich take advantage of those who do not know the laws, those who are undocumented, and those who are too poor or uneducated to get out of the cycle of poverty entrapment. God is against taking advantage of the poor of this world (a rich man appropriates a man's ewe lamb, 2 Sam 12:5–6; Elijah indicted Ahab for moving against a poor farmer, Naboth, 1 Kings 21:1–21).

Isaiah 58 rails against ceremonialism in religion, then he cautions that one should seek "pure and undefiled religion which is to aid the helpless, poor and the weak."[7] Job 29:12–16[8] says

> because I rescued the poor who cried for help,
> and the fatherless who had none to assist them.
> The one who was dying blessed me;
> I made the widow's heart sing.
> I put on righteousness as my clothing;
> justice was my robe and my turban.
> I was eyes to the blind

6. Kaiser, *Toward Old Testament Ethics*, 159.

7. Ibid., 160.

8. All references are NIV.

and feet to the lame.
I was a father to the needy;
I took up the case of the stranger.

In this passage, and Job 31:16–22, we see the proper model for godliness and holiness in relation to the poor and needy.

Jesus' Example

Repeatedly, Jesus taught that compassion for those in need was the feature trait of believer action and the measure of belonging to Christ (Matt 25:31–46). In Luke 4:17–21, Jesus announces what his ministry is all about: righting the situation of the poor, releasing the unjustly imprisoned, insight into real justice, and relief for the oppressed . . . In other words, making things right for everyone. In answer to John's enquiry, Jesus identifies himself as the compassion of God: "Go back and report to John what you hear and see. The blind receive sight, the lame walk, those who have leprosy are cured, the deaf hear, the dead are raised, and the good news is preached to the poor" (Matt 11:3–5). Repeatedly, Jesus included the poor and oppressed in his teaching (Luke 12:17–34).

Jesus also taught by example that we are to take care of the hungry, the sick and those in need. In the feeding of the multitudes (Matt 14:12–21, 15:32–39; Mark 6:32–14, 8:1–10; Luke 9:11–17, John 6:5–13) and the healing of the sick (Matt 9:32; 20:34; Mark 5:18ff; 10:52; Luke 18:43), we see concern not only for the spiritual life of those involved and those observing, but we also see compassion for the people in their physical distress.

Jesus definitely had a sense that to be a disciple of his was to meet the needs of the poor and oppressed on his behalf.

Early Church Example

In the earliest days of the first century church, believers held everything in common and gave to any who had need (Acts 2:44–47; 4:32–37). As a matter of fact, the first official act of the church was to feed the poor (Acts 6:1–6). Imagine how the cities of the world today would be if we had kept up that practice!

James, the pillar of the church in Jerusalem, said "Religion that God our father accepts as pure and faultless is this: to look after orphans and widows in their distress and to keep oneself from being polluted by the world" (Jas 1:27). In fact, James points out that it is the poor who are the primary beneficiaries of the gospel (Jas 2:5). Remembering the poor was the primary mission of the early church (Gal 2:10).

MOTIVATIONAL SHIFT

Change has taken place over the last centuries in both style and motivation for urban ministry. We could even say that over the past decade, we are seeing a revolution in urban ministry. Along with the massive increase in population and need in the cities, has come an awareness by many in the church and ministry that the whole person must be loved.

We are now starting to see clearly a shift from strictly evangelistic ministry to holistic ministry.

At the Lausanne II conference, held in Manila in 1989, these commitments were upheld by declaring, "The authentic gospel must become visible in the transformed lives of men and women. As we proclaim the love of God we must be involved in loving service; as we preach the kingdom of God we must be committed to its demands of justice and peace."[9]

Serving In

Attitudinally, there are three main strategic ways to approach urban ministry. The first is *Serving In*. In this category, someone goes to the "urban" area and does ministry and then returns to their safe place, their home and security. Service is definitely a part of the ministry, and the intentions are good. This person invests in the urban dweller from a point of safety, reserving engagement to specified periods before withdrawal again to their usual surroundings. For example, recently I took a group of my college students to serve for the day at Union Rescue Mission in Los Angeles. We worked hard that day, sorting donated food and cleaning. Following a successful day of work, they went home, though during their day of serving in urban ministry, not a single one had had a serious conversation with anyone in the area. No risk was involved on their part, and their commitment to the people and their needs was limited.

This type of urban ministry is needed, but the world will not be changed by short-lived uncommitted forays into the urban world. In order to be successful and life-changing *Serving In* urban ministry must be paired with a longer-term, deeply committed ministry.

Serving By

Serving By is a style of urban ministry strategy that has been very popular for many years. There is recognition of the need to be more deeply committed to the community and the individuals, so the urban minister takes a more active role in the life of the community–possibly planting and serving a church in the neighborhood. He visits the local hangout and talks with the people he runs into there. The *Serving By* minister even makes the effort to involve the church leaders and some of the community in his ministry efforts. The intentions are good and the ministry effect is much stronger than the *Serving In*. He is standing by the people in their situation, trying his best to help them.

David and his wife Marge are committed to the people of Kibera, Nairobi, Kenya. They moved to Kenya to work there ten years ago. Many lives are changing and a fair number of people have been introduced to the Lord through their work. They have tried to see the needs of the people from their perspective as much as possible. Still, when day is done, they return home, to the safety of their home and their much more comfortable neighborhood. This style of urban ministry strategy is most often paired with the *Serving In* style.

9. Lausanne II, Manila 1989, *Manila Manifesto*, 4.

Serving With

The largest shift in recent years has come with the attitude of *Serving With* in urban ministry. In this style, the minister commits completely to the urban neighborhood, moving into the community, and living life with the people–sharing life with those they minister to daily. This style demands the most of the urban minister, demanding risk and vulnerability. They become even more than what Francis O'Gorman refers to as a "companionate facilitator"[10] (a person who walks alongside as a friend would). They become friend, family, advocate, and resource.

TYPES OF URBAN HOLISTIC MINISTRY

Just as the growth of the world's cities is increasing at an astronomical level, so are the many types of urban ministry possibilities. Ministry in the urban setting, when done from a holistic perspective, "affirms the functional uniqueness of evangelism and social responsibility, it views them as inseparable from the ministry of the kingdom of God."[11] Where there is a new need, there is a new manner of doing urban ministry. As brothers and sisters in Christ, we seek to show the way to God through Jesus in every aspect of our ministry—evangelism, relief, recovery, development—all lead to the goal of transforming lives for Christ.

There are so many ways of approaching the many neighborhoods of the world. Here, we will touch on some of the more prominent, or fast changing. Because of the nature of survival issues in urban slums, relief often must play a pivotal role in ministry.

Physical Needs Being Met

Relief can be defined as the provision of critically needed resources to sustain life and reduce suffering caused by natural or human-induced disasters. Because disasters often cause great life threatening need and human suffering, compassion and respect for all people compels Christians to action. Not all relief agencies are Christian-based, however. Those based in the United States alone number approximately 300 Christian agencies. Widespread media coverage of disasters and globalization has contributed in the last two decades to a trend on the part of Christians around the world to consciously increase their efforts to alleviate suffering of fellow humans. Interestingly enough, as economic difficulties have resulted in a lower contribution rate among many secular agencies, religious based organizations have seen an increase in funding of their projects and ministries.[12] Relief, as a response, treats symptoms of urgent need.[13] Food, shelter, protection and safety issues call for immediate action to avoid catastrophic results.

During a severe drought in Zimbabwe in 1992, I was involved in food distribution in an area where we had planted several fledgling churches. As more and more people were added to the list of those who needed food for survival, we involved the church leaders in

---

10. O'Gorman, *Charity and Change*, 47.

11. Moreau, *Evangelical Dictionary of World Missions*, 448.

12. Banks, "Some Religious Charities Buck Lower Giving Trends," 19.

13. O'Gorman, *Charity and Change*, 4.

the regular distribution. Four thousand people gathered on an announced day to receive food. Several of the church leaders came to me with a question, "All these people have come for food, but we are only giving to Christians, aren't we?" I responded with a question, "Are they hungry?" The reply was an immediate, "Yes, but they aren't Christians! If we tell them only Christians get food, they will join us to get food!" Again, I asked them a question, "Which message will speak louder to these hungry people, telling them they have to be Christians to get food, or that Christ loves them and so do we—and here is your food?" The leaders stood and looked at me for a moment, thinking this over. As the nature of human need dawned on them, they said, "People cannot listen if their stomach is growling too loudly." That year, the churches in that area grew considerably, in scope, not because people were told they had to be Christians to eat, but because they were shown the unconditional love of Christ in very real and relevant terms, answering urgent needs.

Compassionate relief ministry calls for the balancing of personal introspection and purpose. We must continually ask ourselves, "Why are we doing this?" Well-meaning efforts can become little more than the phenomenon of "Rice Christianity," which is the tendency to use efforts of compassion as a means to promote acceptance of Christ by dangling the prize of much needed food and services in front of people as a reward for accepting Christianity, or at least spending time listening to the message.[14]

Relief ministry, done from the Christian perspective, should involve the whole person; the spiritual as well as the physical. Bryon D. Klaus[15] suggests some key theological objectives to keep in mind as we minister:

1. Relief work must always be done as efficiently and effectively as possible, meeting the real needs of the people in a way that honors God.

2. Relief efforts must be done in a way that respects the dignity of the people and their culture.

3. The lifestyles and manners of relief works are the first evidence that the good news is true. Relief works must always demonstrate God's love with their actions and words.

4. There should not be any attempt to convert, capitalize on tragedy, or discriminate in distribution of supplies.

5. The way in which the gospel message is presented should be adapted to the context and culture of the people being served.

6. The relief worker should always consider that their actions have long-term, eternal, implications. How the worker responds to the disaster today may well impact how a person in the midst of tragedy responds to the Gospel in the future.

---

14. Moreau, *Evangelical Dictionary of World Missions*, 817.

15. Ibid., 818.

From Relief to Recovery to Transformation

The goals and functions of relief and development are intertwined in that each seeks to provide improvement of the human condition. Relief seeks to save human life, providing for the immediate needs of the people involved in the disaster. The action is normally transitory and short-lived. The goal is to provide what is needed today so there actually can be a tomorrow for these people. Recovery takes those people who have been helped in the midst of unexpected and unplanned adversity and asks the question, "How can we now begin to rebuild the lives of this community, on an individual basis and a community basis?" Recovery, then, is the process of providing assistance to restore, reconstruct, and recreate that which already was at some point in the past of the person or community. "Like an individual recovering from an illness, each society builds its own defenses and rebuilding methods metaphorically paralleling the healing capabilities of the human body."[16] Slums are most often "built" in areas that no one else wants, such as on hillsides, on riverbanks, or in other flood plains. Location contributes regularly to devastation and the need to rebuild everything. Recovery style ministries are constantly needed in urban ministries.[17]

Development, on the other hand, assists the local community in providing for themselves for the long term. "Development is a process that enables a community to provide for its own needs, above previous levels. Development must be indigenous, comprehensive, and aimed at improved self-reliance."[18] Microenterprise and fair trade initiatives are an excellent example of development at work. Urban Neighbours of Hope, in Bangkok, assists in the development of small businesses that are run by residents for the specific purpose of uplifting the people. The profits go toward helping improve their quality of life, as well as providing dignity and teaching new skills.[19] The recognition of the value of human life, the realization that people's needs are both physical and spiritual, and the development of a faith community sharing Christ with their neighbors within the context lead to transformed lives in Christ.

The challenges of urban ministry are so great that one person, or one organization cannot work alone effectively. Collaboration is required in urban ministry. Networking and collaboration are necessary to achieve success in the long-term change of individuals and communities.

16. Whitmer, S. *Approaching Benevolence in Missions*, 13.

17. On an individual level, among the many types, recovery programs from drugs and alcohol abuse are the most prominently known. By its very nature, the impact of slum living leads to efforts by the individual to alleviate that pain. Many people turn to drugs, alcohol, or sex as a temporary mitigation.

18. Moreau, *Evangelical Dictionary of World Missions*, 818.

19. Urban Neighbours of Hope, 2011.

Examples of Current Challenges

GANGS

Gang violence has turned many areas of our cities into war zones. No longer limited to large, violent cities, smaller cities and towns are also dealing with the repercussions of street gangs. As the influence of family and other socio-institutional sources of support break down, young adults and early adolescents turn increasingly to gangs for their source of identity and support. A yearning to belong and a desire to be part of a larger more connected group tempt youth to the life of the street gang. Repercussions from a low-income life, ethnic isolation, and problems at home can be extremely problematic to young people. When these factors combine, "it is the streets that become the main socialization agent in their lives."[20] "Group affiliation often entails embracing the external signs that characterize the group. Gangs, like many youth groups, are notorious for encouraging their members to dress, talk, and act in a certain way to show that they belong and identify with peers."[21] There are numerous gang types and affiliations within any given city. Generalizations are difficult and within any given gang territory, intermingling of gang types may occur. With this in mind, some overall generalizations are feasible. Of the three distinct types of gangs in cities today,[22] the most common, and most benign, is the *social* gang. This group "hangs out" together and is typically not violent unless they are threatened. These gang members are together not because of a need for self-preservation but because they enjoy the company and feel a close connection to each other. *Delinquent* gangs, the second type, derive their financial gain from illegal activity. Their members depend upon one other for mutual support and exact executions of activities. Survival depends upon their fellow gang members. Criminal activity is typically carried out in their own neighborhoods.[23] The third type of gang centers on *violence*. Power and the associated emotional gratification are central, with both leaders and followers often overestimating "the importance, size, and power of their group. These gangs tend to have a highly structured hierarchy of leaders and followers. The *violent* gang is also characterized by intragroup violence."[24]

Ministry with gangs and those who live among gangs specifically has taken on a more focused and intentional trend in recent years. Giving young people a family to belong to is fulfilling a basic need of life.[25]

One Santa Ana, CA ministry outreach organization has taken on a very distinct tactic. Every Saturday evening, trained volunteers with Lives Worth Saving don their identifying t-shirts and jackets, then go out into the streets. There they spend the evening in the high

20. Vigil, *Barrio Gangs*, xiii.

21. Ibid., 109.

22. For a more extensive analysis of gangs and their psychological makeup, see Ruble and Turner, "A systemic analysis of the dynamics and organization of urban street gangs," 117–132.

23. Fagan, "The Real Root Cause of Violent Crimes," 157.

24. Ruble and Turner, "A systemic analysis of the dynamics and organization of urban street gangs," 117.

25. Abraham Maslow's Hierarchy of Need proposed that the need to feel love and a sense of belonging was fundamental to human nature. Maslow, "A Theory of Human Motivation." 370–96.

crime neighborhoods walking, talking with people, and using only one weapon—God's love. Fear was the impetus for the mission, not the founder's fear, but fear he saw in the faces of those around him. This police officer had one method in mind, "Train everyday people to understand what's happening on the streets. Teach them to read the graffiti, to recognize the tics of a drug addict. Then send them out to talk to the people who live with those issues every day—to offer them a prayer, a phone number or a word of advice, a shoulder to lean on."[26] People in the neighborhoods recognize the jackets. They are not afraid of "the Christians." Lives Worth Saving works through a collaborative effort of faith-based organizations that work side-by-side with local and federal government agencies. Together they make sure communities can receive resources to help youth, educate parents, and bring change to the hurting community.

DEVELOPMENT

The words poverty and slums too often go together in today's world. No matter what they are called–slums, barrios, shantytowns, or *favelas*—they have been with us for thousands of years. The poverty, homelessness, and fear of these slums have not changed. What has changed is the sheer scale of the numbers of people living in these desperate conditions. In 2007, the United Nations reported that one in every three people who lives in urban areas is a slum dweller. One in six of the world's population lives in a slum—that is at least one billion people!

While slums occur all over the world, more than 90 percent of slum dwellers today are in the developing world. "The majority are in South Asia, followed by Eastern Asia, sub-Saharan Africa and Latin America. China and India together have 37 percent of the world's slums. In sub-Saharan Africa, urbanization has become virtually synonymous with slum growth; 72 percent of the region's urban population lives under slum conditions, compared to 56 percent in South Asia. The slum population of sub-Saharan Africa almost doubled in 15 years, reaching nearly 200 million in 2005."[27]

With the explosion of slum living in the world, ministry has needed to adapt and expand into areas that were considered by many as peripheral ministries until recently. Recognition of the need and opportunity is trending into the forefront of mission. Need—because there are so many people living in such great need daily. Opportunity—because we have the opportunity to make a difference in so many people's lives, physically and spiritually.

People in the slums, however, do not just need evangelization, or alleviation of poverty, or even education. Those in the slum areas need help in many areas of their lives. There must be recognition of the holistic need of people who live in the urban context. Recognition of the ramifications of building in one area of life, while leaving others unattended, has led to the urban ministry that is more holistic in nature and more grounded in Christ's overarching love of all. Christ-centered holistic ministry leads to change with Christ at the center of the community. This is transformational ministry.

---

26. Irving, "Missionaries Wage War: God vs. Gangs."

27. UNFPA, *State of the world Population 2007*, Chapter 2.

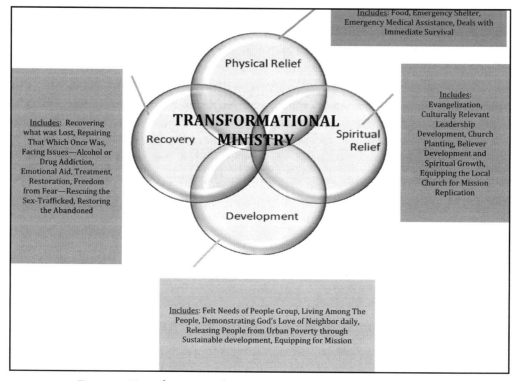

Figure 3: Transformational Ministry Requires Acknowledgement
of Both Spiritual and Physical Needs

THE MAJOR TREND IN URBAN MINISTRY TODAY IS TRANSFORMATIONAL

> Evangelism is primary because our chief concern is with the gospel, that all people
> may have the opportunity to accept Jesus Christ as Lord and Savior. Yet Jesus not
> only proclaimed the kingdom of God, he also demonstrated its arrival by works of
> mercy and power. We are called today to a similar integration of words and deeds. In
> a spirit of humility we are to preach and teach, minister to the sick, feed the hungry,
> care for prisoners, help the disadvantaged and handicapped, and deliver the op-
> pressed. While we acknowledge the diversity of spiritual gifts, callings, and contexts,
> we also affirm that good news and good works are inseparable.[28]

Keeping Christ's gospel central to the ministry changes the focus of the person, the family,
and the community. For example, a young Christian-based organization in Fullerton, CA,
Solidarity, was started a few years ago by a group of young people who saw a need in a
community near their university. The community was filled with undocumented people,
unemployment was high, families were in trouble, gang activity was rife, and crime
was high. Instead of walking away and hoping someone else, someone older and more
experienced, would step in to make a difference, this group decided to make the move
themselves. Today, they, and others who have joined them, live in the community and

---

28. Lausanne II, Manila 1989. "From the 21 Affirmations of the Manila Manifesto." *The Manila Manifesto*,
3–4.

conduct after-school programs, community development, immigration reform, mentoring, education, gang prevention and intervention. The community is changing. Christ was there all along, but now people are noticing.

CONCLUSION

All over the world, cities are growing at an unprecedented rate. Along with that growth rate comes an unprecedented challenge for urban ministry. As we look at biblical precedence, needs of the urban context, and the current approaches used in meeting those needs, effective urban ministry must answer the real questions of the people. Some people in the city need immediate attention for survival; others need assistance in lifting themselves out of the cycle of poverty and pain; still others are lost without a relationship with God; some need all three. If a ministry addresses one need exclusively, even in a Scriptural way, it will be incomplete. As Jesus said, "Whatever you did for one of the least of these brothers and sisters of mine, you did for me" (Matt 25:40). As Jesus is, we must be concerned for the whole person.

Transformed lives should be the ultimate goal of all ministries, urban or otherwise. The challenges of the urban life are unique and call for unique ways to answer the questions people are facing in their lives. Christ has the permanent answer for everyone's life.

14

Islam: How Christians Are Learning to Create A Bridge Over Tumultuous Waters

by Robert Douglas

THIS CHAPTER FOCUSES ON the Muslim world, Islam as a system, and various considerations in Christians responding to Islam in constructive ways. Given the size and complexity of the Muslim world, its long history and centuries of Muslim-Christian interaction, what follows is at best an introduction.

FEAR, FEELINGS, AND FAITH

The mere mention of the word Islam provokes a host of responses from non-Muslims. In too many cases fear is the initial emotion that surges through the thinking of non-Muslims. The world situation today, and the manner in which it is reported by the media, often serves only to feed a frenzy of fear. In worst case situations fear evolves into hatred and what many call "Islamophobia."

Websites abound which spell out the nature of Islam and its supposed agenda for the West, usually in very negative terms. Is Islam a religion of peace or not? Are Muslims playing coy political games to take advantage of Western freedom and tolerance while hiding their real intention? Many think so. Whatever the truth, when such negative emotions prevail, it is difficult for faith to speak with much power and credibility.

The good news always challenges us to believe that God is in charge. With that foundational stone in place, we are called upon to reach out to Muslims in love, building relationships that allow the gospel to be presented in meaningful ways. Rather than dividing the world into us and them camps, scripture reminds us that whatever the deficiencies of Islam, Christians are far from perfect. John tells us that we cannot say we have no sin and that we have not sinned.[1] Paul suggests that it is by God's grace that we are what we are and it is God's intention that this grace is not in vain.[2] While Muslims do not know the fullness of the good news many, like us, are people (sinners together) on a journey, seeking to know more of God and becoming more like him. On this basis we can meet

1. 1 John 1:10.
2. 1 Cor 15:10.

Muslims in a spirit of a common search for the kingdom and its righteousness. Faith can overcome fear and other negative feelings to allow for constructive work to take place. Without first getting our own hearts in order nothing productive can occur.

THE WORLD OF ISLAM

Islam Worldwide

One of our first tasks is to gain a sense of the Muslim world. Ultimately our Christian responsibility is to see Muslims as people, as individuals with their own particular needs and desires. But first we must see them within the wider world of Islam. The number of Muslims in the world is estimated at 1.6 billion. That means that one out of every five people is a Muslim. It is sometimes said that Islam is the world's fastest growing religion. If that is true, it is due to biological increase not conversions.

Muslims are found on every continent on earth with the greatest concentrations in Asia. Generally Westerners immediately think of Islam and the Middle East. It is true that the Middle East, especially the Arabian Peninsula, is the historical and emotional heart of Islam. It is incorrect to equate Islam with Arabs and Arabs with Islam. Only one in five Muslims is an Arab; one out of twenty Arabs is a Christian. There are as many Indonesian Muslims as there are Arab Muslims.

A list of top Muslim countries based on the sheer number of Muslims within their borders (not percentages) would look like the following,

1. Indonesia
2. India
3. Pakistan
4. Bangladesh
5. Turkey
6. Iran
7. Egypt
8. Nigeria
9. China
10. Algeria

Only two of the ten countries are Arab nations, Egypt and Algeria. More than 55% of all the world's Muslims live in the first four nations listed. It is also important to note that Turks and Iranians are not Arabs but of totally different racial makeup. There are approximately 60 nations that designate themselves Islamic nations; some very small like the Maldive Islands. The Islamic nation designation suggests that Islam is the official religion of the country and/or the basis of its social and political system.

Today Muslims are found in ever-increasing numbers in Western Europe. France, Germany, and Great Britain have the largest number of Muslim residents. Generally Muslims in Western Europe trace their origin back to areas once part of a European colonial empire. For example, most Muslims in France come from North Africa; British Muslims are predominately Indo-Pakistani.

In the United States it is estimated there are three million Muslims. Different sources vary widely on the estimated number. About half of America's Muslims are African Americans who have converted to Islam, often for social reasons. The largest immigrant Muslim population comes from South Asia (India and Pakistan). Arabs are the next most numerous. Muslims in America can be found all across the country though the largest concentrations are in big urban areas. America's first Muslim immigrants came mainly from Lebanon and Syria and settled in the Midwest. One of America's oldest mosques in located in Iowa.

Ethnic Groups

Variations within the Muslim world are far more extensive than nation of origin. The Muslim world consists of hundreds of different ethnic (people) groups. Some have calculated more than seven hundred different groups, each with its own heart language, cultural expressions, traditions, and view of what it means to be Muslim. Within Indonesia alone there are more than two hundred different ethno linguistic groups. Afghanistan has dozens, as do Pakistan and India.

Each of these different groups recognize its own uniqueness, marries principally within its own group, worships separately, has its own way of life, and its own language or dialect. Within a given area groups may periodically band together to achieve a common goal or oppose a common outside threat. Once the emergency is over they revert to their previous life of rivalry. The fact that different ethno linguistic groups exist requires those who would minister among them to tailor make strategies for each situation, no one size fits all in terms of ministry and missions.

Denominational Differences

Then there are the denominational differences within Islam. Muslims often want to downplay the existence of such, but they are real and deep. The majority of Muslims (approximately 85 percent) are Sunnis, a term derived from "sunna," meaning the way. By their label Sunnis say they embody the true or right way to be Muslim. The balance of Muslims are Shia (or Shii or Shite). The term "shia" means party, as in a political party. They claim to be of the party of Ali, a relative of Muhammad who died in the seventh century. Today Sunnis are scattered across the Muslim world. Shias are largely concentrated in Iran and parts of India or wherever people from these areas migrated as for instance, East Africa.

For purposes of apologetics, Muslims tend to minimize Sunni-Shia differences. However the division is deep, theologically profound, and long standing since the seventh century. The initial split came shortly after Muhammad suddenly died (632 AD). The point of contention was the qualifications needed by a suitable candidate to follow

Islam's prophet as head of the community. Put simply, the Sunnis said you choose the best Muslim. The Shia countered by saying, no, you choose the best relative of Muhammad. This quarrel led to a bitter split among Muslim succession and was finally settled on the battlefield! Over time Shia became divided among themselves over who was the correct successor. Today there are at least four major Shia denominations.

A second point of contention focused on (to use terms Christians might relate to) how one is to know the will of God. The Sunni said it is enough to consult what is written, meaning the Qur'an (Islam's holy book and the Hadith or collections of traditions). The Shia argued that in addition to considering what is written one also needed to listen to the living voice of God. For the Shia the living voice of God resided with the successor to Muhammad. Remember, they have a different list of successors. The Sunnis scoffed at this idea and the Shia mocked the Sunnis as unbelievers out of touch with whatever God might want to say today. This division remains to this day. The depth and implications of Sunni-Shia division somewhat parallels Protestant-Catholic arguments over authority and correct doctrine, and reconciliation is a long way off.

Variations in How Faith Is Lived

Further variations characterize Muslims. These have to do largely with how one goes about practicing one's faith. Some Muslims are fundamentalists, that is, they are very conservative when it comes to their understanding and application of the Qur'an to life. They take its words literally; it says what it means and means what it says. On occasion they can be very reactionary. For the fundamentalist there is no need for commentary or textual criticism, or any attempt to determine when and why a certain verse came into being. It is! And that is enough.

Other Muslims, while quite convinced the Qur'an is God's word, are not committed to literalism but to identifying principles and asking how they apply today. Still others, who might be labeled progressive or modern, are quite open to textual and historical criticism of the Qur'an. In fact, they often suggest that large portions of the Qur'an have no relevance for today's world. Much, in their opinion, was applicable only in Arabia and only in the seventh century. Naturally the fundamentalists see progressives as betraying Islam, and, in fact, as not being Muslims at all.

Other Muslims are essentially secular. They do not go to the mosque, pray or read the Qur'an. They may not be concerned whether God exists or not. However, culturally they are Muslim. They keep certain customs like circumcision, inheritance procedures, and burial practices.

Still other Muslims are the Islamic equivalent of charismatics. They are known as Sufis, a term thought to come from the Arabic world for wool. Sufism cuts across denominational lines. Thus there are Sunnis who are Sufis and there are Shia who are Sufis. Sufism has its own system of denominations built around practices of knowing God as originally devised by each order's founder. Among the chief concerns of Sufis are experiencing God in a mystical way, becoming one with God and developing a deep personal spirituality.

Sufis are found in most parts of the Muslim world and are generally appreciated, except by some fundamentalists.

Finally, there are Muslims whose religious practices are a mixture of magic, occultism, saint worship, and superstition. They are usually referred to as folk Muslims (popular Islam). The majority of Muslims in the world are influenced by folk religious practice to some degree. Folk Muslims are primarily concerned with power and protection from the many forces and beings they believe exist who threaten them. They seek spiritual aid from saints, dead and alive, as well as rituals designed to keep evil at bay. Many literalists work day and night to rid Islam of folk practices, usually with little success.

From the above description it is clear there are many Islams. In ministry it is of critical importance to know who is being addressed. Discovering that may involve time and patience.

CHALLENGES ISLAM PRESENTS

The Muslim world has sometimes been described as the last frontier and the biggest challenge facing God's people. There are elements of truth in such descriptions. Besides its sheer size—1.6 billion people scattered all around the world and its many faces, ethnically, denominationally, and in actual practice, all of which require missions to think creatively, there are other challenges.

History

Muslims and Christians are not just now encountering each other. There has been a long history of give and take, sometimes relatively peaceful, other times characterized by exploitation, violence, and a mixing of commerce, politics, and colonialism. Different periods have given rise to different tactics in interacting. Both sides have to live with this legacy which often colors relations and interaction. Twenty-first century events from 9/11 to the invasions of Iraq and Afghanistan stand out in people's minds. As does the ongoing tension over Palestine embodied in Israeli-Arab conflicts. Westerners are often called upon to explain why they have participated in these events (as though they had a personal responsibility for what happened), questions not easy to answer.

Holism

Islam also challenges evangelical Christianity because of its holism, a term variously defined, but suggesting that religion should touch on all aspects of life, not just worship or the spiritual. Islam's refusal to divide life in secular and sacred realms runs counter to much current Evangelical thought. In many cases, Christians are forced to re-think their understanding of the gospel and its implications for the whole of life or leave Muslims wondering why they should be interested in such a partial faith.

Urban Emphasis

Another uniqueness of Islam which presents a notable challenge is its urban character. This is not to say that Islam does not have a vast rural constituency, it does. But historically Islam has always been a religion of the cities. It was born in a city, Mecca, realized its first power in a city, Medina, and went on to create spectacular urban areas, for example, Cairo and Baghdad. In some ways the same could be said of Christianity. The difficulty comes in modern times. Western churches have more and more abandoned urban areas for the more comfortable suburbs. Missionaries have historically come more from rural settings than urban. Even the language so popular in contemporary Christianity thrives on rural analogies and symbols. In fact, in many cases today's Christians find cities threatening. Costs, crime, and congestion have caused believers to turn away from the world's greatest concentrations of people. Islam all too easily and eagerly fills the vacuum. Meeting this challenge calls for new strategies and renewed courage.

Theological Challenges

A huge arena of challenge involves theology. Islam presents a fairly simple theology over against the complexity of major biblical doctrine, for example the trinity, incarnation, Jesus' role as perfect man and perfect God, and the substitutionary death of Christ. There is also the question of the Bible's make up (many authors, time periods, and emphases), its reliability, and translation. Muslims come with pointed questions expecting clear simple to understand answers, but feel they meet fancy verbal footwork that to them is ultimately illogical and unreasonable. Answering Muslim theological challenges is one of the biggest hurdles facing those who wish to present an understandable gospel. There are proven answers, but patience and persistence are needed in responding meaningfully.

Resources

The search to find adequate resources to carry on ministry is another area where the church often seems at a great disadvantage. Muslims with their oil reserves spend with great abandon to promote their cause. As long as oil reserves last, Islam can out spend Christian missions by a large margin. It is important to remember as Zechariah said, "It is not by might nor by power says the Lord, but by my Spirit."[3] In the meantime, this challenge looms large.

Changing World

Today's world is not the world of the nineteenth century. Not only has life speeded up but many old established orders have vanished. One is the colonial era with its influence in Muslim territory. In earlier generations missionary visas were often available because of European overlords; in today's new world of independence, easy to come by visas have all but disappeared. Now would-be missionaries often need to be kingdom professionals or bivocational workers. Most Muslim lands will not admit religious workers, but in-

3. Zech 4:6.

stead look for those with some practical skill that will improve the lives of their citizens. Christians are again challenged due to being wed too often to a system that prepares people to preach or minister, but to do little else. To even think of becoming bivocational with all the changes needed in orientation is often more than believers want to wrestle with, yet it must be done to access Islamic areas.

The list of challenges goes on: adequate preparation, commitment to fluency in a heart language, sufficient biblical training, and appreciation of contextualization and its limitations. Yet for all the challenges, many great things are occurring in ministry to Muslims.

WHAT'S GOING ON AMONG MUSLIMS?

To appreciate what's going on among Muslims today, a bit of perspective is needed. Evangelical missionaries first made a systematic effort to minister to Muslims beginning in the early 1800s. Their principle areas of concentration were the Middle East, British India, and Indonesia, in each case colonial influence aided in access. Within half a century agencies that entered the field with high hopes had largely given up on bringing Muslims to faith in Jesus and instead turned almost exclusively to educational and social ministries.

The first Lausanne Conference (1974) with its emphasis on unreached peoples and people groups did much to spur a renewed interest in the Islamic world. Agencies that had work among animist minorities in Muslim lands determined to spend more resources on Muslim majorities. New agencies came into being, such as Frontiers, with its exclusive Muslim focus, while other groups made definite efforts thereafter to give Muslims a fair proportion of resources and personnel. Some groups, like the Assemblies of God, created institutes devoted solely to Muslims. Others like SIM[4] and the Southern Baptists, developed special task forces to work among Muslims. The Adopt-a-People emphasis led many congregations to seek a way to be involved with Muslims.

A quick overview of Muslim areas gives cause for encouragement. (In most cases specific numbers are hard to come by due to security concerns.) In North Africa, small convert groups (Muslim background believers, MBBs) have come into existence. There are reports of hundreds of Berbers embracing Christ largely influenced by dreams and visions. In Egypt brave souls are reaching out to Muslims with positive results. And stories of semi-secret believers abound.

Fifteen years ago the number of missionaries in Turkey was greater than the number of MBBs. Today MBBs outnumber missionary personnel by ten or fifteen to one. In Central Asia MBB groups are rapidly multiplying often in the face of severe restrictions and persecution (for example, Uzbekistan). Bangladesh now has thousands of former Muslims who follow Christ. In Indonesia the numbers are not thousands but hundreds of thousands.

A most encouraging development is the rise of national agencies committed to Muslim outreach. In many parts of Africa agencies that are completely rooted and con-

4. SIM, Serving in Mission, formerly Sudan Interior Mission.

trolled by nationals are spreading the good news to Muslims, Nigeria is an example. In Indonesia, a national agency has church planters in every province of the country and is seeing MBB groups arise with regularity. MBB groups in the West are networking together while seeking to disciple believers of their ethnicities in their home countries. In addition, more efforts are underway to use technology to spread the gospel—film, internet, video, satellite, email, ipods—and the list of new ingenious ways goes on and on.

All of the above is cause for rejoicing, and yet, the needs of the Muslim world are hardly being met.

BASIC MUSLIM BELIEFS AND PRACTICES

To Muslims, Islam is a divine religion, revealed by God from heaven and intended as the faith of all humankind. The Qur'an is its holy book, a document given directly to Muhammad and containing all the truth people need. Islam believes God has spoken to humankind through prophets and messengers from the beginning of time. Included in the list of prophets are Abraham, Moses, David, and Jesus. However, Muhammad is the last seal of the prophets. His message, embodied in the Qur'an, reflects what God has always said through prophets and supercedes any earlier books, including the Old and New Testaments.

Religious authority in Islam rests with God's revealed word, the Qur'an, and with it, Muhammad, especially in terms of his decisions and actions . Since he is the last messenger, his behavior takes on an authoritative nature. Extensive collections of traditions attributed to Muhammad, known as Hadith or Sunna, take their place with the Qur'an in sketching what a Muslim life and world would look like. From the Qur'an and Hadith, along with decisions by educated religious judges, comes Muslim law (shari'a), an extensive legal collection describing numerous aspects of life, both for the individual and for the state.

Dr. Amir Ali, former director of the Chicago based Institute of Islamic Information and Education, has outlined an approach to basic Islamic beliefs and practices that is both commonplace and unique in its comprehensiveness. Under the overarching heading of "requirements for the salvation of man," he divides requirements into physical and spiritual. Most Muslim scholars do not mention the physical. Included in physical requirements are cleanliness issues, in terms of body, clothing, and environment.

The description of spiritual requirements is more extensive. It begins with beliefs and includes the kinds of things all primers on Islam note: belief in one God, belief in prophets culminating with Muhammad, and acceptance of revealed books, the Qur'an being the last. Belief in angels comes next followed by acceptance of the doctrine of the last days and life hereafter, which supposes resurrection, judgment and one's final destiny in paradise or hell.

Attention is then given to works (deeds or practices). Dr. Ali, true to most introductions to Islam, first lists what have been called the five pillars, the recitation of the creed (or declaration of beliefs) with the added note that the recitation presumes a commitment to live by the faith declared. The other pillars follow in quick order: ritual prayer five times daily, the giving of alms, fasting during Ramadan, and the pilgrimage to Mecca.

It is at this point that Dr. Ali's broadens his material by including deeds not usually spoken of. The first is excellence in knowledge and conduct. Second, Islam's moral code is summarized in the frequent Quranic expression, enjoining the good and forbidding evil. Then comes rights and duties, noting obligations of individuals to God, to other humans, to one's community, and to the environment. The final three are submission to shari'a in all its civil and criminal provisions, conveying the message of Islam (what Christians might call evangelism), and working to implement the rule of God on earth.

The initial rubric was one of requirements for salvation. The conclusion is that those who attempt to meet the above requirements do so in an effort to deserve Allah's forgiveness, grace, and mercy. Clearly from this Muslim scholar's perspective Islam is a system of works done in an attempt to deserve grace, a far cry from the biblical system. When asked by students, "If you died today, do you know you would go to heaven?" Dr. Ali always answered, "you cannot know until the time. We cannot know how God will judge." His answer points to a traditional understanding of God. He is absolute sovereign whose main characteristic is will or power. He is not bound by anything, including the Qur'an, but can change his mind as he wills.

There are a number of points at which Islam and the Bible, at least superficially, seem to agree, doctrines such as the oneness of God, God's sovereign lordship and power, his creative acts and maintenance of the world, his revelation of his will, and his role as final judge. In all of these Islam and Scripture use the same language. However, there are also serious differences. For example, biblically, God is not only one but also triune. He becomes incarnate, loves unconditionally, and is true to his word as reflected in the idea of covenant. He also is known and enters into personal relationships with people. Islam denies all of these doctrines.

With regard to Jesus, Islam has several things to say that Scripture supports, his virgin birth, miraculous work, sinlessness, continued existence in heaven, and second coming. The Qur'an even uses a multitude of positive terms to describe Jesus, including Messiah, Word of God, and Spirit of God. But Islam rejects the deity of Christ, his atoning death and resurrection, as well as Jesus being Lord, Son, and Judge, among other things.

With regard to humanity, both Islam and scripture agree that God created people, that humans are accountable, and all have sinned. However Islam has no place for the fall, nor humankind existing in the image of God. When it comes to a solution to sin and evil, Islam relies on a book, the Qur'an, and works of obedience. There is no Savior, nor is there a need for one. Scripture points to God's intervention in a substitutionary sacrifice, the transforming power of the Holy Spirit, and the need for a trusting relationship with a person, namely Jesus.

With regard to the Bible, Muslims affirm that it has been changed and consequently is unreliable except where it agrees with the teachings of the Qur'an.

BIG ISSUES MUSLIMS FACE TODAY

Within the world of Islam today there are several big issues that are being debated by Muslims. These revolve around questions of the relationship of Islam to the modern world. For many conservatives, the debate is an expression of Muslims being seduced by modernity and secularism. For them there is nothing to discuss. Instead Islam today ought to be what it was in the seventh century. Age-old traditions are to be obeyed as they always have been.

For Muslims influenced by contemporary politics and education, there is a sense that Islam needs to modernize if it is to be relevant to the twenty-first century. Key areas for re-consideration are Islamic law (shari'a), the nature of the text, meaning of the Qur'an, and issues of democracy and human rights, especially the rights and role of women. To these can be added questions of freedom of thought and freedom to change one's religion.

With regard to Islamic law, some are championing the need to update and modify Islamic law. To traditionalists this seems unwarranted and is an attack on one of Islam's basic pillars. The Qur'an is one of Islam's most sacred elements and a basic contributor to Islamic law. Traditionalists assume the Qur'an came directly from God to Muhammad, uninfluenced by his times, cultural setting, or personality; it was written down verbatim and has remained unchanged through fourteen hundred years. Muslims of a more secular inclination question the actual text of the Qur'an, speak of variant readings, and believe the Qur'an needs to be read and interpreted in the light of the specific historical and cultural settings which gave rise to it. Their desire for serious textual and historical-cultural criticism is anathema to fundamentalists.

Muslim feminists challenge traditional understandings of passages associated with the nature and role of women. Some insist that traditional applications are invalid; others are so bold as to say Muhammad made up certain passages to satisfy situations where he wanted a specific outcome. Thus, the texts in question are not divine at all, but the result of personal desire and ambition on Muhammad's part. Again, the reaction of traditionalists is outrage at such suggestions.

The outgrowth of these debates will be difficult to predict. One thing is clear, these are not arenas into which Christians should venture. No benefit can come from outside involvement. Family quarrels should be left to the family to resolve.

APPROACHES IN MINISTRY TO MUSLIMS

Over the last quarter century, with greater insights provided by applied anthropology and communication theory, Christians have become more sensitive, at least at a superficial level, to what helps and what hinders. A simple survey of MBBs in Cairo some years ago pointed to some commonalities in their journey to faith. All reported repeated exposure to the Word of God. Each confessed to have simply fallen in love with the Jesus of Scripture. All had a good Christian friend who stuck with them through good times and bad. With many there were supernatural experiences such as dreams, visions, and healings. For others, a high degree of contextualization in terms of means, message, and body of believers was cited. None was drawn as the result of well-reasoned arguments or superior logic.

Contextualization, a commitment to take the cultural setting of Muslims seriously, has been embraced more and more by workers with increasingly positive results. The very idea of contextualization implies there will be many ways to reach Muslims, for there are many contexts and these cannot be ignored or minimized. Any consideration of contextualization requires a serious look at core values which drive Muslim people.

A strategic value include, the place of community, in contrast to strong Western individualism, patterns of communication, which tend to be more indirect, and issues that matter, and above all, the dynamics of honor, Islam's central emphasis. Any effort at taking Muslims cultures seriously necessitates adjustments in approach as it relates to these and other values.

Jesus himself provides the ultimate endorsement of contextualization. In his case it is usually referred to as incarnation. He became flesh and lived among the people he was ministering to. Both elements (flesh and lived among) were critical to his credibility and to being understood. His conformity was extensive; at the same time he confronted certain elements in Jewish life which he deemed against God's will. In John's gospel his commission to the disciples reflected his incarnation, "As the father sent me so I am sending you," John 20:17.

Jesus provides a wonderful model for ministry to Muslims because he lived among Muslims! The people of his day, in their understanding of God and the life of faith, were Muslims in heart and practice. For example, they were strict monotheists having no room for God appearing in the flesh. Their religious practice was law and tradition based and specialized in externals. They were convinced of their heritage in the prophets. They were the people of God, the children of Abraham. For them religion was ritual, place, and a blend of the spiritual and political. One could go on with such statements, all of which are as true of Muslims as they are of first century Palestinian Jews. Jesus understands Muslims because he experienced them long before Muhammad came on the scene. What principles then can we learn from his example?

The Example of Jesus

Jesus shows that process is of great importance when people, like his disciples, are being guided to a radically different understanding of life, righteousness, and God. Jesus was a master at modeling what he taught. He met people where they were theologically and sociologically, and then guided them to new insights. He was a master at timing his statements and deeds. He utilized the place of stories, a common communication vehicle in his society. And he allowed people to move forward at their own pace, giving them time to wrestle with new ideas.

The concept of honor (mentioned earlier) has been used as a way of trying to explain Jesus, his life, and death. Muslims understand the concept of honor and the obligations associated with it. Jesus' life and death are explained in terms of a loyal son, or representative, being true to the one who sent him, the Father, even to the point of being willing to suffer death. The death of the son would have been viewed as an act of dishonor directed toward the Father. It would necessitate that something be done to remove the shame, hence the resurrection, which renders God blameless and shows Jesus superiority over all other forces and beings.

Sometimes the idea of *Christus Victor*, Christ the victory, is woven into the honor presentation, showing Jesus' victory over the one Muslims fear most, namely Satan. Satan is seen as having struck his best blow, the crucifixion, but was defeated forever in the resurrection of Jesus, an act that reinforced the honor of God.

It is important to note a couple of responses to Muslims that may be tempting to undertake, but are disastrous. 1) Never criticize Muhammad even though there are aspects of his life and character that deserve criticism. 2) Never belittle the Qur'an, Islam's holy book. There are a number of things about it that trouble non-Muslims, but to attack it is fruitless in terms of winning Muslims to Jesus. The issue is not Muhammad or the Qur'an, but Jesus and who he is as revealed in scripture. When Muslims come to faith, the place and importance of Muhammad and the Qur'an seem to fade from view.

SPECIAL CHALLENGES

Within a consideration of the Islamic world there are several items that deserve a special word. All that has been noted previously applies to these issues, but each of the following has its own special qualities.

Women

When the subject of women and Islam arises, it is typical to think almost exclusively in terms of the situations facing women who are Muslim. However, an equally important consideration has to do with Christian women who attempt to live among and minister to Muslim women. Given the rather rigid separation of the sexes in much of Islam, ministry of any kind among females will fall almost exclusively to devout Christian women. Effectiveness on their part necessitates knowledge of Islam, its values and worldview, and also a sense of how Islamic values are expressed as they relate to women of any ethnicity or religion.

Muslim women are as varied culturally, socially and religiously as the larger Muslim community. Stereotypes abound usually picturing Muslim women as beaten down, lacking freedom, and generally exploited by Muslim men. While there is some truth within these caricatures, there are also many Muslim women who do not match this common picture held by Westerners. One must know the individuals. The Christian woman worker has yet another layer of insight and sensitivity to deal with.

Many Muslim women live in small worlds consisting of home, husband, relatives, and children. In many cases, their freedom of thought and movement is limited. For many within this category, the religious practice of the mosque is not part of their life.

Rather, they deal with issues of magic, spirits, and fear. Access to them is a challenge and often depends on the willingness of the males within their family. Those men in turn are very concerned to protect their women from their perception of the corruption and rebelliousness of Western women. A Christian woman's acceptance often has to begin with her husband first being accepted by the men of the clan. They would especially be interested in seeing that the worker's wife was not rebellious, was in submission to her husband, and always maintained high standards of honor, especially sexual purity.

Development

For the most part missionary visas are no longer available for Muslim areas. Christian workers must consider other avenues of entrance. Social service programs or development may be an answer to access issues. In some cases development is seen as little more than a practical way in. This is unfortunate. Good mission practice needs a solid theological basis. The gospel is all encompassing and so provides for good biblical grounding of development activities. The challenge from the Christian side is to re-connect development with evangelism and church planting and to do so from a biblical point of view. This effort raises issues about assumptions regarding the length and breadth of the gospel and the meaning of a holistic approach.

From the Muslim side, it is easy to assume that development activities are simply a cover for evangelism. Many Muslims view Christian based social services as deceptive. Hence they oppose them, resisting efforts at doing social good. Situations differ from one another. Thus it is important to try to discover what social activities might best meet local needs and stir the least opposition. Contextualization is vital in development work.

Persecution

Another area of special need involves persecution of workers among Muslims as well as new MBBs. Jesus reminds us that persecution is to be expected. MBBs have a keener sense of what the possibilities for persecution are as they live in the midst of Islamized societies. Foreign workers face a far less serious threat. Likely, if trouble comes, it will result in their expulsion and little more. However, for national believers there can be severe social and economic consequences. How can those working among Muslims help prospective believers prepare for the inevitable? Efforts are underway to address this question.

CONCLUSION

By way of summary the following factors should be considered. 1) The Muslim world is vast, complex, and sophisticated. 2) There is a long history of Muslim-Christian interaction in many arenas of life, where a huge amount of negative baggage has accumulated. This history cannot be ignored. 3) For the work of world evangelization to be completed, the Muslim world needs far more well informed attention than it has received up until now. 4) Effective ministry requires far more attention to social, cultural, and theological issues than has been the case in the past. 5) New strategies need to be developed, strategies that are heavy in contextualization while giving due consideration to Scripture. 6) The process is going to be long, difficult, and at times discouraging, but God's people must resist the temptation to write-off the Muslim world. And finally, 7) a new era of prayer and dependence on the Holy Spirit is needed, for in the final analysis God must lead the way, open doors, and soften hearts.

15

Short-Term Missions: A Cup of Cold Water in My Name?

by Donovan Weber and Bill Weber

THE INITIAL CHALLENGE IN any discussion on the evangelical short-term mission movement (STM) is defining what it is. This has never been more true than in the current age of globalization. In the modern mission movement the term STM has been used to describe mission service of up to two or three years. Since the term STM was introduced over fifty years ago, the duration has become shorter and shorter and today is more commonly identified as a two-week trip or even a weekend trip to the inner-city.

In a relatively short period of time this movement has grown to include millions of Christians around the globe spending billions of dollars. The growth and influence has created new interest on the part of local congregations, colleges and seminaries, mission organizations, and long-term missionaries serving in a cross-cultural context. It is a movement that has demanded attention from the missiologist who studies developments within missions to the local youth minister whose job description includes organizing and leading an STM each summer.

DEFINING SHORT-TERM MISSIONS AND ITS PURPOSES

STMs in the context of evangelical Christianity were born out of a long tradition of evangelizing. The term "short-term missions" developed within the modern mission movement as a way to describe trips that were taken in the spirit of the evangelical mission tradition, but by those who were not ready or able to make a career or long-term commitment. Although the institution of cross-cultural missions has been active for over 2000 years, the STM movement is brand new. The STM movement has evolved and expanded quickly in step with the acceleration of other transnational activities over the past five decades of globalization.[1] The *Protestant Mission Handbook*[2] describes STMs as trips lasting two weeks to one year. However Robert Priest's research suggests that a large proportion of

---

1. Globalization is recognized as a process of diminishing local and regional constructs into global ones that has been developing over centuries of empire building, colonialism and now post-colonial migrations. Due to new technologies in travel and communications this process has accelerated significantly over the past 50 years.

2. *Mission Handbook*, 12–13.

STMs last from seven to 10 days.[3] The number of junior high and high school students who go on these trips each year as part of church programming may account for the growing number of shorter trips. Although the *Protestant Mission Handbook* also describes STMs as overseas trips it is beneficial to expand this boundary due to the number of STMs that travel to places within the United States such as Native American reservations, urban centers like New Orleans, and impoverished rural areas such as parts of Appalachia. These trips may not involve the greater cultural differences (cultural distance) and expense of trips taken to Africa and Southeast Asia, but they still fit a broader definition of Christian mission work in a cross-cultural context.

As the STM movement has developed in relation to the long-term mission movement and other forms of globalization, new ideas have arisen to inform how the movement is defined. The average amount of time that STM trips involve is still a valuable way of thinking about what an STM is. But STMs may be better defined by what they can reasonably accomplish based on the time constraints of such trips. Defining STMs by what they can do is different than defining them by their intentions.[4] For example, many STMs claim to do friendship evangelism. However, it is not reasonable to think that this type of evangelism can take place within a 10-day period when the STM participant does not know the language or cultural and spiritual nuances of the people they are visiting.

The work that STMs can reasonably accomplish fall under these six categories:

1. Preaching/Teaching (leadership development, evangelistic meetings, Vacation Bible Schools, etc.)

2. Service Projects (construction, medical projects, community development projects, etc.)

3. Spiritual Pilgrimages (spiritual retreats, prayer walks, rites of passage)

4. Long-term Missionary Care (provide emotional/spiritual support to long-term workers)

5. Exploratory Trips (to determine whether to make a long-term commitment)

6. Learning Experience (to learn about cross-cultural ministry, contextualization, ethnocentrism, globalization, social justice issues, etc.)

DEVELOPMENT OF THE SHORT-TERM MISSION MOVEMENT

Describing the early years of this movement in evangelicalism is a difficult task largely due to the lack of research early on and also to the grassroots nature of the movement. Because of the unwieldy and disjointed nature of Christendom in the United States it is difficult to generalize the origin of many sociological trends that develop within it. It could be argued

3. Priest, "Researching the short-term mission movement." 433.

4. Scott Moreau offers five categories of STM goals based on his research of the stated primary activity of mission agencies from the U.S. and Canada, including; 1) Evangelism/Discipleship; 2) Education/Training; 3) Mission Agency Support; 4) Relief and Development; 5) Other. Moreau, "Short-Term Missions in the Context of Missions, INC.," 16–19.

that STMs have existed as long as Christian missions have. However, there has been an obvious growth in the movement in both numbers and its perceived value within the evangelical church over the past fifty years.

The popularity of STMs across the entire evangelical demographic spectrum has increased disproportionately to other travel trends in the age of globalization. As travel has become more accessible to the middle class in the US over the past thirty to forty years, increased international travel has allowed for large growth in the service tourism industry, which is non-faith-based travel focused on relief and development work. However, there is a twofold reason for the disproportionate participation of evangelicals in this area: 1) the perceived urgency and obligation to participate in fulfilling the great commission; 2) the communal funding of STMs making international travel more affordable. The first reason provides an ideological framework for the STM phenomenon, whereas the second reason provides an important practical framework.

Regarding communal funding, there is a long tradition of mission work being funded by the church dating back to the Apostle Paul in the book of Acts. The understanding of the church in Antioch financially funding Paul and Barnabas' mission work in Acts 13 has served as a norm for the Christian church for two thousand years and has been easily adopted by the STM movement. There are some self-funded STMs, but today funding for mission trips typically involves participants writing a letter to solicit funds. This letter is distributed to members of their church community and is typically also distributed to family and friends who are sympathetic to their cause. The soliciting of funds is the responsibility of the individual, however, money is often contributed to a communal fund that offsets the excesses and shortcomings in the fund-raising efforts of individual participants. Many evangelical churches have mission funds that are used to support long-term career individuals and mission organizations, but there are a growing number of churches that have budget allocations specifically to fund STMs for their members.

NUMERICAL GROWTH

There has been at least one attempt to estimate the numerical growth of this movement since the late 1950s by McDonough and Peterson. Although this study lacks evidential support for its estimations, it is important because of its ubiquitous use in the early literature discussing STMs. The authors attribute the STM movement in evangelicalism to two different individuals, George Verwer with Operation Mobilization (OM) and Loren Cunningham with Youth With a Mission (YWAM). These men separately decided that young people could be involved in Christian mission for short periods of time. According to McDonough and Peterson this decision sparked a movement in the late 1950s. This is the period that is identified as the beginning of the current phase of globalization that grew from 540 individuals involved in STMs in the beginning to 120,000 in 1989. Using an estimation by John Kyle, the director of the Evangelical Foreign Missions Association (EFMA), they suggest that the movement had grown to 450,000 participants annually in

1998.[5] By this time the authors assumed that their estimations were fairly conservative based upon the trends they were observing.

Roger Peterson observed that the STM movement has continued to grow over the past fifty years, and that there was a significant boom during the 1990s in comparison to the first three decades of the movement. While qualifying that these numbers were virtually impossible to reproduce, he attempted to construct a conservative estimate of STM participants in the USA. His findings show that 35,000 churches, 3,700 North American agencies and 1,000 North American schools were involved in planning and implementing STMs at this time. Based on these numbers he conservatively estimated that the number of Christian STM participants in the United States had exceeded one million per year by 2003.[6]

This estimation has been supported by two recent studies. Robert Wuthnow, Professor of Sociology and Religion at Princeton University, conducted a national survey (n=2,231) of active church members in the United States in 2005. Wuthnow conservatively estimates that 1.6 million Christians participate in STMs to other countries each year with a cost of approximately $1.1 billion with transportation costs conservatively estimated at another $1.6 billion.[7] Robert Priest from Trinity Evangelical Divinity School surveyed 120 Master of Divinity students and found that 62.5 percent had already participated in an STM trip and that 97.5 percent of these students expected to participate in an STM trip in the future.[8] These numbers are noteworthy not only because they highlight the popularity of such trips with American students training for ministry, but also because they point to another trend in the STM phenomenon, participation in multiple STMs. The proliferation of STM not-for-profit organizations and an increase in the "how-to" literature on the subject of STMs are further indicators of the movement's growth.

The research of Wuthnow and Priest also represents a more critical examination of the STM movement than Peterson and his associates had previously offered. Based on the numerical growth and the billions of added dollars to support this growth, the STM movement was bound to draw critical interest from those in the evangelical missions movement and from non-evangelical scholars as well. These researchers are asking what effectiveness the STM movement is having on the larger evangelical mission movement as well as what effect it is having on larger trends in globalization.

TENSIONS BETWEEN SHORT-TERM MISSIONS AND LONG-TERM MISSIONS

The growth and prominence of the STM movement has created tension within the evangelical mission movement. The main critique from missiologists is that even a basic understanding of cross-cultural mission work is absent from the work of many STM practitioners. This is what Priest and Priest call the "amateurization of missions" where

---

5. McDonough and Peterson, *Can Short-Term Mission Really Create Long-Term Missionaries?* 1.

6. Peterson, *Maximum Impact Short-term Mission,* 252–255.

7. Wuthnow and Offutt, "Transnational Religious Connections." 218.

8. Priest, "Researching the short-term mission movement." 434.

they "see everything but understand nothing."[9] This critique is well founded as there exists a mentality within the movement that anyone who is spiritually mature and willing to travel is qualified to organize and lead a cross-cultural STM. However, this definition of spiritual maturity rarely includes an understanding of self in relation to the "other."[10] This is significant as the evangelical movement has a tradition of racial segregation in many church groups consisting of fairly homogenous populations. When spiritual leaders have little experience with other races and ethnicities in their own community, it is difficult to imagine that the same ideologies that created a lack of engagement with the other is not transferred into this new environment.

Many within the evangelical movement who are aware of the disconnect between amateur STM travelers and missiologists are not concerned about it; in fact, they applaud it. Churches and independent evangelical organizations that have not traditionally been involved in cross-cultural mission work are now getting involved through STMs regardless of whether they have the support of either missiologists or long-term career missionaries. Much of this is due to the lack of cohesion within the movement, but this trend is also attributed to a shift in thinking from the baby-boomer generation. David Dougherty, a member of Overseas Missionary Fellowship International (OMF) as well as a former church minister, has identified what he calls "two major streams of action."[11] These two streams are: 1) missions as process, and 2) missions as project. According to Dougherty, the former represents the methodical, ongoing activities of mission organizations and independent missionaries. The latter represents a new interest in reaching out to unreached, or least-reached people groups through more intensive efforts. Another way of stating this difference is that missions as process focuses on the activities of missionaries while the project movement focuses more on the accomplishments of mission efforts.

This new approach is influenced by a generation of people who want to use their spiritual gifts, or talents, as a way to contribute to the great commission. Dougherty believes that this interest is born out of an entrepreneurial spirit in the United States among baby boomers who have more time and resources to participate in STMs. These entrepreneurs include such people as retired teachers, contractors who own their own businesses, and business professionals who have more vacation time at this point in their careers. The latter example is particularly relevant to this conversation as there is currently an interest in business partnerships in the modern mission movement as a way to establish sustainable churches in impoverished communities around the globe.

Implying that these two approaches are neutral, apolitical methods for accomplishing the same task is overly simplistic. There is a palpable tension between missiologists, traditional long-term missionaries and their sending organizations, and the ever-growing STM movement. Those advocating the traditional process approach to missions are grap-

---

9. Priest and Priest, "They See Everything, and Understand Nothing," 1.

10. Otherness (other, othering) is helpful in understanding the dynamics of STM participants encountering cultures different than their own. Like ethnocentrism, otherness recognizes cultural differences such as development and wealth, but also ways of thinking, relating and doing. Othering uses the perceived inferiority of another group to establish the perceived superiority of one's own identity.

11. Dougherty, "What's Happened to Missions Mobilization?" 276–278.

pling with the explosion of STM interest, trying to figure out how to best channel this emerging new voice in evangelicalism. The purpose of that voice is to more effectively use the STM movement for the intended purposes of Christian mission, but also to do damage control. Christian Westerners visiting the slums and villages of the developing world with little or no preparation have the potential to be counter-productive for Christian mission, but it also creates scenarios for unethical human interaction and exploitation.

COMPETITION FOR RESOURCES

Another issue in this tension between long-term and short-term missions is the competition for resources. The proliferation of STM organizations and professionals has occurred in the context of a powerful and salient assertion within the movement. This assertion states that as people participate in STMs they are more likely to give money to support missions and more likely to become long-term missionaries. For missiologists concerned about Christian mission, the implication is that resources must now be shared with this growing movement with little evidence of the validity of this assertion. A missions pastor from Minneapolis describes STMs this way, "I think it is a stimulation to missions. I don't think it is robbing missions dollars from long-term supporters but rather widening the pool of informed missions supporters, both the returning short-termers as well as the support networks they have tapped into."[12] While this may be true, this assertion is only supported by anecdotal evidence at this point. What must be noted in relation to this is that this pastor now has a vested interest in the STM movement. His paycheck and his career rely upon people from his church involving themselves in STMs. This is an especially sensitive issue in the Christian mission movement because of the not-for-profit status of churches and parachurch organizations like those that organize mission trips. Essentially both streams, borrowing Dougherty's term, are raising their funds from the same donor pool, which is evangelical churches and the individuals that these churches represent.

The magnitude of this movement and the various ways in which North American Christians are getting involved is exemplified in the recent STM activity of a Midwestern evangelical megachurch (a church with average worship attendance exceeding 2,000). In April, 2006, this church organized an STM for 300 people to travel to a southern African country. This trip was received well by the sending church, so then they organized two trips of 300 each to travel to the same location in July 2007. What developed was an ongoing partnership where smaller groups of professionals traveled to this same location throughout the year helping to support and continue projects that the larger group worked on. The church conducted another trip in 2008 and a fourth trip in 2010. According to the church's reporting, these groups consisted of medical professionals, IT professionals, business professionals, teachers, and contractors who participated in projects related to their fields, as well as agricultural and construction projects. This church highlights some of the positive trends in the STM movement of prolonged engagement with distant communities and involving participants in areas of service that may not be able to be filled by nationals within those communities. However, while this church's activities may be

12. Guthrie, *Missions in the Third Millennium*, 111.

reflecting trends in globalization and service tourism, the long-term missions movement would ask how much does it cost to send 900 people to Africa over a two-year period? And, what else might this money be used for? Furthermore, there is no information about how so many people are received or accommodated by the host community. Nor is there mention of any investigation into the host community's perception of these visits. Also missing is follow-up research with the participants.

STMS AND CHANGE IN PARTICIPANTS

Despite the objections raised to the STM movement by a minority of stakeholders in Evangelicalism, such as missiologists and long-term missionaries, attitudes among evangelicals as a whole toward the movement are positive. This positive disposition toward STMs in the larger evangelical community is due to the myth that participants' actions and thoughts are changed significantly during and after a trip, and that the world is a better place because of these activities. This myth has recently been critiqued, raising questions about the overall effectiveness of STMs on participants and the possibility of the movement's complicity in unjust global patterns.

The assumption that the actions and thoughts of participants are changed significantly because of their participation in STMs most likely developed out of anecdotal evidence and narratives from a variety of people about their cross-cultural travels. This assumption holds strong within evangelicalism despite the research concluding that an STM experience is just as likely to reinforce previously held stereotypes and to increase ethnocentrism among participants.[13] It is not difficult to envision throngs of American Christians going on a cross-cultural adventure for two weeks returning with stories of exotic foods and poor people with brown skin who truly appreciated their presence. However, within missiological circles this myth has also been supported by the research from the Short-term Evangelical Missions (STEM) organization in Minneapolis, MN.

As mentioned before, there is very little quantitative research that has been done on STMs. Of the studies that do exist, the most influential has been one conducted by STEM, which is an organization that organizes STMs and provides training for those interested in leading trips of their own. Their study, *Can Short-Term Mission Really Create Long-Term Missionaries?*, suggested that those who participated in STMs upon their return engaged more in positive activities like prayer, were more likely to consider full-time mission service as a career, and were inclined to give more money to fund mission services because of their experience.[14] However, the recent influence of this survey is far greater since the authors claim that this study validates an earlier study from 1991 by the same organization titled *Is Short-Term Mission Really Worth the Time and Money? Advancing God's Kingdom Through Short-Term Mission*. These outcomes suggest a win-win situation for those who go on STM and those who host them. The popularity of this widely cited study has contributed to an already well-established myth within the evangelical world as a whole, that STMs make a valuable contribution to the mission of the church. The

13. Rickett, "Short-Term Missions for Long-Term Partnership," 43.

14. McDonough and Peterson, *Can Short-Term Mission Really Create Long-Term Missionaries?* 10–18.

residue from this study has also guarded the movement from further critical analysis for almost two decades.

At first glance there seems to be some validity to McDonough and Peterson's work since it includes a large percentage of the sample population (n=432 of a possible 2,035) and the longevity of the study (ten years). Their method was to administer an attitudes and behavior survey to participants in STEM-organized STMs from 1985 to 1995 shortly after returning from their trip. The survey inquires about participants' giving habits, spiritual activities, and their knowledge on the subject of cross-cultural evangelical missions after they returned from their STM experience. However, a closer inspection reveals that there was no pretest before the trip and that no effort was made to compare their findings with other data, such as actual giving records of participants or other observable indicators. Instead, participants were asked to estimate how much money they gave to and how often they prayed for missions as far back as three years before their trip. Besides the suspicion that one might have about the ability to accurately remember what they were doing before they went on an STEM STM, there is concern for the research bias of both the STEM researchers and the STM participants to portray a positive image of their efforts. These are both issues that the researchers acknowledge in their report.[15] The most significant weakness was the researchers' inability to triangulate the data with another source of data.

IMPACT ON HOST COMMUNITIES

McDonough and Peterson's study, along with other less influential projects, have come under scrutiny for their research methodology. Missiologist Kurt Ver Beek notes that most STM research by evangelical organizations focuses almost exclusively on the impact on American participants and not on the host communities. Of the 44 papers he reviewed that focused specifically on quantitative research on STMs, only four attempted to survey the effects of STMs on host communities. This highlights the trend in the growth and development of the STM movement on the emphasis of benefits for individuals who are thought of as providers of service rather than the beneficiaries of service.

In his own research on the experiences of North Americans who traveled to Honduras to build homes after Hurricane Mitch in 1998, Ver Beek's findings varied greatly from McDonough and Peterson. Ver Beek surveyed 127 STM participants. He also had a Honduran social worker and a North American social worker interview thirty families whose homes were built by the Americans. In a similar fashion to the STEM research project participants were asked about whether or not they had made positive life changes in a variety of areas. One of the tangible areas that could be triangulated by third-party data was whether or not participants had increased their giving to the Christian International Development Fund (CIDO), the sending STM organization. Of the 113 responses to the question of whether or not participants would be giving money to CIDO, 10 percent reported that their financial support had increased significantly two years after the trip, and 49 percent claimed that their giving to CIDO had increased somewhat. According to CIDO's donor records 75 percent of the 162 participants who

---

15. Ibid., 21–22.

had participated in their Honduras trips had not made any financial contribution to the organization during the two years after the trip. Furthermore, the total giving of the STM participants only went up 6 percent after the trip. Averaged out, this represented a change from $31 per year per participant to $33.[16]

Besides providing research findings that challenge the results of the seminal STEM research project, Ver Beek's study went a step further by surveying the recipients of the CIDO STM projects. These were the Honduran families who received a new home. Although the Honduran families helped in the building process and agreed to pay back some of CIDO's investment, they were generally grateful for the assistance. However, what Ver Beek did find was that "the North American work teams seemed to have no greater impact on the communities than the Honduran Christian organizations—either positive or negative."[17] This finding is all the more potent considering that the Honduran Christian organizations built the same houses for $2,000 that it cost the North American groups $30,000 to build once travel and accommodation expenses were figured into the cost. For those who are concerned with the goals of Christian mission, these findings are alarming on two fronts. First, the implications seem to be that national Christian organizations can be just as effective without the presence of STM workers regardless of their skill sets. Second, the most basic form of cost/benefit analysis would question whether this is the most effective way for an organization or community to reach its stated goals.

STMS AND TOURISM

Andrew Root echoes Ver Beek's concern that little to no positive life change takes place in STM travelers. However, he offers a second critique with implications that exceed the concerns of Christian mission. Root's critique questions the second part of the dual myth surrounding the STM movement that it recruits long-term missionaries and increases giving to mission organizations, by instead suggesting that the STM movement is participating in larger global patterns that both highlight and take advantage of inequality and injustice in the world. Root grounds this claim in Zygmunt Bauman's theory that the globalized world creates two types of travelers, tourists and vagabonds. According to Bauman there are no natural borders anymore because technology and the ease of travel in a globalized world have established the sense that no matter where somebody is in the world, they could always be elsewhere.[18] However, because this new postmodern world is stratified according to social class there are the welcomed travelers—the tourists who move freely through passport controls and borders, and there are the unwelcome travelers—the vagabonds who are immigrants, refugees, and those who desire to move but who do not have the means.

Root places the STM traveler in the tourist group because of their obvious resources but also because of the contradictions and paradoxes of their activities. Based on his own experience Root paints the STM as a strange space where travelers go to exotic places in

---

16. Ver Beek, *Lessons from the Sapling*, 485–86.

17. Ibid., 478.

18. Bauman, *Globalization*, 77–78.

the developing world and spend one day in the slums and the next day at a resort on the beach. This description would not be accurate of all STMs, but certainly many of them include explicit tourist activities in the vein of learning more about the country they are visiting or as a time of relaxation from the challenging work they have accomplished. Other trips might be recognized as nothing other than a vacation. By associating STM activities with Bauman's dichotomy of tourists and vagabonds in the globalized world, he recognizes that STMs need poor and disenfranchised people to justify their activity. It is because of poor vagabonds that Christians give money to STM travelers. Root states, "The mission trip is a tourist event, but most insidiously, a tourist event that uses vagabonds as its activities."[19]

Root uses Bauman's common understanding of postmodern people's desire to consume experiences as a way of understanding tourist activity. Tourists like to do things like visit museums, sample foods and visit interesting sites, but once they have consumed these things, they are ready to move on to the next experience. Root believes that the lack of positive life change in STM participants can be attributed to this desire to consume. Once the experience of feeding homeless people in a developing country is completed, the STM tourist can move on to the next experience leaving this experience as just another memory. The reason that this is possible is because STM travelers can occupy their minds with accomplishing tasks that can be easily measured within the context of a ten-to fourteen-day trip.

Instead, Root suggests that "our mission trips should not be about doing anything, but simply about being with people. They should be about seeing, hearing, and sharing existence with others, others who live as unwanted vagabonds in our world of tourism."[20] This is not to say that STM travelers should go and do nothing, but rather that their focus should be about reflecting on the plight of those in the developing world and how those in the developed world benefit from it.

This is an explicit departure from the conventional wisdom of the STM movement, which has traditionally focused on acts of physical service. Much of this emphasis has been based as much on Maslow's hierarchy of needs as it has been based upon any spiritual conviction, it making sense that a person's physical needs should be addressed before their spiritual needs can be met. However, there is a far more practical reason for physical acts of service (i.e., medical services, feeding programs, construction) based on the time restraints that define STMs. Although many STMs still claim to engage in forms of friendship evangelism and relationship building, it has been recognized that it is far more effective for a group of Americans in a foreign culture to build a house or assist in a feeding program due to their lack of cultural competency. Root's reasoning for abandoning such pragmatism is that "when our mission trips are about doing something, then like good tourists we are free to move on and eventually forget them, for we have done our part and now it is time to move on to another experience."[21]

---

19. Root, "The Youth Ministry Mission Trip as Global Tourism," 317.

20. Ibid., 318.

21. Ibid., 318.

STMS FOR CRITICAL REFLECTION

Root brings an important critique to the STM movement that is categorically missing from the literature on this subject. His suggestion of being with people and reflecting, rather than to be preoccupied by doing things for them, is his way of prompting life transformation and minimizing global injustice. Asking STM participants to reflect on the experiences of others is a doorway to the possibility of considering social inequality in the world. Reflection on the experiences of others may also help STM participants confront the privilege and power they have as travelers from the developed Western world over those in the developing world. It further raise the question of whether STM participants are perpetuating the dichotomy of helper and helpless without confronting the global political and economic arrangements that ensure that the helpers will continue to benefit from the system while those who are helpless are trapped in their place.[22]

Furthermore, at one time people in the developing world may have accepted American Christians into their communities with few presuppositions about their connectedness through the streams of globalization. Those days are coming to an end. Americans no longer travel to the developing world as innocent observers and good Samaritans who are in no way connected to or involved in the lived experiences of the host-nationals who receive them. Thomas Friedman describes those in the developing world as the three billion people who now have the means and the desire to collaborate and compete in the global world through new technologies that have made a disconnected world connected.[23] As these three billion people are more aware of the world and its interconnectedness, they will no longer receive American missionaries as just purveyors of the gospel but as the "haves" in the "haves and have nots" dichotomy. Missionaries must recognize that the message of their tourist lifestyle is as valued as their gospel message.

POSITIVE IMPACT OF SHORT-TERM MISSIONS

Anecdotal information provides a long list of positive results stemming from STMs. However, the absence of significant reliable empirical research limits the veracity with which these are presented. There is no doubt that STMs have brought new energy to the modern mission movement. It has also brought significant change to the modern understanding of missions. Those who plan and lead STMs should recognize both their contributions and limitations, and design trips that promote these positive outcomes.

First of all, STMs can be useful in recruiting long-term missionaries. Young people participating in trips organized for high school or college students are exposed for brief periods of time to cross-cultural living and ministry. The experience can have a profound impact on their sense of being called to a particular cultural context to engage in an ongo-

22. This is to say that an American traveler who is interested in helping the impoverished in the developing world might more effectively involve themselves in the Free Trade and Fair Trade movements rather than distributing clothing and rice somewhere in Africa. Scholars like Terence Linhart further raise the question of whether it is ethical to use these exotic locations as a staging ground for adventure and spectacle. Linhart, "They Were So Alive!" 451.

23. Friedman, *The World Is Flat*, 181.

ing ministry. Some long-term missionaries point to a particular STM experience as either a contributing or deciding factor in their pursuit of mission service.

Secondly, there is some evidence that STMs develop an increased interest and passion for missions in people who are active in churches in the US. As noted earlier, participants often report changes in their attitudes and behaviors regarding missions. One particular change is STM participants traveling with mission organizations are more likely to provide for the care of a child through a sponsorship program.

Third, STMs can provide valuable learning experiences that help people better understand a world that requires more cross-cultural interaction. With extensive and appropriate preparation, an STM can provide meaningful learning experience. Increased awareness of how people live, what they eat, how their families function, as well as expressions of faith, enable participants to better understand their world.

Fourth, there is a growing emphasis within Evangelicalism on STMs as a tool for spiritual and identity development in young people. The acts of service that define the trip within a Christian context are important components in this new emphasis.

Finally, STMs can and often do have a positive impact on career missionaries serving on the field. Numerous missionaries tell of timely visits by people who are significant to them. Welcoming these people into their homes has made a difference in their spiritual and emotional well-being. The stress of cross-cultural living, isolation from family and friends, and the absence of worship opportunities in their own language can create a desire for some contact with "back home."

CONCLUSION

The evangelical STM movement developed out of a long history of Christian efforts to evangelize people all over the world. These efforts have been diverse in their methods and in their effects on the world and its communities. The steady growth over fifty years, and the sheer number of people who are traveling cross-culturally in the vein of Christian mission, make STMs a significant factor in modern missions.

The challenges facing the evangelical STM movement to produce positive life change in participants, and to have a positive impact on the communities they visit, is an increasingly complex task. Although Christianity may offer a spiritual and moral framework to address these concerns, they can too easily be lost in the evangelical zeal for evangelism. This is an ideal time to evaluate both the social and spiritual impact of Short-Term Missions.

16

Crossing Language Barriers

by Greg Pruett

ALL THE IMPORTANT LEADERS in the area came to hear the preaching and eat some beef. My Christian friends in the small West African village had erected an ornate, grass-covered conference hall in front of the church with intricate care. We needed a place to host the crowd of esteemed guests we had invited to celebrate Christmas with us—all of them leaders in the world religion that dominates that region. Clusters of curious children peeked over the grass walls to catch a glimpse of the assembly while kicking up enough red dust to gradually deposit a layer of caked sediment in my lungs. Most of the church members were feverishly cooking the Christmas cow in anticipation of the feast to come after the preaching and singing—the highlight of the year.

Every weathered face in the crowd squinted at my interpreter and me in interested concentration as I stood up front pouring out the message of Jesus' love like water on cracked, thirsty souls. I did not yet know how to preach in the local language, but I played the part of the esteemed guest speaker that year anyway, with my friend, the pastor, straining to translate my message. If I close my eyes, I can still see those elders and chiefs hanging on every word we spoke, listening with rapt attention—probably the first real encounter with the message of Jesus for some of them. I had sucked the well of my limited experience completely dry in preparation for the message. I came up with a sermon illustration I thought would be sufficiently physical to translate. At the height of my message I announced: "When God says, 'Be holy as I am holy,' it is like telling people to jump to the moon. Some of us can jump higher than others, but no one can jump to the moon." Every head nodded vigorously in unison and many exchanged knowing glances. A great "Aha" moment rippled across the crowd complete with raised eyebrows. I felt in my heart that this could well be the beginning of a great movement to Jesus. I passed a sweet night in my delusion of competency.

Only the following day did one of my Christian friends have enough pity for me and the courage to burst my bubble: "Do you remember when you were preaching yesterday and everyone nodded and exclaimed their agreement . . . ?" It turns out that the moon is a religious symbol representing their world religion, and the local leaders had debated for decades whether it could be true that an unbelieving American had really flown to the moon. I also had not yet learned that the word for "jump" in the local language was the same as the word for "fly." The way they heard it, I had loudly proclaimed: "No one can fly to the moon!" thereby putting to rest all remaining doubt. Finally an American had publically admitted what every local religious leader intuitively suspected: The United States actually had perpetrated a hoax on the population of the world and no one had flown to the moon. That was not the sermon I had intended to preach, but I learned that day that nothing changes gospel into gibberish faster than language barriers.

What is the role of language in the Great commission? My experience has taught me that language barriers are the greatest obstacle to the spread of the good news about Jesus. At the same time, there is nothing quite like language in the world: until addressed, it remains an impenetrable obstruction, but once an outsider begins to communicate in the local language, the very barrier that prevented the communication of the message becomes the bridge on which the ideas cross. It becomes the winsome attractive force for people to identify with the message and know that it belongs to them. What does the great commission obligate us to do with regard to language barriers?

WHAT MUST WE DO TO OBEY JESUS?

There have been many trends, pendulum swings, and fads over the years in missions, but because Jesus is the one who sent us out, the most valid approach in mission is to carefully obey Jesus' mandate. We must obey his words, emulate his example, and live out the values of his kingdom. When Jesus commanded us to teach people of all nations to follow Jesus, he used the Greek word *ethne,* challenging us to reach people of every culture and ethnicity on earth. In the command, he included instructions to teach them to obey everything he commanded, Matt 28:18–20. Unless the people of every ethnic group hear or read Jesus' commands in a language they understand well, they cannot truly learn how to obey. When Jesus sent us out to the nations, he obligated us to cross all the language barriers on earth with his profound message of grace, salvation, and justice.

How can the nations and languages learn to obey all that Jesus commands if they cannot understand the commands? Jesus said that people cannot truly live without every word that proceeds from the mouth of God, Matt 4:4. They may be breathing and eating, but they are not really alive—they are not thriving spiritually—unless they live in the light of God's Word. Jesus wants the lives of the peoples of the world to be transformed by the power of God's Word. That they would cross from death to life—eternal life in heaven above as well as the vibrancy of living out the truth of the values of God's kingdom on the earth. That each would bring blessing and justice on the earth to the people around them: That blind people would see, the hungry would be satisfied, thirst would be quenched, and the good news would be proclaimed to the poor. Jesus announced the coming of his kingdom so that the peoples who are being saved would also receive on earth a foretaste of the beauty of the kingdom of heaven to come.

For the peoples of the earth to learn to follow Jesus and obey the teachings of his kingdom, we must cross every language barrier in the world with three things:

- Church

- Scripture

- Transformation

People following Jesus need the ongoing ministry and teaching of the church, the gathered followers of Jesus Christ spurring one another on to greater love and living out the values of the kingdom in their community. The church in turn must have Scripture in a language that opens their eyes to the transforming truth of God. However, it is not enough to have church and Scripture; the churches must be using the Scripture to transform their communities for Christ.

Therefore, the next major benchmark I see on the pathway to obeying the great commission is this: churches with Scripture transforming every language community on earth. We must cross every language barrier on earth with church, Scripture, and transformation. The mission's movement of our time has properly emphasized crossing every culture barrier to make disciples among all peoples to obey Jesus' commission.[1] That will happen in the more distant future, but in order to cross all the culture barriers well, right now we must also intentionally cross the 6,900 language barriers.[2]

CROSSING THE LANGUAGE BARRIERS

The idea that everyone should have a Bible they can understand first began to gain traction in the 1940s when both Wycliffe Bible Translators and the United Bible Societies were founded. By the late 1970s when the Bible translation movement was becoming a global movement with increasing momentum, only 420 of the earth's 6,900 languages had a New Testament.[3] Most people still did not have Scripture in their language. Since then, teams of missionaries from numerous Bible agencies have devoted epic efforts to translation in impenetrable jungles and mushrooming cities the world over. Verse by verse, language by language, God has painted through these last decades the careful strokes of a meticulous masterpiece. By 1996 the New Testament was available in the languages of 84 percent of the world's population.[4] Now only about 353 million people remain in the world with no Scripture at all, roughly 5 percent of the world's population.[5] I estimate that between 700 and 900 million people remain in the world without the whole New Testament in their language, only about 10 to 13 percent of the world's population. The dream born in the 1940s has been about 90 percent realized over the last seventy years. The Bible translation movement is now poised to finish the job.

The trends in Figure 1 show that, for the great majority of the world, if the Bible translation movement continues to build momentum as it has over the past thirty years,

---

1. Joshua Project, 2011.

2. Some of the 6,900 languages will not require translation work because their speakers are adequately bilingual in some other language with Scripture or the language is nearly extinct.

3. Grimes, *Ethnologue*.

4. Wycliffe Bible Translators, 1996.

5. Forum of Bible Agencies, 2011.

most every remaining translation project needed will begin during the next 20 years.[6] Back in 1999 a new translation project started every eighteen days. Now a project starts every five days.[7] The Bible translation movement has made great progress in the last seven decades and now has greater momentum, greater unity, and is starting new projects faster than ever before.

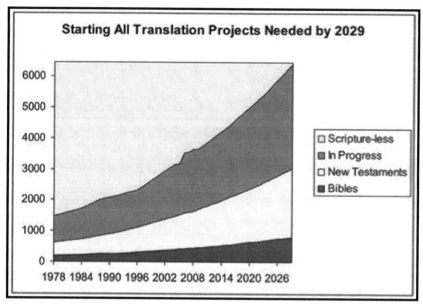

Figure 1: Translation Progress Trend Projection Based on Last 30 Years Data

Travelling around the world I can note the real world evidence of the numeric trends shown in Figure 1. In many places the members of the Forum of Bible Agencies and related partners are starting to see the light at the end of the tunnel. In parts of West and East Africa we have begun to establish projects among the last remaining language groups without God's Word. In North and South America the work has been for the most part handed over to local agencies and is nearing completion in many cases. New Bible agencies are starting up to join the cause around the world from many different nations. Bible translation for the sign languages of the world has begun to gather momentum, and now the first deaf Bible translation consultants are spearheading new translation efforts worldwide.

In the Bible translation agency in which I work, in the past year or so, when we have chosen to begin a project for a language community with more than one hundred thousand speakers, we have found that some other team that we knew nothing about has also just started it simultaneously. We are running out of the really big languages on which to start work. Soon we will be translating primarily for languages with between one hundred thousand and fifty thousand speakers. In another ten years, we may be working mostly on starting projects in languages with less than fifty thousand speakers. If the trend estab-

6. I estimate that all the Bible translation projects needed will have begun by around 2029. I have seen other estimates varying from 2037 to 2038 (www.wycliffe.org). The number of new projects still needed will likely be small by the early 2030s.

7. Wycliffe Bible Translators, 2011.

lished in Figure 1 is projected even further into the future, it predicts that every language in the world could have at least a complete New Testament by 2063. Whether the trend holds true or not, it is definitely up and to the right. A time is coming in which every language on earth will have the New Testament. We are now training and sending out the generation of Bible translators who could achieve a great benchmark toward obeying the great commission. This next generation could leave behind the legacy of a world in which everyone can have at least the New Testament in his or her language.

However, to achieve the milestone of churches with Scripture transforming every language community on earth, some heavy lifting still remains: 1) Some language groups have no Scripture, 2) others lack church, 3) still others lack both, 4) and yet others have Scripture and churches, but the churches are not yet using the Scriptures to transform their language context.

LANGUAGE GROUPS LACKING SCRIPTURE

Language communities that have churches without Scripture in their language suffer a lack of life transformation. Their spiritual growth remains hindered because they cannot easily access the transforming power of God's word. Recent research data collected over four years from over 80,000 people in 200 different churches in the US concluded: "The Bible is the most powerful catalyst for spiritual growth. The Bible's power to advance spiritual growth is unrivaled by anything else we've discovered. Reflection on Scripture is by far the most influential spiritual practice."[8] Another study of over one thousand Christian households showed that people who reported reading their Bible more frequently also reported that they had less debt and gave more to their church.[9] God's word has the power to transform people's lives. Without the word of God in a language they can understand well, churches lack the power to truly transform the lives of people and their communities.

Sadly, many language communities will continue to do without the word in their language for the coming decades. While the trend in Figure 1 shows that the Bible translation movement may start all the projects needed over the next twenty years or so for most places on the earth, some places may take much longer. The low-hanging fruit has been picked and the remaining languages often are spoken in countries that will not allow a missionary to hold a visa. Other world religions vigorously oppose the work of Bible translation. Challenging pockets of extreme linguistic diversity lie scattered over the earth. Their breathtaking numbers of languages require tremendous, creative efforts to meet the need. Much of the continent of Asia remains an ocean of languages without Scripture. For example, languages with unmet translation needs in Papua New Guinea number in the hundreds. A mountain range in North Africa has a different Scripture-less-language group on every mountain. Overwhelming needs in parts of West Africa remain largely unmet. Figure 2 characterizes the locations of the final frontiers of the Bible translation movement. If we grow complacent with current methods, we will not be able to maintain our momentum. We will not be able to compensate for the increasing difficulty of the task as we penetrate more and more complex and resistant areas of the world.

8. Hawkins, *Follow Me*, 104–105.

9. Kluth, *Bible Reading Helps Your Financial Health*.

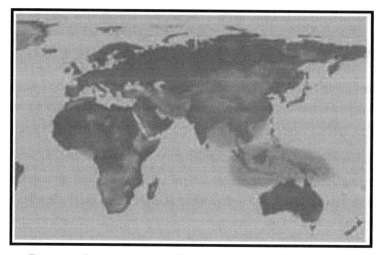

Figure 2: Concentrations of Remaining Translation Needs

Consequently, Bible translation agencies are re-tooling to meet the challenge of pioneering work among these last 2,252 languages spoken by 353 million people[10] in the most remote, marginalized places on earth. Over the next twenty years, innovative efforts will be necessary to build capacity in the various partnering Bible translation agencies to face these last great frontiers of translation need. The Bible translation movement is currently using primarily three methods to accelerate progress: 1) better technology for collaboration, information, communication, and translation, 2) adapting existing translations into related languages, and 3) training and helping the local people to do the translation more independently.

Better Technology

No longer do you hear stories about translators losing decades of work when a manuscript was lost in a canoe accident. Today's Bible translators take advantage of cutting-edge technology. Even though their work is still remote, they can communicate with teammates over satellite modems and internet-based collaboration tools. They no longer need to transport massive tomes like commentaries and Hebrew dictionaries. Now Bible translation software keeps all the information they need within a few clicks on the computer. The Paratext software has begun to be one of the greatest accelerations of the Bible translation movement yet. Paratext software was created by the United Bible Societies, but now is being developed further by a cooperative effort with Summer Institute of Linguistics, SIL.[11] Some agencies are even experimenting with crowd sourcing technologies in which all the pastors of a language cooperate over the internet to generate a Bible translation for themselves.

---

10. Forum of Bible Agencies, 2011.

11. SIL, Summer Institute of Linguistics, is one of the largest translation agencies in the world (http://www.sil.org/) and historically related to Wycliffe Bible Translators. For more information about the software Paratext see http://paratext.ubs-translations.org/about/pt.

Related Language Adaptation

As the Bible translation movement shifts over time to working on smaller and smaller languages, we will find that more and more of them are related to languages that already have a complete Bible. Because of this trend, software that helps adapt translations from one language to another will become exponentially more important. Because little is known about these minority languages, software like Google Translate and others like it cannot help with the process. However, other tools under development are becoming more powerful and user-friendly, proving useful to generate at least a first draft. Language adaptation software will help, over time, to complete remaining projects by adapting existing New Testaments or Bibles to other contexts. These adaptations become especially strategic in closed-access countries where expatriate translation specialists are not allowed to enter the country for long periods of time.

Training and Enabling Local People

The most powerful acceleration of the Bible translation movement remains training the local people to do the work with less outside help. Many Bible agencies are shifting almost exclusively to this approach. As Christianity grows stronger and more mature in more areas of the world, many capable partners are joining the work from a variety of countries and in virtually every context. Where once there was only one mission in the world known as "Wycliffe Bible Translators," now sixty different related missions have started in other countries partnering worldwide in the Wycliffe Global Alliance.[12] As more of the local people have access to higher degrees of education, the progress will be greatly accelerated as Bible agencies focus more effort on enabling the local people. Many of the remaining translation projects are being grouped together in cluster projects designed to leverage the achievement of more projects with fewer expatriate translation specialists. More funding has come available for innovative projects like this than ever before from agencies like The Seed Company.[13]

If the Bible translation movement can create enough innovative capacity through visionary leadership and leveraging all possible methods to accelerate the process, if they can increase capacity enough to overcome the increasing complexity and difficulty of the contexts where the last remaining languages are located, then it should be possible to complete most or all the remaining translation projects at least to the New Testament stage by 2050.

LANGUAGE GROUPS LACKING CHURCH

But having Scripture is not enough! What good is a Bible translation if you do not have churches or people who can read? For people to have their lives transformed by the power of God's word, faith-filled communities of followers of Christ must be proclaiming the word and engaging their context with the life-changing truth of Scripture. Every language group needs churches using these translated Scriptures to transform their communities.

---

12. For a more information on the Wycliffe Global Alliance see http://www.wycliffe.net/.
13. For more information see www.theseedcompany.org.

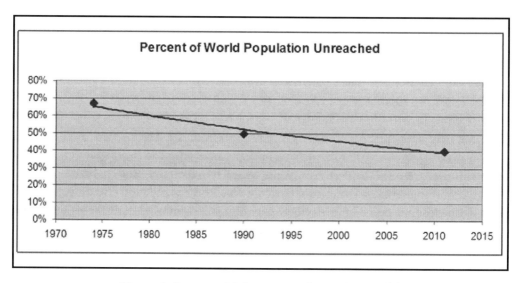

Figure 3: Progress Making Disciples in the World

In 1974 the Lausanne Covenant stated, "More than 2,700 million people, which is more than two-thirds of all humanity, have yet to be evangelised. We are ashamed that so many have been neglected; it is a standing rebuke to us and to the whole Church."[14] When I was training to be a missionary in 1990, the often quoted statistic was that half the population of the world was unreached. Now the Joshua Project website reports that 41.5 percent of the population of the world is unreached, or better stated "least reached."[15] The International Mission Board reports 40 percent.[16] Figure 3 shows these data points graphed with a possible trend line. If nothing else, the trend seems to indicate that we are making progress. When extended into the future, the math indicates that the earliest we could expect the percent of the world's population living with the label "least reached" to go to zero would be 2070 and more probably 2080 or later. One trend analysis indicates that we may drag out the process well past 2100.

Now is the time to mobilize the church to cross these remaining language barriers with the gospel. We can begin to take action today to position the coming generation of missionaries to finally succeed at a major benchmark in the task Jesus gave us to make disciples of all nations. If we effectively mobilize the church and focus some of our attention on intentionally crossing the language barriers, as well as the culture barriers, the coming generation could leave behind the legacy of a world in which every language community has a vibrant church movement ministering to the whole range of community needs.

14. The Lausanne Congress, 1974.

15. Joshua Project, 2011. According to the Joshua Project, "An unreached or least-reached people is a people group among which there is no indigenous community of believing Christians with adequate numbers and resources to evangelize this people group. The original Joshua Project editorial committee selected the criteria less than 2% Evangelical Christian and less than 5 percent Christian adherents. http://www.joshuaproject.net/definitions.php.

16. International Mission Board, 2011.

LANGUAGE GROUPS LACKING CHURCH AND SCRIPTURE

As bad as it would be to live without Scripture or without the hope that vibrant churches can offer, it can be worse. There are language communities in the world that have neither a vibrant church movement nor Scripture. About 900[17] language groups suffer the worst spiritual poverty on earth. They are both Scripture-less[18] and "least-reached"[19] lacking any hope of being able to have their lives transformed either by a vital Christian witness or by encounter with Scripture. Figure 4 reveals that about 200 million people speak a language in which they have virtually no spiritual resources.

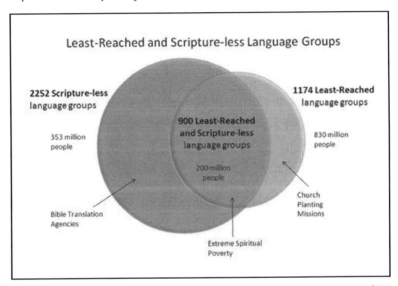

Figure 4: No Church and No Scripture; the Plight of Extreme Spiritual Poverty

There is a reason that these are the last languages in the world that have neither Scripture nor church. The church has shied away from them for generations. They live in unstable, under-resourced corners of the planet, their lives under threat of disease or violence, their populations passionately pursuing the other major religions of the globe. Some of these minorities are oppressed by their own governments or targeted for extermination by neighboring powers. No church, no Bible, and usually, no resources. What greater need could attract Jesus' passion?

Crossing these language barriers with Scripture and church will require groundbreaking strategies. The vast majority of innovation in the Bible translation movement is about training the local church, but what about these places where there are few if any Christians? Who then will we rely upon? Most Bible translation agencies are understandably focused on places with an established church. After all, most Bible agencies do not plant churches. If one works for 20 years on a New Testament for a group with no Christians, who would then benefit? Most church-planting agencies are also not

17. Calculated from data downloaded from www.joshuaproject.net.

18. I use the term "Bible-less" to mean people without a whole New Testament or Bible in their language. I use the term "Scripture-less" to mean without any portion of Scripture in their language.

19. Joshua Project, 2011.

consciously prioritizing these minority groups because of the current strategic emphasis on urbanization and the "gateway cities of the 10/40 window."[20] In order for the church to obey the great commission and eliminate the extreme spiritual poverty illustrated in Figure 4, multi-disciplinary teams and partnerships will need to be formed, incorporating the elements of church planting and Bible translation in order to cross each of these 900 language barriers with both church and Scripture at the same time.

LANGUAGE GROUPS LACKING TRANSFORMATION

Some language communities have church and they have Scripture, but for a variety of reasons, the church is not using the Scriptures in their language to transform their communities. Often because the pastors and evangelists and church planters are trained in a majority language, they use that language to establish the church. The church naturally follows the example by worshiping, praying, and preaching in the majority language. Because Bible agencies prioritize language communities that already have established churches, usually the worship patterns of the church are already well ensconced in a majority language before the translation project ever gets started. If the translation project does not pay sufficient attention to promoting the use of the Scriptures they are producing, often the church will not begin to use the Scripture. Decades of translation work go to waste.

The Bible translation agencies specialize in rapidly generating Scripture relying on the church planters and pastors to use it to transform the people and communities that speak that language, but sometimes the church planters and the pastors do not get the memo about the power of the word in the local language. The church planters themselves may never have considered the possibility of learning the mother tongue of the people to whom they minister. The pastors may have never been told that it would be permissible and advantageous to use the local minority language. Sometimes they just do not know the translation exists.

I met a church planter in South Asia who spoke one of the majority languages of the area. I found out that the local people spoke a different language than the one he was using to plant the church. I asked him, "Would these people like to use the Bible in their own language?" He replied with enthusiasm, "Oh that would be great. They would love the Bible in their own language, but it does not exist." When I consulted the Find-a-Bible website,[21] I found that there was a New Testament as well as a variety of audio Scripture tools and the *Jesus* film in the local language. In West Africa I handed a copy of the Psalms in the local language to a pastor. "This is great!" he gushed, "What do we do with it?" Without someone teaching or modeling the use of the local language for evangelism and discipleship, local pastors will not always intuitively know the value of the Bible in the local language.

The whole success or failure of the church-planting endeavor hinges on being able to communicate the complexity of the gospel and discipleship. How do we hope to succeed without using the most effective language possible? Imagine trying to understand the

---

20. One may simply search for the phrase on the internet to see how common the idea has become.

21. www.findabible.net . Forum of Bible Agencies, 2011.

book of Romans in a second or third language! Our lack of strategic use of language may be one of the great hindrances remaining in world evangelization.

The God-ordained accelerator for the process of world evangelization is the use of the mother tongue. When the Holy Spirit descended upon the first believers in order to begin the church, people came together "from every nation under heaven," Acts 2:5. They came running in fascinated bewilderment not because of the tongues of fire or the sound like a rushing wind. They wanted to know: "How is it that each of us hears them in his own native language?" Acts 2:8. The Greek means "in our own dialect in which we were born." We would be wise to finish the task of world evangelization mindful of the way God started it—with each person attracted to the message by hearing the wonders of God in his own heart language.

Whether in West Africa, the Pacific, or South Asia, the pastors are the key to Scripture use. If we train them to use the majority language, they will. To overcome this gap in the Bible translation movement, our Bible schools and seminaries that train pastors and church planters must be retooled to include training in using the local minority languages when advantageous. Otherwise the Bible translation movement remains on a path to generate all the tools needed without anyone using some of them to transform the minority language communities of the world. We must find ways to train pastors using the majority languages, but then add training to help them evaluate which Scriptures and languages will be most effective. Our training must help them learn how to transition to using the local Bible translation where helpful. Without that training for pastors worldwide, our evangelistic effectiveness will remain hindered. There will be churches and Scripture, but the churches may not be using the heart language Scriptures to profoundly transform the lives of the people.

CHURCHES WITH SCRIPTURE TRANSFORMING EVERY LANGUAGE COMMUNITY BY 2050?

If the momentum of the Bible translation movement continues to build as it has for the last 30 years, we may well begin all the projects needed by the early 2030s. We may well be in a position to use new technologies and new methods to finish most all the projects needed over the following twenty years at least to the New Testament level. With conscious intentional effort, church-planting agencies should also be able to cross every language barrier remaining on earth by 2050, or not long thereafter. All of this means, we could now be recruiting, training, and sending the generation of missionaries that will leave behind them a world in which there are churches with Scripture transforming every language community on earth. If Jesus has not returned by then, that generation will tell their grandchildren, "Kids, it was not always like it is today. There was a time when not everyone could have Scripture in their language. There was a time when not every language community could have a church to attend." It will be unthinkable to that generation because they will hold in their hands a cell phone with access to the New Testament in every language on earth. In that day, "the earth will be full of the knowledge of the Lord as the waters cover the sea," Isa 11:9.

We live in a strategic moment in salvation history. We stand on the threshold of making possibly the greatest contribution to the accomplishment of the great commission in history. We have the potential of being the John the Baptist[22] generation of the Bible translation movement. We are not the fulfillment, but we can see it coming, and we can prepare the way. The steps we take now to position this coming generation for success and to mobilize the church to focus in strategic directions may make all the difference when it comes to the church of Jesus Christ finally crossing all the language barriers on earth with church, Scripture, and transformation in the coming decades.

CROSSING ALL CULTURE BARRIERS BY 2070?

Jesus is accomplishing his plan through us. Our role is to know Jesus and cooperate with his plan for the world and to accept the privilege of investing our lives in his work. Figure 5 shows one possible future trend for crossing the remaining language and culture barriers in the world as Jesus commanded it: making disciples of every *ethnos*—every ethnic group. Over the coming four decades or so we will likely cross the last remaining language barriers with church and Scripture.

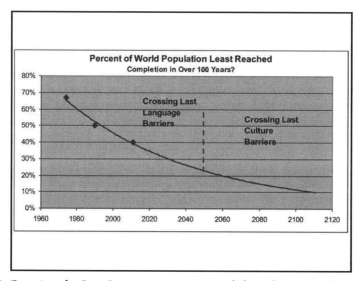

Figure 5: Crossing the Last Language Barriers and then the Last Culture Barriers

When the time comes that at least one people group in each language context has a vital church movement, crossing the remaining culture barriers with church will be more feasible. Each language context will have at least one network of churches with which we may partner to help cross the remaining culture barriers. It will be more powerful to evangelize the remaining people groups in partnership with mature Christians who speak the same language. Will the church proactively cross the remaining culture barriers in 2080, or will the future efforts drag on into the next century? The question should be posed in every church on earth.

22. Luke 3:4–6, 16.

The challenge is for all Christians to ask, "How can my church help a least-reached, Scripture-less language group come to know Jesus? How can I personally help cross a language or culture barrier with church and Scripture?" Everyone who calls Jesus "Lord" has the obligation to get involved by supporting missionaries financially, or in prayer, or by going themselves.

ENDURING ACCESS TO SCRIPTURE

Jesus said, "Heaven and earth will pass away, but my words will never pass away."[23] The Word of God is more durable and valuable than all the splendor of heaven and earth. What if we do see churches with Scripture transforming every language group on earth by 2050, will that be the end of the Bible translation movement? Even when the New Testament has been translated into every language on earth, much work will remain to ensure that every language community has enduring access to Scripture.

OLD TESTAMENT TRANSLATION AND ONGOING REVISIONS

Many of the languages of the world will still need Old Testament translation well into the future. Many of the older translations of the Bible will need to be revised preferably by the local churches. Some of the translations done in the early decades of the Bible translation movement were accomplished in a literal style that does not communicate effectively. In the larger languages of the world, some settings may justify a second translation project aimed at a different target audience.[24] There will need to be ongoing development of relevant evangelistic audio/visual Scripture tools to help the churches to evangelize the rest of their people. A people cannot be considered to have enduring access to Scripture unless they have a network of churches using Scripture to grow and multiply, and an ongoing way to continually revise, print, and distribute the Scriptures.

Digital Distribution

In the past, the finished product of a translation project took the form of boxes full of Bibles stored and distributed in a tropical climate. Over time those books would be destroyed by termites and humidity. Enduring access to Scripture can now be better achieved by digital means. New technologies have not simply opened the door to faster progress in the translation task; they have also created new possibilities for distribution of Scripture.

Today digital Scripture distribution is a reality. Downloadable over the internet, print-on-demand, live streaming audio, and text via cell phones—these abilities will only grow in the coming decades giving people unprecedented access to the Bible in whatever their situation. Around the world cell phone usage has become prevalent even in the most impoverished, remote societies. Scripture text and audio files have begun to spread from phone to phone. Dramatized Scripture recordings can now be made available to the

---

23. Mark 13:31.

24. For example, World Bible Translation Center works on developing "common person" versions of the Bible in the mega-languages of the world. See http://www.wbtc.com/.

most isolated villages with small solar-powered listening devices.[25] A few years ago if a neighbor spoke an obscure language from Asia, no one would be able to find a Bible to give to him or her. Now the Forum of Bible Agencies International has created the "Find-a-Bible"[26] website designed to help people discover sources for Bibles and Scripture tools in any language.

Recently the Every Tribe Every Nation[27] partnership has developed the Digital Bible Library with which they intend to provide the standard repository for all Scriptures in the world. In the future, digital Scripture distributers such as YouVersion[28] will be able to provide digital access over cell phone to the standard copy of any language in the world by accessing the Digital Bible Library. Likewise, instead of needing to keep a stock of all Bible products on hand, print on demand services will be able to access the Digital Bible Library and print and ship a copy of a Bible in any language in the world on an as-needed basis.

In countries that do not allow Scriptures to be distributed over the internet or by cell phone, new compression technologies are making entire libraries of written, audio, and video-based Scripture tools as well as Bible teaching available. A single SD chip,[29] no bigger than the tip of a person's finger, can now contain an entire library of Christian Scripture tools, videos, teaching, and commentaries. No more do people need to smuggle Bibles into closed countries in hidden compartments in buses. Now whole libraries can discreetly enter a restricted access nation carried on tiny chips that can plug into any laptop.[30]

Literacy and Orality

There will always be a need for ongoing literacy efforts to help church leaders learn to be able to read the Bible for themselves. Literacy among minority language communities will always be a great struggle, but one well worth waging.

In the past the Bible translation movement assumed that in order for people to have enduring Scripture access, they must learn to read; but now people are recognizing that minority language communities tend to emphasize oral communication. While literacy still maintains a strategic significance for church maturation, especially for leaders of churches to be able to nourish themselves spiritually, now the Orality Movement has gained wider acceptance in the Bible translation movement. Oral Scripture distribution methods such as "storying" are taking greater prominence than ever before. Many of today's translators assume that standard practice for new translation projects begins with developing oral story sets before they do a written translation. This approach gets

---

25. For more information on solar-powered listening devices see: http://www.faithcomesbyhearing.com/ and http://megavoice.com/.

26. www.findabible.net.

27. For more information see http://everytribeeverynation.org/.

28. http://www.youversion.com/.

29. SD Chip stands for a Secure Digital (SD) flash Card.

30. For more information see http://www.dbsbible.org/english/index.htm.

Scripture content out circulating quickly in the culture in a powerful form appropriate to the cultural setting of oral based societies. The process of story formation also develops potential local translators who understand the significance of using the natural story telling patterns of the culture in the translation.

EVEN TO THE END OF THE AGE

One day a West African friend of mine told me about how the Bible that my wife and I helped translate into his language had changed his world. The passion in his eyes drew my full attention. I could tell from the sheer concentration on his face that he was about to make a once-in-a-lifetime statement. He said, "I cannot imagine any way to explain how grateful I am. For as long as I live, I will never be able to tell you the thanks I have in my heart for this Bible in my own language. Sometimes I think about it at night. I used to read the Bible in English or in French, and I could understand a little bit, but now when I read it in my language, the meaning just comes right into my mind." Not many years ago, this man had little access to Scripture and no church where he lived. Now he uses Scripture to plant churches in the villages around his home. For his community, the command of Jesus is coming to fruition—they have churches with Scripture transforming their language context.

God foretold to Abraham, ". . . through your offspring all nations on earth will be blessed . . . ," Gen 22:18. For 4,000 years God has been working the fulfillment of this prophecy through his people. One day the blessing of the message of Jesus will reach every nation, every language, and every culture.

Two thousand years ago, Jesus gave us a command, and he said that he would accompany us and accomplish this work through us "even to the end of the age," Matt 28:18–20. When we complete this task to his satisfaction, that will be the end of the age. Are not 2000 years enough? Will we now decide to get serious about Jesus and his command? We are potentially one generation away from accomplishing arguably the greatest milestone toward the accomplishment of the great commission in the history of the world—churches with Scripture transforming every language group and community. Prophets and holy people longed to see this day, but we are the ones living in this time with these choices ahead of us. A great opportunity lies before us now, but will we seize it? Every church and every Christian has the responsibility to play a part in this movement to strive for transformed lives through God's Word in every language.

17

Stress and Perseverance in Crossing Cultures

by Janice Lemke

Good intentions for mission work can be derailed by unrealistic expectations of the culture, co-workers, and God. Perseverance requires growth in how we relate to our host country, people close to us, and the One who asked us to go in the first place.

AFTER YEARS OF PREPARATION, it seemed too good to be true. "I can't believe we're actually moving to Ukraine next week," I told my friend Lori, a former missionary. "We've raised our support and got our shots. I just need to finish packing and I'm ready to go."

"I remember what it's like," she replied. "You can't wait to get there and once you do, you wonder why you ever came."

I shrugged off her comment and thought, *I'm sure I will never feel that way.* After all, this was not my first encounter with a new culture. I had traveled throughout Europe. I had gone on mission trips to Mexico, Belize, and Jamaica. I spent five years in Kenya as a single missionary.

Two weeks after my husband and I arrived in Ukraine with our two small children, I wrote in my journal: "I'm covered with bug bites and my intestines churn. I'm tired of camping and want an indoor bathroom and a refrigerator. I can't even engage in small talk, much less expound the great truths of Scripture to a lost and needy world. I feel as helpless as a small stick of wood carried by the surf." As the hardships continued, I wondered why we ever came.

CULTURE STRESS

We arrived in Ukraine not long after its independence from the Soviet Union, during a time of great economic and political turmoil. Support from the church we went to help was spotty. Not knowing Russian, we used the "sink or swim" method for learning the language. These details differ from other missionaries, but we experienced many common emotions.

Clueless

Getting an indoor bathroom and refrigerator helped, but didn't eliminate the stress of adjusting to a new culture. I knew how to live in the United States, but life in Ukraine contained many mysteries. Where do I buy stamps? How do I make a telephone call? Groceries weren't packaged the same. What's in those mysterious jars and cans? How do you know if the meat is fresh? On my first shopping trip, I came back with a bottle of amber colored liquid. I thought it was apple juice. I was thirsty, so I took a swig—and got a mouthful of cooking oil.

Fear

Will I get sick from eating this stuff? Can I drink the water? Who can we trust? We heard rumors of mafia crime and a helpless police department. The medical system was in shambles. What if something happens to our little girls?

Even after I learned my numbers and knew how to say, "How much does this cost?" a trip to the market felt like jumping into a cold mountain lake. I'd take a deep breath and brace myself. Would I understand their reply? What if they took advantage of my ignorance and me?

It's Odd

The locals eat raw garlic and uncooked pig fat. They believe sun tanning makes you healthy and cold drinks will make you sick. I think Russians look unfriendly—they think Americans smile too much.

Even church traditions are different. Local believers cherish scriptures Americans pass off as first-century culture. Women ought to cover their heads, and we should greet each other with a holy kiss. Good Christian women don't wear make-up or jewelry.

Anger

Old ladies tell me my girls aren't dressed warmly enough and scold my toddler for sucking her thumb. I want to say, "Mind your own business," but they think it *is* their business. The electricity and water goes off when I needed it. I hate to wait in line. I can't understand these stupid rules and bureaucratic blockades. My husband and I take out our frustrations on each other—who else is there? Other missionaries have conflicts with co-workers, but we have no other missionaries nearby.

Guilt

The average wage is $50 per month. Many are unemployed. Old women try to sell knitted socks or sunflower seeds so they can buy bread. Sick people can't afford medical care. I pass beggars on my way to the meat store. Most families eat meat just once a week, if that often. Are we extravagant to eat it every day? I'm more comfortable when I'm not surrounded by so much poverty.

Helpless

We went to Ukraine with plans of training leaders and helping them plant more churches. We arrived and felt like grasshoppers confronted by giants. The issues are more complex than we imagined. Our goals seem lofty, and we feel inadequate to make any impact in the culture. We can't even keep our sink attached to the wall.

STAGES OF CULTURE SHOCK

We had lived in Ukraine about eight months when we got a visit from David Giles, who worked in our mission agency office. Since he had spent eight years in Kenya, he knew what it's like to adjust to another culture.

He told us, "At first, I used to lay awake at night wondering, 'What am I doing here' and 'What am I doing to my family,' but after a while, it starts to feel like home." He explained that everyone will experience stress when they move to a new country. "Your sense of comfort is based on predictability. Since so many things are different, it's normal to feel some tension while getting used to a new culture. The term 'culture shock' sounds so abrupt, when it's actually the little things that wear you down."

I did more research on the subject. Many have written about different stages of culture shock. While the labels they give sometimes vary, each agrees that adjustment to a new country includes several phases. Some writers tried to give a timeline, but the amount of time spent in each phase will vary from person to person.

One can define culture as "accepted beliefs and behaviors within a group." Someone from a time-oriented culture believes it is rude to be late or keep someone waiting. Those in relational cultures believe it is more important to properly greet and interact with people they see on the way—to ignore someone is much more offensive than being late. When one encounters different attitudes about time, property, personal space, relationships, work, and leisure, one wonders, "What's wrong with these people?"

Honeymoon Stage

During the honeymoon stage, the visitor enjoys cultural differences. This is the euphoria that accompanies vacations in exotic places. Different sights, sounds, and foods seem exciting. My husband thinks our Ukrainian mission experience skipped this stage, other than our enthusiasm and anticipation before arrival.

Frustration Stage

The frustration stage sets in as cultural differences seem annoying. One longs for familiar characteristics of his or her homeland. For example, one may feel anxious about hygiene and safety, angry, depressed, or overwhelmed. If unable to return home, some simply withdraw, avoiding contact with the host culture.

Some call this the "rejection stage," as the visitor struggles to see anything good. My own world faded to shades of black and white when all I could see was scattered trash, gray buildings, and dirt. I felt deep loneliness. When a visitor asked, "What do you like best about Ukraine?" I could not think of a single thing to like.

Adjustment Stage

When feeling more comfortable and confident, one reaches the adjustment stage. One accepts differences and appreciates the positive qualities of the new culture. The fog lifted as I gained more language, enjoyed fabulous local fruit, and swam in the Black Sea. My husband collaborated with like-minded local leaders to form a training program.

Some authors stop with three stages, giving a "u" curve to one's sense of comfort and satisfaction. Some add two more, "*depression*" and "*assimilation*" for a "w" in the journey through culture shock. This acknowledges that the journey to becoming bi-cultural includes different levels of adjustment. Our experience contained multiple "w's," with each wave bringing us closer to high tide.

OVERCOMING CULTURE SHOCK

How can missionaries cope with culture shock? Some people get so depressed they spend the day in bed. Others withdraw from contact with local people. Some end up going home early. Returning home early is not a sin, but the goal in coming is to adapt and do ministry. I talked with other missionaries and compiled their advice for personal use and an article on the subject.

Be Flexible

I might think "on time" means five minutes early, but others feel no guilt arriving an hour late. I might want beef but end up serving eggs when I don't find meat at the market. If the immigration official is out for the day, we postpone our visa renewal. One missionary said, "I learned to think of each day as a trip to Disneyland. It took the edge off of not knowing what to expect."

Learn the Language

Multiple languages at Babel brought confusion and isolation. The best way to overcome confusion and loneliness in a new country is to learn the language as soon as possible. Whether you plan to be in the country five weeks or fifty years, make language learning a priority.

Unfortunately, there are no short-cuts. Some missionaries attend language school; we used a local helper. Feelings of isolation drove me to improved language skills. Each new word helped me feel more comfortable. As a home-schooling mom, I never learned Russian perfectly, but I could get around alone, eavesdrop, and make friends.

Lower Expectations

After six weeks with an outhouse, we finally found an apartment and moved in. It took two weeks, though, before I found time to sweep the floor. Besides finding furniture, I had to study Russian, care for children, and sort rocks out of the rice. A year later, we still had not won the whole city for Christ.

The smallest tasks take more time. One missionary told me, "I never expect to accomplish everything on my to-do list." Another veteran gave this advice, "Don't feel as if you have to do it all today." So what if the lady downstairs keeps her floors so clean you can eat off of them.

Disengage

Moving to a new country isn't like changing clothes. Though you work to adopt a new language, culture, and customs, you retain some of the "old you." Sometimes you will get tired of coping with everything that's new and need a break. If you liked eating in restaurants back home, find a good one and go. My husband likes to play computer games, and I relax by keeping a journal. *Reader's Digest* and Calvin and Hobbs helped us more in the beginning than our stack of theological books.

Make Local Friends

Some missionaries tend to isolate themselves and need no encouragement to disengage. Building relationships cross-culturally takes a lot of work, especially when you don't know the language well. We relied a lot on mime while working to increase our vocabulary.

Local friends brightened our life and lightened the load. They taught me how to cook borscht, buy stamps, go shopping, and use the train. They gave gifts beyond their means, played with our children, and overlooked our language blunders.

Forgive

Mission work provides many opportunities to forgive. You may encounter crazy drivers, unfriendly government officials, and people who don't know how to wait in line. Someone may steal your laundry. Other missionaries may not provide the support you expect. Local believers will let you down. Your spouse might be hard to live with for a while.

We can't be too surprised when non-believers act un-Christian. After all, if everyone followed Christ, there would be no need for missionaries. It's harder to take, though, when we experience conflict with other Christians. Regarding non-believers, Jesus forgave "for they know not what they do;" but he also forgave his friends, the ones who should have known better.

Look Up

Most advice about culture shock applies to any cross-cultural worker, from anthropologist to diplomat. Many articles contain helpful advice, but my biggest boost came from the Bible. In order to run the race with perseverance, I need to keep my eyes fixed on Jesus.

When Jesus said, "Go into all the world and preach the gospel to every creature," he added, "I am with you always, even to the end of the age." The command may give me incentive to go, but his promise enables me to stay.

When I can't communicate with anyone else around, Jesus understands. Though friends and family live an ocean away, he knows what I'm going though.

Jesus experienced "culture shock" too. He exchanged heaven for human skin. He had to learn the language. People rejected him and his message. He wasn't always comfortable either, but said, "I have come down from heaven, not to do my own will, but the will of Him who sent me" (John 6:38, NAS).

Since Jesus is with me, I don't need to be afraid. Circumstances beyond my control are not beyond his. When I feel inadequate, he is strong in my weakness. His faithfulness is my anchor.

INTERPERSONAL CONFLICT

A research project on missionary attrition, "Reducing Missionary Attrition Project" (ReMAP), which became the basis for the book, *Too Valuable to Lose: Examining the Causes and Cures of Missionary Attrition*[1] shows various types of interpersonal conflict as a source of preventable attrition. Problems with peers or local leaders, marriage and family conflict, and disagreement with the sending agency all brought missionaries home from the field.

Those who think missionaries belong on pedestals as super saints probably don't know any very well. My husband's missions professor used to say, "Missionaries are like manure. Heaped together, they stink. If you spread them out, they can do some good." It takes some stubbornness and independence to get to the field in the first place. These qualities can also cause conflict.

Stress of life on the field intensifies conflict between co-workers or husbands and wives. Lacking familiar supports, new missionaries can expect more of co-workers or spouses than they can give. I have heard of new missionaries who pulled down others on the team, blaming them for a difficult adjustment. In one case, the resulting conflict brought home both the existing missionary and the newcomer.

Missionary education is helpful, but even for the well prepared, going to the mission field is a little like jumping into the deep end of the pool when you don't know how to swim. It's one thing to practice strokes while standing on land, but quite another to jump in and try to stay afloat.

Survey

At a women's retreat in Ukraine, I surveyed the participants, asking them to evaluate their level of stress and its effect on relationships. I also wanted to hear what had helped them and see what advice they could give.

Of the forty women who responded, twenty-two reported that they felt more stress on the mission field, ten thought it was about the same and three said they had less stress. Three women wrote in "different."

1. Taylor, W. D., *Too Valuable to Lose.*

Loss of A Support System

They reported the loss of a support system as the highest contributing factor. They left behind friends, family members, and enjoyable outlets. Without familiar props and ways to "vent," the husband and wife sometimes take out their frustrations on each other. Single missionaries can resent other team members when they don't feel adequate support. Some feel let down by their sending organizations.

New Roles

New roles also ranked high as a source of stress. The missionary once felt like a competent adult but becomes an infant in language learning. One might have more household tasks with fewer conveniences or be expected to supervise house help. Instead of a job with easily measurable results, the missionary has the ambiguous task of building relationships. He or she may have left an efficiently-run business to spend hours waiting in line.

Difficult Living Conditions

Difficult living conditions add stress. I became irritated by frequent outages of power and water. I carried groceries home from the market. Our Russian washing machine ate holes in our clothes, and I had to rinse laundry by hand. I heated water on the stove. One woman wrote, "It takes so much time and energy just to live here." Men also feel the stress of trying to provide for the family and keep them safe in a foreign land.

Singleness

Some single missionaries see their singleness as a handicap and feel like a matrimonial target from nationals wanting a free ride to a wealthier country. When struggling with loneliness, some believe married missionaries have it easier. Single women may need to take extra precautions for their safety. They may need help from male colleagues in ways they previously felt independent, adding stress to relationships.

Unequal Sense of Fulfillment

Married women can feel an unequal sense of fulfillment. While the man is out having mission adventures—or waiting in line—the wife is more likely to be stuck at home. One woman wrote, "I love teaching and would like to be more involved in ministry, but it takes more time to live here: cooking, shopping, etc. Plus, we have not yet found someone who is trustworthy and available to help with the children." Another wrote, "It was as if he was the missionary and I was the 'wife.' I wanted to be involved in the ministry aspect and was unhappy to be home every day for weeks."

THE MISSIONARIES SURVEYED LISTED OTHER SOURCES OF STRESS

- Concerns for well-being of children
- Finances, support

- Sharing a translator
- Unequal language skills and opportunity to study and progress
- Sinfulness exposed in each other in cramped living condition
- No place to get away
- The bribing or "gift" system. "Sometimes we feel used"
- Facing your own personal weaknesses, which become more obvious on the field

OVERCOMING CONFLICT

Stresses that can torpedo a marriage or team can also strengthen relationships. The following tips can help relieve strife.

Recognize Your Real Enemy

Jesus prayed his followers would love one another, so the world might know him. It's no wonder, then, that Satan seeks to disrupt Christian unity. Ultimately, it's not flesh and blood we should fight against, but the enemy of us all.

Give Each Other Permission to Struggle

It helps to remember you aren't perfect either. You don't provide perfect support, nor can you. Do what you can to encourage others, but trust that God can help in ways you can't. Likewise, look to God to meet your needs in ways others can't.

Forgive

After three years on the mission field, I realized I had not forgiven my husband for not providing the kind of support I wanted during a difficult first year on the field. He was struggling too, though. Without forgiveness, it was easier for me to focus on the things he did wrong instead of the things he did right; and all those "wrong things" justified and fueled my anger. Giving and asking forgiveness fosters harmony in a marriage and team.

Affirm the Good

When courting, we notice the other person's good traits and compliments flow freely. Under stressful conditions, our spouse or teammate may not behave admirably, but affirmation builds bridges. Look for opportunities to say "Thank you" and "I appreciate the way you . . ." and "You handled that situation well."

Take Your Complaint to God

God knows what you can handle. Saying "Yes, Lord" to unpleasant circumstances in life will reduce the need to take out frustrations on others. Inner peace will extend to your relationships.

Take Time for Fun

One woman wrote, "Have a weekly, non-cancelable date for fun and another appointment for business, planning, etc. Do not mix them. Pray together. Communicate."

Another said, "Put your vacation on the calendar a year ahead if necessary because time gets swallowed up if you wait until you have a break in your schedule. We need a break to look forward to."

Cultivate Your Relationship with God

Time spent praying and reading God's Word will uphold you in ways others cannot. God provides strength for the journey and perspective on stresses you face. Pray for and with your spouse and teammates.

Seek Support

As one part of the Body of Christ, we need the other members. E-mail gave us a way to share our struggles with those who care. We receive encouragement and advice when we need it instead of months later.

You don't need to broadcast your deepest problems in a newsletter, but a little honesty doesn't hurt either. Our financial support did not drop when we admitted we felt inadequate and life was hard for us. People want to know how they can pray more specifically for you.

Seek also to develop a network of friends in your host country with nationals and other missionaries. You can't drink tea or coffee together over e-mail.

Change What You Can

Learning the language will increase your confidence and ability to make friends. Learning the bus system can improve your independence. One missionary says, "Don't be afraid to appeal to your sending agency if you feel you need some structural change in responsibilities, situation, etc."

Changed expectations can help too. One woman said, "After struggling for a while, I realized I could not do a lot of ministry and take care of my family too."

Develop Resilience

In a paper titled, "What Is a Healthy Missionary Family?" Laura Mae Gardner of Wycliffe Bible Translators defines resilience as "that internal sturdiness which enables people to endure hardship, profit from the experience and move on to new challenges with confidence."[2] She says it includes freedom from bitterness, anger, and resentment. It accepts life as it is, doesn't live in a fantasy of what life should be. Resilience is not dependent on good health, an abundance of money, or a supportive network close at hand. "Like most skills, resilience can be learned and developed."

---

2. Gardner, "What Is a Healthy Missionary Family?"

A respected former missionary privately told my husband and me that he thinks many missionaries return home as "wounded warriors." This term often applies to military veterans, but missionaries are engaged in a spiritual battle.

Since he now promotes missions in seminars and teaches missions at a Bible college, I asked, "If many come home wounded, why do you try to encourage people to go into missions?"

He replied, "Because there is a need, and Jesus' Commission is still valid."

Do missionaries get "wounded" more than others on the front lines of ministry or service? I don't know. Pastors get beat up too. Being president or being a mother is also a thankless task. Anything worthwhile is difficult.

Mission-field stress need not cause shipwreck. The Apostle Paul also writes about resilience: "We are hard pressed on every side, but not crushed; perplexed, but not in despair" (2 Cor 4:8, NIV).

SUSTAINED BY GOD

I have often heard, "Give your life to Christ and you will find true happiness," or "Follow God and you will be blessed." I don't think I went to Ukraine looking for what I could get out of it, but when circumstances remained difficult for so long, I felt as though God had let me down. God's definition of blessing often differs from my own.

We went to the mission field because people need Jesus. During my college years, I came to understand that true Christianity requires more than church attendance on Sunday—I must live my life with the same priorities that motivated Jesus. Jesus loves people, millions of them who don't know him. I do, so I have a responsibility.

Sometimes though, it's not enough to see the need or feel responsible, especially when I'm lonely, confused, angry, or feel inadequate. Pre-missionary enthusiasm can go only so far. Like wheat planted in shallow soil, my zeal fades when hardships come and hope for harvest seems far away.

Americans grow up in a society where we are encouraged to change circumstances to our liking. If you don't like your laundry soap, or car, or house, or job, or spouse, then get a new one. "You deserve it." Everything worthwhile has a cost. Nevertheless, we are tempted to give up too soon. Missionaries who spent years preparing for the field will find many good reasons to go home early. What is the Christian to do when life or ministry isn't fun or fulfilling?

Review Sense of Call and Priorities.

When winter came, cold wind blew through cracks in the window frames of our apartment. We had little heat and no hot water. If I hung laundry outside to dry, it simply gathered coal smoke under solid gray skies. Hanging wet clothes inside contributed to the problem of condensation on the ceiling and moldy wallpaper. I lay awake at night listening to my three-year-old daughter cough. Our goals seemed lofty and unreachable.

I wondered, *what are we doing here, going through all this discomfort?* I looked forward to completing our four-year term so we could get back to "normal living." Then I read Paul's letter to the Corinthians and remembered why we came. "For the love of Christ controls us . . . he died for all, so that they who live should no longer live for themselves, but for him who died and rose again on their behalf" (2 Cor 5:14–15, NAS).

Who's in charge of my life? There will never be a time I can say, "I've done my good thing for God. I can go my own way now." He gave us the ministry of reconciliation . . . we are ambassadors for Christ. Before moving to Ukraine, I felt this strongly—that I need to live for God—but during difficulty, I forgot and had to be reminded.

Adjust Expectations

During a brief visit to the US during our first term, people often asked us, "So, how do you like it over there?" I thought a well-adjusted missionary should be able to say, "I've never felt so fulfilled." Or at least, "It's rewarding in spite of the difficulties." I could only reply, "It's a difficult place to live, but that's where we feel God wants us for now." I decided that was not a lesser answer.

How did Moses like leading the Israelites? Did Paul enjoy getting beaten and ship-wrecked? If you had asked Jesus, "So, how do you like living on earth?" what would he have said? They all had a mission to accomplish. It would have been easier for Jesus to stay in heaven, "but for the joy set before him, he endured the cross." Hebrews 11 lists men and women who chose to do difficult things, not for immediate reward, but in faith that something good would result. Good people suffer, even those doing God's will. To say that the Christian life offers constant happiness, or to suggest that service to Christ is always fulfilling is false advertising.

Learn to Abide

I gained new insights from a women's conference in Kiev where Elizabeth Elliot was the featured speaker. She had become a widow as a young missionary when Auca Indians killed her husband. Discouraging self-pity, she spoke on the value and necessity of suffering. If Christ, our Lord, suffered, why should we expect anything different? Hard times help shape our character, to make us more like Christ. In acceptance, there is peace. She talked about "blessed inconveniences" and urged us to thank God for the things we find unpleasant or difficult. I thought of how people used the entry to our apartment building as a toilet. I was used to the urine smell, but we got a more solid "present" the previous week. I finally cleaned it up, since it didn't go away by wishful thinking. How could I thank God for that? I *could* be thankful that Jesus willingly left a perfect realm to live in our polluted world.

In another session, Elizabeth Elliot told the story of a woman who dealt with a series of difficulties, including the sickness and death of her mother. The stress could have crushed her, but with each new crisis, she continued to say, "For this, I have Jesus."

After returning home, I found another "blessed inconvenience" in the entryway. I took our garbage pail and a piece of thin cardboard down the stairs, trying to be grateful for the opportunity to serve my neighbors. *For this, I have Jesus.*

Recognize the Benefits of Hardship

Our new roles brought new kinds of stress, which like a refiner's fire, brought impurities to the surface. Some days, I woke up growling. I felt angry, more often than I had in my whole life. I disliked the inconveniences, the sense of isolation, the language barrier, the hard work. I wondered, *will I ever feel at home?* Family, especially my husband, got the brunt of it.

I wrote in my journal: *Some people believe in purgatory, the idea of getting cleaned up for heaven after death. I think God uses life to get us ready for Glory, to burn up the chaff so we can look and act like Jesus. I want to shine like gold, but I don't like the fire.*

Wash day was always a chore in Ukraine. Our Russian washing machine had a centrifuge chamber for spinning out water, but I still had to rinse by hand. One wash day, our three-year-old daughter Alicia gave *The Jungle Book* cassette a bath. Irritated, I took the wet tape apart to dry. She discovered the open cassette sitting on a windowsill and had to inspect its innards. As I struggled to rewind the sprawling tape, Alicia tried to crawl on my lap. I pushed her away. With her attempt at reconciliation ignored, she burst into song, "He's still working on me." Four-year-old Janelle asked, "Is he still working on you too, Mommy?"

Press On

I couldn't wait until the end of our four-year term so we could leave without losing face. I was too proud to quit early and tell people we couldn't handle it; but if we made it through four years, we would not have to apologize to anyone—not to our supporters, mission agency, not even to God. It seemed a little un-Christian to leave God out of the decision entirely, so I changed it to: If God gives me the desire to come back, I'll consider it. I figured that was safe, knowing I would never have the desire to return.

I admitted this to an old friend when I had the chance to visit her in Kiev. I told her all about our situation and concluded, "It's just so hard! Cory doesn't like it either."

She asked, "Is God leading you on to something different?"

"No, I just want an easier life."

She replied, "That's not a good reason to quit. Sometimes God asks people to do hard things. When he does, he gives the strength."

I returned home and read Galatians 6:9: "Let us not become weary in doing good, for at the proper time we will reap a harvest if we do not give up" (NIV). Those who give up too soon, miss out on seeing the results of their labor.

Reap with Rejoicing

When I stopped fighting with God over my future, life in Ukraine became more enjoyable. Our water and electricity continued to go off, and the entry to our apartment building still smelled like an outhouse, but I stopped looking for things to justify my discontent.

Ministry opportunities improved. God linked my husband with two national men with a similar desire for planting new churches. Together, they started a training program for church planters. We served fifteen years in Ukraine and still see fruit. When I meet people whose lives have been changed though the outreach of these evangelists, I am grateful for God's sustaining grace.

The difficulties of our early years clearly showed us our inadequacy so we can never say, "Look what we did." God was strong in our weakness. He loved these people more than we did but used us anyway. He loves us too—we got a front row seat to watch what he is doing in Ukraine.

Those who sow with tears will reap with rejoicing. Ps 126:5.

REASONS TO PERSEVERE

Gal 6:9	Let us not become weary in doing good, for at the proper time we will reap a harvest if we do not give up.
2 Chr 15:7	But as for you, be strong and do not give up, for your work will be rewarded.
Ps 126:5–6	Those who sow in tears will reap with songs of joy. He who goes out weeping, carrying seed to sow, will return with songs of joy, carrying sheaves with him.
1 Cor 15:57–58	But thanks be to God! He gives us the victory through our Lord Jesus Christ. Therefore, my dear brothers, stand firm. Let nothing move you. Always give yourselves fully to the work of the Lord, because you know that your labor in the Lord is not in vain.
Heb 6:10–12	God is not unjust; he will not forget your work and the love you have shown him as you have helped his people and continue to help them. We want each of you to show this same diligence to the very end, in order to make your hope sure. We do not want you to become lazy, but to imitate those who through faith and patience inherit what has been promised.

18

New Streams: Looking to the Future

by Mike Sweeney

IN DEUT 18:22, IN speaking of true or false prophets, the writer tells us that if a prophetic claim does not come true, the speaker was being presumptuous and was not actually speaking a prophetic word of the Lord. This chapter, though looking toward the future, makes no such claim (especially since it merited the death sentence!). Modern "futurists" may enjoy a period of respect, but frequently their predictions neglect to pan out and, seen from a decade later, are usually less than impressive.

The world is changing rapidly, and because of that our approach to missions has been changing rapidly. It is not just technology and communications that has changed. Boundaries have become obsolete. Cultures are merging. The worldview of many people in Western churches differs greatly from that of people in those same churches only a generation ago. Foreign governments open and shut their doors to church workers every day. The future of missions, at least in its details, is very hard to predict.

But there are significant trends on the global front—ongoing developments and shifts in attitudes as well as approaches to theology that can give us an idea, at least in broad terms, of what is around the corner in world outreach. You will notice echoes in this chapter of previous chapters in this book, because the current state of missions is the foundation for the future of missions. Of course, whether or not all of these changes turn out to be entirely positive is another matter altogether, and one that we will not be able to evaluate for some time.

There are two major missiological shifts, both of which have been mentioned in previous chapters, that are, themselves, based on major socio-political movements around the world, and will continue to influence our approach to world mission in the years ahead. The first shift has to do with the transition of Christianity from a Western, northern hemisphere religion to something less-connected to any specific geographic region, worldview, or culture. Indeed, in terms of numbers, we can now say that the geographic center of Christianity is in the South, particularly Africa and South America. But there is also significant growth in many parts of Asia and a continued receptivity to the gospel among certain sectors in North America. In other words, Christians, as a whole, are now more culturally diverse than at any other time in history.

The second shift, which appears to rise out of the first, has to do with a broadening, more holistic view of the purpose of missions. While evangelism will always be a major part of our task, the church is coming to see that people are complex beings, and that it is not possible to separate the "spiritual" aspects of life from the physical, emotional, economic or social aspects of life. The point of missions, now, is not just to make converts, but to be a living, active expression of the reign of God on earth, a reign that touches every part of a person's life and environment.

Andrew Walls has shown us how, throughout church history, changes in cultural and political concerns have had an impact on the church's self-understanding.[1] In an era when international boundaries are becoming irrelevant in realms of business and economics, we find a similar transformation occurring in global Christianity which is creating major changes in the way the church is coming to define its mission.

In this chapter, we will be looking at seven areas that will continue to be significantly affected by these global changes: missions from everywhere to everywhere, the increasing role of technology in missions, mission entrepreneurialism, foreign-supported indigenous workers, short-term missions, the growth of Pentecostalism, and increased mission networking and partnerships.

MISSIONS FROM EVERYWHERE TO EVERYWHERE

For the past half-millennium, what we think of as missionary work has primarily been from Western nations to non-Western nations. Whether it was Jesuits accompanying merchant ships to Brazil, William Carey moving to India, or a modern medical team setting up a two-week clinic in Ghana, by and large, over the past four centuries, the majority of missionaries have come out of Western nations and gone to developing non-Western nations. The history of Western Civilization has also been, in many ways, the history of the church, so Europe and the United States had come to be regarded as "home base" for Christianity. European nations and the United States were also economic powers, with the financial resources to act as sending nations.

We have seen a gradual shift from this "Western to non-Western" tendency over the past several decades, especially as we note the large numbers of missionaries who have been coming out of Korea. But as the church in Europe has been in decline, and the church in North America has almost "flat-lined" in growth, we are finding an increased need for Christian workers in those nations that, not that long ago, were the primary recruiting grounds for missionaries. European nations, in particular, are seeing an increase in missionary activity. Indeed, some European nations that once were closely identified with Christendom are now considered to be among the world's more resistant fields, as global pluralism and complacency toward the state church have created an air of cynicism about all things religious.

Samuel Escobar, a Peruvian who has worked in campus ministries all over the world, reminds us how the new global culture is now making it possible for people from a multitude of nations and cultures to interact with others.

1. Walls, *The Missionary Movement in Christian History*, 16–25.

At the start of the twenty-first century, facilities for travel and the flow of information at the global level through the media, as well as colossal migration movements caused by economic change, allow Christians and churches everywhere to experience rich and diverse expressions of the Christian faith. I have met wandering prophets of independent African churches, native storytellers from Latin American Pentecostal movements, tireless missionary entrepreneurs spreading through the world from the Korean homeland and Orthodox priests regaining political weight in the lands that used to be part of the Soviet Empire . . . Migration patterns and refugee movements have helped to bring a multiplicity of cultures, as well as the different forms that the Christian church has taken among them, to Europe, the United States, and Canada.[2]

The movement of the gospel from everywhere to everywhere is not just about the newly located southern center of Christianity and a reversal in the direction of missions from East to West—the world itself has become more heterogeneous. As populations continue to surge toward urban areas, and as businesses and universities continue to attract talent from other nations and cultures, it is no longer necessary for cross-cultural Christian workers to obtain a work permit and visa in order to share the gospel with people from other ethnic groups and nations. They are all around us, and, if the trends of the last twenty years continue, we will see even heavier immigration to the West in the future—at least with regard to more highly educated peoples from other countries. Domestic cross-cultural mission work will bring increasing opportunities to the church as the years pass.

A part of this new trend has to do with what might be called "diasporic missions." Large numbers of displaced peoples have had to leave their homes and settle, as larger groups, in other countries. Frequently these migrations have come about through persecution. Such groups often go through states of extreme cultural stress where they seek physical refuge from their previous home, but still want cultural refuge from their new hosts. There may be great opportunities for sharing the gospel and ministering to people in these circumstances—but such endeavors need to be done with great sensitivity so as not to mix the message of the gospel with the message of the dominant host culture.

Of course, heavier cultural mixing will also mean that the Western church will need to develop healthy ways of relating to people of other faiths. Mosques and Hindu temples will continue to pop up in Western neighborhoods. Cross-religious dialogue will no longer be the purview of foreign missionaries and diplomats alone. Any congregation located in an urban center is likely to encounter people of different faiths nearby. The ways the church chooses to maintain its witness in such situations will either bring glory to God or turmoil to the neighborhood. Such will be our challenge.

TECHNOLOGY IN MISSION

Technology and ministry have long been awkward bedfellows. There can be no doubt that improvements in communication, transportation, and medicine have made the job of missionaries easier in many ways. Less than a century ago, cross-cultural church workers often left children behind to be raised by grandparents and committed their lives, with

2. Escobar, *The New Global Mission*, 14.

few home visits, to their work. Now, most missionaries have access to almost instant communication through email and are able to visit families and sending churches every few years. Online conferencing and a host of other digital services have solved many of the old problems that were created by the distances between missionaries and their supporters.[3]

The problem has often been that technology has not always been used in ways that enhance relationships. Is an email really the same as a face-to-face encounter? Is a blog an adequate substitute for a sermon? Is a television or radio broadcast as effective at communicating the gospel as an actual person within arm's length? Indeed, it is fair to say that many missionaries have used these technological advances as ways to avoid the inevitable stress that comes from dealing directly with people from other cultures. And more than one missionary has fallen prey to the dark side of the internet, with many leaving the field after succumbing to addictions to internet pornography.

But there are ways that technology seems to be of great benefit to the task of global mission, and will likely become even more useful in the decades ahead. One of these has to do with the area of Bible translation.

Bible translation is an area of missions that requires long-term commitment—often decades to see a completed New Testament, let alone an entire Bible. In some fields, it has become increasingly difficult to find workers willing or able to make such commitments. So Bible translation agencies have had to think creatively to get the most out of the work force they have. One result of this has been the development of computer programs that enable the users to start with a completed translation of a book in one language, and create a usable rough draft of the same book in a related language in the fraction of the amount of time it would have taken to do the same work from scratch. Translators can then take the computer-generated rough drafts and, through workshops involving indigenous speakers, bring a book to the point of publication far more efficiently than what they were able to do a few years ago.

The internet itself is creating change in how we can go about the task of bringing Christ to the nations. The missionary is no longer in the driver's seat. As Thomas Friedman has noted in his book *The World is Flat*, the internet, for all its problems, has empowered groups and individuals all over the world to become more involved with their own development. The ease and relatively low cost of digital communications has created a situation in which Christian organizations may, through the use of social networking and blogs, touch millions of people around the world in seconds. On the other hand, other religious groups may do the same. Christian organizations do not have a privileged position in cyberspace.

One major area where we may see dramatic change in the coming years is that of theological education at a distance. The rise in online learning and the availability of online resources means that a professor in Missouri can teach a class on the book of Romans with students enrolled from the United States, India, Kenya, the Czech Republic, and Brazil—all of whom may interact and cooperate on projects. While several developing

3. A good overview of the issues related to both the operational and the strategic challenges of using new technologies in mission can be found in Esler and McConnell's article, "Technological Solutions to Missionary Problems," 40–48.

nations may not have internet access in most households, there are few nations where the service is not available at some level.

Beyond that, in an age of specialization, even specialization in the world of missions, mission organizations are now able to create networks and cooperate jointly on projects to an extent never before imagined. Thus, a mission that specializes in church planting may venture into a special outreach project by coordinating with another organization that specializes in Community Health Evangelism. Using digital and wireless communications, both organizations are able to bring together their separate strengths to create greater impact among the people they hope to reach than they would have separately.

And then, of course, there is social networking. People around the globe have discovered Facebook and Twitter. Within those networks, special Christian sub-networks develop in which people can have a voice that can be heard in a hundred countries at once. We are only beginning to tap the potential of this relatively young relational tool in the world of Christian missions.

MISSION ENTREPRENEURIALISM

There was a time, in the not-too-distant past, where the words *missionary* and *entrepreneur* would not have been found in the same sentence. Indeed, the church has long avoided any mixing of *business* with the work of the church. The church, it was thought, is about the care and keeping of people's souls, not their wallets. But even those boundaries are breaking down as the dividing wall between secular and sacred has been breached. "Business," we have found, does not need to be driven *solely* by profits, although a business that does not earn money will not last long.

The old aphorism "give a man a fish, and you will feed him for a day; teach a man to fish, and you will feed him for a lifetime," does not go far enough. The man will still need equipment to fish with. He will need to understand how to sell his catch. He will probably need some start-up money to get things going. He will have to learn what it means to pay taxes and take care of employees. Fishing, in the larger picture, is not just about food—it is about business. But if a man or woman can reach the point where, through the help of others and a great deal of effort on his or her own part, he or she has overcome the cycle of poverty and helped others to do the same, then a major victory has come about that will have long-term results. Once a person has found success in one major area of life, such as running a fishing business, it is possible to begin to understand oneself as a victor instead of a victim in life. God can thus be seen in a far healthier light.

And so, finally, entrepreneurialism has found its place in the world of missions.[4] We have seen this begin to take off since the turn of the millennium, and it is sure to grow exponentially in the future. There are two areas where we have seen major progress along these lines, but the future is limited only by our own creativity.

---

4. In truth, people have been involved in some forms of business on the mission field for centuries, but normally more along the lines of carrying on their own "tent-making" ministry.

The Business as Mission (BAM) model has been developing rapidly around the world.[5] A common model is that of an experienced Christian businessman or woman, often an expatriate, setting up a business that trains and hires others while at the same time creating a work environment with Christian values and opportunities for witness and growth. The success stories have been significant enough that we will certainly see more of this in the future. In addition to the obvious benefits to the employees, it allows people with skill and experience in the realm of business to make a marked contribution to the work of the church.

Micro-loans are also on the rise in the Majority World. Frequently, all a person needs to become self-sufficient is some basic training in how to manage a small business and enough money, at a reasonable interest rate, to get established. The rest is up to the new businessman or woman. It is an arrangement in which everyone gains. We are bound to see this area expand in the years to come.

Ken Eldred[6] speaks of a number of trends that are taking place in the world that point to a future wherein this blend of business and mission will become more prevalent. Among those listed is the realization that the world has become a smaller, more connected place. Socialism has run its course, and many countries have embraced capitalism, but often without good spiritual values. Many countries are open to business opportunities but closed to traditional missionaries. The cost of supporting missionaries in other countries is going up rapidly, while overall funding has not increased in years. Private investment to developing nations has also increased strikingly in recent years. And the movement to integrate faith and work is spreading in the church.

As business people within the church see opportunities to use their knowledge for kingdom purposes, we will no doubt see new types of creative enterprises emerge in the years to come. God is, after all, interested in every aspect of a person's life. As the church learns to free itself from old models of mission and looks to holistic solutions that involve things like job training and venture capital, we may see the church cast in an entirely different light in nations that were otherwise resistant to the gospel and its messengers.

FOREIGN-SUPPORTED INDIGENOUS WORKERS

With a few very notable exceptions, the idea of a Western church directly supporting indigenous workers in their home country has had a spotty, and sometimes disappointing, history. The few major success stories normally have come out of situations where the indigenous worker was educated in the United States and developed strong relationships with people and churches outside of their own country. In these cases, a relationship of trust with Western congregations has grown to the point where they are able to operate effectively within their own society through strong external funding.

---

5 As of yet, this phenomenon has not settled comfortably under one label. But whether one calls it "marketplace ministries" or "kingdom business" or any other name, the idea of combining the world of business and the work of the kingdom of God is the same.

6. Eldred, *God is at Work,* 252–256.

Part of the problem has been accountability. Western missionaries report to their own Stateside officers, who, in turn, report to their Board of Trustees. They have salaries and must turn in expense reports to account for mission-related expenditures. Their finances are audited. They make regular trips home and report to supporters to assure them that their money is going toward the Lord's purposes. Western missionaries frequently have college degrees and do additional special training to prepare them for the field. But indigenous workers, especially those in the Majority World, are sometimes lacking in formal education. They are unable to make trips to the United States to visit with supporting congregations and individuals. They may find it difficult to account for every dollar (or whatever type of currency they use). Frequently they have poor English skills. As the head of one missions committee said, "This is a missions committee. We support missionaries. Those people aren't missionaries, they grew up over there." Statements like this indicate how easily Christian people can lose track of the overall goal.

But there are changes on the horizon for foreign-supported indigenous workers. Consider the advantages they have over traditional missionaries: They already speak the language of the people they are working with. They are familiar with existing networks and who the influencers are in their society. They understand the culture and worldview from the inside out. They already know the hot issues and problems that must be avoided. They have no need for work permits and visas. They can often live on a fraction of the amount that a Western missionary would require.

In truth, with the right person in place, an indigenous worker could be many times more effective than a foreign missionary and would not have to go through years of language and culture learning or relationship building in order to start doing the job. Remember, the church's first missionary, the apostle Paul, was already a cultural insider (a Jew and a Roman citizen) everywhere he traveled. Jesus, a Jew, took the message of the kingdom primarily to the Jews. If the church hopes to have any major breakthroughs among resistant peoples, it will need to make better use of indigenous workers.

What we are really talking about here is partnerships. It means growing past a sense of the Western big brother and the indigenous little brother to a kind of relationship where the native worker and the foreign agency learn to cooperate and trust one another on a very high level. It means avoiding structures that contribute to one-sided dependencies and creating structures that support mutuality. Daniel Rickett poses the greatest challenge in a question:

> Have we contributed to the self-development of our partners? The surest way to prevent dependency is to pay close attention to development. It is also the best safeguard against paternalism. By focusing on development, we are forced to ask whether our involvement makes our brothers and sisters better able to serve God according to their own gifts and calling. Are we helping to build their capacity or are we simply relieving their needs?[7]

Rickett goes on to insist that the real answer is a sense of interdependence between partner organizations. It should never merely involve sending money to individuals, fi-

---

7. Rickett, *Building Strategic Relationships,* 3–4.

nancing local churches, or, heaven forbid, using indigenous workers to run Western programs. It will require a clear understanding of the responsibilities of each agency involved and open communication. It will mean that the funding partner and the indigenous ministry partner must each learn to trust the judgment of the other in the areas of their responsibility.

In the future, though, we will find that even developing nations will have a good supply of well-qualified national church workers. With the large number of Asian, African, and Latin American students that have studied for ministry, either in Western nations, or in mission-based schools at home, there are hundreds of workers ready to be sent into their own fields, if only the funding, logistics, and terms of responsibilities can be worked out. Indigenous workers will understand the task in ways that will not always line up with the notions of their Western partners. Issues of accountability will always be there, as there are for Western missionaries. But creative approaches to cross-cultural church agency partnerships should be a significant part of the future wave of missions.[8]

SHORT-TERM MISSIONS

No other area of missionary activity has grown as much as short-term missions since the 1980s. In fact, the very definition of short-term missions seems to have changed. At one time, many missions regarded any person who was serving on the field for two years or less as a short-termer. Now, the vast majority of short-term missionaries are participating in one or two-week trips. The value of these brief jaunts is often debated, and is, in fact, very much related to the purpose and participants of each individual trip. Certainly, it can be argued that short-term missions typically have a greater impact on the participants and their view of the world than upon the people to whom they go. While, the topic of short-term missions has already been dealt with in this book, in this chapter we are considering what the future holds for this rapidly growing area in the world of missions.

One question that arises is where short-term missionaries will be going in the future. Ken Walker suggests that there may be a future trend toward domestic short-term missions.[9] Due perhaps to the added expense and complexity of crossing national borders, there has been, in recent years, an increase in domestic mission trips and a decrease in international trips among many agencies and church groups. But is this a real trend, or is it more related to current circumstances?

It seems to be part of the nature of short-term missions that people prefer to go where they can have the greatest impact during their short stay on the field. This means that short-term missions are often focused on immediate human need; they can be crisis-driven. Hence, in 2005 when Katrina and other hurricanes devastated New Orleans and areas of the Gulf coast, the crisis happened within US borders. New Orleans became the short-term mission field of choice. In January of 2010, an earthquake flattened a good portion of Haiti, and Haiti saw a sharp increase in short-term missions. Wherever there is great need, we will see Christian groups organizing and sending available workers to that field.

8. Porter lays down some excellent ground rules for this type of partnership arrangement in "The Role of Best Practice Principles in a Partnership Culture," 344–347.

9. Walker, "Homeward Bound: Short-Term Missions May Be Shifting Domestic," 15.

Beyond human need, a negative component for short-term missions might be the perceived risk to the short-term missionaries, especially with regard to youth groups. In 2007 Robert Priest, Douglas Wilson, and Adelle Johnson surveyed several hundred mega-churches regarding their missions programs. Their survey revealed that the top destination for short-term mission trips was Mexico[10]. But when the swine flu and violence over drug trafficking hit the headlines in the US, short-term trips to Mexico decreased sharply. Parents were unwilling to allow their teenagers to venture into harm's way.

In the future, both of these factors, human need and risk, will continue to play a part in short-term mission destinations, along with the issues of accessibility and expense. We will always see more short-term mission activity in areas within driving distance.

At one time, short-term missions were primarily routed through organizations that specialized in these trips for church groups. On average, six to ten people, either adults or youth, would join teams somewhere in the world to build houses, or run VBS programs for children. Organizations like YWAM (Youth With a Mission) or OM (Operation Mobilization) would take college students for two months during the summer to do outreach programs in various countries. Physicians and nurses would join medical teams to set up one-week clinics in needy areas. And even though these traditional programs are still running strong, the megachurch movement has created a new wave of short-term mission trips. Frequently these large churches have a staff member whose job is dedicated to planning short-term trips for people connected with the church. Depending on the situation, groups as large as 100 people may travel to another continent to help the people in multiple areas of concern simultaneously: medical programs, children's programs, women's programs, building programs, evangelistic programs, sports programs, and adult educational programs—all going on in a kind of Christian blitz into an area, with groups returning to the same place annually as the sending church and receiving church create a sibling-church relationship. In other words, for large churches, short-term mission trips are becoming incorporated into a larger strategy for the congregation, often in an effort to strengthen relationships with either a long-term missionary who is connected to the church or with an indigenous congregation in another country. This movement will continue to expand along with the megachurch movement.

Many missiologists have questioned the efficacy of short-term missions, noting that changed lives and true discipleship grow out of long-term relationships, not one-week semi-tourism forays. Some churches have recognized this problem and have redefined their short-term mission goals in terms of the life-changing impact on the participants. The greatest strength of short-term mission trips will always be how they broaden the world of those that go. Those are the people who become the great mission promoters of the future, perhaps even long-term missionaries themselves. We will likely see even more growth in the short-term missions' movement.

10. Priest, "U.S. Megachurches and New Patterns of Global Mission." 98.

THE GROWTH OF PENTECOSTALISM

According to a survey reported by the Barna Research Group in March of 2010, Pentecostal Christians now comprise 25 percent of people who claim to be Christians in the United States.[11] Estimates of worldwide Christianity run the same, with some claiming up to 500,000,000 Pentecostals around the world, including those within traditionally Pentecostal denominations and those who regard themselves as Charismatics within other denominations. This is spectacular growth, considering that Pentecostal Christians comprised only 6 percent of Christians worldwide in 1970.[12] The global shift from North to South has also been a shift to Pentecostal forms of the faith. Latin America alone claims more than 60,000,000 evangelical Pentecostals and Charismatics.

But it must be noted that "Pentecostal forms of the faith" are varied to the extreme, from the somewhat traditional, denominationally-related groups coming out of the West, to independent African movements that center around charismatic miracle-workers, to underground Chinese congregations whose teachings remain a mystery to the rest of the world. The umbrella terms "Pentecostal" or "Charismatic" cover such a wide range of beliefs and practices that they are barely helpful as modern categories.

Normally we think of Pentecostals as believing in a second act of the Holy Spirit, as evidenced mainly in speaking in tongues, but also in other miraculous outpourings, such as healings, spirit-induced insights, prophetic utterances, and other extraordinary events. Miracles seem to have a special appeal to the impoverished and exploited peoples of the world, who can find no hope for a better life anywhere else. There have been reports of mass conversions among the Islamic populations of northern Africa based on ecstatic visions. There is something very attractive about a God who is immediately available and willingly involved, in powerful ways, in the lives of his followers.

Three major trends among this group of Christians point to what is likely to be the future of the Pentecostal movement worldwide. First, it will continue to grow rapidly, at least for the next several years. In a world where mainline denominations are struggling and standard evangelical groups are barely keeping pace with the population, Pentecostal groups are growing and will continue to grow at rates far out-pacing any other religious group in the world. The movement carries a message of both grace and supernatural power and adapts easily to many contexts. In short, there is very little that can hold it back.

Second, it will become more acceptable, at least in its most common expressions, to missiologists and religious leaders around the world. Whereas at one time the charismatic movement was regarded as schismatic and theologically naïve by many Christian thinkers, Pentecostal theologians and church leaders have found their voice in the Christian world. They have produced their own theologians and biblical scholars. They participate in Christian gatherings alongside of other evangelical groups and are able to relate spectacular success stories working among people who have been resistant to all other forms of Christianity. Certainly there will always be fringe groups that will give rise to doubts

11. Barna Group, "How Different Generations View and Engage with Charismatic and Pentecostal Christianity."

12. Hartford Institute for Religious Research, "A Quick Question: Is Pentecostalism Christianity's next Reformation?"

and suspicions, but Pentecostalism is becoming a respectable form of the faith in many of its more common varieties.[13]

Third, Pentecostals will be even more heavily involved in missions. From its very inception, the Pentecostal movement has been fervently missional. The amazing growth of Pentecostal churches in Latin America and Africa has spurred the movement on to even greater outreach, relying on the power and gifts of the Holy Spirit to get the job done. Certainly there is no indication that this trend will, in any way, subside in years to come.

But Pentecostalism is, by its very nature, a difficult beast to tame. The great emphasis on supernatural experiences and individual gifts often leads to syncretism and over-reliance on charismatic leaders instead of biblical truth. Growth, by itself, does not guarantee that the gospel is being preached. And while the same might be said of other Christian movements, the Pentecostal bent toward extremes will continue to produce some groups whose orthodoxy may seem questionable to many.

MISSION NETWORKING AND PARTNERSHIPS

There is a tendency within organizations, especially as they move into their second generation, to become more focused on self-preservation and regulation than about their mission. Bylaws become sacrosanct, methods become clearly defined, innovation becomes more difficult, decisions come mainly from top administrators, and people within those organizations can begin to feel as if this is just another job instead of a role within a group that is making a real difference. A by-product of this tendency is the additional inclination for organizations, even mission organizations, to seek to set themselves apart from other organizations that are competing for the same donors' money. The distinctions may be doctrinal, methodological, geographical, or based on some other factors—but the end result has often been one of competitiveness and ill-feelings.

Such attitudes have done great harm to the church in many areas of the world, as Western missionaries have exported their divisiveness alongside of the gospel. Missions had to develop contractual agreements called "comity agreements" to set boundaries and ensure that other mission groups would not trespass into their areas of influence. Cooperation, in that environment, meant that church groups agreed to remain separated.

But since the 1970s, a growing number of people have found this self-centered approach to mission to be both ineffective and unsatisfying. As the evangelical world has become less denominationally-oriented, the stress on superiority and distinctiveness on the mission field has revealed itself to be both sinful and counterproductive for the work of the kingdom. It was impossible for missionaries caught up in this culture of alienation to agree with Jesus' prayer for unity in John 17 with any kind of integrity. And, from a purely practical standpoint, missionaries were not able to do their jobs well when situations required expertise that their own organizations did not possess. So we have seen an increase in the number of Christian networks and organizational partnerships as church groups attempt to work more closely to obey the Commission given to us by Christ.

13. Evans, "Pentecostals: Missions Movement or Voting Bloc?"

Phill Butler makes a distinction between networks and partnerships. In his words, a network is "any group of individuals or organizations, sharing a common interest, who regularly communicate with each other to enhance their individual purposes." Whereas a partnership is, "any group of individuals or organizations, sharing a common interest, who regularly communicate, plan, and work together to achieve a common vision beyond the capacity of any one of the individual partners."[14] In other words, partnerships take things a step farther than networks, actually coming to agreements and working together for a common goal.

The rise of the internet and the ease of modern communication has given birth to a number of new networking initiatives in recent years. Often these initiatives are based on information-gathering and sharing that will allow interested organizations to go the next step to develop partnerships with other organizations who share a common purpose and have resources or expertise to contribute to the effort.[15] Indeed, the network explosion among mission organizations has been one of the chief characteristics of missions in the 21st century.

Dan Sinclair and Dick Scoggins have envisioned a new networking system, roughly analogous to the internet, wherein traditional mission agencies (TMAs) connect through nodes called "Apostolic Service Providers" (APOs) that are essentially purpose-based in order to combine their own special ministries in a loosely-based cooperative network that would be at the same time more flexible and more effective than what the traditional approach to missions is able to be. All of these APOs would be connected within a worldwide network they call "ApNet." Field–based ministries could make use of the most applicable service providers, allowing them to stay focused on their overall mission while keeping costs down and efficiency high.[16] Will we see something like this happen? Probably not exactly as they have described, but it is easily within the realm of possibility. Certainly it follows the trends of globalization and connectivity that have been taking place in recent years.

CONCLUSION

What will the world of missions look like in 2020? No one can predict the details, but we can say with assurance that it will be less culture-bound, more connected, more global, more innovative, more holistic, and more dynamic than ever before. The challenge will always be to keep the main mission in mind, not losing focus on what we have been called to do in the face of all that we will be able to do. The fields are still white unto harvest. They will still need workers. They will still need to hear the message of the gospel. The kingdom of God must continue to be fleshed out. But the possibilities for how we will go about this great mission are endless.

14. Butler, *Well Connected: Releasing Power, Restoring Hope through Kingdom Partnerships,* 34.

15. Some of the more well-known networks would include the Finishing the Task Network, Call 2 All, and resource organizations such as The Joshua Project, Gordon Conwell's World Christian Database and Indigitech.

16. Sinclair and Scoggins, "Introducing the ApNet: a 21st Century Approach to Apostolic Ministry," 13–16.

Bibliography

Addison, Steve. *Movements That Change the World*. Smyrna: Missional Press, 2009.

Adeney, Miriam. *Daughters of Islam: Building Bridges with Muslim Women*. Downers Grove: InterVarsity Press, 2002.

Ahlstrom, Sydney. *A Religious History of the American People*. New Haven: Yale University Press, 1972.

Aldridge, Alan. *Religion in the Contemporary World: A Sociological Introduction*. Hoboken: Wiley, 2007.

Allen, Roland. *Missionary Methods: St. Paul's or Ours?* Grand Rapids: Wm B. Eerdmans, 1962.

Anderson, Allan. *An Introduction to Pentecostalism*. Cambridge: Cambridge University Press, 2004.

———. *Religion in the Contemporary World: A Sociological Introduction*. Cambridge: Polity Press, 2007.

Andrews, Dave. *Compassionate Community Work: An Introductory Course for Christians*. Carlisle: Piquant, 2006.

Archer, Gleason. *A Survey of Old Testament Introduction*. Chicago: Moody Bible Institute, 1994.

Bakke, Ray. *The Urban Christian*. Downers Grove: InterVarsity Press, 1986.

Bakke, Ray and Samuel Roberts. *The Expanded Mission of Old First Churches*. Valley Forge: Judson, 1986.

———. *The Expanded Mission of City Center Churches*. Chicago: International Urban Associates, 1998.

Bailey, Kenneth. *Southern White Protestantism in the Twentieth Century*. New York: Harper and Row, 1964.

Banks, Adelle M. "Some Religious Charities Buck Lower Giving Trends." *The Christian Century*, Oct. 29, 2010.

Barbour, Claude Marie. "Seeking Justice and Shalom in the City." *International Review of Mission* 73 (1984): 303–09.

Barker, Ash. Urban Workshop at National Missionary Convention, Lexington KY., 2010.

Barna Group. "How Different Generations View and Engage With Charismatic and Pentecostal Christianity." http://www.barna.org/barna-update/article/12-faithspirituality/360-how-different-generations-view-and-engage-with-charismatic-and-pentecostal-christianity?q=pentecostals.

Barrett, David B., Todd M. Johnson, Christopher R. Guidry, and Peter F. Crossing, eds. *World Christian Trends, AD 30—AD 2200: Interpreting the Annual Christian Megacensus*. Pasadena: William Carey Library, 2003.

Barrett, David B., George T. Kurian, and Todd M. Johnson, eds. *World Christian Encyclopedia*, 2nd Edition. New York: Oxford University Press, 2001.

Bartchy, S. Scott. "Community of Goods In Acts: Idealization or Social Reality?" in *The Future of Early Christianity: Essays in Honor of Helmut Koester*, ed. Birger Pearson. Minneapolis: Fortress Press, 1992.

Bauer, Susan Wise. *The History of the Ancient World: From the Earliest Accounts to the Fall of Rome*. New York: W. W. Norton, 2007.

Bauman, Zygmunt. *Globalization: The Human Consequences*. New York: Columbia University Press, 2000.

Bavinck, J. H. *An Introduction to the Science of Missions*. Phillipsburg: Presbyterian and Reformed Publishing Company, 1960.

Beattie, John H. *Other Cultures*. New York: The Free Press, 1964.

———. "On Understanding Sacrifice." In *Sacrifice*, edited by M. F. C. Bourdillon and Meyer Fortes, London: Academic Press, 1980.

Bebbington, David. *Evangelicalism in Modern Britain: A History from the 1730s to the 1980s*. Abingdon: Routledge, 1989.

Bellah, Robert, et al. *Habits of the Heart: Individualism and Commitment in American Life*. Berkely: Unviversity of California Press, 1996.

Bevans, Stephen B. and Roger P. Schroeder. *Constants in Context: A Theology of Mission for Today*. Maryknoll: Orbis Books, 2004.

Bickford, Eric. "White Flight: The Effect of Minority presence on Post World War II Suburbanization." www .eh.net/clio/publications/flight.shtml.

Billings, Todd J. "Incarnational Ministry and the Unique, Incarnate Christ." *Contend Earnestly.* http://contend earnestly.blogspot.com/2010/03/incarnational-ministry-and-unique.html.

Blauw, Johannes. *The Missionary Nature of the Church: A Survey of the Biblical Theology of Mission.* Cambridge: The Lutterworth Press, 1962.

Bonhoeffer, Dietrich. *Life Together.* San Francisco: Harper, 1954.

Bonk, Jonathan. *Mission and Money: Affluence as a Missionary Problem . . . Revisited.* Maryknoll: Orbis Books, 2006.

Bosch, David J. *Witness to the World: The Christian Mission in Theological Perspective.* Eugene: Wipf & Stock Publishers, 2006.

———. *Transforming Mission: Paradigm Shifts in Theology of Mission.* Maryknoll: Orbis Books, 1991.

———. "Reflections on Biblical Models of Misison." In Phillips, James M, and Robert T. Coote, eds. *Toward the 21st Century in Christian Mission.* Grand Rapids: Wm. B. Eerdmans, 1993.

Bourdillon, M. F. C. "Introduction." In *Sacrifice,* edited by M. F. C. Bourdillon. London: Academic Press, 1980.

Brewster, E. Thomas and Elizabeth Brewster, *Language Acquisition Made Practical.* Colorado Springs: Lingua House, 1976.

Brauer, Jerald C., ed. *The Westminster Dictionary of Church History.* Philadelphia: The Westminster Press, 1971.

Bruce, F. F. *The Book of Acts.* Grand Rapids: Wm. B. Eerdmans, 1956.

Brunner, Frederick. *Matthew: A Commentary.* Vol. 2. Grand Rapids: Zondervan Publishing, 1990.

Burgess, Ernest. "The Growth of the City: An Introduction to a Research Project." Publications of the American Sociological Association. 18: (1924): 85–97.

Burris, Stephen E. "Biblical Basis for the Homogeneous Principle." Lincoln Christian Seminary, MA Thesis, 1980.

Bush, Evelyn L. "Measure Religion in Global Civil Society." *Social Forces* Volume 85, Number 4, 645–65.

Butler, Phill. *Well Conneted: Releasing Power, Restoring Hope through Kingdom Partnerships.* Waynesboro: Authentic Media, 2006.

Buxton, Jean. *Religion and Healing in Mandari.* Oxford: The Clarendon Press, 1973.

Campolo, Bart. *Kingdom Works.* Ventura: Vine Books, 2001.

Carey, William. *An Enquiry into the Obligations of Christians to Use Means in the Conversion of the Heathen.* Leicester: Ann Ireland, 1792.

Carmichael, Joel. *The Death of Jesus.* Hammondsworth: Penguin, 1966.

Carson, D. A. "Matthew." In *The Expositor's Bible Commentary.* Grand Rapids: Zondervan Publishing, 1984.

Cate, Mary Ann and Karol Downey. *From Fear to Faith: Muslim and Christian Women.* Pasadena: William Carey Library, 2003.

Chapman, Colin. *Cross and Crescent: Responding to the Challenge of Islam.* Downers Grove: InterVarsity Press, 2003.

Christenson, Michael J. *City Streets: City People.* Nashville: Abingdon, 1986.

Clouse, Robert G., Richard V. Pierard and Edwin M. Yamauchi. *Two Kingdoms: The Church and Culture Through the Ages.* Chicago: Moody Press, 1993.

Conn, Harvie M. *A Clarified Vision for Urban Mission.* Grand Rapids: Zondervan Publishing, 1987.

———. *The American City and the Evangelical Church.* Grand Rapids: Baker Books, 1994.

Conn, Harvie, and Manuel Ortiz, eds. *Urban Ministry.* Downers Grove: InterVarsity Press, 2001.

Conquest, Robert. *Reflections on a Ravaged Century.* New York: W. W. Norton, 2000.

Corbett, Steve and Brian Fikkert. *When Helping Hurts.* Chicago: Moody Publishers, 2009.

Cornille, Catherine. *The Im-Possibility of Interreligious Dialogue.* New York: Crossroad Publishing Company, 2008.

Costas, Orlando. *The Church and Its Mission: A Shattering Critique from the Third World.* Wheaton: Tydale House Publishers, 1974.

Dark, K. R. "Large-Scale Religious Change and World Politics." In K. R. Dark, ed. *Religion and International Relations.* London: Palgrave Macmillan, 2000.

Dawson, Christopher. *Religion and the Rise of Western Culture.* New York: Doubleday, 1991.

Dayton, Edward R. and David A. Fraser. *Planning Strategies for World Evangelization.* Grand Rapids: Wm. B. Eerdmans, 1980.

Dodds, Larry and Lois Dodds. *Collected Papers on the Care of Missionaries*. Liverpool: Heartstream Resources, 2000.

Dougherty, D. "What Happened to Mission Mobilization?" *Evangelical Missions Quarterly*. 34 (1998): 3, 276–80.

Douglas, Mary. *Natural Symbols: Explorations in Cosmology*. London: Barrie and Jenkins, 1970.

———. *Implicit Meanings: Essays in Anthropology*. London: Routledge and Kegan Paul, 1975.

DuBose, Francis. *How Churches Grow in an Urban World*. Nashville: Broadman, 1978.

Duncan, Michael. *Mission: The Incarnational Approach: The Journey Series,* No. 2. Christchurch: Servants to Asia's Urban Poor, 1991.

Easterly, William. *The White Man's Burden*. New York: Penguin Books, 2006.

Eckheart, Jeleta and Fran Love, eds. *Longing to Call Them Sisters*. Pasadena: William Carey Library, 2004.

Eldred, Ken. *God Is At Work: Transforming People and Nations Through Business*. Ventura: Regal Books, 2005.

Elliston, Edgar J. "An Ethnohistory of Ethiopia: A Study of Factors that relate to the Planting and Growth of the Church." Fuller Theological Seminary, MA Thesis, 1968.

Elliston, Edgar J. and Stephen E. Burris, eds. *Completing the Task: Reaching the World for Christ*. Joplin: College Press, 1995.

Engel, James F. and William A. Dyrness. *Changing the Mind of Missions: Where Have We Gone Wrong?* Downers Grove: InterVarsity Press, 2000.

Escobar, Samuel. "Evangelical Missiology: Peering into the Future at the Turn of the Century." In *Global Missiology for the 21ˢᵗ Century*, edited by William D. Taylor. Grand Rapids: Baker Academic, 2000.

———. *The New Global Mission: The Gospel from Everywhere to Everyone*. Downers Gove: InterVarsity Press, 2003.

Esler, Ted and Douglas McConnell. "Technological Solutions to Missionary Problems." *Evangelical Missions Quarterly* 39 (2003): 1, 4–48.

Esposito, John. *What Everyone Needs to Know About Islam*. Oxford: Oxford Univ. Press, 2002.

Evans, Justin. "Pentecostals: Missions Movement or Voting Bloc?" *Lausanne World Pulse*, January 2007. http://www.jausanneworldpulse.com/research/php/594/01-2007?pg=all.

Evans-Pritchard, E. E. *Neur Religion*. Oxford: The Clarendon Press, 1956.

Fagan, Patrick. *The Real Root Causes of Violent Crime: The Breakdown of Marriage, Family and Community*. Heritage Foundation, 1995.

Farhadian, Charles, ed. *Christian Worship Worldwide: Expanding Horizons, Deepening Practices*. Grand Rapids: Wm. B. Eerdmans, 2007.

Filbeck, David. *Yes, God of the Gentiles, Too*. Wheaton: Billy Graham Center, 1994.

Fishman, Robert. *Bourgeois Utopias*. New York: Basic Books, 1987.

Friedman, Thomas. *The World is Flat: A Brief History of the Twenty-First Century*. New York: Picador, 2008.

Firth, Raymond. *Symbols: Public and Private*. Ithaca: Cornell Univiversity Press, 1956.

Fortes, Meyer. "Anthropologist and Theologians: Common Interests and Divergent Approaches." In *Sacrifice*, edited by M. F. C. Bourdillon and M. Fortes. London: Academic Press, 1980.

Forum of Bible Agencies. *Find a Bible*. 2011. www.findabible.net.

———. *Forum of Bible Agencies International*, 2011. www.forum-intl.net.

Foster, John. *Beginning From Jerusalem*. New York: Association Press, 1956.

———. *To All Nations: Christian Expansion from 1700 to Today*. New York: Association Press, 1960.

———. *Church History I: AD29–500: The First Advance*. London: SPCK, 1972.

———. *Church History II: AD 500–1500: Setback and Recovery*. London: SPCK, 1974.

Frost, Michael, and Alan Hirsch. *The Shaping of Things to Come: Innovation and Mission for the 21ˢᵗ Century*. Peabody: Hendrickson, 2003.

Gardner, Laura Mae. "Missionary Care and Counseling: A Brief History and Challenge." In *Enhancing Missionary Vitality: Mental Health Professions Serviing Global Mission*. Eds. John Powell and Joyce Bowers. Palmer Lake: Missionary Training Institute, 1999.

———. "What Is a Healthy Missionary Family?" Paper presented at International Congress on the Family, Denver, Colorado, July 5, 1995.

Garrard, John, and Carol Garrard. *Russian Orthodoxy Resurgent: Faith and Power in the New Russia*. Princeton: Princeton University Press, 2008.

"GeoResponse." In David B. Barrett, Todd M. Johnson, Chrstopher R. Guidry, and Peter F. Crossing, eds. *World Christian Trends, AD 30–AD 2200: Interpreting the Annual Christian Megacensus*, Pasadena: William Carey Library, 2003.

Gill, Brad. "Reassessing the Frontiers." *Mission Frontiers*. 32 (2010): 20–21.

Gittins, Anthony J. *Gifts and Strangers: Meeting the Challenge of Inculturation*. New York: Paulist Press, 1989.

Glasser, Arthur F. et al. "The Kingdom of God," in Evangelical Dictionary of World Missions, ed. Scott Moreau, Grand Rapids: Baker Books, 2000, 539-40.

———. *Announcing the Kingdom: The Story of God's Mission in the Bible*. Grand Rapids: Baker Academic, 2003.

———. Gletcher, Richard. *The Barbarian Conversion: From Paganism to Christianity*. Berkeley: University of California Press, 1999.

Gluckman, Max. "Les Rites de Passage." In *Essays in the Ritual of Social Relations*, edited by Max Gluckman. Manchester: Manchester Univiversity Press, 1962.

Goldin, Ian, Geoffrey Cameron, and Meera Balarajan. *Exceptional People: How Migration Shaped Our World and Will Define Our Future*. Princeton: Princeton University Press, 2011.

Gonzalez, Justo. *The Story of Christianity: The Early Church to the Dawn of the Reformation*. Vol. 1. New York: Harper Collins, 1984.

———. *The Story of Christianity: The Reformation to the Present Day*. Vol. II. New York: Harper Collins, 1985.

Gorrell, Donald. *The Age of Social Responsibility*. Macon: Mercer University Press, 1988.

Green, Michael, *Evangelism in the Early Church*. Grand Rapids: Wm. B. Eerdmans, 1970.

Greenway, Roger S. "Eighteen Barrels and Two Big Crates: How and Why Our 'Stuff' Gets in the Way of Our Witness." *Mission Frontiers*. March/April 1992.

Greenway, Roger, and Timothy Monsma. *Cities: Missions' New Frontier*. Grand Rapids: Baker, 2000.

Greer, Peter and Phil Smith. *The Poor Will Be Glad*. Grand Rapids: Zondervan Publishing, 2009.

Grigg, Viv. "Sorry! The Frontier Moved." In *Planting and Growing Urban Churches*, ed. Harvie M. Conn. Grand Rapids: Baker Books, 1987.

———. *Cry of the Urban Poor*. Monrovia: MARC, 1992.

Grimes, Barbara F. *Ethnologue*, 8th ed, 1978, Huntington Beach: Wycliffe Bible Translators.

Grunlan, Stephen A. and Marvin K. Myers. *Cultural Anthropology: A Christian Perspective*. Grand Rapids: Zondervan Publishing, 1988.

Gundry, Robert H. *Matthew: A Commentary on His Handbook for a Mixed Church Under Persecution*. Grand Rapids: Wm B. Eerdmans, 1994.

Guthrie, Stan. *Mission In The Third Millennium: 21 Key Trends for the 21st Century*. Waynesboro: Paternoster Press, 2000.

Hadaway, C. Kirk. "Church Growth and Decline in a Southern City." *Review of Religious Research* 23:4: 372–77.

Haddad, Yvonne, ed. *The Muslims of America*. Oxford: Oxford Univ. Press, 1991.

Hagner, Donald A. *Matthew 14—28*. Word Biblical Commentary, Vol. 33b. Nashville: Thomas Nelson, 1995.

Halman, Lock and Veerie Draulans. "How Secular is Europe?" *The British Journal of Sociology*, 57 (2006): 2:263–88.

Handy, Robert, *The Social Gospel in America 1870–1920*. New York: Oxford University Press, 1966.

Harris, Dorothy, "Incarnation as a Journey in Relocation." In *Sharing the Good News with the Poor*, ed. Bruce J. Nicholls and Beulah R. Wood. Grand Rapids: Baker Books, 1996.

Hartford Institute for Religious Research, "A Quick Question: Is Pentecostalism Christianity's Next Reformation?" http://hirr.hartsem.edu/research/quick_question32.html.

Haviland, William A. *Cultural Anthropology*. 2nd ed. New York: Holt, Rinehart, and Winston, 1978.

Hawkins, Greg L. and Cally Parkinson. *Follow Me*. Chicago: Reveal, Willow Creek Resources, 2008.

Hayes, John. *Sub-Merge: Living Deep in a Shallow World*. Ventura: Regal Books, 2006.

Hedlund, Roger. *The Mission of the Church in the World: A Biblical Theology*. Grand Rapids: Baker Books, 1991.

Heschel, Abraham Joshua. *The Prophets*. New York: Harper Collins, 1962.

Hiebert, Paul G. *Anthropological Reflections on Missiological Issues*. Grand Rapids: Baker Books, 1994.

———. *Transforming Worldviews: An Anthropological Understanding of How People Change*. Grand Rapids: Baker Academic, 2008.

———. *The Gospel in Human Contexts: Anthropological Explorations for Contemporary Missions*. Grand Rapids: Baker Academic, 2009.

Hirsh, Alan. *The Forgotten Ways: Reactivating the Missional Church*. Grand Rapids: Brazos, 2006.

Holmes, T. H., and M. Masusu. "Life Change and Illness Susceptibility." In *Stressful Life Events: Their Nature and Effects*. eds. Barbara Snell Dohrenwend and Bruce P. Dohrenwend. New York: Wiley, 1974.

Hopkins, C. Howard. *John R. Mott, 1865–1955: A Biography*. Grand Rapids: Wm. B. Eerdmans, 1979.

Horsley, Richard. *Jesus and the Powers: Conflict, Covenant, and the Hope of the Poor*. Minneapolis: Fortress Press, 2011.

Howell, Brian M. and Jennell Williams Paris. *Introducing Cultural Anthropology: A Christian Perspective*. Grand Rapids: Baker Academic, 2011.Kindle e-book.

Howells Douglas, Kendi. "Facing the Challenge of the Urban Frontier: Creating Effective Church Congregations in the Cities of the United States". Asbury Theological Seminary, DMiss Dissertation, 2004.

Hubert, H. and Marcel Mauss. *Sacrifice: Its Nature and Function*. Chicago: Univiversity of Chicago Press, 1964.

International Mission Board. *Global Research*. Richmond: International Missions Board, 2011.

Irving, Doug. "Missionaries Wage War: God vs. Gangs." *The Orange County Register*, April 16, 2009.

Jenkins, Philip. *The New Faces of Christianity: Believing the Bible in the Global South*. Oxford: Oxford University Press, 2006.

———. *The Next Christendom: The Coming of Global Christianity*. Rev. Ed. New York: Oxford Univiversity Press, 2007.

———. *The Lost History of Christianity: The Thousand Year Golden Age of the Church in the Middle East, Africa, and Asia—and How It Died*. New York: Harper One, 2008.

Jeyaraj, Daniel. "The Re-Emergence of Global Christianity." In Todd M. Johnson and Kenneth R. Ross, eds. *Atlas of Global Christianity, 1910 to 2010*. Edinburgh: Edinburgh University Press, 2009.

Johnson, Todd M. and Kenneth R. Ross. *Atlas of Global Christianity, 1910–2010*. Edinburgh: Edinburgh University Press, 2009.

Jones, Ezra Earl, and Robert Wilson. *What's Ahead for Old First Church*. New York: Harper and Row, 1974.

Joshua Project. "Unreached Peoples of the World. Joshua Project 2011." www.joshuaproject.com.

Kaiser, Walter C. *Toward an Old Testament Theology*. Grand Rapids: Zondervan Publishing, 1978.

———. *Toward Old Testament Ethics*. Grand Rapids: Zondervan Publishing, 1983.

———. *Mission in the Old Testament*. Grand Rapids: Baker Academic, 2000.

Keener, Crag S. *Matthew*. The IVP New Testament Commentary Series. Downers Grove: InterVarsity Press, 1997.

Kelly, J. N. D. *Early Christian Creeds*. 3rd ed. New York: Continuum Books, 2006.

Kinnaman, David and Gabe Lyons. *unchristian*. Grand Rapids: Baker Books, 2007.

Kittel, Gerhard, *Theological Dictionary of the New Testament*. Edited by Gerhard Kittel and John Friedrich. Grand Rapids: Wm. B. Eerdmans, 1985.

Kluth, Brian. *Bible Reading Helps Your Financial Health*. http://www.stateoftheplate.info/Bible-reading-helps -your-financial-health.htm.

Kostenberger, Andreas J. and Peter T. O'Brien. *Salvation to the Ends of the Earth: A Biblical Theology of Mission*. Downers Grove: InterVarsity Press, 2001.

Kraft, Charles. *Christianity With Power*. Ann Arbor: Servant Publications, 1989.

———. *Anthropology for Christian Witness*. Pasadena, William Carey Library, 1996.

———. *Culture, Communication and Christianity*. Pasadena: William Carey Library, 2001.

———. *Appropriate Christianity*. Pasadena: William Carey Library, 2005.

———. *SWM/SIS at Forty: A Participants/Observer's View of Our History*. Pasadena: William Carey Library, 2005.

———. *Worldview for Christian Witness*. Pasadena: William Carey Library, 2008.

Kuhn, Thomas S. *The Structure of Scientific Revolutions*. 2nd Ed. Chicago: The Univiversity of Chicago Press, 1970.

Larson, Harry. "Eras, Pioneers, and Transitions." In *The World Christian Movement*, ed. Johathan Lewis. Pasadena: William Carey Library, 1994.

Latourette, Kenneth Scott. *A History of Christian Missions in China*. London: SPCK, 1929.

———. *A Short History of the Far East*. Rev. Ed. New York: Macmillan Company, 1951.

———. *The Chinese Their History and Culture*. New York: Macmillan Company, 1964.

———. *A History of the Expansion of Christianity*. Contemporary Evangelical Perspectives Ed., 7 Vols., Grand Rapids: Zondervan Publishing, 1970.

———. *A History of Christianity: Beginnings to 1500*. Rev. Ed. Peabody: Prince Press, Seventh Printing, 2007.

———. *A History of Christianity: Reformation to the Present*. Rev. Ed. Peabody: Prince Press, Seventh Printing, 2007.

Lee, Moonjang. "Future of Global Christianity." In Todd M. Johnson and Kenneth R. Ross, eds. *Atlas of Global Christianity, 1910–2010*. Edinburgh: Edinburgh University Press, 2009.

Levitt, Peggy. "Redefining the Boundaries of Belonging: The Transnationalization of Religious Life." In Nancy T. Ammerman, ed. *Everyday Religion: Observing Modern Religious Lives*. Oxford: Oxford University Press, 2007, 103–20.

Lewis, Jonathan, ed. *World Mission: An Analysis of the World Christian Movement*. Pasadena: William Carey Library, 1987.

Lienhardt, R. G. *Divinity and Experience: The Religion of the Dinka*. London: Oxford Univiversity Press, 1961.

Lingfelter, Judith and Sherwood G. Lingenfelter. *Teaching Cross-Culturally: An Incarnational Model for Learning and Teaching*. Grand Rapids: Baker Books, 2007.

Linhart, Terence D. "'They Were So Alive!': The Spectacle Self and Youth Group short-Term Mission Trips." *Missiology: An International Review*. 34 (2006): 4:451–61.

Longmead, Ross. *The Word Made Flesh: Towards an Incarnational Missiology*. Lantham: University Press of America, 2004.

Loss, Myron. *Culture Shock: Dealing with Stress in Cross-cultural Living*. Winona Lake: Light and Life Press, 1993.

Luzbetak, Louis J. *The Church and Cultures*. Techny: Divine Word Publications, 1970.

Ma, Jule, and Allan Anderson. "Pentecostals (Renewalists), 1910–2010." In Todd M. Johnson and Kenneth R. Ross, eds. *Atlas of Global Christianity, 1910 – 2010*. Edinburgh: Edinburgh University Press, 2009.

Magnuson, Norris. "Salvation in the Slums: Evangelical Social Work." *ATLA Monograph Series, No. 10*. Metuchen: The Scarecrow Press, 1974.

Mandryk, Jason. *Operation World*. Colorado Springs: Biblica Publishing, 2010.

Markham, Ian. "Theology." In Robert A. Segal, ed. *The Blackwell Companion to the Study of Religion*. Malden: Blackwell Publishing, 2006.

Marshall, I. Howard. *New Testament Theology: Many Witnesses, One Gospel*. Downers Grove: IVP Academic, 2004.

McDonough, D. P., and R. P. Peterson. *Can Short-Term Mission Really Create Long-Term Missionaries?*, Minneapolis: Stem Press, 1999.

McGavran, Donald A. *The Bridges of God*. New York: Friendship Press, 1955.

———. *Understanding Church Growth*. Grand Rapids: Wm. B. Eerdmans, 1980.

McGavran, Donald A. and C. Peter Wagner. *Understanding Church Growth*, 3rd ed. Grand Rapids: Wm. B. Eerdmans, 1990.

Miller, Donald E. and Tetsunao Yamamori. *Global Pentecostalism: The New Face of Christian Social Engagement*. Berkeley: University of California Press, 2007.

Miller, Roland. *Muslim Trends*. St. Louis: Concordia Publishing House, 1996.

Mission Handbook: U.S. And Canadian Protestant Ministries Overseas, 2004–2006, 19th edition, Wheaton: EMIS, 2004.

Moffett, Samuel Hugh. *A History of Christianity in Asia: Beginnings to 1500*. Vol. 1. Maryknoll: Orbis Books, 1998.

———. *A History of Christianity in Asia: 1500–1900*. Vol. II. Maryknoll: Orbis Books, 2005.

Mohler, Johann Adam. *Symbolism; or, Exposition of the Doctrinal Differences between Catholics and Protestants as Evidenced by their Symbolic Writings*. New York: E. Dunigan, 1844.

Moreau, Scott. "Short-Term Missions in the Context of Missions, INC." In *Effective Engagement in Short-Term Missions: Doing it Right!* ed. Robert Priest. Pasadena: William Carey Library, 2008.

———. Charles Van Engen, and David Burnett. *Evangelical Dictionary of World Missions*. Grand Rapids: Baker Books, 2000.

Moucarry, Chawkat. *The Prophet and the Messiah: An Arab Christian's Perspective On Islam and Christianity*. Downers Grove: InterVarsity Press, 2001.

Muggeridge, Malcom. *Something Beautiful For God*. Garden City: Image Books, 1977.

Musk, Bill A. *The Unseen Face of Islam*. London: Monarch Books, 2003.

———. *Touching the Soul of Islam*. Toribti: Monarch Books, 2005.

Myers, Bryant L. *Walking With The Poor*. Maryknoll: Orbis Books, 2000.

Myers, Ched. *Binding the Strong man: A Political Reading of Mark's Story of Jesus*. Maryknoll: Orbis Books, 1988.

Naugle, David. *Wordview: The History of a Concept*. Grand Rapids: Wm. B. Eerdmans, 2002.

Neill, Stephen. *A History of Christian Missions*. London: Penguin Books, 1990.

Nida, Eugene A. *Customs and Cultures*. New York: Harper and Row, 1954.

Noll, Mark A. *The New Shape of World Christianity: How American Experience Reflects Global Faith*. Downers Grove: InterVarsity Press, 2009.

O'Callaghan, Rob. "What Do We Mean by 'Incarnational Methodology?'" *The Cry* 10, no. 3 (2004): 3: 6–8.

O'Donnell, Kelly, and Michele Lewis O'Donnell, "Perspectives on Member Care in Missions." In *Missionary Care: Counting the Cost for World Evanglization*, ed. Kelly O'Donnell. Pasadena: William Carey Library, 1992.

O'Gorman, Francis. *Charity and Change: From Bandaid to Beacon*. Australia: World Vision, 2000.

Orr, J. Edwin. *The Light of the Nations: Evangelical Renewal and Advance in the Nineteenth Century*. Milton Keyes: Paternoster, 1965.

———. *The Flaming Tongue: Impact of Twentieth Century Revivals*. Chicago: 1973.

———. *The Eager Feet: Evangelical Awakenings 1790–1830*. Chicago: Moody Press, 1975.

———. *Evangelical Awakenings in Southern Asia*. Minneapolis: Bethany Fellowship, 1975.

Osborne, Grant, "New Testament Theology of Missions." In *Evangelical Dictionary of World Missions*. Moreau, Scott, ed. Grand Rapids: Baker Book House, 2000.

———. *Romans*. The IVP New Testament Commentary Series. Downers Grove: InterVarsity Press, 2004.

Pao, David W. *Acts and the Isaianic New Exodus*. Grand Rapids: Baker Book House, 2002.

Parshall, Phil. *New Paths in Muslim Evangelism: Contemporary Approaches To Contextualization*. Waynesborough: Gabriel Publishing, 2003.

Pate, Larry D. "The Changing Balance in Global Mission." In *Perspectives on the World Christian Movement*: A Reader, Rev. Ed. Winter and Hawthorne, eds., Pasadena: William Carey Library, 1992.

Perkins, John. *With Justice for All: A Strategy for Community Development*. Ventura: Regal Books, 2007.

Perrin, Norman. *The Resurrection: According to Matthew, Mark, and Luke*. Minneapolis: Augsburg Books, 1995.

Peterson, Eugene. *The Message: The Bible in Contemporary Language*. Colorado Springs: NavPress, 2007.

Peterson, Roger, et.al., *Maximum Impact Short-Term Mission: The God-Commanded Repetitive Deployment of Swift, Temporary, Non-Professional Missionaries*. Minneapolis: Stem Press, 2003.

Pierson, Paul E. "Historical Development of the Christian Movement." Syllabus and Lecture Outlines, Fuller Theological Seminary, 1990.

———. *The Dynamics of Christian Mission: History Through a Missiological Perspective*. Pasadena: William Carey International Univiversity Press, 2009.

Pocock, Michael, Gailyn Van Rheenan and Douglas McConnell. *The Changing Face of World Missions: Engaging Contemporary Issues and Trends*. Grand Rapids: Baker Academic, 2005.

Pohl, Christine, *Making Room: Recovering Hospitality as a Christian Tradition*. Grand Rapids: Wm. B. Eerdmans, 1999.

Poplin, Mary. *Finding Calcutta*. Downers Grove, IL: InterVarsity Press, 2008.

Porter, Eldon. "The Role of Best Practice Principles in A Partnership Culture." *Evangelical Missions Quarterly* 46 (2010): 3:344–47.

Poston, Larry. *The Changing Face of Islam in America*. Camp Hill: Horizon Books, 2000.

Priest, Doug. *Doing Theology with the Maasai*. Pasadena: William Carey Library, 1990.

———. "Balancing Word and Deed." *Christian Standard*. 144 (2009): 4–5, 8.

———. "Back On Track: With God, With His Creation, With One Another." Sermon delivered at Atlanta Christian College, East Point, Georgia. September 1, 2010.

Priest, Doug and Nicole Cesare, eds. *Get Your Hands Dirty*. Knoxville: Mission Services, 2008.

Priest, Robert J. and J. P. Priest. "'They See Everything, and Understand Nothing': Short-Term Mission and Service Learning." *Missiology: An International Review*. 36: (2008): 2:53–73.

Priest, Robert, Douglas Wilson and Adelle Johnson. "U.S. Megachurches and New Patterns of Global Mission." *International Bulletin of Missionary Research* 34 (2010): 98.

Priest, Robert, et.al. "Researching the Short-term Mission Movement." *Missiology: An International Review.* 34 (2006): 431–50.

Putnam, Robert D. *Bowling Alone: The Collapse and Revival of American Community.* New York: Simon and Schuster, 2000.

Randall, Max Ward. *The Great Awakening and the Restoration Movement.* Joplin: College Press, 1983.

Richardson, Alan. *The Political Christ.* London: S. C. M. Press, 1973.

Richardson, Don. *Eternity in Their Hearts.* Rev. Ed. Ventura: Regal Books, 1984.

Rickett, Daniel. *Building Strategic Relationships: A Practical Guide to Partnering with Non-Western Missions.* Minneapolis: STEM Press, 2008.

———. "Short-Term Missions for Long-Term Partnership." *Evangelical Missions Quarterly.* 44 (2008): 1:42–46.

Ridderbos, Herman. *Paul: An Outline of His Theology.* Grand Rapids: Wm. B. Eerdmans, 1997.

Robert, Dana L. *The Modern Mission Era, 1792–1992.* Macon: Mercer Univiversity Press, 1997.

———. *Christian Mission: How Christianity Became a World Religion.* West Sussex: Wiley-Blackwell, 2009.

———. "Missionaries Sent and Received, Worldwide, 1910–2010." In Todd M. Johnson and Kenneth R. Ross, eds. *Atlas of Global Christianity, 1910–2010.* Edinburgh: Ediburgh University Press, 2009.

Robert, Dana L., ed. *Gospel Barriers, Gender Barriers: Missionary Women in the Twentieth Century.* Maryknoll: Orbis Books, 2002.

Rogers, Glenn. *Holistic Ministry and Cross-Cultural Mission in Luke-Acts.* Mission and Ministry Resources, 2003.

Root, Andrew. *Revisiting Relational Youth Ministry: From a Strategy of Influence to a Theology of Incarnation.* Downers Grove: InterVarsity Press, 2007.

———. "The Youth Ministry Mission Trip as Global Tourism: Are we OK With This?" *Dialog: A Journal of Theology.* 47 (2008): 4:314–19.

Ross, Kenneth R. *Edinburgh 2010: Springboard for Mission.* Pasadena: William Carey International Univiversity Press, 2009.

———. "Edinburgh 1910: A Defining Movement." In Todd M. Johnson and Kenneth R. Ross, eds. *Atlas of Global Christianity, 1910–2010.* Edinburgh: Edinburgh University Press, 2009.

Ruble, Nikki M. and William L. Turner. "A Systemic Analysis of the Dynamics and Organization of Urban Street Gangs." *The American Journal of Family Therapy* 28 (2000): 117–132.

Sachs, Jeffrey D. *The End of Poverty.* New York: Penguin Books, 2005.

Sanford, Mark, and Steve Wilkins. *Hidden Worldviews: Eight Cultural Stories that Shape Our Lives.* Downers Grove: InterVarsity Press, 2009.

Sanneh, Lamin. *Disciples of All Nations: Pillars of World Christianity.* New York: Oxford Univiversity Press, 2008.

———, *Translating the Message: The Missionary Impact on Culture,* Rev. Ed. Maryknoll: Orbis Books, 2009.

Schnabel, Eckhard J. *Early Christian Mission: Jesus and the Twelve.* Vol. 1. Downers Grove: InterVarsity Press, 2004.

———. *Paul the Missionary.* Downers Grove: InterVarsity Press, 2008.

Shorter, Aylward. *African Culture and the Christian Church.* Maryknoll: Orbis Books, 1973.

Showalter, Nathan. *End of a Crusade: The Student Volunteer Movement for Foreign Missions and the Great War.* Lantham: Scarecrow, 1998.

Sider, Ronald J. *Rich Christians in an Age of Hunger: Moving from Affluence to Generosity.* Rev. Ed. Nashville: Thomas Nelson, 2005.

Sider, Ronald J., Philip Olson and Heidi Unruh. *Churches that Make a Difference.* Grand Rapids: Baker Books, 2002.

Siemens, Ruth E. "Tentmakers Needed for World Evangelization." In *Perspectives on the World Christian Movement: A Reader,* Rev. Ed. Winter and Hawthorne, eds. Pasadena: William Carey Library, 1992.

Simson, Wolfgang. *The Starfish Manifesto.* Antioch: Asteroidea Books, 2009.

Sinclair, Dan and Dick Scoggins. "Introducing the ApNet: a 21st Century Approach to Apostolic Ministry." *Mission Fronteirs,* 28 (2006): 13–16.

Sire, James W. *The Universe Next Door.* 4th ed. Downers Grove: InterVarsity Press, 2004.

Slimbach, Richard. "The Mindful Missioner." In *Effective Engagement in Short-Term Missions: Doing it Right,* edited by Robert J. Priest. Pasadena: William Carey Library, 2008.

Smith, James K. A. *Desiring the Kingdom: Worship, Worldview, and Cultural Formation.* Grand Rapids: Baker Books, 2009.

Smith, Susan E., *Women in Missions: From the New Testament to Today*. Maryknoll: Orbis Books, 2007.

Stanley, Brian, ed. *Missions, Nationalism, and the End of Empire*. Grand Rapids: Wm. B. Eeerdmans, 2003.

———. *The World Missionary Conference, Edinburgh 1910*. Grand Rapids: Wm. B. Eerdmans, 2009.

Stark, Rodney. *The Rise of Christianity*. San Francisco, CA: Harper San Francisco, 1997.

Stark, Rodney, and Roger Finke. *Acts of Faith: Explaining the Human Side of Religion*. Berkeley: University of California, 2000.

Stokes, Charles J. "A Theory of Slums." In *Land Economics*. Vol. 38, No. 3 (Aug, 1962).

Stott, John. *Christian Mission in the Modern World*. London: Falcon, 1975.

Strauss, J. D. "God's Promise and Universal History: The Theology of Romans 9." In *Grace Unlimited*, edited by Clark Pinnock. Minneapolis: Bethany Fellowship, 1975.

Swanson, Eric and Sam Williams. *To Transform a City: Whole Church, Whole Gospel, Whole City*. Grand Rapids: Zondervan Publishing, 2010.

Swantz, Marja-Liisa. *Ritual and Symbol in Transitional Zaramo Society*. Uppsala: Gleerup, 1970.

Tabar, Charles R. *The World is Too Much With Us: "Culture" in Modern Protestant Missions*. Macon: Mercer Univiversity Press, 2003.

Taylor, W.D., ed. *Too Valuable to Lose: Examing the Causes and Cures of Missionary Attrition*. Pasadena: William Carey Library, 1997.

The Free Dictionary, http://www.thefreedictionary.com.

The Lausanne Congress. *The Lausanne Covenant*. 1974. http://www.lausange.org/covenant.

Thompson, Heather. "The Fight for Freedom On The Streets and Shopfloors of Postwar Detroit." Panelist Paper presented at the Rainbow Coalition Program on African American Freedom Struggle in the Midwest. http//americanhistory.si.edu/paac/libpaac.htm. United States Government, Census Bureau (U.S. Census) 2000 www.census.gov 2003 www.census.gov table 2:10 2010 www.census.gov.

Tippett, Alan R. *Introduction to Missiology*. Pasadena: William Carey Library, 1987.

———. *The Ways of the People*. Pasadena: William Carey Library, forthcoming.

Tsoukalas, Steven. *The Nation of Islam: Understanding the Black Muslims*. Phillipsberg: P & R Publishing, 2001.

Tucker, Ruth A. *From Jerusalem to Irian Jaya: A Biographical History of Christian Missions*. Grand Rapids: Academie Books, 1983.

———. *Guardians of the Great Commission: The Story of Women in Modern Missions*. Grand Rapids: Academie Books, 1988.

Turner, Victor. *The Forest of Symbols*. Ithaca: Cornell Univiversity Press, 1967.

———. *The Dreams of Affliction*. Ithaca: Cornell Univiversity Press, 1968.

———. *Revelation and Divination in Ndembu Ritual*. Ithaca: Cornell Univiversity Press, 1975.

Tylor, Edward Burnett. *Primitive Culture*. Part One. New York: Harper and Brothers, 1958.

Van Engen, Charles. *God's Missionary People: Rethinking the Purpose of the Local Church*. Grand Rapids: Baker Books, 1991.

Van Engen, Charles, Dean Gilliland, and Paul Pierson. *The Good News of the Kingdom: Mission Theology for the Third Millennium*. Maryknoll: Orbis Books, 1993.

Ver Beek, K. "Lessons from the Sapling: Review of Quantitative Research on Short-term Missions." In *Effective Engagement in Short-Term Missions: Doing it right!*, edited by Robert Priest. Pasadena: William Carey Library, 2008.

Vanhoozer, Kevin J. *The Drama of Doctrine: A Canonical–Linguistic Approach to Christian Theology*. Louisville: Westminster/John Knox, 2010.

Vigil, James D. *Barrio Gangs: Street Life and Identity in Southern California*. Austin: University of Texas Press, 1988.

Wagner, C. Peter. "Those Amazing Post-Denominational Churches." *Ministries Today*. July/August 1994.

Walker, Ken. "Homeward Bound: Short-Term Missions May Be Shifting Domestic." *Christianity Today*. 54 (2010): 15.

Walls, Andrew F. *The Missionary Movement in Christian History: Studies in the Transmission of Faith*. Maryknoll: Orbis Books, 1996.

———. *The Cross-Cultural Process in Christian History*. Maryknoll: Orbis Books, 2004.

Walls, Andrew and Cathy Ross, eds. *Mission in the 21ˢᵗ Century: Exploring the Five Marks of Global Mission*. Maryknoll: Orbis Books, 2008.

Wallstrom, Timothy C. *The Creation of A Student Movement to Evangelize the World*. Pasadena: William Carey International University Press, 1980.

Warren, Rick. *The Purpose Driven Life*. Grand Rapids: Zondervan, 2002.

Westerholm, Stephen. *Understanding Paul: the Early Christian Worldview of the Letter to the Romans*. Grand Rapids: Baker Books, 2004

———. *Understanding Matthew: The Early Christian Worldview of the First Gospel*. Grand Rapids: Baker Books, 2006.

Wetzel, Tom. "What is Gentrification?" *Processed World*. May 2000:1–4.

White, Ronald C., and Howard Hopkins, eds. *The Social Gospel: Religion and Reform in Changing America*. Philadelphia: Temple University Press, 1976.

White, Mortan and Lucia White, *The Intellectual Verses the City*. New York: Oxford University Press, 1977.

Whiteman, Darrell L. *Anthropology and Mission: The Incarnational Connection*. Chicago: Chicago Center for Global Ministries Publications, 2003.

Whitmer, Steven M. "Approaching Benevolence in Missions." Johnson University, MA Thesis, 1995.

Wilkins, Michael J. *The Concept of Disciple in Matthew's Gospel: As Reflected in the Use of the Term "Matthetes."* Leiden: E. J. Brill, 1988.

Willis, Avery. *Indonesia Revival: Why Two Million Came to Christ*. Pasadena: William Carey Library, 1977.

Wilson, Marvin R. *Our Father Abraham: Jewish Roots of the Christian Faith*. Grand Rapids: Wm. B. Eerdmans, 1989.

Winter, Ralph D. *The Twenty-Five Unbelievable Years 1945–1969*. Pasadena: William Carey Library, 1970.

Winter, Ralph and Steven Hawthorne, eds. *Perspectives on the World Christian Movement: A Reader*. Rev. Ed. Pasadena: William Carey Library, 1992.

———. *Perspectives on the World Christian Movement: A Reader*. 3rd edition. Pasadena: William Carey Library, 1999.

———. *Perspectives on the World Christian Movement: A Reader*. 4th Edition. Pasadena, CA: William Carey Library, 2009.

Witherington, Ben III. *Imminent Domain*. Grand Rapids: Wm. B. Eerdmans, 2009.

———. *We Have Seen His Glory: A Vision of Kingdom Worship*. Grand Rapids: Wm. B. Eerdmans, 2010.

World Christian Database, http://worldchristiandatabase.org. Leiden: E. J. Brill Online, 2011.

Wright, Christopher J. H. *Knowing Jesus Through the Old Testament*. Downers Grove: InterVarsity Press, 1992.

———. *Truth With A Mission: Reading Scripture Missiologically*. Cambridge: Grove Books Limited, 2005.

———. *The Mission of God: Unlocking the Bible's Grand Narrative*. Downer's Grove: InterVarsity Academic, 2006.

———. *Salvation Belongs to Our God: Celebrating the Bible's Central Story*. Downers Grove: InterVarsity Press, 2007.

———. *The Mission of God's People: A Biblical Theology of the Church's Mission*. Grand Rapids: Zondervan Publishing, 2010.

Wright, N. T. *Jesus and the Victory of God*. Minneapolis: Augsburg/Fortress, 1996.

Wuthnow, R. and S. Offutt. "Transnational Religious Connections." *Sociology of Religion*. 69 (2008): 2:209–32.

Wycliffe Bible Translators. *Bible Translation Needs Bulletin*. Dallas: Wycliffe Bible Translators, 1996.

———. Wycliffe Bible Translators. 2011. http://www.wycliffe.org/Explore/WhenWillWeFinishtheTask.aspx.

Wycliffe Bible Translators Canada. *Vision 2015: A Vision for You?*, 2011. http://www.wycliffe.ca/aboutus/vision2015.html.

Yamamori, Tetsunao, Bryant L. Myers, and Kenneth L. Luscombe, eds. *Serving with the Urban Poor*. Monrovia: MARC, 1998.

Yamamori, Tetsuanao, and Kenneth A. Eldred, eds. *On Kingdom Business: Transforming Missions Through Entrpreneurial Strategies*. Wheaton: Crossway Books, 2003.

Yunus, Muhammad. *Banker to the Poor*. New York: Public Affairs, 2003.

———. *Creating a World Without Poverty*. New York: Public Affairs, 2007.

Subject Index

A

Abel, murder of, 42
abiding
    in Jesus, 70
    learning to, 238
Abraham, God's promise to, 6
Abram, 44, 45, 51
absolute poverty, living in, 19
accountability, avoiding, 149
acculturation, 154
action(s)
    of a people, 128
    taking, 13
activities
    of the church, 8
    totality of, 127
Acts of the Apostles, 8–9, 56, 76, 80
actual culture, 130
Adam, 42
adaptation, from related languages, 219
adjustment stage, of culture shock, 231
Adopt-a-People emphasis, 194
affluence, as a barrier, 33, 34
Africa, 110, 116
African Americans
    converted to Islam, 190
    seeking economic opportunity, 167
African church, 85n38
African Independent Pentecostal renewalists, 118n27
agnostic growth, due to secularization, 120
agnostics, 109n7, 111
AIDS virus, contracted by Phanice, 22
Ali, Amir, 195–196

allegorical commands, 65n7
Allen, Roland, 107
amateurization of missions, 204–205
Anderson, Rufus, 154
anger, in a different culture, 229
anthropology
    Christian mission and, 132–133
    discipline of, 125
    influential in Third Era, 97
    understanding ritual and symbol, 135–146
ApNet worldwide network, 252
Apologies (Martyr), 83
Apostle Paul. *See* Paul
apostolic band, 95
Apostolic Service Providers (APOs), 252
applied anthropology, 125–126n2
Arabia
    Christian prior to Islamic conquest, 85n39
    early Christian missions in, 84n37
archaeology, 125
Asia
    least access to the Gospel, 121
    most religiously diverse major area of the world, 111
    ocean of languages without Scripture, 217
Assemblies of God, 194
Asset Based Community Development (ABCD), 156
atheists, 109n7
attractional method, 29
Augustine, 83
authority, from Christ, 40

B

Bailey, Kenneth, 165

Bangkok, Thailand, living in a slum in, 147

Bangladesh, former Muslims following Christ, 194

baptism, symbol of, 137

Baptist Missionary Society, 95–96

Baptistic-Pentecostal renewalists, 118n27

Barbour, Claude Marie, 170

Barker, Ash, 170

barrios. *See* slums

"Bebbington Quadrilateral," 119n33

beginning point, for a new model incorporating Kingdom Missionary paradigm, 103

Being in the Way Strategy, 149

beliefs and practices, basic Muslim, 195–196

believe and abide commands, of Jesus, 66

believing, in Jesus, 70

benevolence, essential praxis for believers, 75n21

Berbers, 85n38, 194

Bible

    in the language of the people, 92

    missional reading of, 1, 2

    most powerful catalyst for spiritual growth, 217

    points of agreement with Islam, 196

Bible translation

    movement, 215–216

    present in other paradigms, 94

    requiring long-term commitment, 244

Bible-less, defined, 221n18

biblical revelation, 48

biblical text, making sense of, 104

biblical transformation, 12n70

biblical worldview, 44, 48

Billings, Todd, 30

black theology, in the United States, 123

blessed inconveniences, 238

Boas, Franz, 127

bodies, as living sacrifices, 60

body of Christ, 35, 36

Boniface, 88

Bonk, Jonathan, 34–35

bottom line, of God's promise to Abram, 45

bottom-up programs, addressing poverty, 156

Brahmin class, Robert Nobili concentrating on, 90

Brazilian/Portuguese Pentecostal renewalists, 118n27

bridge, building across a river, 157

Buddhists, 111, 122, 123

business, not driven solely by profits, 245

Business as Mission (BAM) model, 246

C

Cain, fate of, 42–43

called-out ones (*ekklesia*), 106n64

Can Short-Term Mission Really Create Long-Term Missionaries? 207

Canaanite woman, 52

Capernaum centurion, 52

career missionaries, positive impact of STMs on, 212

Carey, William, 94–96

Caribbean, Moravians sending missionaries to, 91n78

Catholic Charismatics, 118

Catholic mission communities, ancient model of, 172

cattle, 144

Celtic monastic movement, 87–88

centripetal model, 7

changes, making to reduce conflict, 236

charismatics, Islamic equivalent of, 191

CHE committee, forming, 156

children

    honoring, 73

    learning languages, 129

    shunned in adult world in Jewish culture, 73n15

China

    Christianity in, 85

    family altars dedicated to ancestral spirits, 135

    Jesuit mission work in, 89

    reaching interior provinces of, 96

Chinese Charismatic renewalists, 118n27

Christ. *See also* Jesus, reaching the world for, 121–122

Christian activists, identifying with a particular people group, 37

Christian agencies, formation of many, 163–164

Christian baptism, symbol of, 137

Christian based social services, Muslims viewing as deceptive, 200

Christian Century, 108

Christian Commonwealth Colony, 165

Christian community development, 103

Christian denominations, increasing number of, 117

Christian financial resources, majority in global North, 119

Christian International Development Fund (CIDO), 208, 209

Christian leadership, transitioned from North to South, 114

Christian mission, anthropology and, 132–133

Christian Missionary Fellowship (CMF), 150

Christian outreach, never reaching non-Christians, 121

Christian radio programs, contextual produced from another country, 151

Christian slum movements, 33

Christian speeches, in Acts, 76

Christian unity, impact of trends on, 122–124

Christian women, attempting to live among and minister to Muslim women, 199

Christianity
    decline in the North, 120
    expansion and endurance of, 82
    first thousand years stronger in Asia and North Africa than in Europe, 79n6
    geographic changes in, 113
    going out from Jerusalem in all directions, 79
    renewal worldwide, 118–119
    shifted dramatically to the South, 112
    spread outside of the Jewish boundaries, 78n2
    status of global, 108–124
    transition from a Western, northern hemisphere religion, 241
    trends outside global, 120–122
    trends within global, 112–120
    as a tri-continental religion, 79n5
    Western phenomenon in 1910, 116
    Western-dominated history of, 114

Christianization, 98

Christians
    in Africa increasing dramatically, 110
    by continent (1910 and 2010), 113
    involved in various renewal movements, 118–119
    largest population of, 117
    martyred each year, 54
    in the United States, 117

Christ's gospel, keeping central to the ministry, 186

Christ's kingdom, unworldly exhibitions of, 54

Christus victor (Christ the victory), 199

church
    activities of, 8
    of affluence, 77
    as Christ's continuing incarnation, 35–36
    cultural penetration of, 82
    first official act to feed the poor, 179
    growth of, 8
    language groups lacking, 219–222
    as representation of God's love, 79
    with Scripture transforming every language community, 223–224
    structures at work within, 95
    traditions, facing different, 229

church and Scripture, language groups lacking, 221–222

church leaders, importance of, 83–84

church planters, 195, 222, 223

church-planting agencies, 221–222

Church-planting movements, 33

CIDO STM projects, surveying recipients of, 209

circumstances, dictating witness, 12

cities
    in colonial America, 162
    focusing on in the Fourth Era, 99–103
    marginalized people of, 177
    migration to all over the world, 175
    negative perception of, 169
    populations of the world's, 175–176
    problems of, 177
    to the suburbs (1945–2000), 166–168

The City of God (Augustine), 83

civilized culture, definitions of, 130

cleansed people, as God's covenant people, 5

clueless, in a different culture, 229

coastlands, focus on in the First Era, 94–96

collaboration, required in urban ministry, 183

collective sacrifice, for Nuer, 144

Collins, son of Phanice, 22

colonial apparatus, collapse of, 99

colonial models, of civilizing local cultures, 30

colonialization model, 103

Columba, 88

comity agreements, 251

commands
    categorized, 65–69
    implementing into the commission, 74–77
    of Jesus, 64–65

common humanity, calling attention to, 59n62

common media, using all over the world, 149

communal funding, of STMs, 203

communal lifestyle, for inner band of Jesus' disciples, 75

Communism, rise of, 109, 120

community
    impact on host of STMs, 208–209
    place of for Muslims, 198
    specific needs of, 19

Community Health Evangelism, training session on, 22

Community Health Evangelism (CHE) strategy, 156–157

community projects, simple, sustainable, 156

companionate facilitator, 181

compassion
    demonstrations of our, 10
    of God, 10, 11

compassionate relief ministry, 182

complaints, taking to God, 235

compression technologies, 226

computer programs, translating a book, 244

concentric zone model, of a city, 161

conceptual transformation, taking place during a paradigm shift, 93

conduct, excellence in, 196

Confessions (Augustine), 83

conflict, overcoming, 235–237

conflict resolution, as a function of ritual, 139

Confucian scholar, Matteo Ricci living as, 89n68

Conn, Harvie, 100

conscious culture, 130

consecration, during a sacrifice, 141

conservative Christianity, compared to liberal, 164

conservative Christians, rift with liberal Christians, 16

conservative churches, promoting new efforts of evangelism, 17

conservatives, concentrating efforts on evangelism, 16

Constantine, Emperor, 82

consumption, desire for, 210

context, indicating emphasis, 12

contextual churches, in Indonesian cities, 155

contextual theology, 153n9

contextualization
    process of, 131
    regarding Muslims, 197–198
    vital in development work, 200

conversion, including a change in behavior and beliefs, 44n8

Coptic Church, Bible in its vernacular language, 85n38

Council of Jerusalem, significance of, 78n2

covenant, nature of, 45

covenant loyalty, essential to ancient Jews, 63

cows, sacrificing, 143, 145

creation, brokenness of God's, 43

creation and purpose, God's orderly, 41–42

Creation theme, in the Old Testament, 4

Creator God, as a missionary God, 4

crisis-driven short-term missions, 248

critical reflection, STMs for, 211

cross-cultural message, of God, 48

cross-cultural missionaries, remaining outsiders or semi-insiders, 29

crossing cultures
    humility in, 30
    incarnation as, 28–31
    stress and perseverance in, 228–240

cross-religious dialogue, 243

crowd sourcing technologies, for Bible translation, 218

crusade evangelism, as commonplace, 17

Crusades, 87, 87n51

cultural anthropology, 125, 126–132

cultural bias, of an author, 79

cultural competency, STM participants lack of, 210

cultural institutions or systems, 132

cultural relativism, 131

cultural translatability, needed today, 113

cultural unity, rituals and symbols used to promote, 139

culture
    changing, 130
    characteristics of, 129–130
    defined, 127–129, 230
    levels of, 44n8
    meeting basic needs of its members, 130
    relationship to, 28–31

culture barriers, crossing, 215, 224–225

culture shock
    overcoming, 231–233
    stages of, 230–231

culture stress, 228–230

cultures, complexity of, 130

Cunningham, Loren, 203

customs, understanding other people's, 132

D

Dark Ages, 84

David, covenant with, 45–46

Davidic reference, establishing Jesus as ruler of Israel, 50

death
    nonultimacy of, 105n62
    of the victim in a sacrifice, 142

deity, not the same as culture, 30

delinquent gangs, 184

deliverance, from whatever enslaves, 5

denominational difference, within Islam, 190–191

dependency, preventing, 247

depressions, economic, 163

desire for gain, as a function of many sacrifices, 141

developing world, 90 percent of slum dwellers in, 185

development
    assisting local communites, 183
    re-connecting with evangelism and church planting, 200
    required for lasting change, 23

Dialogue with Trypho (Martyr), 83

diasporic missions, 243

Digital Bible Library, 226

digital distribution, of Scripture, 225

Dinka, sacrifice of animals, 144–145

disciple, being a, 70

disengagement, overcoming culture shock, 232

disinvestment, as an economic issue, 169

distinct people, creating, 46

divine grace, extended to Gentile world, 60

divinization, 51, 51n13

domestic short-term missions, 248

dominant symbols, 137

Dooley, Kevin, 77

Dougherty, David, 205

drama, ritual as a form of, 136

Duncan, Michael, 28

Dynamics of Christian Mission, 80n12

E

early Christianity, far from monolithic, 117

Eastern church, 86n43

eastward spread, of Christianity, 79n6

eating, the animal sacrificed, 142

economic changes, in cities during white flight, 168

economic egalitarian practice, of the church, 75

economic system, 132

ecumenical branch, of the church, 1n3

Edessa (city), 80n9

Edict of Toleration, 82

Edinburgh World Missionary Conference (1910), 108

education, strategy opening doors of opportunity, 92

Eldred, Ken, 246

Elliot, Elizabeth, 238

Emily, in Zimbabwe, 174

empowerment
    as feature of CHE strategy, 157
    of the Holy Spirit, 50

enculturation, process of, 129

enemy
    loving, 72
    recognizing your real, 235

enfleshing, 25, 26

Enoch, walking with God, 43

entrepreneurial spirit, among baby boomers, 205

entrepreneurialism, finding a place in the world of missions, 245

epistles, reading, 57

eschatological preparedness commands, of Jesus, 67

Escobar, Samuel, 158, 242–243

ethics, Jesus at center of, 71

Ethiopia, 80, 135

ethne, 126

ethnic groups, in the Muslim world, 190

ethno, 126

ethnobotany, 126

ethnocentrism, 130–131, 205n10

ethnohistory, 126

ethnomedicine, 126

ethnoreligions, declining, 111

ethnos, making disciples of every, 224

ethnosemantics, 126

ethnotheology, 126

evaluation, key component in developing a strategy, 149

evangelical branch, of the church, 1n3

Evangelical Foreign Missions Association (EFMA), 203

Evangelicalism in Modern Britain, 119n33

Evangelicals
    number of, 118–119
    structural definition of, 119n31

evangelicals
    defined, 119n32, 119n33
    less knowledgeable about world religions, 122
    number of, 119

Evangelicals for Social Action, 165

evangelism
    compared to social transformation, 15
    as primary aim of a mission, 96
    as primary with social action as secondary, 18
    ultimacy of, 20, 105n62

evangelism vs. social action, 16

evangelized person, 121n42

Every Tribe Every Nation partnership, 226

everyone, making things right for, 179

evil, 42, 61n71

Exile theme, in the Old Testament, 5

exodus, from city to suburb, 166

Exodus Covenant, 45

Exodus theme, in the Old Testament, 5

expectations, adjusting, 238

F

Facebook, 245

faith, 32–33, 63

faith missions, 96

faith principle, regarding support of the work, 96

faithful servant, becoming the Passover Lamb, 46

faithfulness, compared to faith, 64

family peace, achieved at funeral of a parent, 139

fastest Christian growth, over last ten years, 116
Father. *See also* God, send the Son, 27
faults, wiping out via sacrifice, 144
favelas. See slums
fear, in a different culture, 229
Federal Council of Churches, 165
Federal Housing Administration, 166
feminists, Muslim, 197
financial principles, of Jesus, 68, 71, 75
"Find your own Calcutta," 170
"Find-a-Bible" website, 226
Finishing the Task Network, 252n15
First Churches, 163, 166–167
First Era: focus on coastlands (beginning about
    1800), 94–96
five pillars, 195
flexibility, overcoming culture shock, 231
flood, as result of arrogant sin, 43
"flying toilets," 21
following Jesus, commands, 65–66, 70–71, 74
forgiveness
    overcoming culture shock, 232
    of spouse, 235
Forum of Bible Agencies, 216, 226
fountain and sprinkler structure, turning water
    back on, 171
Fourth Era: focus on cities, 99–103
Friedman, Thomas, 244
friendship evangelism, 32
Frontiers, with exclusive Muslim focus, 194
Frost, Michael, 29
frustration stage, of culture shock, 230–231
fulfillment
    concept of, 50n8
    of God's promise, 50
    unequal sense of, 234
full circle, missions coming, 106–107
fun, taking time for, 236
fundamentalists, Muslim, 191
funerary sacrifices, by Mandari, 143
future
    issues for, 103–106
    looking to, 241–252

G

Gabriel, Isaias, 160
Galilee, of the Gentiles, 51n12
gangs, 184–185
Garden of Eden, 42
Gardner, Laura Mae, 236
Genesis 1–11, 4, 41
Genghis Khan, 86, 86n44

Gentile mission, of Jesus, 51–52
Gentile mission story, in Matthew's gospel, 52
Gentiles, acceptance of, 76
gentrification, as an economic issue, 169
geography, awareness of during the First Era, 95
Gerhard, Johann, 95
gift of hope, 173
Giles, David, 230
Gladden, Washington, 165
global changes, areas affected by, 242
global front, trends on, 241
global North, 109n7
global purpose, of God, 46
global South, 98n31, 101, 112–118, 112n11
globalization, defined, 201n1
globalized world, creating two types of travelers,
    209
God. *See also* Father
    actions in redeeming his good creation, 10–11
    as missionary God, 11, 78
    pre-existing creation, 41
    sustained by, 237–240
    walking with Adam and Eve in the garden, 42
godliness, proper model for, 179
God's mission, *missio Dei*, 2, 5, 11
good, affirming, 235
gospel
    movement from everywhere to everywhere,
        243
    presenting to the hearts of the people, 81
Gothic Bible, produced by Ulfilas, 81
grand finale vision, 61
grand strategy, for Ethiopia, 150
great commission
    earlier, 44–47
    implementing commands into, 74–77
    Jesus,' 73
    Matt. 28:18–20, 7, 50
    as process of making disciples of all ethnic
        groups, 63
    restating commission given to Abraham, 78
Great Commission Christians
    equivalent to "evangelical," 119n32
    number of, 119
Greeks, allowing to become Christian, 78n2
Greenway, Roger, 33
Gregory the Great, Pope, 88
Gregory X, Pope, sending two Dominican Friars
    to Mongols, 86
Grigg, Viv, 33
guilt, in a different culture, 229

H

Hadith or Sunna, 195
hardship, recognizing benefits of, 239
Hari Raya Haji, Muslim holiday, 136
haves, 154, 155
healing, 114
health problems, associated with open sewage, 21
helper and helpless, perpetuating dichotomy of, 211
helpless, in a different culture, 230
hidden peoples, 94n6
Hiebert, Paul, 100
Hierarchy of Need, Abraham Maslow's, 184n25
Higher Criticism, described, 16n3
Hindus, 111, 122, 123
Hirsch, Alan, 29
The History of the Expansion of Christianity, 80
holiness, proper model for, 179
holism
    of human needs, 11
    of Islam, 192
holistic mercy of God, achieving, 72
holistic ministry
    aiming for both spiritual renewal and social renewal, 21
    confronting sin and fostering transformation at every level, 23
    described, 19
    explosion of, 24
    including demonstration and proclamation, 19
    shift to, 180
holistic mission, 18, 103
    defined, 3n17, 103n52
    recapture of emphasis on, 105n62
holistic nature, of mission of God in Christ, 54
holistic need of people, in slums, 185
Holy Spirit, 50, 78
home culture, of Christian workers, 39
homeless, with "nowhere to lay his head," 34
homogeneous unit principle, 151
homogeneous units, discipling, 98
honeymoon stage, enjoying cultural differences, 230
honor, concept of, 198
hope, enfleshing, 25
hospitals, started by Christians, 16
household, crucial medium for evangelism, 9n53
houses, depreciating in older neighborhoods, 167
Howard, John, changing prison conditions, 16
human behavior, principles or laws underlying, 127

human factors, contributing to spread of Christianity, 83–84
human identity, secured in the image of God, 42
humankind, 42, 126
humans, 42
humility, Jesus demanding, 71
Huss, John, 91n75

I

ideal culture, 130
identification
    for all classes and types of people, 39
    with a group of people, 29
identity theologies, 114–115
imitating, 70
imperial collapse, great era of, 99n33
incarnation
    church as Christ's continuing, 35–36
    as crossing cultures, 28–31
    of God in Christ, 12
    as influencing others, 31–33
    as Jesus' endorsement of contextualization, 198
    methodology of, 26
    as a particular methodology, 25
    as relocation, 27–28
    as simple lifestyle, 33–35
incarnational approach, value of, 25
incarnational identification, with a group of people, 29
incarnational methodology, steps and aims involved in, 26
incarnational ministry, basis of, 12
incarnational mission
    as a methodology, 29
    as a specific methodology, 36–40
    as a specific model to emulate or copy, 26
    steps of, 26
incarnational model, 12, 30
incarnational strategy, 151–153
Incarnational witnesses, for our Lord, 134
independent churches, rise of, 99
Independent tradition, 117
India, early church in, 90
indigenous church, defined, 99n35
indigenous ministry, developing as soon as possible, 92
indigenous theory strategy, 153–155
indigenous workers, 246–248
Indigitech, 252n15
individual or personal sacrifice, for Nuer, 144
individualistic perspective, interpreting from, 97

Indonesia
    in the 1970s, 153
    hundreds of thousands following Christ, 194
    national agency with church planters in every
        province, 195
    process of Islamization, 155
    sheep offered as sacrifices, 135–136
influencing others, incarnation as, 31–33
inner cities, 162, 169
inner city mission presence, 160, 161
inner-city American, relocation in, 28
Institute of Islamic Information and Education,
    195
interdependence, between partner organizations,
    247–248
interiors of continents, as focus during Second
    Era, 96
intermediate strategy, 150
internal analysis, coupled with external analysis,
    148
internet, 244
interpersonal conflict, 233–235
invocation to divinity, in Dinka sacrifices, 145
*Is Short-Term Mission Really Worth the Time and
    Money? Advancing God's Kingdom Through
    Short-Term Mission*, 207
Isaiah, 46, 55–57
Isaianic Exodus story, in Luke, 56
Isaianic mission, of "light to the nations," 56
Islam
    challenges presented by, 192–194
    needing to modernize, 197
    rejecting deity of Christ, 196
    religious authority in, 195
    setback to church initiated by, 84–85
    system of works done in an attempt to deserve
        grace, 196
    top mother tongues of, 111
    world of, 189–192
Islamic law, need to update and modify, 197
Islamic nations, designating themselves, 189
Islamization, in Indonesia, 155
Islamophobia, 188
Israel
    redeeming from Egypt, 45
    rejection of her messiah, 57
    unrepentant idolatry and unholy lifestyle, 60
itinerant lifestyle, of Jesus, 35

J

James, looking after orphans and widows in their
    distress, 179

Jerusalem church, expectations of, 8
Jesuits, gaining favor of Chinese ruling classes, 89
Jesus. *See also* Christ
    abiding in, 70
    actual experiences of, 40
    balanced ministry of, 18–19
    believe and abide commands, 66
    believing in, 70
    calling for subversive political evasion of
        Roman fidelity, 70n11
    commands about following, 65–66, 70–71
    commands of, 64–65
    Davidic king of the Jews and gentiles, 50–51
    demanding humility, 71
    endorsement of contextualization, 198
    eschatological preparedness commands, 67
    example of, 198–199
    experiencing culture shock, 233
    financial principles, 68, 71, 75
    following, 74
    gentile mission of, 51–52
    as the Incarnate One, 25
    included poor and oppressed in his teaching,
        179
    Islam on, 196
    itinerant lifestyle of, 35
    listening to commands, 66
    ministry, 18, 30
    mission to Jews, 247
    model centered on, 38
    model for contextualization, 30
    model for ministry to Muslims, 198
    as model for mission practice, 133
    money commands, 68, 71, 75
    obeying, 214–215
    preaching and persecution commands, 69,
        73–74, 76–77
    preferential option for poor, 18
    as receptor-oriented, 102n49
    religious piety commands, 67, 71, 74
    relocating of, 26
    sole means of getting to God, 70
    son of Abraham, 51
    son of David, 46
    taught compassion for those in need, 179
    treatment of others commands, 68–69, 72, 76
Jewish culture, Jesus part of, 30
John of Monte Corvino, 86, 86n49
John the Baptist, doubt of, 53
The Joshua Project, 252n15
The Joy Program, 151
judging others, banned from, 72
judgment passage, in Matt 25, 6
justice, poverty linked with, 23–24

K

Kangemi slum, in Nairobi, Kenya, 157
Kingdom Missiology
    aspects of, 9–12
    incorporating all that Jesus did and taught, 2
    as a new missiological paradigm, 3
    performing whole work of kingdom of God, 1
kingdom mission, 24
kingdom model, in the New Testament, 7
kingdom of God
    holistic view of, 7
    unleashing, 53–55
    vision of, 6
"kingdom of priests," God's people as, 45
kingdom vision of reality, 49
kingdom worldview, reminding us of God's grace, 60
knowledge, excellence in, 196
Kraft, Charles, 102
Kroeber, A. L., 127
Kublai Khan, 86
Kuhn, Thomas, 93
Kyle, John, 203

L

LAMP method, of language learning, 153n8
language(s)
    contextual relationship with religion, 111
    of global Christianity, 111–112
    importance of learning, 151
    "sink or swim" method for learning, 228
    strategic use of, 223
language adaptation software, 219
language barriers
    crossing, 213–227
    Jesus obligating us to cross, 214
language groups
    lacking church, 219–222
    lacking church and Scripture, 221–222
    lacking Scripture, 217–219
    lacking transformation, 222–223
language learning, overcoming culture shock, 231
Larson, Harry, 105
Latin-rite Catholic renewalists, 118n27
Latourette, Kenneth Scott, 80, 108
Lausanne Conference (1974), 194
Lausanne Congress on World Evangelization (1974), 17
Lausanne Covenant (1974), 220
leader in a community, finding, 156
leaders, emphasis on training, 150

leadership development, importance of, 92
learning experiences, provided by STMs, 212
Leo the Great, centralized government of Western church, 84
levels, of strategy, 150–151
"Levels of Conversion," discussion of, 44
liberal Christianity, compared to conservative, 164
liberal Christians, rift with conservative Christians, 16
liberals, engaging in social action, 16
liberation theology, in Latin America, 114–115, 123
lifestyle, characterized by Christian communities, 81
lifestyle challenges, raised by mission in slums, 34–35
lifestyle priorities, importance of, 38
Lingenfelter, Judith and Sherwood, 30
linguistic distinctions, separating peoples, 97
linguistics, 125
listen to Jesus commands, 66
literacy, fostered by Bible translation, 16
literacy efforts, need for ongoing, 226
Lives Worth Saving, volunteers with, 184
living conditions, difficult, 234
living voice of God, for the Shia, 191
local church, as Christ incarnate, 36
local friends, overcoming culture shock, 232
local people, training and enabling for translation, 219
long-term missionaries, STMs useful in recruiting, 211–212
looking up, overcoming culture shock, 232–233
loving, an enemy, 72
lower expectations, overcoming culture shock, 231–232
Ludwig, Nicolas, 91
Luke
    Isaianic Exodus story, 56
    pragmatic ethic of possessions, 8
Luke-Acts, as missiological document, 57
Lutheran church (Protestant), 118

M

Maa language, 152n7
Maasai
    bias toward traditional or rural educated Maasai, 151–152
    living with, 133
    working with, 151
Madoya, at the very bottom of Mathare Valley, 21

Majority World
    context of Christianity, 17
    cross-cultural missionaries sent from, 101
    half a billion people living in absolute poverty, 19
Majority World missions
    growing influence and participation of, 101
    rise of, 98
managerial missiology, 158
Mandari, 142–143
married women, allowed to be involved in mission work, 96
Martyr, Justin, 81, 83
martyrdom, 81n18
Maslow, Abraham, 184n25
material culture, notes on, 133
Mathare Valley, 20, 21, 22, 23
Matthew, 49, 50
McGavran, Donald A., 98
megachurch movement, creating a new wave of short-term mission trips, 249
mega-cities, growth of, 176
mental map, culture providing, 128
mercy, importance of, 73
Messiah, of Jew and Gentile, 51
Messiah-Mission motif, in Luke's writings, 50
messianic advents, 54
messianic genealogy, of Matthew, 50
messianic reading, 100n37
micro-loans, on the rise in Majority World, 246
Middle Ages (500–1500 AD), 84–89
Midwestern evangelical megachurch, recent STM activity of, 206
migrants, building bridges across cultures, 123
migration
    increasing religious and ethnic diversity around the world, 111
    to the suburbs after World War II, 162
Millennial generation, rising concern for justice, 23–24
ministry of inconvenience, 178
minjung theology, in South Korea, 123
minority language communities, emphasizing oral communication, 226
Missio Dei (God's mission), 2, 5, 11
missiological shifts, two major, 241–242
missiology, 97n23
mission(s)
    anthropology and, 132–133
    biblical foundation of, 3–9
    end of, 104
    from everywhere to everywhere, 242–243
    existing to bring praise to God, 46

    more holistic view of the purpose of, 242
    new inter-denominational type of, 96
    new model of, 103–104
    in the New Testament, 7–9
    in the Old Testament, 3–7
    Pentecostals even more heavily involved in, 251
    as process, 205
    as project, 205
    source of, 11
    ultimate purpose of God's, 46
mission activity, Winter's four stages of, 94
mission entrepreneurialism, 245–246
mission movement, Holy Spirit initiator of, 78
mission networking and partnerships, increased, 251–252
mission of God, service of, 58
mission station approach, producing a limited response, 103
mission strategies
    rethinking, 147–159
    traditional ineffective, 170
mission tasks, being involved in a variety of, 106
mission tension, 104–105
Mission Year, *modus operandi* of, 170
missional hermeneutic, 41, 100n37
missional reading, 100n37
    of the Bible, 1, 2
missionaries
    going to specific places and particular people, 12
    immersing themselves in the new culture, 132
    number sent and received by continent in 2010, 101
    residing among urban poor, 147–148
    sharing a new vision with present, 106
    supporting and honoring veteran, 105
    wearing dress of local people, 96
missionary churches, task letters to, 57–58
missionary personnel, allocating to most strategic task, 106
missionary strategies
    described, 148–151
    examining some specific well-known, 151–159
    process of determining, 149
    for today, 158–159
missionary work, maintaining a strategic balance, 106
mission-in-reverse, 170
Missions and Money: Affluence as a Missionary Problem (Bonk), 34
modality, 95
modeling, of teaching, 198

modern Muslims, 191

modernization, displacing traditional Javanese culture in Indonesia, 155

monasticism, influential in China, 86

money commands, of Jesus, 68, 71, 75

Mongols, 85–87

monotheists, having no room for God appearing in the flesh, 198

moral code, Islam's, 196

Moravians, 91, 95

Mother Teresa, 173

    d, 169–170

motif, found throughout scripture, 172

motivational shift, in urban ministry, 179–181

Mott, John R., 97

movements, bringing possibility of transformation, 33

Muhammad, last seal of the prophets, 195

multitudes, feeding of, 179

Muslim areas

    missionary visas no longer available for, 200

    quick overview of, 194

Muslim background believers (MBBs), 194

Muslim feminists, 197

Muslim law (shari'a), 195

Muslims

    approaches in ministry to, 197–199

    big issues facing, 196–197

    Crusades as a living factor still, 87n53

    disastrous responses to, 199

    give and take with Christians, 192

    modern, 191

    number in the world, 189

    proximity with Christians, 123

    reaching out to in love, 188

    remarkable gains by, 111

    responsive to the Gospel, 122

    tending to minimize Sunni-Shia differences, 190

    in the United States, 190

    in Western Europe, 190

    what's going on among, 194–195

N

Nairobi, Kenya, 20, 147

National Defense Highways Act of 1950, 166

nations

    bringing justice, righteousness, and light to, 55

    reaching all, 78–79

    rise of new, 99

Nazareth manifesto, 2

needs, struggling to address, 19

neighborhood, moving into, 27

Neill, Stephen, 95

Nestorian version of Christianity, 85

networks, 252

new exodus storyline, Isaiah chapters 40–66, 55

new heaven and a new earth, 47

New Testament, 7–9, 62

New Testament pattern, return to, 103

New World religious naturalization, civil pattern of, 103n57

Nida, Eugene, on cultural anthropology, 126–127

Nightingale, Florence, founder of modern nursing, 16

Nilotic sacrificial practices, summary of, 145–146

Nilotic tribes, illustrations from, 142–145

nineteenth century, as a great century for Christianity, 108

Noah, covenant with, 45

Nobili, Robert De, 90

Nod, land of, 42

non-Christian neighbors, hospitality to, 123

non-incarnational methods, using, 37

non-poor Christians, trying to identity with those born into poverty, 39

nonreligious, in Asia, 111, 120

North Africa, church identified with more elitist Romans and Romanized populations, 85n38

North Korea, religions, 111n8

Nuer, 143–144

O

O'Callaghan, Rob, 29

oddities, of a different culture, 229

oil reserves, of Muslims, 193

Old Testament

    Christ-directed reading of, 51n8

    covenants throughout, 45

    future Day of the Lord, 53

    mission in, 3–7

    presenting a consistent message, 47

    response toward those marginalized in society, 178–179

    revealing God's calling of a people, 41

    as revelation, 46

    translation and ongoing revisions, 225

Old Testament Law, provisions for poor and strangers, 178

online learning, 244

Operation Mobilization (OM), 203, 249

Oral Scripture distribution methods, 226

Orality Movement, 226

organizations, focusing on self-preservation and
regulation, 251
Origen, 83
Original Sin, doctrine of, 59n62
Orthodox churches, tied to ethnic lines in Europe,
118
orthopraxis, required in community
transformation, 37
otherness (other, othering), 205n10
Overseas Missionary Fellowship International
(OMF), 205
ox, sacrificial made object of hostility of the group,
145

P

Palestine, tension over, 192
Pao, David, 56
parachurch structure, 95
paradigm shifts
changes caused by, 93
introduced by Carey, 95
during modern missions period, 93
principles involved in, 93n2
paradigmatic disciple, 65n7
paradigms, 93, 105
Paratext software, 218
Parthians, 79–80
participants, overall effectiveness of STMs on, 207
Participation stage, of mission activity, 94
partnership, compared to indigenous theory
model, 155
Partnership stage, of mission activity, 94
partnerships
described, 252
of native workers and foreign agency, 247
pastors, 222, 223
Paternal stage, of mission activity, 94
paternalism, safeguarding against, 247
Patrick, return to Ireland, 87–88
Paul
cultural insider, 247
funding of mission with Barnabas, 203
long-awaited visit to the Roman church, 58
missionary journeys, 9
persecution of, 76–77
on resilience, 237
theory of evangelizing a province, 107
peace-making efforts, social relations to be
marked by, 72
peasant class, grinding poverty of, 75
penalties, for sins, 87n51

Pentecostal forms of the faith, varied to the
extreme, 250
Pentecostal/Charismatic renewal, 118
Pentecostalism
emerging in early 1900s, 118
growth of, 250–251
Pentecostals, number of, 119
people
God moving through, 78
referring to a group of individuals, 127
people groupings, as one way of establishing the
church, 100
people groups, 98
people of God, 7, 79
People's Movement (1–500 AD), 80–84
persecution
high probability of, 73
important factor in expansion of Christianity,
81
of workers among Muslims, 200
perseverance, scriptural reasons for, 240
Persia, 82, 83
Persians. *See also* Parthians, persecution by, 83n31
personal influence, Jesus' model of, 31
Pesce, Mauro, 58n54
Peterson, Roger, 204
Phanice, 21–22
Pharisees, opposition from, 73
physical anthropology, 125
physical requirements, of Islam, 195
Pierson, Paul E., 80, 103
piety, commands about practicing, 67, 71
pillars, five, 195
Pioneer stage, of mission activity, 94
plague, during Middle Ages, 15
Plan So Far Strategy, 149
plastic bags, people relieving themselves in, 21
political system, 132
pollutions, to Mandari, 142
poor
in Old Testament times, 178
as primary beneficiaries of the gospel, 179
solidarity with, 39
possessions
accumulating in front of poor people, 33
intermingled with every other's possessions, 75
selling, 8
Post-Denominational Churches, 102
potential strengths, of incarnational missions,
37–38
poverty
attacking, 24
being willing to embrace, 29
linking with justice, 23–24

macro-approaches to, 156

overcoming cycle of, 245

praxis, importance of in the urban world, 37

prayer, 71, 74

preaching, aimed at conversion and on needs of people, 92

preaching and persecution commands, of Jesus, 69, 73–74, 76–77

pressing on, 239

presumption, of sin, 43

Priest, Robert, 204

primary schools, in Ethiopia, 15

priorities, reviewing, 237–238

private symbols, 137–138

progressive Muslims, 191

promise-fulfillment, concept of, 50

prophets, Muslim list of, 195

Protestant Mission Handbook, describing STMs, 201–202

Protestant tradition, 117

psychological changes, in cities during white flight, 169

psychology, impact on the Western mind, 97

public character, of symbols, 137

pull hypothesis, on white flight, 167

push theory, of white flight, 167–168

Putnam, Robert, 37

Pythagoreans, communalism of, 75n20

Q

Qumran community, practice of, 75

Qur'an, 191, 195, 196, 197

R

Rahab, 63–64

rain sacrifices, of Mandari, 143

rational thinking, infused with prayer and scriptural reflection, 149

Rauschenbusch, Walter, 165

Rayburn, Jim, 31

receptor-oriented approaches, 102

reconciliation, shalom as, 5–7

recovery, described, 183

"Reducing Missionary Attrition Project" (ReMAP), 233

reflection, on the experiences of others, 211

Reformation, limited missionary activity in early years of, 91–92

Reformation/Pietistic movement (1500–1800 AD), 89–92

rejection stage, of culture shock, 230–231

rejoicing, reaping with, 239–240

relational cultures, 230

relational model imitation, as incarnational mission, 32

relationship webs, organized on a more voluntary basis, 100

relationship with God, cultivating, 236

relief, 181, 183

relief agencies, Christian-based, 181

relief ministry, 182

religion

genuine, 58

pure and undefiled, 178

religionists, contact with other, 123–124

religious communication, taking place through symbols, 140

religious freedom, restricted, 122

religious piety commands, of Jesus, 67, 71, 74

religious system, 132

religious workers, most Muslim lands not admitting, 193–194

relocation, incarnation as, 27–28

renewal movements, unprecedented, 118

renewalists, 119

rescue missions, diverse group of, 164

resilience, developing, 236–237

resource distribution, inequality of Christian, 119–120

resources

allocating to most strategic task, 106

competition for between long-term and short-term missions, 206–207

of Islam, 193

restricted access countries, creative strategies for entering, 102

resurrection, importance of, 40

Revelation (book), 49, 61–62

Ricci, Matteo, 89–90

Rice Christianity, phenomenon of, 182

Rickett, Daniel, 247–248

risen Christ, preaching with relentless tenacity, 74

risen Jesus, focusing on, 40

ritual and symbol theory, of sacrifice, 136–140

rituals

attribute of efficacy, 138

changing, 138

defined, 136–137

masking conflict, 139

properties of, 137–138

relating to worldview, 138

used to assert a hierarchy and order to reality, 138–139

river of God, 2, 6
roles
in a culture, 129
new, 234
Roman centurion, reaction at the crucifixion, 52
Roman Empire, 84
Roman missionaries, 88–89
Romans epistle, 58–61
Rome, Jesus calling for subversive political evasion of, 70n11
Root, Andrew, 31–32, 209–210, 211
root causes, growing awareness of, 23
rural paradigm, shifting to an urban and then suburban one, 169

S

sacrifice(s)
anthropological treatment of, 141–142
definition of, 140
functions of, 141
Nuer occasions of, 143–144
purposes for offering, 140
ritual and symbol theory, 136–140
as a symbolic ritual, 140–146
understanding from the point of view of participants, 140
sacrificial animals, colors of, 145
sacrificial lifestyle, similar to that of Jesus, 34
sacrificial rituals
experiences of seeing, 135–136
stages of for Nuer, 144
sacrificial service, of Christ, 38
Sadducees, opposition from, 73
salvation
attaching to specific works, 64n5
described, 78–79n3
meanings of, 1
Salvation Army, 164
salvation history, strategic moment in, 224
salvation today, liberals talking about, 16
Sanneh, 103
Sarkaktani Beki, Nestorian princess, 86n44
Satan, waging war upon people of God, 57
schools, started by Christians, 16
Scoggins, Dick, 252
Scripture
ensuring access to, 225
for every language community on earth, 217
high view of, 104
language groups lacking, 217–219
need for vernacular, 85n41
unity moving to God's ultimate purpose, 48

Scripture-less, defined, 221n18
SD chip, containing an entire library of Christian Scripture, 226
Second Era: focus on the interiors (beginning about 1865), 96–97
Second Great Migration, 167
secondary symbols, 137
secular Muslims, 191
secularization, 109, 120–121
seed-project, CHE committee selecting, 156–157
self support, as major tenet of "indigenous theory," 152
self-centered self, emerging, 97
sending church, assisting in development of strategies, 106
sense of call, reviewing, 237–238
Sermon on the Mount, commands in, 65n8
Servant Song chapter, Isa 52:13–53:12, 55
servant-messiah, functioning as a Second Moses, 56
service tourism industry, 203
Serving By, approach to urban ministry, 180
Serving In, approach to urban ministry, 180
Serving With attitude, in urban ministry, 181
sewage, running downhill, 21
Shaftesbury, Lord, 16
shalom
bringing into the community, 13
concept of, 5–7
as the goal, 6n39
shanties, homemade, 20
shantytowns. *See* slums
The Shaping of Things to Come, 29
sheep, Maasai sacrificing at the birth of a child, 135
Shia (Shii or Shite), 190–191
shopping mall, introduced, 166
short-range strategy, 150
Short-term Evangelical Missions (STEM) organization, 207
short-term mission movement, development of, 202–203
short-term missionaries, perceived risk to, 249
short-term missions (STMs)
categories of, 202
for critical reflection, 211
defined by accomplishments, 202
defining, 201–202
future of, 248–249
numerical growth, 203–204
participants more likely to give money to support missions, 206
participation in multiple, 204

positive disposition toward in larger evangelical community, 207
positive impact of, 211–212
tensions with long-term, 204–206
sick, healing of, 179
sickness, as result of sin for Nuer, 144
Siemens, Ruth, 102
sign languages, Bible translation for, 216
SIM (Serving in Mission), formerly Sudan Interior Mission, 194n4
simple lifestyle, incarnation as, 33–35
sin(s)
 eternal and temporal penalties for, 87n51
 Islam's solution to, 196
 polluting the sinner, 142
 wiping out via sacrifice, 144
sincerity, Jesus demanding, 71
Sinclair, Dan, 252
Singapore, religions, 111n8
singleness, causing loneliness, 234
slaughtering, distinguished from sacrifice, 140–141
slavery, abolishment of, 16
slum movements, Christian, 33
slums, 20–23, 40, 185
"slums of hope," 174n1
small businesses, development of, 183
social action, 16
social action vs. evangelism, dichotomy of, 3
social capital, decreased, 37
social change movements, 33
Social Christianity Movement, 165
social engagements, revolutionary rules for, 73
social gang, 184
Social Gospel, 16, 163
Social Gospel movement, 164–166
The Social Gospel (periodical), 165
social issues, considering root causes of, 23
social justice, seeking for the powerless, 73
social justice issues, modern missions toward, 76
social networking, 245
social problems
 church involved in addressing, 15
 due to injustice, 23
social structures, 128, 132, 139–140
societal structures, present in the city, 100
societies, great age of, 95
society
 defined, 128
 described, 129
 relationship with culture, 127
Society for the Propagation of the Faith, 88
socio-cultural barriers, overcoming, 38

socio-economic barriers, reducing, 34
sociological changes, in cities during white flight, 168
sociological paradigm, 33
sodality, 95–96
soldiers, becoming Christians, 81
Solidarity, 186–187
South Korea, five religions, 111n8
Southern Baptists, 194
specialization, coordinating in the world of missions, 245
specific rain, 143
speeches, in Acts, 76
spigots, for water throughout Mathare Valley, 21
spiritual explanations for happenings, 114
spiritual poverty, plight of extreme, 221
spiritual power, 104
spiritual requirements, of Islam, 195
spiritual salvation, 1
St. Louis, MO, working in inner city, 171
Standard Solution Strategy, 149
statistical center of gravity, of global Christianity, 115, 116
STEM-organized STMs, 208
stewards
 humans as, 4
 obligation to be, 7
stewardship
 avoiding, 149
 given to humans, 42
STM goals, categories of, 202n4
STM participants, desire to consume, 210
STM travelers, placed in tourist group as welcomed travelers, 209–210
"storying," 226
strategic planning, 148
strategic plans, temporal dimension, 151
strategic thinking, as valid endeavor for Christians, 149
strategy
 components of, 148–149
 contextual, 153
 levels of, 150–151
 not ensuring success, 158
 types of, 149–150
 understanding, 148
street level, transformation at, 172–173
stress, 230, 234–235
The Structure of Scientific Revolution (Kuhn), 93
struggle, giving each other permission to, 235
Student Volunteer Movement, 97
sub-Saharan Africa, 116, 185

suburbs
from the city to, 166–168
migration to after World War II, 162
subversive pacifism, as an effective social
mechanism, 72n12
Summer Institute of Linguistics (SIL), 218
Sunnis, 190–191
Sunni-Shia division, depth and implications of,
191
support, seeking, 236
support system, loss of, 234
Surfis, 191–192
sustainability
as feature of CHE strategy, 157
growing trend toward, 23
Swahili, national language of Tanzania, 152
SWOT analysis, 148
symbolic ritual, sacrifice as, 140–146
symbolism, in Dinka sacrificial practices, 145
symbols
in any ritual, 137
attribute of efficacy, 138
changing, 138
conveying many meanings, 137
defined, 136–137
properties of, 137–138
public and a private domain, 137
relating to worldview, 138
of a society, 139–140
timeless quality of, 138
as vehicles of communication, 138
systems, cultural, 132

T

Tanzania, compared to Kenya, 152
task letters, to missionary churches, 57–58
Taylor, Hudson, 96
teaching, content of in great commission, 63n2
technology
availability and use of, 102
Bible translators taking advantage of cutting-
edge, 218
increasing role in missions, 243–245
tension
existing between missionaries, 104–105
steps to reduce, 105–106
tentmakers, defined, 102
theological challenges, of Islam, 193
theological education, at a distance, 244–245
theological implications, of global trends, 123
theological metaphors, taking too literally, 38
theologies, contextual, 153

theology, in the academy versus in the
congregations, 114
theses, proposed by Pierson, 80
Third Era: focus on unreached peoples (beginning
about 1935), 97–99
The Third Great Wave: The Industrial City, 163
Third World, missionary agenda in, 18
Thomas, carrying gospel to India, 82–83
thought communication, 137
three-selves, 154, 155
time-oriented culture, 230
toilet facilities, need for, 21
*Too Valuable to Lose: Examining the Causes and
Cures of Missionary Attrition*, 233
top line, of God's promise to Abram, 45
top-down approaches, to poverty, 156
tourism, STMs and, 209–210
tourist event, using vagabonds as activities, 210
Townsend, Cameron, 97
traditional mission agencies (TMAs), 252
traditions, attributed to Muhammad, 195
training, covering basics of CHE development
philosophy, 156
transformation
as bridge to evangelism, 20
language groups lacking, 222–223
in slums, 20–23, 40
taking place, 13
through disciple-making, 12
transformational development, 18, 19
transformational ministry, 185, 186–187
translation needs, concentrations of remaining,
218
translation process, of the Christian message, 113
transportation technology, expanding, 163
treatment of others commands, of Jesus, 68–69,
72, 76
Turkey, MBBs outnumbering missionary
personnel, 194
twentieth century, religious change in, 109–112
Twitter, 245
Two-Thirds World Protestant missions movement,
101
Tylor, Edward Burnett, 127

U

Ukraine, life in, 229
Ulfilas, 80–81, 80n13
Ulrich, Anthony, 91n78
ultimacy, of evangelism, 20
unconscious culture, 130
Unique Solution Strategy, 149–150

Unitas Fratrum, small remnant of, 91n75
United Bible Societies, 215
United Nations Populations Fund report, 175
United States
    black theology in, 123
    Muslims in, 190
    number of Christians in, 117
    urbanization patterns in, 162
universal rain, 143
unknown, making known, 139
unreached peoples, 94n6, 97–99
unwelcomed travelers, 209
urban, defined, 161
urban America, move from rural to, 163–164
urban churches, made up of members of the
    middle-class, 155
urban emphasis, of Islam, 193
urban holistic ministry, types of, 181–185
Urban II, Pope, objective of the Crusades, 87
urban industrialization, migrating to cities for, 163
urban ministry
    change in style and motivation, 179–181
    changing, 178–179
    as key to expansion of the church, 9
    strategic ways to approach, 180–181
urban neighborhoods, poverty in, 163
Urban Neighbors of Hope (UNOH), 170, 183
urban poor
    missionaries residing among, 147–148
    responding to plight of, 163
urban populations
    exceeding rural populations, 175
    by major geographical area, 177
    in U.S. cities (1800–2010), 162
urban state, changing, 175–177
urban work, in terms of motif, not model, 170
urbanization
    effects of, 37
    focus on, 100
    in Indonesia, 155
    patterns in the United States, 162
    unprecedented rush to, 175

V

vagabonds, 209
Vandals, invasion by, 84
variations
    within the Muslim world, 190
    practicing in Muslim faith, 191–192
VBS programs for children, 249
Venn, Henry, 154
Ver Beek, Kurt, 208
Verwer, George, 203

victimization, sacrificial rite first and foremost an
    act of, 145
Vietnam, four religions, 111n8
violent gangs, 184
Visigoths, invasion by, 84
vitilla tournament, 172, 172n48
Volunteers of America, 164

W

Wagner, C. Peter, 102
Waldo, Peter, 91n75
Walker, Ken, 248
Walls, Andrew, 242
warfare, in the twentieth century, 109
Way, designation for the church, 56
weaknesses of the people, transferred to the ox for
    Dinka, 145
webs, of relationships, 100
welcomed travelers, 209
Wesley, John, 91
West Indian slaves, evangelization of, 91n78
Western Christianity, imposed on other cultures,
    114
Western missionaries, reporting to Stateside
    officers, 247
Western to non-Western tendency, gradual shift
    from, 242
Western women, Muslim perception of corruption
    and rebelliousness of, 199
What's Ahead for Old First Church (Jones and
    Wilson), 163
white elephant syndrome, 167
white flight, 167
wholeness, in the kingdom of God, 6
widows, caring for, 76
Willis, Avery, 153
Winfrith. *See* Boniface
witness, 8, 10
women
    Islam and, 199
    married allowed to be involved in mission
        work, 96
word, seen as primary and as priority, 18
word and deed, 15–16
    prioritizing between, 20
word or deed, choosing between, 16–19
word over deed, 17–18
word with deed, 18–20
works
    attaching salvation to specific, 64n5
    vs. faith, 63–64
    in Islam, 195–196

world
    entering into the church, 82
    as smaller, more connected place, 246
World Christian Database, 252n15
world Christian movement, 80, 124
World Council of Churches, development of, 165
The World is Flat (Friedman), 244
world population, percentage not evangelized, 220
world religions
    by adherents (1910 and 2010), 110
    opposing work of Bible translation, 217
worldview
    of a culture, 128
    differences, 128
    essential questions of, 43–44
    reflecting values of a society, 139
    of a society, 138
worldview thinking, central issues of, 44
worship, as goal of mission, 47
Wuthnow, Robert, 204
Wycliffe Bible Translators, 97, 215
Wycliffe Global Alliance, 219

X

Xavier, Francis, 89

Y

YHWH. *See* God
Young Life, 31
Young Men's and Women's Christian Associations,
        164
youth groups, risk of short-term missions, 249
youth ministry, 32
Youth With a Mission (YWAM), 203, 249
YouVersion, 226

Z

Zimbabwe, severe drought in 1992, 181–182